Plays by French and Francophone Women

Plays by French and Francophone Women

A Critical Anthology

Edited and Translated by
Christiane P. Makward and
Judith G. Miller

with an annotated bibliography by
Cynthia Running-Johnson

Ann Arbor
THE UNIVERSITY OF MICHIGAN PRESS

Copyright © by the University of Michigan 1994
All rights reserved
Published in the United States of America by
The University of Michigan Press
Manufactured in the United States of America
ⓧ Printed on acid-free paper

1997 1996 1995 1994 4 3 2 1

A CIP catalogue record for this book is available from the British Library.

Library of Congress Cataloging-in-Publication Data

Plays by French and Francophone women : a critical anthology / edited
and translated by Christiane P. Makward and Judith G. Miller.
    p.   cm.
    Includes bibliographical reference and index.
    ISBN 0-472-10263-X
    1. French drama—Women authors—Translations into English.
2. French drama—French-speaking countries—Translations into
English.   I. Makward, Christiane P., 1941– . II. Miller, Judith
Graves.   III. Running-Johnson, Cynthia.
PQ1240.E5P53 1994
842'.91408—dc20   94-30885
                                                                 CIP

to the memory of Laurent Karim Makward and Judith Gershman

Acknowledgments

We wish to express our appreciation to LeAnn Fields, general editor of the theater series for the University of Michigan Press, who brought this project to completion; Jack Patterson, who critiqued our translation of Maillet's Acadian French; Marie-José Cérol and Mariann Mathéus, who spent many hours teaching us about Creole and Antillean culture; Maurice Chappaz, who generously gave us access to Corinna Bille's unpublished manuscripts; Andrée Chedid, who shared her unpublished work and incomparable hospitality; Michèle Foucher, who came to the United States with *La Table,* and Chantal Chawaf, who came with her fairy tales and special poetry; Denise Boucher, Ina Césaire, Hélène Cixous, and Antonine Maillet, whose work has helped us dream and react; Bruno Browning and the Learning Support Services of the University of Wisconsin, for their lessons in technology; Judith Miller's Wisconsin students, particularly Nina Dibner, who have read, interacted with, performed, and commented on these plays for a number of years; Sue Grass-Richard, who can read impossible handwriting; and friends and colleagues in Aix-en-Provence, London, Madison, New York City, Paris, and State College, who have cared.

Grateful acknowledgment is given for permission to publish English-language translations of the following:

La Table: Paroles de femmes (The Table: Womenspeak) by Michèle Foucher © Michèle Foucher 1977.

Mémoires d'isles (Island Memories: Mama N. and Mama F.) by Ina Césaire © Editions Caribéennes 1985.

Les Crasseux (The Rabble) by Antonine Maillet © Editions Leméac 1973.

Les Fées ont soif (When Faeries Thirst) by Denise Boucher © Faeries Editions Intermède 1978.

La Déesse lare ou des siècles de femmes (The Goddess Lar or Centuries of Women) by Andrée Chedid © Andrée Chedid 1977.

La Chemise soufrée (The Scent of Sulphur) by S. Corinna Bille 1963 © Estate of S. Corinna Bille, Maurice Chappaz, Executor.

Chair chaude (Warmth: A Bloodsong) by Chantal Chawaf © Editions Mercure de France 1976.

Le Nom d'Oedipe (The Name of Oedipus: Song of the Forbidden Body) by Hélène Cixous © Editions des Femmes 1978.

Contents

Judith G. Miller

Introduction

In the Provençal village of Villeneuve-lez-Avignon, just across the bridge from the site of one of the world's most famous theater festivals, the local museum features a remarkable composition entitled *Le Couronnement de la Vierge* (The Coronation of the Virgin). This fifteenth-century painting by Enguerrand Quarton depicts identical images of God the Father and God the Son crowning a sunken and passive Mary. The Dove-Spirit, final member of the Trinity, hovers directly over the Virgin's head. While gripping the diadem in its beak, the holy bird extends its wings from the lips of the Father to those of the Son. Thus is Mary dominated by three manifestations of metaphysical authority, each bearing down on her with a collective "tongue."[1]

Submerged in the multiplied voices of the Lord and, one might infer, deprived of her own speech, Quarton's Mary stands, with few exceptions, for the place of women's voices in the history of French theater. Throughout the "grand" theatrical tradition in France the producing, writing, or originating voice of the text has overwhelmingly been male. Major women playwrights only appeared after World War II, and to date only one of these has been honored by a performance in the Papal Courtyard of the Avignon Festival.[2] Moreover, there has not yet been a re-evaluation of the canon that has discovered or recuperated lost women playwrights whose interest can be termed other than "sociohistorical."[3] Rather, as might be expected from a country that so much enjoys debating and prizing "the feminine" and "femininity" and whose language possesses no term that is equivalent to *gender,* the place of women in theater has mainly been as unquestioned representation of "Woman," as flesh and blood image—as unproblematized actress.[4]

In those regions of the world that have been grouped together as "La Francophonie"—that is, in which French is a major language and/or in which there is a significant cultural production in French—theater by women or even theater that examines women's social, psychological, or political situation is still rarer, if it exists at all. Calvinist Switzerland, birthplace of theaterphobe and misogynist Rousseau, for example, having long proscribed all theater practice, only allowed the radio to become a locus of dramatic expression for men (and eventually women) after World War II.[5] Quebec has a thriving theater by women but only since the mid-1970s. In French-speaking Africa and the Caribbean—which began producing plays in considerable numbers in the late 1960s and in which oppression takes the form of the Gallic rooster as well as the spiritual dove—plays by women are strictly a phenomenon of the last decade.[6]

A body of recent theatrical works of compelling interest by both French and Francophone women writers can, however, be discerned, despite the continuing, if differing, histories of theatrical and political subjugation that characterize the place of women in all regions of the French-speaking world. The following overview of the emergence of significant women playwrights and performances—as well as the analyses of individual plays, the anthologized plays themselves, and the appended annotations—intend to convey the diversity and importance of French and Francophone women's theatrical projects. These are endeavors that can be read together, and in response to writer and teacher Hélène Cixous's injunction, as a political gesture aimed at changing theater's means of production and expression, as a refusal of complicity with the model of the patriarchal family, and as a grasping toward a representational structure in which women are no longer "victims."[7]

The history of an identifiable women's theater in French begins, at least for the European and Québécois components, in the post-1968 years, when progressive women were forced to come to terms with the fact that their concerns as women were neglected or dismissed by most of their male comrades. For women in theater the issue became one of investigating the status of playwrights, actresses, and directors, as well as rethinking images of women onstage and, indeed, the act of representation itself. Some theater women engaged in agitprop theater. Many invaded the café-théâtre circuit and even the commercial Boulevard stage. Several sought inspiration in the lives of exceptional historical figures. And a few dedicated their talents as innovative poets, prose writers, or directors to the invention of new theater forms. Not all of these women called themselves feminists, but all of them had to deal with what it meant to be a creative woman in an institution and a practice still markedly dominated by men.[8] Furthermore, they produced and continue to produce a body of works that lends itself convincingly to feminist reading and directing strategies. They therefore pose a feminist challenge to the social and theatrical status quo—provided that their audiences are equally willing to question the vision of a unitary Woman, which mainstream theater has taught them to see.

Most of the French and Québécois women writers who came to a clearly intended feminist, or "women-centered," theater project in the early 1970s had been directly involved in antiwar protests or other forms of political activism. Québécois women writers, for example, in particular in 1976, after militating in the ten-year struggle for cultural and political emancipation from dominant Anglophone Canada, discovered that the finally elected Parti Québécois had no intention of addressing the repressive situation of women in Quebec. These artists, like their French contemporaries, consequently trained their well-honed agitprop or consciousness-raising techniques on an analysis of women and society.

To cite one instance of the trend in France, the Parisian troupe La Carmagnole, which took its name from a song popularized during the French Revolution, worked up a series of sketches foregrounding patriarchal authority. Their performances encouraged the audience to discuss with the actors the ramifications of the use and abuse of power within the domestic arena.[9] Another successful variation of this type of participatory theater was the production of Lo Teatre de la Carriera's *L'Ecrit des femmes: Paroles de femmes des pays d'oc* (Women's Writing: Voices from Occitania) in 1981.[10] Actresses from La Carriera developed four sketches in conjunction with communities of rural Provençal women, who were then prompted to delve into their doubly alienated status as speakers of Occitanian, a regional dialect, and women in an agricultural society. In a similar endeavor the actress-director Michèle Foucher surveyed Alsatian women about the place of the table in their lives. Their edited responses resulted in a production, *La Table: Paroles de femmes* (The Table: Womenspeak), in 1978, which elicited debates on how the rituals of food preparation and eating define women's lives in France.[11] A final French example that continues to draw attention through an agitprop format to patterns of dominance in the family is the Reims-based La Théâtrelle. La Théâtrelle creates sketches from interviews with local women. After performances the audience engages in critiquing scenes it may itself have generated.[12]

Theater troupes with similar goals in Quebec—for example, Le Théâtre des Cuisines and Le Théâtre Experimental des Femmes—have produced plays on abortion rights and on sexual stereotyping. In Le Théâtre des Cuisines's *As-tu vu? Les maisons s'emportent!* (Have You Noticed? Our Houses Get Carried Away, 1980) actresses carried clumsy cardboard homes on their backs.[13] The clarity and dramatic impact of this central image of "women's burden," the commitment to theater based in women's quotidian reality, and the transporting of the experience from the stage to the public make Le Théâtre des Cuisines's work representative of the best of the early forms of theater practice defining itself as feminist.

Trenchant cabaret pieces that teased their public in send-ups of everyday sexism became another major category of theater by women. Such is the case of the work of the French trio Les Trois Jeanne (The Three Joans), who in their 1977 satire *Je te dis, Jeanne, c'est pas une vie la vie qu'on mène* (I'm Telling You, Joan, This Is Not Life We're Living) captured in quick images the omnipresent reminders of women's status as "the second sex" in French society. In the mid- to late 1970s women's cabaret shows, frequently written and performed by an actress working alone, accounted for almost 20 percent of the programming at Paris's café-théâtres.[14] Many of these took the form of "talking cures," with characters such as Victoria Thérame's Fifi (L'Escalier du bonheur [The Staircase to Happiness, 1982])[15] jauntily chatting themselves, and often an alter ego, out of suicidal depressions. As explained by the actress Liliane Rovère, who wrote and acted in the one-woman show Lili (1984), these pieces allowed actresses to take risks, to put their "selves" in danger in ways that conventional theater—with its play of masks—rejected.[16]

French and Québécois women writers and theater women in general, like many women historians throughout the Western world, also set out to recover the lives and achievements of forgotten or undervalued women artists, thinkers, and activists. French actress and director Anne Delbée, for example, in Une Femme (A Woman, 1982)* dramatized the life of sculptress Camille Claudel, who had all but disappeared from history. In her play Delbée shows a complex and many-faceted personality, an artist who would have been commissioned to create what was to become Rodin's The Doors of Hell had the jury felt that a woman were capable of handling the project's hefty budget. In another instance of reclaiming "foremothers," Marseilles-based Anne Roche and Françoise Chatôt wrote and produced Louise/Emma (Louise/Emma, 1982),* in which they pay tribute to the radical political daring of Louise Michel and Emma Goldman. Jovette Marchessault, Québécois artist, writer, and modern-day shaman, brought together in her Saga des poules mouillées (The Saga of the Wet Hens, 1981)* predecessors "Anne Hébert," "Laure Conan," "Germaine Guèvremont," and "Gabrielle Roy" to discuss what it means to be a woman author in today's Quebec.

Taking quite another tack, established writers such as Andrée Chedid and Chantal Chawaf (France) and Louky Bersianik and Marchessault (Quebec) focused their lyric gifts on the theater in order to create dramas based specifically in what they believe to be the unique experience of being female. In their works questions of Woman's difference, her rhythms, rites, and specific codes are central. Such theater pieces are frequently delicate, ritualistic, and often choral—as, for example, Chedid's La Déesse-Lare (The Goddess Lar, 1978), which pits the character Gynna's happiness against ingrained notions of what her duties to the home must be, or Chawaf's Chair chaude (Warmth: A Bloodsong, 1976), which heralds the mother-child bond.[17] Marchessault's Tryptique lesbien (Lesbian Tryptique, 1980)* passionately calls for women's rights to control their own bodies and to pursue their sexual preference without fear,[18] while Bersianik's Le Pique-nique sur l'Acropole (Picnic on the Acropolis, 1983)[19] exuberantly takes on the founding myths of Western patriarchy. In Bersianik's riotous send-up of Plato's Banquet Socrates' wife, Xanthippe, back from the grave, leads a tribe of timeless sisters through healing rites that demonstrate, among other things, Xanthippe's many legitimate reasons for adopting the persona of the married shrew.

Even that bastion of bourgeois and patriarchal values, French Boulevard theater, found itself infiltrated by comedies of manners sympathetic to feminist enthusiasms. Loleh Bellon's *Les Dames du jeudi* (Thursday's Ladies, 1977)* and Françoise Sagan's *Château en Suède* (Castle in Sweden, 1960)[20] topple accepted images of the primacy of the family and the inevitability of romantic love. Dysfunctional families, running the gamut from urban poor to upper middle class, are indeed preferred targets of many contemporary Frenchwomen playwrights. Those whose approach tends toward realism, such as Denise Bonal (*Portrait de famille* [Family Portrait, 1983])* and Jeannine Worms (*Avec ou sans arbres* [With or without Trees, 1979]),* still manage to put into question by a sense of excessiveness or overflow both the "real" world and its representation. Similarly, Denise Chalem's *A Cinquante ans elle découvrait la mer* (The Sea between Us, 1980)* and Constance Delaunay's *Olympe dort* (Olympia Is Sleeping, 1977)* disrupt their mimetic frames through hysterical depictions of mother-daughter relationships. In fact, in most of these plays hysteria stands for a kind of doomed resistance to the terrifying conundrum of family loyalties. Only in the recent manifestation of the undeniable talent of Yasmina Reza (*Conversations après un enterrement* [Conversations after a Burial, 1987])* is there a return to a theatrical narrative that does not query in any manner its own ability to tell a story. Reza seeks, rather, through sustained and rich dialogue, to portray the heightened communication among grieving family members.

All of these plays refuse to reinforce for their audiences the ideologically correct model of the happy family. They contrast pointedly with the many plays of Françoise Dorin, the leading playwright of the Boulevard, whose nostalgic and sophisticated melodramas uphold the conventions of France's grande bourgeoisie. When Dorin creates a "liberated woman," as in *L'Autre valse* (The Other Waltz, 1976),* the character is a hateful schemer. Needless to say, not all women playwrights wish to undercut a male-centered universe.

Undoubtedly, the three most important Frenchwomen to articulate the necessity of rethinking the representation of women in theater are Hélène Cixous, Marguerite Duras, and Simone Benmussa. Their influence began to be felt especially in the late 1970s, although Duras had been writing plays since the 1950s and Benmussa, through her work with the Renaud-Barrault Company, had been instrumental in staging plays by women (including those of Duras and Cixous) onward from 1958.[21] Cixous's early essays, especially *La Jeune née* (The Newly Born Woman), written with Catherine Clément (which includes an extended version of Cixous's essay "The Laugh of the Medusa"),[22] and the exemplary productions of Duras and Benmussa have had a decisive impact on theater practice by women. Not only in France but almost everywhere in the world where women write theater, Cixous's, Duras's, and Benmussa's texts and productions have energized, empowered, and challenged women to create.[23]

Cixous, one of the first and most provocative theoreticians of *l'écriture féminine*—or a feminine writing based on polysemy, nonlinearity, wordplay, and generally the notion that language usage contains the potential for radical psycho-social transformation—published her feminist theatrical manifesto "Aller à la mer" ("Going to the sea," homonymically "Going to the mother") in *Le Monde* in the spring of 1977. In it she accused traditional theater of being sadistic and destructive of women by its continuing insistence on the androcentric family. In *Portrait de Dora* (Portrait of Dora),[24] which Benmussa directed in 1976, Cixous had already taken issue with the patriarchal structure privileged by Freud by questioning the key Freudian concept of infantile sexuality. Her *Dora* indicts the theoretical basis on which the psychoanalytical establishment has constructed its definition of Woman. Through multiplying subject positions and destabilizing the audience's ability to identify with specific characters, Cixous reframes Freud's narrative of Dora's illness, showing how Freud chose to ignore much of the information Dora gave him so that he could interpret her coherently as a hysteric.

In *Le Nom d'Oedipe: Chant du corps interdit* (The Name of Oedipus: Song of the Forbidden Body, 1978),[25] Cixous again breaks up unified subject positions and reassesses a central Freudian construct. Jocasta, rather than Oedipus, is the character who acts to solve the enigma in this play. Yet in her action she refuses to conform to the laws of the patriarchal city and, instead, effects a transformation that creates a new Oedipus. Neither strictly masculine nor feminine, the Oedipus of the play's end ultimately transcends gender by incorporating within him- or herself his mother/lover.

Cixous's recent work, in concert with the extraordinary talent of director Ariane Mnouchkine, is an attempt to come to grips with major historical events of the modern world. Cixous and Mnouchkine have staged the disintegration of traditional cultures in Southeast Asia and the havoc wrought by Western imperialism in *L'Histoire terrible mais inachevée de Norodom Sihanouk, roi du Cambodge* (The Terrible but Unfinished Story of Norodom Sihanouk, King of Cambodia, 1985). They have also examined, in *L'Indiade, ou L'Inde de leurs rêves* (The Indiad or India of Their Dreams, 1987),[26] the painful independence and partition of India—that mixture of metaphysics and power politics that has resulted in a series of bloody religious wars. In both productions, but particularly in *The Indiad,* Mnouchkine's staging seemed to flesh out Cixous's notions of women's writing as she expresses it in "The Laugh of the Medusa." The productions' sweep and color and their championing of transcendant love as an organizational principle can be understood as suggesting that theater itself, which gives birth, which allows multiple transformations and transgressions, is a maternal space, a space that permits actors and spectators to grow.[27] The exceptional quality of both productions also indicates what theater can be when women directors such as Mnouchkine—or her contemporaries Viviane Théophilidès, Anne-Marie Lazarini, Jeanne Champagne, Brigitte Jaques, Simone Benmussa and their younger colleagues Sophie Loucachevsky, Saskia Cohen-Tanugi, Gilberte Tsai, Stéphanie Loïc, and Chantal Morel— combine superb directing skills with an attitude that abandons hierarchy and includes the actors in the creative process.

Duras's dislocated texts, dazed and anguished women characters, and troubling themes of forbidden, if realized, passion in plays of the late 1970s and 1980s (*Eden Cinéma* [1977], *Vera Baxter* [1980], *Agatha* [1981], *Savannah Bay* [1982], *La Musica deuxième* [1985])* and films of the 1970s (*Nathalie Granger* [1973] and *India Song* [1976])[28] seem to echo many of the original preoccupations voiced by Cixous. *Agatha,* for example, reunites brother and sister in incestuous desire, which completely eclipses the father in their family's constellation. *Eden Cinéma* disrupts all the expected conventions of theater and redefines the audience's rapport with the actors. An autobiographical theatricalization of Duras's growing up in Indochina, *Eden Cinéma* uses the techniques of offstage voices to dismantle the process of audience identification. The "characters" narrate their family's story or listen to others' narration of it. Duras's texts also permit readings that demonstrate an awareness of how society constructs Woman as "object" and in addition represses what might be called "feminine space."[29] Particularly in her films, Duras images this space and with it something of the "otherness," or subversive, because passive, energy of Woman—an energy she celebrates as positive, especially at its most witchlike.[30]

Benmussa's adaptations of prose narratives have as their stated goal the sabotaging of the "great reproducing machine" that for her constitutes theater.[31] Her adaptations stem from a feminist rereading and critique of late-nineteenth-century and early-twentieth-century texts by men. For instance, in her work on George Moore's *La Vie singulière d'Albert Nobbs* (The Singular Life of Albert Nobbs, 1977)* Benmussa pictures character "Albert's" nearly untenable situation of having to function as a man in a "borrowed" body while thinking and feeling like the woman she is. Benmussa calls into question the complacency of Moore, the male narrator present in her production, and brings to the fore the issue of gender as determined by social constraints. Likewise in her 1979 adaptation of Henry James's story *Appearances*[32] and her 1984 piece based on Nathalie Sarraute's novel *Enfance* (Childhood), she undercuts, respectively, the authority of the author (by putting him or her into circulation in her play) and the system that declares what female experience should be (by satirizing notions of femininity).

At the same time that readers and spectators were finding Duras's dispossessed characters emblematic of late-twentieth-century women, Cixous's audacious textual experiments liberating, and Benmussa's adaptations indicative of a theater that could both question the act of representation *and* represent, their much admired compatriot Nathalie Sarraute, creator of sparse and mordant verbal dramas such as *Isma* (Izzum, 1970)* and *Elle est là* (1978), rejected all suggestions of affinity with other women writers or any feminist design. In direct opposition to Simone de Beauvoir, who in 1947 had already written an existentialist play with a feminist edge, *Les Bouches inutiles* (Who Shall Die?),* Sarraute claimed her only public identity as that of writer. She has consistently refused to accept that the condescending category of "lady author" has lost its credibility.[33] Nevertheless, throughout Sarraute's work a scathing critique of the patriarchal norm subtends the murky psychological tension that is her hallmark. Better than any other playwright, she points to the power relationship central to the acquisition of language and the process of marginalization that attends those who fail to grasp the dominant mode of expression.

Marguerite Yourcenar, another acclaimed Frenchwomen novelist and playwright—one of only three women to have been elected to the prestigious Académie Française—also resisted identification with a feminist pursuit. Yet her theater gives full and complex representation to women characters, and in *Electre ou la chute des masques* (Electra or the Fall of the Masks, 1944)* she repositions Electra as the driving and unrepentant force behind the double crime of patricide and matricide. Yourcenar would appear to challenge Jean-Paul Sartre's version of the myth in *The Flies* (1943), in which his sniveling and tergiversating Electra retreats from the undaunted heroism of Orestes.

As this overview reveals, the works of women in French and Québécois theater, as indeed the productions of women in theater elsewhere in Europe and North America, fall into several categories and practices. They exalt values and experiences considered to be "feminine," or women-centered, criticize the exploitation of women in patriarchy, dramatize the experience of forgotten women, question and re-vision the myths of the Western tradition, create roles for actresses in which the performers do not feel they are playing out men's fantasies, and show how gender is constructed through social interactions and expectations. While these practices are sometimes mutually exclusive, all of them include a recognition of the ethical dangers inherent in conventional theatrical representation.

Theater women have multiplied alienation techniques in order to question the notion of a unified subject and call attention to the process of representation, in order to negotiate different positions for the spectator and in order to destabilize the preconception of the spectator as male. In a remarkable tour de force a group of six well-established Québécois writers created a piece in 1976 (*La Nef des sorcières* [The Ship of Witches])[34] in which all of these destabilization options were exercised. Each writer developed a monologue focused on a "type" of woman in a typically stultifying situation. The style and tone of the vignettes ranged from lyrically confessional to garbage-can realistic to broadly farcical and stand-up comedic. Connecting the different parts was "the actress," a recurring figure who kept tripping over the men's scripts she was supposed to have learned.

While the preceding discussion has emphasized the similarities between plays by French and Québécois women, it is also crucial to recognize how their works diverge; for women artists are also products of their specific societies, and feminists are further challenged by their culture's particular articulation of notions about "men and women," "masculine and feminine," and "self and other." Most Québécois women playwrights, for example, have not completely divorced themselves from the type of class-based analysis that underlies theater connected to the national liberation movement in Quebec. A great many plays by Québécois women, notably the work of Denise Boucher (*Les Fées ont soif* [When Faeries Thirst, 1978]) and that of the Acadian writer Antonine Maillet (*Les Crasseux* [The Rabble, 1973]), show an awareness of class as a determining factor in the creation of individual identity and in the establishing of differences among women.[35] Furthermore, and related, many plays by Québécois women writers, such as Marie Laberge's *L'Homme gris* (Deep Night, 1983),* are written in Joual, the French dialect of Montreal, a language quite distinct from standard French.[36] Because it is crucial to her particular project, Maillet, in fact, writes not in Joual but in Acadian, a language still spoken by northeastern Canadians and directly issued from the sixteenth-century sailors who accompanied Samuel de Champlain. Québécois (and Acadian) writers' attempts to maintain linguistic specificity help obviate the threat of engulfment posed by France's well-organized cultural "neocolonialism."[37]

Finally, and contrary to the neo-Romantic stance taken toward motherhood in theater by many French women, maternity appears as an affliction or a threat in plays by Canadian writers in French. This probably reflects the critical attitude toward church and state collusion that forced a still potent "bearer mentality" on women transported to North America in the seventeenth century for the purpose of populating the "New World." Whatever the reason for this defamation of motherhood, plays by Québécois women exhibit significant hostility toward the Catholic church and a much greater violence toward men than those written for the French stage.[38] In their theater Québécois women still seem to be working through their anger at men's refusal to see them as consequential human beings.

Just as Québécois theater by women differs markedly from French theater, so do French Antillean and French African productions contrast with those of the North American Francophone contingent. The special characteristics of Antillean and African theater by women, as well as the divergencies in theater from one part of the French-speaking developing world to another, speak to the weakness and even obfuscation of the concept "Francophonie," which damagingly occults the conditions under which people came to speak French in the first place and the reasons why they still produce literature in French. Québécois playwrights, including women, have defined themselves not so much against French hegemony but, rather, against Anglophone Canada and the United States. A Québécois theater practice corresponded to, and to a certain extent led, the struggle in the 1960s and 1970s for recognition of the cultural specificity and autonomy in Canada of what, as "French Canada," had connoted a marginalized territory. The theater of West Africa and the Maghreb, on the other hand, has designed itself from its beginnings in the postcolonial period as a resistance effort— against colonial culture and for the emergence of a collective identity and the recognition of a history and mythology that existed long before the French swallowed their slice of the "African pie." The situation in the French Caribbean speaks to another political and, thus, theatrical constellation: for example, writers of Martinique and Guadeloupe, French Overseas Departments since 1947, have had to deal with what it means to be French people of color, living in the economic ruins of the French sugar empire to which their ancestors had been enslaved for almost three centuries.[39]

African and Antillean women playwrights add another dimension to the concerns of former colonized writers. They wonder how to speak as women and thus valorize their particular existence while at the same time remaining allied with the liberationist ethos of their male counterparts.[40] Given their social reality, for African and Antillean artists the oppressive concept of the Other does not take the shape of Woman but, rather, of "Native." Women playwrights therefore attempt to show not only the constructedness of Woman but also that of "Man"—that is, the colonized or postcolonial male, still called by many Eurocentric myopics the Native. Women playwrights theatricalize their understanding that both gender *and* race are created categories that serve to perpetuate the ideology of the dominant economic power.

These are writers in conflict. Fatima Gallaire-Bourega, one of several Algerian women exiled in France in order to be able to keep on writing—because the increase of fundamentalistic Islamic forces in Algeria has silenced almost all progressive writers there—expresses her dilemma in these terms: "It is very difficult to tear off the last veil, the one we wear on the inside and which insists that a woman always stay modest, discrete, and especially removed from the public sphere which is reserved for men."[41] When she comes to write, the African or Antillean playwright confronts the clash of indigenous cultures with "modernization," *including* feminist thought, brought about through contact with the West. She must come to terms with the patriarchal interdictions of her own culture. She must face the havoc wrought by decolonization, which includes the power vacuum created and often subsequently filled by political tyrants. And she must deal with her particular privileged situation among women in her country.

Gallaire-Bourega feels herself fully engaged as a representative of Algerian women, seeking to end their subordination to twenty-five years of postcolonial patriarchal rule. Yet she must speak to and for them from one of the capitals of European imperialism. In her play *Princesse* (You Have Come Back, 1988),* she depicts the deadly conflict of a woman caught between the West and the culture of her "fathers." In this play maternal guardians of tradition violently resolve the situation by destroying the questioner, a young woman returned to her village from France.

The Zairois writer Diur N'Tumb (*Qui hurle dans la nuit* [Lost Voices, 1987])* treats this cultural conflict in a satirical vein, sending up not only the self-importance of the prodigal son who comes back from a university in Boston to take over the kingship of his village but also the superstitions of the villagers and the impatience of his completely Westernized fiancée. N'Tumb's rowdy humor aligns her with a number of recent African men playwrights, who find the current chaos in their countries better suited to dramatic expression than recriminations against former colonizers.

Caribbean playwrights include several women who are among the most arresting working in French-language theater today. Maryse Condé, a highly productive and versatile fiction writer, has experimented with African and Caribbean history as well as with contemporary Parisian settings in her dramatic texts. Committed to the promotion of Creole, she has even written in the Creole language both a play on the revolutionary events of 1789 and a domestic comedy.[42]

Both Guadeloupian Simone Schwarz-Bart and Martinican Ina Césaire forsake the rewriting of "History" and corresponding fascination with heroes of African or Caribbean revolutionary struggles that structured the plays of the first great Antillean playwright, Aimé Césaire. Instead, they weave portraits of the daily lives and concerns of women characters, rethinking in the process the very concept of "History." Ina Césaire, for example, in *Mémoires d'isles: Maman N. et Maman F.* (Island Memories: Mama N. and Mama F., 1985)[43] places onstage two old women who reminisce about their long lives on their island, where—despite class differences—they have been able to affirm a similar strength and drive. In

Rosanie Soleil (Fire's Daughters, 1992), focusing on the interactions of four women in their home, Césaire allows only glimpses of the Southern Insurrection of 1870, in which angry Martinican farmers and workers burned down over twenty sugarcane plantations.

Schwarz-Bart's *Ton beau capitaine* (Your Handsome Captain, 1987)* employs the offstage voice of character Marie-Ange, who dialogues through a cassette tape with her husband, Wilnor, an exiled Haitian agricultural worker. Through their exchanges both are liberated: Marie-Ange by revealing to Wilnor the complexities of both her adultery and her love and Wilnor by understanding his complicity with the white man's capitalist fantasy, which is responsible for their long separation. By metonymically displacing Marie-Ange to the cassette, Schwarz-Bart also sidesteps in her play the issue of the "male gaze"; she would foreclose the possibility of the actress becoming the site of the audience's desire by keeping her offstage during the performance.

What almost all these plays by Francophone women have in common, be they Canadian or African or Antillean, is the use of music and dance. Through nonverbal elements of specific cultural expression—central to most performances—the playwrights convey their characters' inner dramas and establish a structure of communication that is not controlled by the language of the colonizer, however conceived. They work to effect the *métissage,* of which critic Françoise Lionnet speaks when analyzing work by women of color; that is, they "braid" cultural forms to reevaluate Western concepts and to foreground their own cultural traditions. They found a future on "collective solidarities and in opposition to essentializing approaches to questions of race, class, or gender."[44]

The effort of many Francophone women to break down oppositional categories in their theater and the undertaking of other women writing in French to construct characters with a multiply-based subjectivity speaks to the most urgent task facing all progressive thinkers: how to acknowledge contradictions and difference in human beings without reifying them into immutable categories. Such a representational practice also attempts to rethink what a subject is and allows for the possibility of linking representation with sociopolitical action. This is a practice that actively distrusts what has been handed down as "the real" without denying that a real exists.

In the theater this real, at its most salient, is situated in and through the actor's body, which is physical: textural, material, and sensual. The actor's presence, especially compelling in the theater, can mean danger and subversion.[45] An actor is able to escape from or at least trouble constructed classifications, behaviors, and compulsions—including those of male directors.

In this light it is interesting and frustrating to review the work of the late

Antoine Vitez, probably France's most intellectually exciting director of the past twenty years. When queried about why he directed all the women actors as mindless dolls in his radical staging of four of Molière's most performed plays, Vitez—then about to be named director of France's premier national theater— answered: "Well, I wanted to stage misogyny. . . . It's a problem in vogue today. Am I fundamentally a misogynist? Maybe. But I don't want to analyze myself *ad infinitum*. . . . For a woman to perform Molière well, she has to question who she is, *because it's an oeuvre which is entirely founded on woman represented as object for whom the subject is man*."[46] To understand such an assertion requires us to see that Vitez— although audacious enough to introduce a play by a black Francophone man into the Comédie Française's repertory—was still bound by tradition concerning women. He could not imagine a staging that would disturb the subject-object dichotomy he, in this sense a traditional male director, found at the heart of Molière.

The current generation of stellar French and Francophone women actors and directors (many of whom are also active in film as directors and producers) has demonstrated its ability to counter Vitez's anxious proclamation of the "truth" with plucky questions.[47] These artists would no doubt add their voices to those of the Royal Shakespeare Company's Juliet Stevenson, who, with several of her colleagues, maintains that women can be independent and feminist in their work even while interpreting the great theatrical tradition. Stevenson muses: "But you know, there isn't a fixed end to a play. The script ends. The words run out. But the ending—that's something that has to be renegotiated every performance."[48] No ending means no boundaries—or "out of bounds" in terms of existing structures and expectations.

This anthology might well have been called "Out of Bounds" because the project has meant considering how an emerging theater by French and Francophone women has challenged mainstream theater, not only in form and content but also in practice, thereby locating it "somewhere else," sometimes even out of the conventions that make it possible to recognize theater in the first place. It has meant, moreover, and perhaps more important, addressing the issue of differences among plays by women and especially among plays by women of different cultures, for, while many women now write plays in French, not all came to writing in French the same way. The Martinican or the Algerian who learned to recite in grade school history classes "Our ancestors, the Gauls," as deeply committed as she might be to a feminist project in French, still knows that her sisters never were and are not now descendants of Frankish tribes. The Québécois writer, somewhat more "Gaulish," is in greater danger of cultural colonization by the English-speaking world. She nevertheless recognizes the indelible imprint of a North American existence.

European, African, Antillean, North American—these women are, then, out of bounds in one another's dramatic territories too. Yet they share a willingness to play, to trespass beyond the boundaries that the inherited imagination has set. To return to the reflection at the beginning of this essay, such writers, were they to take their own look at Quarton's painting *The Coronation of the Virgin,* might discover multiple possibilities for refining her image. Instead of a crowned and stunned idol, she might well provide the stuff from which new dreams are made.

NOTES

1. Parts of this essay appeared in Judith G. Miller, "Contemporary Women's Voices in French Theatre," *Modern Drama* 22, no. 1 (March 1988): 5–23.

2. Hélène Cixous's *The Name of Oedipus: Song of the Forbidden Body,* the libretto for André Bourcourechliev's opera of the same name, was performed in the Honor Court in July 1978. The enigmatic production proved very controversial; see the introduction to the translated text.

3. See, for example, the overview of theatrical activity by women in the eighteenth century by Barbara Mittman, "Women and Theater Arts," in *French Women and the Age of Enlightenment,* ed. Samia Spencer, 155–69 (Bloomington: Indiana University Press, 1984); or the survey of women playwrights at the French national theater by Sylvie Chevalley, "Les Femmes auteurs dramatiques et la Comédie Française," *Europe,* no. 426–28 (1964): 41–47.

4. One can, indeed, speak of a distinguished tradition of female performers from the seventeenth century to the present. These include the independent Béjart women of Molière's company and the grand tragedian La Champmeslé in the seventeenth century; the theatrical innovators Adrienne Lecouvreur and Mlle. Clairon and the exquisite comique talent Mme. Riccoboni in the eighteenth century; the respective queens of melodrama and classical tragedy, Marie Dorval and Rachel, and the invincible Sarah Bernhardt of the nineteenth century; and contemporary greats Maria Casarès, Madeleine Renaud, Jeanne Moreau, and Delphine Seyrig. However, despite their verve and vocal gifts, despite their physical dexterity and remarkable memories, these women have excelled for the most part in materializing the imaginative constucts of male authors and male directors, in telling the "great story of MANkind." In fact, it was not until the sixteenth century that women were finally allowed onstage. Up to that point female players were almost completely excluded from the act of representation. Boys had played women's roles, except for that of the Virgin, in medieval mystery plays. And in neighboring Spain, to comply with the decrees of the church fathers, even that role remained "unpolluted" by the presence of real women. In this light it is interesting to note that in commedia dell'arte practice women wore no masks, a woman's face being considered to be the mask of duplicity itself.

5. Among the signs of an awakening of Francophone Swiss women to theater, one must note the work of Simone Collet in Lausanne and, in Zurich, of Anne Cunéo, an

established feminist novelist who also experiments with bilingual (German/French) drama. In Geneva poet Mousse Boulanger has been active adapting literary texts on women for the stage, while Gisèle Sallin, director of the Théâtre des Osses in Fribourg, which has performed short plays by Swiss writer Corinna Bille, works with local mythological materials. More information on Francophone Swiss theater can be found in *Scène,* no. 19 (May 1988); and G. H. Blanc, "La Condition de l'auteur dramatique en Suisse Romande," *Alliance Culturelle Romande,* no. 26 (November 1980).

6. The following have been particularly helpful in considering the question of feminism and the theater: Sue-Ellen Case, "Gender as Play: Simone Benmussa's *The Singular Life of Albert Nobbs,*" *Women and Performance* 1, no. 2 (Winter 1984): 21–24; and her book *Feminism and Theater* (New York: Methuen, 1988); Teresa de Lauretis, *Alice Doesn't: Feminism, Semiotics, Cinema* (Bloomington: Indiana University Press, 1982); and *Technologies of Gender: Essays on Theory, Film, and Fiction* (Bloomington: Indiana University Press, 1987); Elin Diamond, "Brechtian Theory / Feminist Criticism: Toward a Gestic Feminist Criticism," *Drama Review* 117 (Spring 1988): 82–93; and "Refusing the Romanticism of Identity: Narrative Interventions in Churchill, Benmussa, Duras," *Theatre Journal* 27, no. 3 (October 1985): 273–86; Jill Dolan, "Feminists, Lesbians, and Other Women in Theatre: Thoughts on the Politics of Performance," *Themes in Drama* 11 (1989); and her book *The Feminist Spectator as Critic* (1988; reprint, Ann Arbor: University of Michigan Press, 1991); Linda Walsh Jenkins, "'Locating the Language of Gender Experience," *Women and Performance: A Journal of Feminist Theory* 2, no. 1 (1984): 5–20.

7. Hélène Cixous, "Aller à la mer," *Le Monde,* 28 April 1977 ("Going to the Sea," trans. Barbara Kerslake, *Modern Drama* [December 1984]: 546–48).

8. Of the some ninety-four state-subsidized decentralized theaters or national stages in France, for example, only eleven have women artistic directors. Not one of the five prestigious national theaters has a woman at its head. If, however, the state remains conservative, public appreciation of women in theater has led to the establishing in 1987 of Les Prix Arletty, theater prizes subsidized by the popular press and specifically meant to encourage women creators.

9. Monique Surel-Turpin, in "La Prise de parole des femmes au théâtre" in *Le Théâtre d'intervention depuis 1968,* ed. Jonny Epstein and Philippe Ivernel, 56–78 (Lausanne: L'Age d'Homme, 1980), discusses the Carmagnole troupe as well as other feminist agitprop activity in the 1970s.

10. Bibliographical information for this play is included in "Selected Plays by Contemporary French and Francophone Women Playwrights," by Cynthia Running-Johnson, at the end of this volume. All plays mentioned in this introduction that are treated in the annotations will henceforth be marked by an asterisk in the body of the text or in the notes.

11. Michèle Foucher, *La Table, L'Avant-Scène* (October 1978): 23–30. For more information on *La Table,* see Josette Féral, "Writing and Displacement: Women in Theatre," trans. Barbara Kerslake, *Modern Drama* 27, no. 4 (December 1984): 180–94. See also Michel Deutsch and Paul Guérin, "*La Table:* Connexion," *Travail Théâtral* 16 (December 1979): 13–21.

12. Judith Miller spoke with representatives from La Théâtrelle at a conference on women and creativity at La Criée Theater in Marseilles, 5 May 1985.

13. Le Théâtre des Cuisines, *As-tu vu? Les Maisons s'emportent!* (Montreal: Les Editions du Remue-ménage, 1981). The following are very useful in situating the place of women in Québécois theater: Paula Gilbert Lewis, ed., *Traditionalism, Nationalism, and Feminism: Women Writers of Québec* (Westport: Greenwood Press, 1985); Jane Moss, "Les Folles du Québec: The Theme of Madness in Québec's Women's Theatre," *The French Review* 57, no. 5 (April 1984): 617–24; "Théâtre-femmes," *Cahier du Jeu* 3, no. 16 (1980).

14. Christiane Makward, in a paper on women's theater in France delivered at the North East Modern Language Association meeting in March 1985, reported on the number and characteristics of these cabaret pieces during the 1985 theater season. Jane Moss, in "Women's Theater in France," *Signs* 12, no. 3 (Spring 1987): 549–67, discusses in more detail the theater practice of Les Trois Jeanne and other cabaret-style women's theater.

15. Victoria Thérame, *L'Escalier du bonheur* (Paris: Des Femmes, 1982), unpublished translation available from Christiane Makward and Judith G. Miller.

16. Personal conversation with Judith Miller, 14 December 1984.

17. André Chedid, *La Déesse-Lare*, MS given to Makward and Miller by the author; Chantal Chawaf, *Chair chaude, suivi de L'écriture* (Paris: Mercure de France, 1976).

18. In keeping with the more specifically politicized character of Québécois women's theater, a number of major women writers writing for the theater (Marchessault, Pol Pelletier, Nicole Brossard) celebrate the subversive energy of lesbianism. In France the most persistant champion of a theater in which lesbianism finds representation is Monique Lepeu, whose charming *Gertrude morte cet après-midi* (Gertrude Dead This Afternoon, 1985) replays the love story of Gertrude Stein and Alice B. Toklas with the discretion that Toklas herself might have cherished. In France there are no examples of established all-lesbian audiences or "counter-hegemonic reception fields," as described by Dolan, in *Feminist Spectator,* that experiment with an entirely different erotics of theater.

19. Louky Bersianik, *Le Pique-nique sur l'Acropole*, MS adapted from her novel *Le Pique-nique sur l'Acropole* (Montreal: VLB Editeur, 1979).

20. Françoise Sagan, *Château en Suède* (Paris: Julliard, 1960).

21. All three of these artists have given rise to exceptional studies by feminist theater critics. See, in addition to those cited above, Jeannette Savona, "In Search of a Feminist Theatre: *Portrait of Dora,"* in *Feminine Focus: The New Women Playwrights*, ed. Enoch Brater, 94–108 (New York and London: Oxford University Press, 1989); as well as essays by Elin Diamond (on Benmussa) and Sue-Ellen Case (On Duras) in the same volume. See also the excellent overview of Hélène Cixous's theater in Morag Shiach's *Hélène Cixous: A Politics of Writing* (London and New York: Routledge, 1991).

22. Hélène Cixous and Catherine Clément, *La Jeune née* (Paris: 10/18, 1975); "Le Rire de la Méduse," *L'Arc,* no. 61 (1975): 39–54, trans. Keith and Paula Cohen, "The Laugh of the Medusa," *Signs* 1, no. 4 (1976): 889.

23. The brilliant but often dense theories developed since 1970 by feminists and/or feminist poststructuralists have had less of an impact than *La Jeune née* on theater artists

in France. Ironically, the theories of Julia Kristeva and Luce Irigarary, among others, as well as the work of Cixous, Duras, and Benmussa as they have been interpreted by Anglo-American critics, have resulted in some of the most exciting recent work in Anglophone feminist theater and theater criticism. It would seem that few French theater women rely on theoretical models to inspire their work. Many Québécois artists, on the other hand, are quite conversant with feminist and poststructuralist theory. There are also many more performance artists in Quebec than in France, performance art usually being created more consciously within a theoretical frame. There is also a dearth of feminist studies of theater in French—with the notable exception of a volume of probing essays on the work of Hélène Cixous (Françoise van Rossum-Guyon and Myriam Diaz-Diocaretz, eds., *Hélène Cixous, chemins d'une écriture* [Paris: Presses Universitaires de Vincennes, 1990]).

24. Hélène Cixous, *Portrait de Dora* (Paris: Des Femmes, 1976); trans. Anita Barrows, *Benmussa Directs: Portrait of Dora by Hélène Cixous and the Singular Life of Albert Nobbs by Simone Benmussa* (London: John Calder, 1979).

25. Hélène Cixous, *Le Nom d'Oedipe: chant du corps interdit* (Paris: Des Femmes, 1978).

26. Hélène Cixous, *L'Histoire terrible mais inachevée de Norodom Sihanouk, roi du Cambodge* (Paris: Théâtre du Soleil, 1985); *L'Indiade ou l'Inde de leurs rêves et quelques écrits sur le théâtre* (Paris: Théâtre du Soleil, 1987).

27. Without labeling as "feminine" or "feminist" the cathexis of these two talents, one can suggest that their collaboration has heralded a new epoch for French theater. Mnouch-kine herself adapts texts, including her 1979 reworking of Klaus Mann's *Mephisto, Méphisto, le roman d'une carrière* (Paris: Solin et Théâtre du Soleil, 1979); and her 1990–91 adaptation of Aeschylus' trilogy, *The Orestia*. In production she prefaced the latter with Euripides' *Iphigenia in Aulis* to help ballast what could be understood as a feminist interpretation of the "House of Atreus" (*Les Atrides*). In line with their collaboration on The House of Atreus project, Hélène Cixous completed in 1994 a new text for Ariane Mnouchkine's Théâtre du Soleil. This piece, *La Ville Parjure ou Le Réveil des Erinyes* (The Faithless City or Furies Awakening), speaks metaphorically of the contaminated blood scandal that has rocked France's medical and political establishments.

28. Marguerite Duras, *Eden Cinéma* (Paris: Mercure de France, 1977); *Agatha* (Paris: Minuit, 1981); *India Song* (Paris: Gallimard, 1973); *Nathalie Granger* (Paris: Gallimard, 1973); *Savannah Bay* (Paris: Minuit, 1982); *Véra Baxter ou les plages de l'Atlantique* (Paris: Albatros, 1980). All of these texts appear in English translation by Barbara Bray. *La Musica deuxième* (Paris: Gallimard, 1985) was translated by Judith G. Miller as "La Musica: Two" for inclusion in this volume. Unfortunately, Mme Duras withdrew permission to use the text in April 1992. She no longer wishes to participate in collective projects.

29. See Diamond, "Refusing the Romance of Identity"; and Susan Cohen, "La Prés-ence de rien," *Cahiers Renaud-Barrault*, no. 106 (1984): 17–36.

30. Here from the feminist journal *Sorcières* are Xavière Gauthier's thoughts (trans. Erica M. Eisinger) on the subversive energy of women (see Elaine Marks and Isabelle de Courtivron, eds., *New French Feminisms* [Amherst: University of Massachusetts Press,

1980], 203): "If the figure of the witch appears wicked, it is because she poses a real danger to phallocratic society. We do constitute a danger for this society which is built on the exclusion—worse—on the repression of female strength."

31. Simone Benmussa, *Benmussa Directs*, 11.

32. Benmussa, *Apparences* (Paris: Des Femmes, 1979).

33. It is for this reason that she refused to be included in this anthology.

34. France Théorêt, Pol Pelletier, Luce Guilbeault, Marthe Blackburn, Odette Gagnon, Nicole Brossard, *La Nef des sorcières* (Montreal: Quinze, 1976).

35. Denise Boucher, *Les Fées ont soif* (Montreal: Editions Intermède, 1978); Antonine Maillet, *Les Crasseux* (Ottawa: Léméac, 1973).

36. The subversion of French in the Joual dialect has permitted, for example, the creation of feminine forms for writer (*l'auteure*) and director (*metteuse-en scène*), words that are nonexistent in standard French.

37. France has a Ministry of Francophone Affairs, which subsidizes, among other activities, a yearly theater festival in Limoges and the productions and exchanges of an operation entitled the Théâtre International de Langue Française. Despite the neocolonialist tinge, both the festival and the work of the International French Language Theater are immensely helpful in bringing together writers from around the globe and exposing them to one another's work.

38. Jeanne-Mance Delisle's *Un Oiseau vivant dans la gueule* (Montreal: La Pleine Lune, 1987), for example, which won the prestigious 1988 Governor General's Prize, forcefully suggests that men's preferred companions will always be men and that women are "merely" necessary enemies.

39. See Carole Boyce Davies and Elaine Savory Fido, eds. *Out of the Kumbla: Caribbean Women and Literature* (Trenton: African World Press, 1990), for a series of fine essays dealing with Caribbean women writers.

40. In the cultures of Africa and the Antilles, in general, women have had limited opportunity to begin to write; they are still largely responsible for keeping their households functioning. Although there has been a plethora of African women novelists published in France—including the respected Algerian Assia Djebar, who, with Walid Carn, wrote an impassioned prorevolution play in 1960, *Rouge l'aube* (Red Dawn), which was not published until 1969 (Algiers: SNED)—few women's plays have traveled to France. One exception, although still unpublished, is *Imaïtsoanala* by the Malagasy author Volona Andriamoratsiresy. This play, which treats the life of a legendary Malagasy queen, was produced by the International French Language Theater. Another, also by a Malagasy author, Michèle Rakotoson (*La Maison morte* [The Dead House, 1990]),* won first prize for radio theater at the Inter-Africa Theatre Competition in 1989. It is, in fact, quite difficult to find African women playwrights writing in French. There are also very few women engaged in theatrical micropolitical activities. One such artist, however, is truly remarkable: Werewere Liking animates the Village Ki-Yi of the Ivory Coast, writing for and directing a troupe of some fifty actors, musicians, dancers, and painters. Werewere Liking produces theater with and for a pan-African community. Her work, as that of many

Africans these days, is partially improvised and hybrid in form, performed in a combination of French and African languages. See *Singuè Mura: Considérant que la femme . . .* (Singuè Mura: Given that a Woman . . . , 1990).* Liking's dramatic monolgue *La Veuve Diyilem* (The Window Dylemma) has been published in Judith G. Miller's translation in *Plays By Women: An International Anthology, Book 2*, ed. Françoise Kourilsky and Catherine Temerson (New York: Ubu Repertory Theater Publications, 1994). Judith G. Miller has also translated Liking's *Singuè Mura* and *Héros d'eau* (Paper Heroes.)

41. Cited in the program notes to the 1990–91 season at the Théâtre des Amandiers (trans. Judith Miller).

42. Condé's dramatic texts include *Dieu nous l'a donné* (God Gave It to Us) (Paris: Harmattan, 1972); *La Mort d'Oluwémi d'Ajumako* (The Death of Oluwemi d'Ajumako) (Paris: Harmattan, 1974); *Pension les Alizés* (The Tropical Breeze Hotel) (Paris: Mercure de France, 1988);* *An Tan Révolisyion* (Once upon a Revolution) (Conseil Régional de la Guadeloupe, 1991); *Comédie d'amour* (Comedy of Love, 1993). See C. Makward, "Lire le théâtre de Maryse Condé," *Callaloo*, forthcoming.

43. Ina Césaire, *Mémoires d'isles: Maman N. et Maman F.* (Paris: Editions Caribéennes, 1985).

44. Françoise Lionnet, *Autobiographical Voices: Race, Gender, and Self-Portraiture* (Ithaca: Cornell University Press, 1989), xiii.

45. See Lynda Hart's Introduction to *Making a Spectacle: Feminist Essays on Contemporary Women's Theater* (Ann Arbor: University of Michigan Press, 1989); and Sue-Ellen Case's essay "From Split Subject to Split Britches," in Brater, *Feminine Focus*, 126–46, for a longer discussion of the subversive potential of the actor's body.

46. Judith Miller interviewed Antoine Vitez in 1978 at the Avignon Theater Festival (trans. Miller and emphasis by Miller).

47. Isabelle Adjani, once with the Comédie Française, for instance, commissioned, produced, and starred in a 1989 film version of the life of Camille Claudel. Other noted French and Francophone women film directors include Agnès Varda, Nicole Garcia, Yannik Bellon, Colline Serreau, and Chantal Ackerman, who in 1992 wrote her first play, *Hall de Nuit*. One of the most recent theatrical inquiries into the complicated rapport between a woman actor and a male director is Brigitte Jaques's painful evocation of the lessons of Louis Jouvet to theater students during the German occupation of France (*Elvire-Jouvet 40*).*

48. Carol Rutter and Faith Evans, eds., *Clamorous Voices: Shakespeare's Women Today* (London: The Woman's Press, 1988).

Michèle Foucher

MICHÈLE FOUCHER (B. 1941) was a chemist before she became an actor, a profession that attracted her because she was more interested in the alchemy of the body than in her laboratory solutions. She began acting in 1966, working first with director Patrice Chéreau. In 1975 she entered the multifaceted theater company that director Jean-Pierre Vincent created during his tenure as head of the Théâtre National de Strasbourg. Encouraged by Vincent to explore her own interests, she decided to come to grips with the lack of "Everywoman" roles for actresses. She was tired of performing the social stereotypes: servant girl, lovesick heroine, mother, or whore, which were usually available to her. Instead, she wanted to create a role for herself that would be nonnaturalistic, popular, and contemporary and would explore several dimensions of a woman's existence. She therefore set about interviewing working-class women in the Strasbourg area, launching her questioning by a discussion of the place of the table in their lives.

The result, in 1977, was some twenty hours of taped material, which Foucher edited into a one-hour and forty-five minute performance. In collaboration with her friends Denise Péron and Yolande Marzolff, who helped her, respectively, with the staging and choreography, she developed a one-woman show with multiple characters and a fragmented time and space frame. Everything, however, was connected to the central preoccupation with the table.

The following year, after successfully touring *The Table* throughout Europe and the United States, she used the same techniques to develop a play based on her interviews with men about their rapport with pain (*En Souffrance* [In Pain]). In this production she was able to depict men's vulnerability in ways not usually staged. Since then she has, in addition to continuing to act, become increasingly involved in directing and producing.

In 1988, in keeping with her decision to concentrate on projects that focus on the nature and meaning of war, she adapted and directed Christa Wolf's *Cassandra*.

Michèle Foucher portrays two of the many women and attitudes expressed in her play *The Table: Womenspeak*. The top photo depicts a young mother overwhelmed by having to raise children on her own after her husband has deserted them. The bottom shows an outraged housewife listening to a neighbor extoll the sexual exploits of a girlfriend (1977). (Photos by Sabine Strosser.)

The same year she also performed in Michel Deutsch and Philippe Lacoue-Labarthe's dramatic compilation of Heideggerian meditations on power and language. Among her recent projects is her work with a group of actors of her generation, Les Acteurs Producteurs Associés (APA). The partners in APA have commissioned dramatic pieces on madness and anxiety by some of France's most interesting and controversial contemporary writers and philosophers. These have been performed as successful theatrical montages since 1989. Under APA's sponsorship she directed in tandem in 1991 a modern piece on the Vietnam War by Michel Deutsch (*L'Empire*) and an adaptation of Plato's *Ion*. As in all of her recent work, this juxtaposition bears witness to her continuing quest for an answer to exactly what "representation" is and to whether or not human beings can get beyond representation to be able to act on the world.

The Table: Womenspeak consists of twenty-six dramatic moments lasting from several seconds to as many as eight minutes each.[1] These dramatic fragments are anchored in concrete immediate experiences of a woman's material existence, especially her place within the family. While no male characters are ever present onstage, their offstage presence, most often a source of aggression and emotional abuse, is constantly felt.

The performed conversations run the gamut of accepted to contested notions of how women do and should relate to the home and to homemaking. For instance, vignettes explain how women should do the cooking at home but how only men can be great chefs. Others demonstrate how a wife's duty is to figure out how to make ends meet, even if her husband earns hardly enough money for the rent, and, furthermore, how men have the right to beat unruly wives. Others, however, tell stories of resistance to accepted behavior: how, for example, one man stopped going out with his "buddy from work" when he witnessed the buddy's violence toward his family.

In a series of rapid, comic, and sometimes maddening juxtapositions the characters recount, for example, being scolded at table or making love on top of it. The rhythm slows down for the occasional poignant story of abandonment or a triumphant one of revolt. The sketches tend to reinforce the image of woman as both nurturer and reproducer. Yet often, by Foucher's editing as well as by the free-associating of her interviewees, the texts contain a sardonic critique of this image. Such is the case in a raucous exchange about eating horse meat and going to a stud farm: through their ribald conversation the characters unselfconsciously acknowledge the connection between sex and food. They also invest this link with their own perspective. By the semantic displacements in their unintentional parable, the female characters are the ones who end up conquering, not to say cannibalizing, the prize stud.

Foucher played all the roles in *The Table,* moving from one character to the next by changing a hat, a hand prop, a characteristic gesture, or her position around one of the three tables that delimited three separate playing areas. She transformed herself, for example, from spinster to grande dame to frightened wife, thus establishing many different images of women and their rapport with their tables. The tables, in turn, became hiding places, assembly line worktables, seductresses' dens, baby carriages, or school desks. These Brechtian-inspired transformations allowed Foucher to distance herself from the characters and to point out the connections between concepts of the table and forms of women's oppression.

While the interviews she chose allowed Foucher to reflect both positive and negative dimensions of the table in women's lives, the staging permitted her to criticize the texts. Thus, while cataloging the superstitions surrounding menses and the preparation of food, she knelt on the table in a very uncomfortable position, conveying that there is something very wrong in connecting failed hand-churned mayonnaise with menstruation. In a vignette that dealt with a woman's dilemma about what to do with a husband who acted like a tyrant at the table, Foucher, with the awkward movements of a little girl, played with a fork twice her size. The fork, like other objects of the production invested with an emotional charge, signaled how the housewife is controlled by her environment rather than being able to control it. Throughout the performance Foucher's unrelenting physical activity—cleaning, scrubbing, washing, peeling vegetables, setting the table, putting things away, and disciplining children— undercut the dominant notion that homemaking is not a true occupation.

Other sketches tore into the image of the tranquil housewife by highlighting such characteristics as her burlesque imaginative powers. Detailing her fairly banal daily routine, for example, an at-home mother danced a sultry tango to the music of her transistor radio. Throughout all this one silent but constant onstage image—a caged bird at whom Foucher glanced quizzically from time to time— also made its statement about a woman's rapport with her table. Although Foucher's production far from denied the sometimes spectacular personal resources of the French homemaker, especially her ability to cope through humor, this caged bird indicated the dangers of domestic imprisonment. The last words of the play revealed the potential utopia of living without the table as a major source of identity: "I painted my table the same color as my walls: white! That way they fade into each other, and when there's nothing on it, I'm real happy."

By dint of the intratextual and gestual commentaries, by sympathetic characterizations alternating with distanced ones, and especially by the postshow discussions that followed each performance, Foucher's work encouraged her audiences to think about how the table constructs women's lives and creates "meaning." It underscored how biological sex and gender roles manage to be unyieldingly connected. For certain members of her audience—those women whom she had interviewed and who had not, in many cases, ever been to the theater before—just seeing their words given theatrical form made them reevaluate their own possibilities as speaking subjects. *The Table*, then, exemplifies a type of theater that foregrounds considerations of social roles while at the same time appealing to a popular public.

NOTE

1. *The Table*, conceived and performed by Michèle Foucher, opened to full houses at the Théâtre National de Strasbourg in the fall of 1977.

Michèle Foucher

The Table: Womenspeak

1. — This brioche. . . . You break it apart with your hands . . .
   — If you want I'll give you a knife . . .
   — But really you ought to . . . break it apart.
   — Well at our house it all depends.
   — Traditions aren't what they used to be.
   — Before, we used to make a cross on the bread, then we cut it.
   — Oh I still do!
   — But you have to think about what you're doing. You shouldn't just make the cross, you should say to yourself, "God bless this bread!"
   — My mother always said a little grace, "God bless this bread!" And "Thank you." And she prayed before eating . . . That's what *my* mother did.

2. — And what about spilling the salt! That was my father's thing!
   — And knives that get crossed on the table! That means bad luck. We still say so.
   — Salt means a fight. My father would say . . .
   — My husband would always say, "Knives are the gifts of enemies."
   — Sure, they're supposed to split up friends!
   — Yeah, and then there's mayonnaise . . . When my aunt had the. . . . When she had her. . . . Well, you know . . . it was my uncle who made the mayonnaise!
   — It's the same with pickles; they go bad too.
   — And plants, you should never touch a plant or it'll die. . . . It's true!
   — Oh I believe it about plants, but why the hell should it matter with pickles?
   — Well there are lots of things we believe in, but who knows where they come from.
   — How about the number 13, or Friday the 13th, or being 13 around the table? Now I know *that* has to do with Judas, Judas Iscariot.
   — The old folks really . . . but us, what do we know, huh?

3. — In ancient times the Romans used to say, "The gods watch while you're eating." They meant Vesta, the goddess who rules over the table. The guests couldn't be less than three or more than nine, because three is the number of the graces and nine the number of the muses. And for baptisms salt was used to purify the baby. In ancient Rome, before you ate, you'd put the god's share on the altar.

4. — Salt! It used to be, a long time ago, there was even a tax on salt!

5. — Well, the way things are going, I wouldn't be surprised if . . .
— When I saw the price of coffee yesterday at the market, I couldn't . . . eleven francs and something a half pound! It's awful, isn't it?
— And potatoes! My sister had a terrible time this winter trying to keep up with the potatoes. She needed at least ten 10-kilo bags! During vacation she said to me, "God . . . (She was scared!) God, do you realize that means almost 1,000 francs for potatoes?" . . . After we got home, she had to start scratching and saving in order to have enough for the potatoes this winter. Well, she didn't make it, and all winter long she had to ration them out, dole out potatoes . . .
— These days it's hard to make a meal for the whole family.
— Yeah, somebody has to leave before everybody else and then, pretty soon, it's not a real meal anymore, you know what I mean?
— Sure, but Sundays . . . Sundays . . .
— Breakfast on Sunday morning is sacred at my house.
— Because it's the only day you can be together. On Sunday morning . . .
— So we take our time, you bet! Because we don't get up until . . .
— On Sundays you have the time to go for a walk, to eat the way you should. Weekdays, we drink instant coffee, but on Sundays we have the real thing. It tastes great, too!
— You finally have the time, but the rest of the week when you get up at 4 or even 3. . . . I usually take tea in the morning, but, even so, lots of times I forget to drink it.

6. — I made some real nice cloth envelopes for my napkins.
— Girls don't embroider anymore.
— My daughter just makes scenes.
— *Mine* embroiders.

7. — My place at the table? Yeah, always the same one, the kids, too!

— The little ones like to switch, but not the older kids. Well, I guess that's not always true. When her father isn't there my oldest, Michèle, takes his place; that way she thinks she's the boss. That's how it is! But . . . but it's really not right. Nope, it isn't right. When I was little, there was five of us kids and nobody dared talk, you know? . . . We didn't dare say a word. Once we had blood sausage, fresh blood sausage, and my brother says to me, just like that, "That looks like shit!" So I started to laugh. But did my brother ever get it! My father put him to bed, and he didn't have anything to eat all day. And then one time it happened with spinach. He says to me, "We went to the garden to collect duck turds." So my father pours the plate of spinach over my brother's head, so he'll see how good it is. All that spinach. *All that spinach!* All over my brother's head. Why? Because he said it was duck turds! My father . . . all over my brother's head. Boy! You bet we didn't dare talk. Then my mother. . . . She was there too. She'd stare at you with her big eyes! Oh no, there was no way you could make a fuss at our table. When you wanted something, it was, "Would you please pass me? . . . " And now? Now it's "Come on! Hurry up! Hand over that bottle! I'm thirsty. . . . Is it coming or what? Are you helping yourself again? You already had two glasses." That's how it goes . . . with Michèle . . . and Roland, too!

8. — Yes, I think when you're at the table you should, you should. . . . Well, that's what's . . . that's what's nice, isn't it? Otherwise, it doesn't mean . . . anything.

9. — Both of us work at the local hospital, in surgery; there's plenty of work, and we never get bored, you can bet on it! We work in teams, either mornings or afternoons. You know, for married women I don't think it's a bad deal, because by 2 o'clock I'm home. I have all afternoon to myself. Like yesterday. Yesterday— . . . What am I saying? Yesterday, I had to take my daughter to dance class because she's studying ballet. What a circus! Run downtown, do the housework when I get back, cook the dinner, do the errands; I tell you, it's crazy. Sometimes, you wonder how you make it. Right? It just about shoots your nerves for good.

— Especially if you're on a diet.

— I *finished* one fifteen days ago, but I'm still paying for it. The pill makes me gain weight. I start work at 6:30 in the morning, you know? Then between the housework, the meals, the kid, my husband, sometimes I think my nerves won't take it anymore! Anyway! Luckily my husband, I

don't mean to say he's a pushover or anything, but he understands, he
helps out, you know? Because if I had a husband who didn't do anything,
who was "laid back," who came home, plunked himself down, and
plopped his feet on the table—well, that . . . that would be too much.

10. — If there were no tables? . . .
    — If there were no tables, we'd have to sit on the floor, like they do in
      Algeria. Yes they do . . . on the floor! In China they sit on the floor too;
      but they do have a little table, even it it's only 20 centimeters high . . .
    — That changes a lot of things!
    — It changes what you serve. You have to have cold buffets . . .
    — You can live on just fruit . . . and fresh water! Love and water!
    — I've heard that a lot, but I never believed it.
    — You ought to try it, with your family!
    — It'd be too beautiful—I'd finally save some money.

11. — I know some people who can't even think unless they're at a table.

12. — Well, there's on top of the table, and then there's underneath it. But you
      should never end up underneath the table, especially if you're drunk.
      Though it does happen . . .

13. — And why not admit it? There are even people who make love on the
      table, since we're talking about tables! Usually they say, "On a corner of
      the table!"
    — Is that for real? It would never happen to me!
    — Mme Bauer, that's disgusting!
    — They say that it's real good for depression.
    — Do you know anybody . . . who makes love . . . on the table?
    — Oh sure, I do. That's why I can talk about it! Sure. She's the one who
      told me about it! She . . . I mean a friend of mine, she's a little nutty!
      That's the kind of thing you do but don't talk about!
    — That's true.
    — Sure, there are lots of things like that.
    — Of course! Otherwise, I wouldn't have said anything! She was real proud
      of herself, too. And, anyway, she could do what she wanted with her
      husband, right? Mmmm, this is good coffee.
    — And, and she told you everything. Just like that?
    — Everything, absolutely everything. It happened after they finished eating,

on the kitchen table, just before he left for work. He went to look for the quilt, if you want to know everything. Then he put it on the table. He brought a stool for himself. . . . It is too! I already told you so. . . . Well, after breakfast, she'd put the dishes on the sink. . . . And, . . . I don't know, I wasn't there! She's the one who told me, the nut!

— I don't find it amusing, I think it's disgusting. What you're telling is . . . it's disgusting. They can do what they want but. . . . This *is* good coffee! . . . To think what people do on the table. . . . When Yvon was just a baby, in the beginning, I used to *change* him on the table.

14. — My dream? A worktable! That's my dream!
    — With a "twenty-first-century" kitchen, like they say.
    — If I only had my own place. . . . Then . . . oh boy . . . I saw just the thing at the expo, in the Alsatian crafts exhibit, a gorgeous kitchen, but I didn't dare ask the price! Especially because it was all wood; wood's a lot more expensive! Wood's warmer, though!

15. — Incidentally, my husband wants to remove my kitchen table! He wants to set up a bar!
    — Really? That's my husband's idea too!
    — So I said, "Forget it, I need my table! How do you expect me to roll out my dough on something no wider than that?"

16. — Meals? I'm the one who gets them, oh sure, it's the woman!
    — In Alsace there's a saying that goes, "The way to a man's heart is through his stomach."
    — Parisians say almost the same thing.
    — Anyway, isn't it easier now to cook and clean? Used to be, we didn't even have vacuum cleaners!
    — You can even buy mayonnaise in a jar!

17. — Don't you think that the table is losing a bit of its prestige?
    — Oh yes! A beautiful table, perfectly . . . perfectly "decked out." It's lovely!
    — The table setting is half the meal.
    — Well, I don't eat with my eyes!
    — A well-set table is already appetizing.
    — It's what Mama always tells me, "You eat first with your eyes!" She always says that.

—If you don't have the right spot for your table, if it's too dark or crowded, . . . you know, it's depressing. You can lose your appetite. You can get in a mood that's really . . . you know what I mean? It happens.

—Right, a table should always be. . . . You should always be happy with your table.

18. —Setting the table—how to set a table. . . . Should girls learn how to do it?

—You better not ask my daughter!

—But boys do it, too! Christian sets the table. And Didier! It's no big deal!

—No, I really mean staging the meal; setting the table is easy.

—Staging is quite an art.

—Heck, you practically have to go to college to learn how.

—Come on, you can fix things up without that much trouble.

—Sure, if you have a nice tablecloth!

—But, first off, you have to have a fine table. Let's start with the table.

—But you don't even see the table!

—It's completely hidden under the tablecloth! When you put a tablecloth on the table, you kind of "civilize" it. A tablecloth is like sheets!

19. —My husband, who doesn't come home for lunch, wants to see everybody at the table at 7:00 sharp. I agree. The table means being together again, discussing things.

20. —In the Middle Ages, to show they were equal, two lords would not only eat at the same table but also on the same tablecloth, and a knight who quarreled with another would take his sword and slice the cloth in half. That was a very serious insult. They say that Du Guesclin did that.

21. —A table? It's a flat surface, whose height is maintained or increased as civilizations develop. People sit around it, all the same level. That way they think they're equals, or, at least, they make believe so. . . . But think about business dinners. . . . Where you sit is important!

—At my house, when my parents come over, they have the place of honor.

—So . . . tell me, what is the "best" place?

—Well, usually it's . . . at the end of the table!

—Except, well. . . . Take a wedding. . . . The bride and groom aren't at each end. They're in . . . the middle, right? And at the Last Supper where was Jesus Christ?

— In the middle!

— And if you have a round table? What then?

22. — I'm used to seeing a certain person in front of me. . . . So, if I have to sit somewhere else. . . . I'm uncomfortable! Why? I don't know, but . . .

— It's just a habit that you acquire. That's all.

— It's like the bed, exactly the same! When you're . . .

— Boy, yes, me too!

— And I just can't . . . I won't sleep!

— So it gets to be . . . an idea you can't change anymore! That's the way it is! Always the same side. I have to be on *my* side to sleep! Why? . . . I don't know, and at the table it's the same thing! My husband faces me. . . . Well, I guess maybe it's because I get up all the time, and the stove is right behind me . . .

— It's a lot more practical! Maybe that *is* it—just a matter of saving energy! Except, that doesn't make sense because where I keep the dishes is . . .

— Yeah, habit is a funny thing.

— It depends on which habit! We probably ought to try to get to the bottom of it. Something that was drilled into us when we were kids, and it . . . it stuck.

23. — Christmas? Christmas . . . Oh Christmas! Turkey . . . foie gras . . . oysters . . . venison . . . foie gras? Not many people have eaten as much foie gras as I have in their entire lifetimes, because I used to work in a place that made foie gras! So, the first slice that wasn't pink enough I . . . zip . . . and . . . mmmm.

24. — I made some *kougloff* yesterday afternoon! In fact, I made two. I took one to my mother! The dough has to rise first. They say you should let it rise three times. But I let it rise twice, then I knead it some more, then I let it . . .

— My grandfather was a Mongol!

— A real Mongol?

— Absolutely!

— You can tell them just by the slant of their eyes. Really.

— You never know where you come from! You might know how you got into the world, but that doesn't mean you know where you came from.

— Yep, you know your mother. But you don't know your father.

— Oh, come on! *I* know. My mother never fooled around in any kind of black market!

— You can't be sure of that. You really can't!

— And what if it were the Holy Ghost, huh?

— Now *flammekueche* . . .

— Eleven francs at the restaurant!

— You have to have a wood stove. A gas stove isn't the same thing. Myself, I like *baekoff, baekoff* made in a wood stove. I don't make it in summer, but in the wintertime it's really . . .

— It's pretty expensive; it comes to quite a lot if you get the meat you need—mutton—and then you need white wine, some cognac. . . . It used to be. . . . Now everybody does a leg of lamb!

— Yeah, you have to have meat! You really aren't eating properly if you don't have meat!

25. — You know, here we eat horse meat. It's good! With horse you have to marinate it . . . mmmm, to go with a potato salad! Then we call it roast beef! It's really good. Oh beef? Well, we call that roast beef, too, only you don't marinate it. You put it in the oven for half an hour. That way it's still rare! I like it. I make it a lot. But horse meat, you have to marinate it in red wine; yeah, you marinate it for three or four days!

— When's the last time we had horse meat? For your birthday?

— Yeah, no wait a minute, it was Christmas!

— But it's expensive, isn't it? Before the war it wasn't expensive at all. Poor people bought it. It used to be the cheapest meat, and now it's the most expensive. For a kilo of horse meat you pay about 55 francs—50 to 55 if you want a good cut!

— If you're weak; if you don't have any strength at all, you should buy a horse meat steak, it'll build you up!

— You have to be careful not to eat too much!

— Yeah! I guess so! Boy, oh boy!

— Some of my friends from work and I went to a stud farm! *We* saw some horses; with a thing. . . . Wow! . . . like that! Yeah, it was that big!

— All five of us went one morning. We had a little "aperitif." Then they brought out a stallion. . . . We said we couldn't miss that. So, we took a good look!

— And *he* got . . . like . . . like . . . that. Then he jumped a mare, well he sort of did this . . . mmmm . . . and that . . . mmmmm . . . , you know? And then, when he finished, it was on to the next one. So, we were expecting to see his stuff again. . . . But it was over just like that!

— Yeah, we saw him jump on her! Then he . . . caressed her a little . . . boom boom boom! He does it four to five times a day!

— Even as many as seven!

— You have to get him ready, you know. They prepare him with a . . . a machine. They told us.

— Afterward, the mare, well, she didn't want to get into the trailer.

— Oh boy, you should of seen the ruckus she made. . . . The mare doesn't get much . . . no, no, it's over so fast! Everything's set up ahead of time.

— Five to six times a day! . . . the same stallion!

— And you have to pay for it! But he's beautiful, so elegant. You know how much a horse like that—a thoroughbred—is worth? Fifteen million old francs.

— They're beautiful, horses. And the meat's good too, right?

— In restaurants you can always get roast beef, but it's not from horses!

— When my baby was born, to make me strong, they gave me a horse meat steak.

— I think I'll fix some horse meat soon . . .

— Horse meat . . . and what about some couscous?

26. — It's a pleasure to sit down and eat at a beautiful table!

— I have my everyday dishes and a set for the holidays. They're traditional, with a peasant motif! When it's a holiday, the . . . the girls . . . they set the table! And then it's really perfect! They use cloth napkins and everything . . .

— I have those shallow soup bowls and the regular dinner plates . . . and you have to make sure the little people go in the right direction, of course!

— And you have to make sure you've got the same design on the soup bowl as on the dinner plate, the dessert plate, the cup, and the saucer. No, not the saucer, there isn't any design on the saucer.

— Then if you break something, you have to be real careful to note exactly which design it was, don't you?

— What I do is stick the pieces together, I use Scotch tape or even a Band-Aid, then I glue the broken parts, and then, right away, I go buy the same plate!

— Phew! . . . Good dishes are expensive!

— I was at Cora's the other day, 9 francs 50 for a demitasse cup!

— Two of mine just got chipped. Boy . . . that . . . that . . . makes me sick to my stomach.

27. — The budget? You bet it's hard! I figure it by the month.

— I can't make it anymore with 500 francs a week. It's just not enough.

— Just on the milk we drink every day, and a week's supply of bread (I subtract the meat from the paycheck at the end of the month), with the wash, cleaning stuff, the hot water bill, and then the rent, I have to figure 600 to 700 francs. When you don't have a car, it sure helps.

— These days the cost of living has increased so much you can't save anything.

— It's hard. We don't have a car, but even for a bicycle. . . . I keep after my husband. He's been saving for over a year just to buy a chain for his motorbike. It only costs 40 francs.

— A lady was telling me she could never stick to her budget, and by the end of the month she didn't dare tell her husband there wasn't enough. . . . So she'd call her sister to borrow some money and . . . that went on and on!

28. — Is that you, Albert? We said we didn't want any men here! Who's going to watch the kids? . . . Wait a minute! I'll get you a chair. You know I'm not like that. Besides, I'm afraid you'll get varicose veins! It's Albert. The other day we were sitting at the table, and a colleague of his came over. He said, "Women, they're always talking about diseases and stuff! . . ." So, him and Albert, they decided right then to test it: "We're going to launch the color black, it'll turn out to be the hottest color on the market, you'll see; all those women and their death and diseases and all the rest!" That's how they get their kicks! Nice, huh? I say, "Next time, try red." But men wouldn't dare try red! I don't think they'd appreciate what women would have to say about it. First, it'd be "revolution" . . . then, "blood." . . . It's tremendous. It's . . . it's women in revolt, and then . . . well, I, for one, I've had my moments. Sometimes you get to a point where there's so much . . . crap. . . . You just revolt, you know . . . or something like that. . . . You have to evolve. . . . It's part of growing—when you don't just go along anymore. Right, Albert?

29. — There was this woman, her husband hit her because she was . . . well, she drank, smalltown people, you know. . . . She was a drunk, so he hauled off and hit her. She died from it! You know the Arab proverb, "Beat your wife; if *you* don't know why she deserves it, *she* does." That's what my husband always says to me.

— My husband had a buddy from work, and he stopped over at his house. His wife, you know? She'd just bought a new table. She'd been wanting it—for a long time. It was . . . but it was a little unstable, and her husband? He tipped over his drink on it. So, he says, "Why the hell did you buy a wobbly table?" And then he hits her, right in front of my husband. So, my husband says, "You shouldn't have slapped her. It could have happened to you! Just as easy, buying a table that's a little wobbly." Yes, he did. Then he said, "You just have to put a little piece of felt underneath the leg, and it won't wobble anymore; that's how to fix your table!" Yeah. He hit his wife right in front of my husband! So, what does my husband do? He says, "A guy who hits his wife is not a man, that's what I think." And he never went back there.

— One time, some Moroccans, or somebody like that, came by. . . . They were selling those little round tables to put flowers on . . .

— Oh, Alsace, Alsace is known for . . .

— It's got the record for wife beating!

— But it also has the record for faithful wives!

— Maybe there are men who aren't faithful . . .

— Anyway, that's accepted!

— "Couples that fight a lot love a lot."

— Maybe there are couples who manage real well because of the fighting!

— Not for me, thank you! All day long you work, take care of the kids, and at night you're supposed to let him hit you?

— Uh uh. . . . That's not my cup of tea!

30. — When I'm alone I don't eat! If I eat at the table, all alone, I get uncomfortable. If somebody . . . I already told you this! . . . If somebody comes by; if they ring the doorbell . . . I feel guilty because I'm eating by myself, as if I was being caught red-handed, doing something I shouldn't! Somebody rings! And right away I'm ashamed! So, either I throw everything out or I don't open the door.

31. — Let me tell you, when he starts to eat with his fingers, we jab him with his fork.

— How old is he?

— Christophe? Fifteen.

— Some things you can eat with your fingers—french fries, chicken. . . . It's even better that way. But he picks up . . . he eats everything with his fingers! Even sauces. He picks up his potato, and he won't have. . . . So, we say to him, "Don't use your paws!" And he says, "I don't have paws, I have hands!" It doesn't seem to matter how many times we tell him. So, now we don't even bother anymore. But, as soon as he starts, we jab him with his fork.

32. —Composition time! For Mother's Day, children, you're going to tell me
    what a mama is . . .
    —Uh . . . a lady who makes the meals, uh . . . a lady who rides a bike,
    uh . . . a lady who changes the beds . . .

33. —You should see *me* at the table. I have this plastic spoon, huge like this!
    real tough, you know? A wooden one? . . . it'd break. So, in the morn-
    ing, around 6:30, when they wake up, I've already got it on the table.
    You bet they understand! They get the message, for sure!

34. —But when you've got little kids, like that, it's the same thing! You cut
    their meat. You feed this one. You feed that one. And, when you finally
    get around to sitting down, everything's cold!
    —Yeah, and you're not hungry anymore, right!
    —It's too late! You eat bad. Your stomach gets all upset. Sometimes I ask
    myself, "How come?" But then I think: "Well that's the way it is. Those
    are the breaks. A woman is meant to serve, so . . ."

35. —Nowadays children start eating at the table when they're real young! As
    soon as mine could eat with a spoon, I put a fork next to their plates, and
    they ate with us.
    —Like my little Nicolas . . . he has a knife when he eats, even if he can't
    use it to cut.
    —It's all a matter of personality. It depends on the kid.
    —Well, you ought to see my sister's three-year-old! She sits at the table—a
    perfect angel—three years old, with her knife and fork, and she eats! It's
    unbelievable.

36. —At my house. . . . It's always crazy at the table! That's what I like!
    Because when you get right down to it . . . if there was just two of us
    it'd be . . . well, sometimes it's kind of monotonous.
    —I don't know . . . maybe . . .
    —I love it when it's lively. I'm like that, anyway. Everybody says so: I'm
    noisy. Noisy! You know my husband is real quiet. So, I'm always the one
    who has to speak or say something because . . . I have to talk. Even if
    it's not very important, I have to talk! It's like a mania. . . . When my
    little girl starts in . . . boy, do I nag, you know? She won't eat, or she
    takes forever, so I yell: "Caty eat! Hurry up! Sit up! Get your elbows off

the table!" Oh yeah, I can't stand it when. . . . Say, Sunday, you know? I had the day off for a change . . . I work most of them. . . . Well, she was sitting like this! . . . So, I didn't say anything. I just gestured to my husband as if to say, "You see the way she's sitting!" So, he says to her, "Caty, sit up straight!" "Ohhhhh," she says. Then he say, "Caty, is your head *that* heavy?" And she says, "Oh leave me alone!" I suppose she was still sleepy! But you have to see her at the table, just like a monkey, with her legs up in the air . . .

37. — We needed a cup, so Michèle bought one yesterday at the co-op.
   — Why did you need a cup?
   — Because of Grandma! We have quite a lot, but they're either little or like this. . . . And if we have big ones and Grandma has a little one . . . well, there's hell to pay! So, now we have ones with flowers, and Grandma has a big blue one . . .
   — We use coffee bowls.
   — At our house in the morning it's a circus! Saturday, when my husband's there, I have to shut the door so he won't hear me! I try not to say anything, but there's still a racket! There's no stopping me. I check each of the kids one after the other. First the teeth, then the ears. Oh it's my mania, not the teeth, uh . . . I mean . . . not the ears. . . . (When I'm nervous I switch everything around) . . . I mean the teeth. Christophe— well, he's still devouring the toothpaste! I have to hide it! If I buy Signal, he eats it up in no time flat.

38. — You have to think of everything!
   — The man should be able to count on his wife. He needs his rest! There are some women who expect their husbands to discipline the kids. I think that's . . .
   — I think it's stupid! Since the wife is always there with the kids, anyway! Sure, you have to punish the kids! And it's the wife who . . .
   — I agree 100 percent!
   — When my husband comes home at night, he always asks me: "How was your day? How'd it go?" And I always say, "Just fine." I think it's ridiculous when the husband's been away all day and then comes home to "This one did that, and that one did that!" And then the wife expects him to spank them.
   — Nope, not for me!

39. — At our table you can't forget anything. "Mama serves the meals, the kids set the table!" Salt, pepper, napkins; it's a regular routine. You should see it! And they know for sure that if they forget something my husband will get mad. And Michèle? Michèle always says: "If I have to get up, if one of you has forgotten one single thing, you're going to get it, understand! Because I don't want to get the hiccups again!" And if something *is* missing . . . she gets up. . . . And she has the hiccups! Yep! Hiccups! I don't know. She gets upset right away. . . . She's afraid that I'll have to get up so she gets the hiccups! Because my husband would yell!

40. — Well, after Eric's communion I was sick for fourteen days! Yeah, I drank a whole bottle of champagne all by myself! You know. . . . I'd worked all day long; my sisters helped me some, but I'd been at it the whole day. I hadn't eaten a thing, not a bit, just drank a little water! So, in the evening my husband says to me: "OK. Time to relax now! Your turn for some champagne. Come on!" That's all I remember! My husband pours me a glass. . . . Oh, it was cold that champagne, so cold you couldn't. . . . The next day I woke up in bed! They even took a picture of me in my chair!

41. — Left, my husband left! "To live his own life!" That was six years ago! I still feel as much . . . as much a part of a couple! It's . . . it's a mess, you know? I can't . . . I can't get over it. I can't seem to give up on it! I'd say to myself, if three kids can't keep him here, it's because I don't . . . count for anything! So, I . . . I didn't even. . . . Well, I got him to think about it! Afterward, with the kids, when we were all alone. . . . My oldest was eight years old. . . . We were like baby chicks, all in the same room! There we were, all four of us in the bedroom! All four in the kitchen! All four in the. . . . It was . . . phew . . . unbelievable. We were like in a nest, all four of us, everywhere piled on top of one another in the same room. It was. . . . We couldn't breathe. . . . Like baby chicks, traveling together . . . everywhere! And then, the dishes! We had these dishes in Melmac, with this dark sort of design on them. . . . I couldn't stand them! On the table? I couldn't stand anything that dark! Yeah, it was the color, not the Melmac. . . . I needed something bright, flowered. I had to set a table . . . I needed to set *my* table! So, I got out the good dishes! And now, if they're all mixed up, I don't care. If it's a dark plate, I take it for

myself automatically. But before . . . my dark dishes . . . I'd put them at the bottom of the pile. And we didn't talk about it anymore.

— It's funny. There are lots of things like that.

— What? . . . Now? I do everything. At the table I'm the father and the mother! It's not so complicated because . . . well, when Mother's Day came around. . . . But. . . . When there was Father's Day I started to panic. I said to myself, "What now?" But you know what my son did, the littlest one? He said, "I don't have a Papa, but it doesn't matter cuz I've . . . I've got a Mama who takes the place of Papa, so I'm going to draw a picture!" And, instead of drawing a papa who was smoking a cigar or a pipe, he drew a mama. A mama with a cigar and I don't know what else, and he said to me, "Mama, you're our Papa, so you might as well have two presents." I said, "You're right, honey!" So . . . we've made it. We don't miss a father at my house anymore . . . except when there's a broken toy . . . and . . . well, . . . anyway. . . . Anyway, I never have men over, since I don't know any, so. . . . There's no men at our house! But the four of us, we talk! And we laugh . . .

42. — Are there any girls who're master chefs?

— Master chefs? No, there isn't a one of them! There're only men!

— Eric, my seventeen-year-old, is apprenticed to a chef. He cooks. . . . He does all the banquets for . . . for the Council of Europe in Strasbourg! And it's not ordinary meals I'm talking about. Sometimes he brings me back these goodies . . . mmmm! mmmm! Oh, I know there are girls who work in restaurants, but not the master chefs! Because it's real hard. You have to work late at night and . . .

43. — Oh! The new schedule? Well, before, I had an hour and a half at lunchtime. I could make my sauerkraut or some other vegetable and get a head start on dinner. Now I have less than an hour, and I can't manage anymore.

— I wonder what you'd do if we were still paid for piecework, like before?

— Oh, I'd go nuts, for sure! Now we work at a normal pace; but when you're paid according to piecework it's not normal. . . . You go faster and faster!

— And it shows up at home, especially at the table.

— Yeah, the work is still boring and impersonal, but you don't have here . . . in your head, your throat, really, in all your body . . . that little voice that keeps saying, "I've got to make my quota." The pressure is awful!

— And it never stops. Your quota keeps increasing.

— Yeah, and besides, with all this business of "creating needs" . . . well, it's on your mind, and, like Marie says, "We're all patsies!" And even if you know that the whole society is set up to encourage buying . . . you . . . you want to make more money! And sometimes it gets so you don't even make what you made the month before! So, that gets to you. . . . And your nerves are on edge!

— And then they call you into the supervisor's office because . . . "How come you're putting out less?" and all that! So there's this pressure and . . . you know . . . I think . . . yeah . . . I'd croak! I'll never do piecework again. I'd croak from it. I'd stand almost anything, but . . . Jesus . . . piecework . . . it's *unthinkable*! When you've won the battle, and you don't have to work that way anymore. . . . It took me a year to get rid of this funny ball I had in my throat! And when I get nervous now I get it back. I start thinking I'll never finish my lot. And then, right away, like before, it's: "Damn, I can't handle it today. I'm not getting anywhere. I work, work, work. And still I'm not getting ahead. Shit! What'll I make today?" You used to go home, and you'd count what you'd got done. And you'd think: "Nuts, I didn't make anything. Got to work faster from now on." So, the next day you'd have all that on your mind: Crap work. . . . Work that pays nothing. Believe me! You could give me the choice between a year in prison or the rest of my life doing piecework, and, you bet, I'd rather spend a year in the slammer!

— A small group of us women were the first in France to protest and sign petitions. We obtained the first agreement to get rid of piecework. And salaries. . . . The salaries stayed the same! It was a tough fight. . . . Management is still sore about it. You should hear how they're still griping! Oh boy! But I think that, when you start getting involved, having other responsibilities . . . the table, well, it becomes less important. That doesn't mean you don't cook or you don't invite people over. . . . But for a woman the table isn't the most important thing anymore. It's more, "Sit down and let's eat! . . ." In the long run what's important is to be together. It's not always easy. Because the day the woman starts to take some distance from the table, she encounters all kinds of problems with the rest of the family. They want to know, "What's the matter with *you?*" Yup. That's the way it is!

44. — My mother . . . during the war, we lived in Grenoble. Well, Mama with her two suitcases, would take off for the Saône and Loire. And during the

war she'd come back from there, with a pig in each suitcase. At Lyon she had to get across the whole city. And there were no more bridges. She had to get across the Rhone! But my mother's a real trooper. She couldn't even carry the bags off the train, right? So, one time a German wanted to help her: "What do you have there, Fraulein? Are you setting up house-keeping?" "Sure, it's my trousseau!" she says. She was taking a real chance. If they'd shipped her off. . . . It would've been the end. It was even worse because she wouldn't tell them she was Alsatian. During the war Mama would hide Alsatian refugees at our house, and she'd feed everybody. At the time she even wanted to join the Resistance! But they wouldn't let her because she had four little kids. "But what you did wasn't *normal*. . . . Did you think about . . . if they took you away? What would've happened to us kids?" It wasn't *normal*, because, when you get down to it, we weren't dying of hunger at our house! It wasn't normal to go to the Saône and Loire to get a pig. . . . Imagine!!! risking your neck for a pig!

45. — No, I don't have a job, but I call myself a "homemaker," because I don't like it when you have to write "No occupation" on all those forms! The other day I got furious with my husband. The children had some forms to fill out about . . . concerning their religious instruction. So, he writes, for my profession, "Nothing." And, right then I blew up; I said, "Listen, you can take your nothings and. . . ." Even the other times he wrote down "Nothing" I said, "Oh yeah, well, wait'll I show you someday just what 'nothing' means." As if you didn't work in the house! Anyway, I have to admit that the women who have a job outside their home and who do the housework, get the meals, raise the kids. . . . Well, I say, "Hats off to them!"

46. — I painted my table the same color as my walls: white! That way they fade into each other, and when there's nothing on it I'm real happy!

Ina Césaire

INA CÉSAIRE (B. 1941), daughter of Martinique's most famous poet and statesman, is an ethnologist and playwright. Her many years spent analyzing and codifying Antillean folktales have fueled her passionate interest in the structure of Caribbean mythology. They have also resulted in two erudite collections of oral tales: *Contes de mort et de vie aux Antilles* (Life and Death Tales in the Antilles, 1976) and *Contes de nuits et de jours aux Antilles* (Day and Night Stories of the Antilles, 1989).

Her research focuses in particular on the oral tradition that presents a picaresque hero traveling from childhood to adulthood. The prototypical rascal works out his liberation by destroying the past and profiting from miraculous reversals. This is the character she portrays in her 1987 play, *L'Enfant des passages ou la geste de Ti-Jean* (The Child of Passages, or the Adventure of Ti-Jean), a charming and lively history of Guadeloupian folk hero Ti-Jean l'Horizon, who had earlier been the locus of a celebrated novel by Simone Schwarz-Bart.[1]

Ti-Jean succeeds through cunning and egotism, defeating various folk monsters and opponents on the way. He is a likable con artist, a trickster who, by his immorality, counters neatly the model of the Christian "good man." Césaire's fantastic parable can be seen as a depiction of the poor man's way out. In her play Ti-Jean, friends, and enemies dance and sing a startling trajectory to their destination.

Césaire understands her folk heroes, including Ti-Jean, as presenting a morphology of repressed desires. Folk heroes are her culture's way of expressing its need for autonomy from the mentality of the colonizers, of defeating European lessons about humility and endurance. While Césaire obviously relishes such tales, she is also aware of how much of the main character's liberation—the main character being always male—depends on the vilification of women. In oral tales female characters show up primarily as stereotypical sorceresses, mothers, or empty-headed young women. Guadeloupian novelist Maryse Condé and educa-

45

In the Théâtre du Campagnol's production of Ina Césaire's *Island Memories* (1983), the two elderly characters, Aure (Myrrha Donzenac) and Hermance (Marian Mathéus) often acted out moments from an evening of reminiscing about their long lives in Martinique. Here, they recreate the tableau of Hermance's strong-willed mother braiding her daughter's hair. (Photo by Alain Fonteray.)

tors France Alibar and Pierrette Lambeye-Boy have similarly underscored in novels (Condé's *Hérémakhonon*) and essays (Alibar's and Lambeye-Boy's *Le Couteau seul / Sé Kouto sèl* . . . [Only the Knife Knows . . .]) the Caribbean woman's often harrowing status in fiction—as well as in life.

This painful and complicated representation, which barely takes into consideration the matriarchal component of Antillean culture, prompted Césaire to compose *Island Memories: Mama N. and Mama F.* (1985). She began with the biographies of long-lived Martinican women, especially the experiences of her own grandmothers, who had been or were willing to recount their life stories. In *Island Memories* Césaire, therefore, combats the negative mythical heritage of the folktales, with its attendant social consequences, by portraying women who are the heroes of their own lives.

Césaire was greatly aided in her project by actresses Mariann Mathéus and Myrrah Donzenac, who incarnated the principal roles and contributed many of the stories that their own family members or other elderly women had shared with them. The two actresses were guided by Césaire and Jean-Claude Penchenat, the director of the Théâtre du Campagnol, which produced the first version of the piece in 1983. They reworked the original material through improvisations, selected real-life fragments to be dramatized, and, according to their own intimate knowledge of Caribbean culture, discussed every detail of the production with the technicians and designers. Following Penchenat's suggestion, they also developed three separate playing spaces in order to isolate one area of the stage for acting out parts of the stories embedded in the old women's monologues.

The creative team divided the play into two parts: the first, inscribed under the sign of the Caribbean Carnival, presents two vital young women, signaled as "actors" but dressed and made up as she-devils, strutting the *vidé*, the main Carnival dance step. They tell riddles, joke with each other and the audience, and play language games in French and, more significantly, in Creole. This short "overture" establishes the rules of the performance and a certain theoretical underpinning: that women's roles are consciously chosen and can be entertaining for the performers too; that theater (like Carnival) can be the site of subversive activity; that Caribbean culture and Creole language must also be subjects of dramatic expression; and that life might just be a series of metamorphoses and processes—far from stagnant, far from fixed, and far from stable; finally, that this instability is precisely the stuff of "life."

At the end of this fragment the two actresses change their makeup to "become" two old ladies who will, in the second part of the play, recount and act out their stories. They will remember the past and reinscribe the history of the island under the sign of women's quotidian reality. Together, "Aure," the distin-

guished, lighter-skinned, well-educated woman from the calm southern part of
the island, and "Hermance," the seamstress, the underprivileged, the darker-
skinned woman from the wild North, speak, in bits and pieces, their parallel
lives. Hermance often asserts the superiority of her Creole-dominated speech to
Aure's refined French. And Aure acknowledges, albeit often unconsciously, her
acquiescence to Hermance's more creolized version of island life.

They create a doubled version of a Martinican "Everywoman," a legendary but
not exoticized figure anchored, nevertheless, in very specific details. The latter
vary from Hermance's onomatopoeic *tchipp,* a filler word to express disagreement,
dismay, or simply presence, to the carefully composed costume of Aure, which
bespeaks both her character and her status in Martinican society. Their important
differences, including their drastically opposed fates, are ultimately underplayed
in order to give one voice to all those who have kept or been kept quiet in the past.

Their interweaving monologues treat of birthing and raising children, doctor-
ing, marriage and courtship, cuisine, religion, death, and the various physical and
political traumas that have marked Martinican history since the end of the nineteenth century. Hermance and Aure also establish a feminine genealogy by recol-
lecting all the other strong women who have influenced their lives. Finally,
through dance interludes and Creole phrases, they valorize, too, a system of communication that is specifically their own, freed of the language of the colonizers.

Of the many remarkable moments each restores, the most awful is the archetypal rape scene—the only time when a white presence intrudes in their personal
histories. Without their commenting on it, this telling moment of horror foregrounds the double victimization of the African woman, slave for European
colonizers and sexual property for men in general. This one reference to slavery
has a double function: it reminds the audience of something that must never be
forgotten; but it also demonstrates that lives can be built on something other than
unspeakable memories. The formidable tragedy of African peoples does not, then,
overshadow the play's focus on the fabric of aged Caribbean women's lives.

Profoundly connected to the land and the sea of their birth, these women have
built their lives with themselves at the center. They are mothers and wives, of
course, but the metaphors they relish for themselves: woman—dance, woman—
sea, woman—force, woman—racehorse, and woman—daughter of other women,
put forward a multidimensional human being, untethered by any given representation and irrepressibly committed to the act of living itself.

---

1. See C. Makward, "Ethno-dramaturgie d'Ina Césaire," in *L'Héritage de Caliban,* ed. Maryse Condé
(Guadeloupe: Jasor, 1992).

Ina Césaire

Island Memories: Mama N. and Mama F.

We are in Martinique. Two old women take stock of their lives in the course of a festive evening. One is Aure, a refined mulatto from the countryside. Blue-eyed and light-skinned, she was born in the southern part of the island, in the realm of palm trees and aloe, near a transparent, placid sea, white sand, and the inconspicuous greenery of dry climates. Very cultured, she is a retired school-teacher, who hides her indomitable strength and prickliness under real elegance, great gentleness, and an air of modesty. Her youthful and delicate sense of humor tempers a strict sense of duty.

The other, Hermance, also known as Cia, is a very tall black woman. Her background is urban and working-class. She was born in the wild northern part of the island, by a frenetic sea and the dark volcanic sand surrounding Mount Pelée and its tragic memories, in the thick shadow of lush tropical vegetation: fern trees, giant bamboos, and stark ceiba trees—a violent and unstable land. Although uneducated, she is endowed with undeniable charisma, bolstered by keen intelligence and uncompromising will. Loud-mouthed, proud, assertive, controlling— Man Cia is all of these.

These lives, geometrically ambiguous, since they are at once parallel and divergent, are also deceptively banal. Richer in pain than in laughter, they reveal two authentic human beings, both profoundly female and profoundly Caribbean. They reveal, too, a whole cultural and symbolic background born of historical reality (with the ghost of slavery never far behind)—a political, social, and economic situation that suggests itself to us with all the nuances and brutality of life itself, of everyday language and people.[1]

---

1. A first version of this play premiered in Bagneux, a Parisian suburb, in 1983 by the Théâtre du Campagnol, directed by Jean-Claude Penchenat, with Myrrha Donzenac as Aure and Mariann Mathéus as Hermance. Ubu Repertory Theater Company has produced two of Ina Césaire's plays: *Island Memories* (1991) and *Fire's Daughters* (Rosanie Soleil, 1993). The latter piece, translated by Judith G. Miller for *New French Language Plays* (New York: Ubu Repertory Theater Publications, 1993), again treats of women's lives in the French Caribbean.

THE SHE-DEVIL PARADE

Lights. The two actors, dressed as SHE-DEVILS *in the Ash Wednesday Carnival tradition, are putting on their makeup. On a cue from the drum they begin strutting, then dancing the* vidé.[2]

FIRST SHE-DEVIL: (*Bellowing*) Ladies and Gentlemen . . . I said good evening!

SECOND SHE-DEVIL: (*Ironically*) Ladies and Gentlemen . . . I replied!

(*They laugh and dance the* vidé.)

FIRST SHE-DEVIL: (*Dancing*) Sorry if we lose the rhythm.

SECOND SHE-DEVIL: . . . And if we run out of breath . . .

FIRST SHE-DEVIL: . . . And if our feet slip . . .

SECOND SHE-DEVIL: But we have our reasons!

FIRST SHE-DEVIL: Three hundred years, gentlemen and ladies!

SECOND SHE-DEVIL: Three hundred years of dancing Carnival!

FIRST SHE-DEVIL: Without counting the "sweet little waltzes" before that . . .

(*She executes a few energetic African dance steps.*)

SECOND SHE-DEVIL: (*Swirling*) Thank heavens it doesn't last all year!

FIRST SHE-DEVIL: Let's not let night catch us, my friend![3]

SECOND SHE-DEVIL: The night's still far away, my friend! . . .

FIRST SHE-DEVIL: *If you say so, girl. Come on! (*They dance.*)

SECOND SHE-DEVIL: (*Very fast*) *Can you tell me if time has time?

FIRST SHE-DEVIL: (*Same beat*) I can hear time: it has no time.

SECOND SHE-DEVIL: (*Laughing*) *My friend, I'd say that's a riddle!

FIRST SHE-DEVIL: *Here's another: Lordy, lordy! What are we, my friend?

SECOND SHE-DEVIL: Women outside of time, my friend!

FIRST SHE-DEVIL: And outside the ages, by God!

---

2. The *vidé* (like the samba in Brazil) is the traditional Carnival strut. Incarnating the spirit of Carnival itself, the fast-paced *vidé* suggests an explosive liberation from conventions and social rules. Other Antillean dances mentioned in this play include the *haute taille* (a quadrille—a "called dance," unlike the french quadrille, which is not called—and named after the cut of the dress worn by women during the Directory and Napoleonic periods), the *damier* (another form of quadrille, named after the chessboard), and the *mazurka piquée* (a more rapid and rythmically complicated version of the polka, which includes a brusque pause marked by raising one foot). Césaire, an anthropologist as well as a playwright, has researched extensively the importance of music and dance in Caribbean society. *Island Memories* includes references to some fourteen songs and seven dances, ranging from Creole ballads to popular dance music, such as the sentimental *léroz,* which lends its name to an entire evening's activities, held especially after the sugarcane harvest. We have translated song titles in the dialogue in cases in which a translation would facilitate the sense of the exchange. In all other instances the titles remain in the original French or Creole, with an English translation in brackets.

3. Césaire uses Creole phrases and expressions throughout her text. Creole sentences, such as this one, will henceforth be marked by an asterisk. In cases in which only part of a line is in Creole the phrase or expression will also be in italics.

TOGETHER: All these years we've strutted and danced. . . .

SECOND SHE-DEVIL: (*Picking up the phrase*) The *grand vidé* . . .

FIRST SHE-DEVIL: Empty of time and of age . . .

SECOND SHE-DEVIL: (*Asking a question*) Age . . . what's that?

FIRST SHE-DEVIL: Age, well it's . . . (*Questioning*) like time?

(*The second* SHE-DEVIL *registers dissent.*)

FIRST SHE-DEVIL: (*Triumphantly*) Age is like the *kenep,* the hard green fruit whose outside is tough . . .

SECOND SHE-DEVIL: (Taking over) But whose inside is tender as memories!

(*They dance together.*)

FIRST SHE-DEVIL: All these years we've strutted and danced . . .

SECOND SHE-DEVIL: . . . The *grand vidé* . . .

FIRST SHE-DEVIL: . . . Empty of time and of age . . .

SECOND SHE-DEVIL: . . . So much has passed! . . .

FIRST SHE-DEVIL: . . . The past has passed! . . .

SECOND SHE-DEVIL: (*Humming*) It passed by here . . .

(*They dance to the Caribbean round "Le Poteau bleu"* [The Blue Post].)[4]

FIRST SHE-DEVIL: . . . It passed by there . . .

SECOND SHE-DEVIL: . . . The past has been trespassed . . .

FIRST SHE-DEVIL: . . . The past has been surpassed . . .

SECOND SHE-DEVIL: (*Feigning naïveté*) . . . But has the past passed away? (*They laugh.*)

---

4. Much of the impact of Césaire's images depends on direct, even tactile knowledge of the flora, geography, and sociology of the French Caribbean (or Antilles). We have used the English equivalent for such images if we felt it would have the same or similar resonances for an Anglophone public as for a Francophone Antillean one. In other instances we have used description to better convey the charm or the force of Césaire's associations. Some words are quite untranslatable (although we have translated them), because they carry an emotional charge that is specific to the Caribbean. These include, among others: *le béké* (translated as "local white man"), which has often, but not always, a derogatory connotation and refers to the whites (and their descendants) who colonized the islands; *le morne* (translated as "hill" or "hills"), which is always contrasted to *le bourg* (village) and where many slaves (the Maroons) fled to freedom during slavery, connoting therefore a free life away from white domination; *la case* (translated as "cabin" or "house"), which is the basic four-wall shelter of the islands and which, if a family is prosperous, includes a veranda; *le madras* (translated as "head scarf") and *la gaule* (translated as "dress"), typical elements of French Caribbean dress made of Indian cotton, usually plaid, whose cut, as well as how a scarf is tied, can indicate the marital status and psychological profile of the wearer; *le gommier* (translated as "gum tree canoe"), which is the light-weight, square-sailed, fishing vessel omnipresent in the Caribbean; *le flamboyant* (translated as "flame tree"), which is a strikingly tall tree of tropical countries, whose large red flowers often give it symbolic status as the "tree of life"; *le fromager* (translated by its botanical name, *ceiba*), a huge tree often thought to have occult power and under whose branches people gather to talk and tell stories; and *une chabine kalazaza* (translated as "pale-skinned negress"), a mixed-race person characterized by what are commonly thought of as Caucasian facial features and Negroid hair—Antilleans have a complicated system of distinguishing differences among themselves.

FIRST SHE-DEVIL: Let's get on with our dance, my friend!

SECOND SHE-DEVIL: Let's dance to "I'll Be Young," God willing!

FIRST SHE-DEVIL: Let's dance to "I've Been Old," the devil only knows!

SECOND SHE-DEVIL: Let's dance to *"It's Not All Said and Done . . ."

TOGETHER: . . . And tomorrow will be different! (*Uncontrollable laughter. They return to their makeup tables to transform themselves into grandmothers.*)

(*The stage is dimly lit. An old woman is seated in an armchair. Another one enters slowly, obviously tired, while the lights gradually grow brighter. The women are in formal clothes. Bits of music, laughter, and conversation flow in from a door, which is slightly ajar: inside a party is going on. The lighting foregrounds a typical Caribbean veranda at nightfall.*

Behind the two women the slatted shutters create a striped, luminous backdrop, while the latticework between the roof beams projects shadows on the floor.

Sounds of a Caribbean night.

Bright moonlight.

The second old woman hesitates a moment, noticing the other woman's motionless shape in the chair. She continues on her way and settles down in a rocking chair set slightly askance and oriented in such a fashion that, at first, neither woman can look at the other.

One rocks gently, fanning herself. The other massages her foot. Each one starts a sentence at the same moment and interrupts herself almost immediately to allow the other to speak. Embarrassed silence.

The music grows stronger. The orchestra is playing a Creole mazurka. Laughter.

Somewhere onstage there should be two darkly colored screens behind which the actresses will change before performing their various roles.

Throughout the evening their very different pasts will surge forth in short remembrances.

Their conversation, polite and inconsequential at first, will transform itself gradually through both monologues and dialogues into a profound exploration of their personal histories.)

GESTURES, QUIRKS, AND OTHER CHARACTER TRAITS

AURE

—*Rubs her fingers numbed by arthritis, one after the other.*

—*Always has one or two bandages on her fingers because, since her fingers have become insensitive to heat, she often burns herself while cooking.*

—*Never throws away her old chocolate tins: opens ten of them in order to find the most trivial bit of paper.*

—*Is always engrossed in some mysterious task: she cautiously wraps minuscule objects in meticulously crafted, tiny packages.*
—*Discreetly, but without vanity, inspects her careful appearance.*
—*Laughs like a girl, a full-throated, musical, hearty laughter.*
—*Her voice is soft and melodious, bespeaking good breeding. She is, however, afflicted with a chronic sore throat.*
—*Loses her glasses every five minutes.*

HERMANCE

—*Enjoys looking cross, frowns, and pouts.*
—*Often massages a sore leg.*
—*Constantly tosses about her cane. (It had been her husband's.) She brandishes it, loses it, retrieves it, uses it to underscore her speech.*
—*Often emits the* tchiip, *a Caribbean onomatopoeia indicating disdain or irritation.*
—*Has an immense capacity to remain motionless.*
—*Often has musical reminiscences (dance tunes from the Martinique of her youth).*
—*Her laugh is broad, low-pitched, and resounding.*

AURE: Aren't these ceremonies exhausting?

HERMANCE: Heaven's yes, my dear! I'm not so young anymore . . .

AURE: But the service was very moving and the bride so beautiful!

HERMANCE: The mass was too long for me! I don't understand a thing about these masses in French that they do nowadays. It doesn't even sound Christian, if you want my opinion!

AURE: It's progress, my dear! You have to adapt . . .

HERMANCE: Progress! I call it sloppiness, uh huh! Hmmmmm! I think my feet are dead! Oooeee. Oh Lord!

AURE: (*Conciliatory tone, measured*) It sure is funny: your husband's niece marrying my brother's son. Now we're even more family than ever!

HERMANCE: You speaking about me? I'm not from one of your best families.

AURE: My maternal family is also of very humble origin! And, after all, we do have the same father!

HERMANCE: Uh-huh, but I wasn't good enough to be acknowledged. My mother wasn't well enough born—not enough of a mulatto to be taken to the altar!

AURE: Oh, that was such a long time ago, Hermance. And prejudice is so . . . regrettable. . . . The past shouldn't run in front of the future . . .

HERMANCE: Where's my cane? I'm going to ask Joseph to take me home! I'm not sure the maid isn't pinching some of my things. (*She calls out.*) Joseph! Children are so ungrateful. *He's up and gone.*

AURE: Joseph is your grandson, isn't he?

HERMANCE: That's right! These days our sons go to France, make kids with white women, and send them back to finish off their old mothers who've already borne their crosses—I had my own eight children!

AURE: That is the way it is these days . . . but life goes on . . .

HERMANCE: These children nowadays, all they're about is spending money . . . there's no respect left!

AURE: That's true. . . . When I was a child, I wouldn't even think of looking my father in the eyes.[5] (*The light over* HERMANCE *gradually fades out.* AURE *remains in a halo of light.*) He was a very gentle man, though, very affable and a good worker, too; he could do anything! And such a handsome man! A fine mulatto, very straight and slender! His natural father was a white man from France, M. de Vrigny. My father was born in Marin, around 1865. When he finally married my mother, I was eighteen. . . . At that time I was getting ready for the teacher training school exams, and I was helping somebody named Mlle Rosimond with her class. . . . A mulatto-type who did her hair in two big macaroons over her ears. She was a woman who made her students sing every hour of the blessed day: "Snow's falling on Paris, snow's falling on Paris. . . ." *Ever see any snow fall around here?*

HERMANCE: (*Laughing*) Snow!

AURE: So, that's when Papa Bert came and settled at Desmarinières. It was a real woods then! No neighbors. . . . The land he built our house on didn't belong to any local white man, no sir! It was our very own! To build the house my father had to clear trees with his own two hands. We got help from people my mother knew. They burned a patch in the woods. They dug up tree stumps. They hauled off rocks. They settled the foundations. Everybody sang, and my mother served cold drinks. . . . My father didn't just build a hut: four walls and a roof. He made a real house, with a veranda all around, a cooking shed behind, and a little wind hut in case of hurricanes.

He couldn't stop working. He would get up before dawn and tend the farm, the animals, the buildings, without ever losing his smile or his song. . . . (*Dreamily*) People were really fond of him. He was very poor, but he enjoyed giving. He gave away all the vegetables in his garden. He was well loved . . . revered, you might even say!

---

5. Certain cultures of African origin as well as certain African cultures consider looking someone directly in the eyes as rude and disrespectful behavior.

When he died—from a prostate condition—the funeral was enormous! It looked like a public demonstration.

HERMANCE: For me *father* meant Fénio Larochade. That's not to say Monsieur Larochade took care of me, oh no! I can't remember seeing his face for any too long!

Fénio Larochade was a migrant farmworker. He came and went from one plantation to another. He had a bunch of women and a bunch of kids, too. . . . I used to see Monsieur Bernus pass by on his way down to the village, and my mother would say: "There's your real daddy, and if you don't grow up proper, I'm going to send you off to stay with the upper crust, in the woods of Desmarinières!"

My mother always raised her children all on her own. Her first husband died two years before I was born. That's why the other children didn't take to me when I came along. And Uncle Hector didn't like me either. Hector? A rascal, a bad seed! He was always picking fights, never went anywhere without his machete! He said Mama had disrespected his brother, because she had me after he died . . .

One day he came to the house dead drunk while Mama was in the village. He got to the front of the house and yelled twice: *Today I'm gonna kill Hermancia!*" I was nine. I was scared. I hid under the bed while Monsieur was thrashing around outside. He was hollering. He was banging on the door. He was stomping his feet on the ground! I was shaking all over . . .

It was only when Man Da[6] came back from the market that Monsieur Hector stopped acting up. He didn't dare throw his weight around in front of her. God no! My mama! Man Da! That woman had a temper all her own!

AURE: They probably called her Edamine because she was born on St. Côme and St. Damien's Day?[7]

HERMANCE: (*Waving her hand impatiently*) *What's it matter?

AURE: My mother. . . . They called her Ti-piment. (*She laughs.*) "Hot little pepper"—because she was a tiny but very headstrong woman, with light eyes. A half-sized masterful woman. But a masterful woman just the same! There was no trying to fool her. . . . She was born in the south, too, around 1870.

---

6. *Man,* a term of respect, is a common Creole expression used with a grown woman's given name. It is usually combined with a shortened version of the name, hence Hermancia becomes "Man Cia" and Edamine "Man Da."

7. St. Côme and St. Damien's Day falls on 26 September. Those named after this Saints' Day are said to be inventive and resourceful.

That was the year of the big uprising, the year they killed Codé,[8] the white overseer who didn't let the people forget how important he was.

When my mother took up with my father she was twenty-three, but she'd already raised six children—since she'd been a governess.

HERMANCE: *A nanny!

AURE: A governess! She was the wet nurse for a Madame Assur, whose children considered her their real mother; in fact, they visited her every single year at Christmas until she died.

HERMANCE: My mama, Man Da, was a working woman: she took in sewing at home. . . . She had to nearly kill herself to raise all her other children, plus me. When we had a piece of land near Lorrain, she even grew vegetables to put food in our stomachs: white yams, coco yams. . . . At Christmas we had lots of field peas. (*Lost in thought*) I worked with Mama when I was little, barely thirteen, and even before that I worked with her. She's the one who taught me to be a seamstress. I didn't finish grade school. I left in order to help Mama. I helped her prepare the meals: clean the homegrown vegetables, fix the cod. I was the littlest . . .

From time to time fishermen brought part of their catch to us, but not very often. Mostly it was salted meat. For holidays we killed a hen. The rest of the time we ate vegetables and dried cod. After that, when we came to live in the village, Mama supported the whole family with just her sewing. People criticized her a lot, all through her life, but her motto was: "Let 'em talk, just do the right thing." (*Pause*) . . . Life wasn't so good. . . . The only fun we had, I'll tell you, was the balls. I went dancing a lot when I was young. I really loved to dance.

AURE: I never enjoyed dancing. I would go once in a while to a family ball, but I never danced. My father would never have allowed me to go to a dance that wasn't a family affair. He said he wanted to put on a ball by himself, but he never did manage to organize it.

HERMANCE: I organized balls. I was even queen several times. We used an exchange system, with bouquets, too: *You'd do a ball and then everybody invited would do one in turn.* . . . My mama, could she dance the *haute taille!* It was a treat! And the *damier,* you just had to watch her take off! (*Laughing, she ventures a few dance steps, humming a tune to accompany herself.*)

---

8. Codé was one of the white jurors in a case involving the revenge beating of a white man by a black man. The black man was convicted and sent to prison. When the French Third Republic was proclaimed in 1870—implying a new justice system for Martinique—an angry mob took the occasion to sack Codé's place and begin a general insurrection. Codé was killed and the insurrection put down with difficulty. The incident signals the growing revolutionary consciousness of Martinicans of color.

AURE: My father didn't want me to mix with young men.

HERMANCE: . . . What I liked best was the *mazurka piquée* and the Creole waltz. Féfé, my husband, loved to do the Creole waltz. (*She swings slowly while listening to a few bars of waltz music in her head.*)

AURE: At Carnival time there were classical music concerts in many of the town's drawing rooms. Sometimes I went to those. . . . But for me studying came before everything else! No, I never liked balls . . .

(*Motionless,* HERMANCE *is still humming her nostalgic tune. Only her foot keeps time with the music.*)

HERMANCE: As a matter of fact, we met at a ball. We loved to be together so *we decided to set up house.* My mama was happy because Ferdinand *was such a good match:* he worked for the tax administration! The only thing was, Man Lili, that's Ferdinand's—my husband's—mother, didn't like it at all. Mama Lily, short, very dark, *standing straight as an arrow and really tough to boot.* You should have seen her with her head scarf on and her walking stick! She looked like royalty! But, then, she was African! She kept saying that her parents' parents had come from Mali! From Mali! I ask you, did she even know where Mali is? She ran a little state-licensed store, and her cabin was the first one you saw when you entered the village. She had only four years of school, but her longhand was beautiful! As for liking education, well, she really loved it! She taught all her grandkids to write. She was so proud that her son Ferdinand had a middle school diploma. You'd have thought he was the first black man in the world to have one!

She sure was a character! A grande dame! She was a great Catholic, belonged to all the religious groups. When a new priest arrived he had to report to her first. And all the transactions between the hill people and the villagers went through her.

It was also at her place that the girls freshened up and put on their shoes before entering the village. She organized marriages and prepared children for Renunciation.

AURE: (*Correcting her*) Confirmation . . .

HERMANCE: *Well, I say:* Renunciation! (*She hums part of a hymn: "Chez nous, soyez reine"* [Be Queen in Our House].)

AURE: My mother had a very close friend, an Indian lady. . . . This woman invited me to name one of her children. I was sixteen, and it was my first godchild. I was so proud!

I left the hill on foot to walk the eight kilometers into the village. It was Lent. When I got to the village I washed up properly in cold water to take off the dust from the road.

My partner was my cousin Benoît. He was thirteen years older than me. After the ceremony he invited me for a walk in the moonlight. The dark was full of sounds. . . . When we came back I was so hot and tired that I lay down on a mat on the floor, right in a draft. They found me burning up with fever and stiff as a stick. Benoît took me back home, to Desmarinières. He held me up in front of him so I wouldn't fall down. My mother was so scared she thought she'd die. She put me in her own bed and watched me day and night. The fever was so strong I had visions. I told Mama I was visiting the virgins' home in Heaven. The Holy Virgin herself was showing me around, after she had lifted me up and drawn me toward her. She stood there erect, wrapped in veils from head to toe. She held her arms out to me, and then, very gently, she raised them, and I ascended into the light. . . . In the virgins' space, in Heaven, it was all very simple and pure, a great white sweep decorated with garlands and long sheer drapes, a lot of pretty sparkling things and singing girls crowned with flower wreaths, all smiles and softness. And a light . . . a light.

(HERMANCE *hums a hymn.*)

AURE: (*Taking up her story*) My parents though I was at death's door. They held séances to cure me. In those days we didn't count on medical science, especially in remote areas like ours. They told me that the healer prescribed cleansing baths. So, they macerated herbs in special water. They rubbed me to exorcise the evil cast on me. They said prayers. And there were even sessions of hypnosis—and fumigations . . .

I must say that I don't believe in such nonsense, but the point is . . . I got well.

HERMANCE: When you think, you can sometimes go a long way . . .

AURE: My first memories are of Mama and me visiting my sick great-grandma. We had to go by canoe and brought her herb teas. Her name was Amante. She wore huge gold earrings that pulled so much on her lobes they were de- formed. She was a tall, dark, smooth-skinned woman, wearing a madras head scarf and heavy chains—convict style—around her neck. She did her hair in two braids tied together in the back. She had a tick that drew down her mouth, and she ground her teeth. She used to beat her children and her grandchildren. They were very afraid of her.

She had several children by her former master, a short white man named Lafleur. Her last child was Malvina, my mother's mother . . .

(*Semidarkness sets in abruptly. This is the archetypal rape scene.* MALVINA *is startled when the door opens. We can hear the creaking of a bed across which a body has thrown itself.* MALVINA *stands up slowly and leans over the bed. She raises her arm; is it a gesture of love or aggression? In the distance we can hear hunting dogs barking and remote screams. Deaf to the tumult, the other woman, rocking in her chair, hums a Creole ballad, "Papa moin mô, man pa pléré . . ."* [My Daddy Died, I Didn't Cry . . .]. *Total darkness invades the stage. This will be the only time the slavery era is recalled.*)

HERMANCE: When I was little we didn't talk about slavery and all that non-sense. . . . My grandmother was already dead before I was born. I only knew my mama, Man Da.

I can't understand people who want to go far back into their ancestry. . . . They did tell me about somebody named Firmin, a runaway slave, a maroon, during slavery times . . .

But, as far as I'm concerned, life today's enough of a handful! The past doesn't interest me. It's all too far, too far away, the whole thing. Right now all that interests me is my leg, and it hurts . . .

When I was little life wasn't so easy, heavens no! You couldn't throw away money! *These days all they do is squander money. They have cars; we had nothing like that!* The first thousand-franc note I saw, I was already married. *We worked our tails off. (Her childhood comes back to her.)* I went to school in the village of Lorrain. I came down to the village from Morne Capot. It was seven kilometers down and seven back up again. There was no time to be idle or to fool around along the way!

All the children from the hill went down together. We walked together because the way was so long. It wasn't a road with . . . not fixed like now. It was trails with rivulets everywhere. *We used to call it "the wetlands." And the children often fell down.* You had to pay attention to walk right: the rain had ravaged the earth. We used to get up real early, as early as five. You had to fix your food, and then, while it was cooking, someone did your hair. After that you had to fetch water, tidy up the house, and then, if there were errands to do, you did them. And then we left for school. We walked down the seven kilometers. But you couldn't go to school barefoot. So, we had shoes and socks with us. We washed our feet when we entered the village, put on our shoes, and went to class. And in school we had to wear black jumpers . . .

(They both laugh.)

AURE: I went to school for the first time in the country around Rivière-Pilote, in the Epinay district. . . . That was January 1900. I was seven and had never spoken a word of French. All I spoke was Creole. . . .

When we heard that a school was going to open the district about burst with joy! Two communes accepted to share in the expenses. The day school opened, sixteen-, even seventeen-year-old girls turned up. They begged to be registered. They cried when they were turned away because of their age.

There was an enormous need for education. My mother insisted that I go to school with shoes and a broad-rimmed hat on.

In the country the other children attended school barefoot.

I only had plaid cotton dresses, and I really admired the outfits of the schoolteacher's daughter. She was my age. She wore a pleated skirt, a sailor blouse, and a Breton hat. I thought she was very chic! (*Laughing*)

There was this girl . . . born to a white gendarme and a black peasant woman. Her name was Ludivine. That girl was always competing with me. She played up to the schoolteacher. While all the children went down to the river at noon to get water, Ludivine stuck to the side of the teacher and flattered her! She was very affectionate. And I've always been a little standoffish . . .

There was only one book for class: it was the teacher's. You had to learn from what you could take down during the lessons. When we had to prepare for the grade school certificate, the teacher would lend her book to the girls who were taking the exam. Well, Ludivine kept the book as long as possible on purpose so that I couldn't study. She was a very jealous person. Maybe because I was doing so well in school . . .

Ludivine and I were the only ones allowed to take the exam for the certificate. But Ludivine's mother—and this infuriated the schoolteacher— did not send her to the exam, under the pretext that her daughter would not be as well dressed as me. I passed the exam. My mother was very proud, but my father said: "These days, it seems that girls want to know more than their fathers!" But he was proud, too, in spite of that!

HERMANCE: (*Still deeply immersed in the childhood she is reliving*) One day I was coming down the hill to go to school with the neighbor's little boy, named Edwige—not the neighbor, mind you, the little boy! He was shorter than me and I was holding him by the hand. That day I had the greatest scare of my life, *I swear it*. . . . We walked past Man Doudou's cabin, and after that there were no more houses. At that time it wasn't all built up like now. We stopped just for a minute to gather some wild cherries. There was one tree, which was almost completely weighted down with fruit! We ate and ate. . . . And then . . . all of a sudden we heard blood-curdling, really blood-curdling screams. . . . All I knew was there's no beast that can produce a scream like that, not a Christian either, no human creature! Even a lion can't roar like that! At that moment a shower of stones fell on the cherry tree. I yelled: "Why are you throwing stones? Go ahead and throw stones, but please leave me alone!" I left the cherries behind, grabbed the kid in my arms, and ran and ran . . . the village was still far away. . . . At one place called "Four-à-Chaux" there were huge rocks and old cannons. It was like an old fort, and that's where a white baby had been found, a dead newborn. (The mother was sent to jail when they found her.) So, then, there at Four-à-Chaux I felt as though I was being lifted up. I wasn't walking on the ground anymore. My feet weren't touching the earth. I was walking like this, way up in the air. (*Waves her arms to demonstrate.*)

I told the child, *"*Edwige, turn your cap around."* He turned his cap. I said, *"Good God in Heaven!"* and kept on going.

Then I saw a big steer come out of the bushes. He was dragging a chain behind him. But there wasn't really a steer there. He was, it looked like, walking over the road. And I wasn't even sure if I myself was on the road. I said: "Good God, help us! Jesus, Mary, and Joseph, help us!"

It sounded as if the entire river was up and running behind us! *An incredible mayhem!* Then I saw the steer pass me, and then he wasn't there anymore. *Completely vanished!* We didn't see where he went, whether he went into the sea, whether he went into the pond. . . . We ran with all our might, and we got to the village. (*Half-laughing*) And so, up till this very day, I never ate wild cherries again in my life . . .

AURE: I never believed all those stories about magic! And yet I've seen some strange things in my life. . . . The biggest fright for me was the hurricane of '28! We saw all those wagons passing by the house! And a lot of people gathered at our home for protection. The next day there wasn't a cabin left standing! What devastation, my God! The river was carrying along palm trees, dead animals . . .

HERMANCE: That morning day didn't break at all! The sky was dark, and not a tree was moving. The chickens stayed out, never opening their beaks to cackle or to eat. . . . People started nailing down doors and shutters. Pounding and hammering, hammering and pounding. That was all you could hear all over the neighborhood.

At midday my mama gave us flatbread and pan-fried cod. She had no time to cook: she was fixing the cabin with Monsieur Isidorin, our neighbor, who came over to give her a hand.

We were nine children in the house because we had the two boys of a friend of my mother's. They were staying with us through another one of her pregnancies.

My mother gave us lemongrass tea and made us wear socks, just like for the procession of the Virgin . . .

(*They both laugh.*)

So then, about eight in the evening, a wind rose. The little kids got frightened. They started crying. My mother told them: "I've had lots of hurricanes go right over my head, and here I am, alive and hardy!" But it was just to reassure us! No, that hurricane was not a normal one. The shutters started flying off: "whoof. . . whooof, . . ." even though Monsieur Isidorin had nailed them down! . . .

At one point we heard a great crash close by; it was a tree that had landed right there, right in front of the house.

Mama Da, my mama, said: "My, oh my God, it's the old flame-tree! Who knows if the roots aren't what holds up the house!"

And the house started cracking leeward and starboard. And the wind was playing such havoc! The house shook. It shook but it stayed anchored to the ground. You could hear iron sheeting whistling by in the air.

It was like the end of the world. . . . My mother knelt down, with all her children around her, and we prayed as best we could: "Ave Maria," "Our Father," . . . "Praise to the Lord." There was a huge noise. We only found out the next day: the neighbor's roof had flown off!

They found Mme Titine under her bed with her youngest daughter. She had the shakes. She was all right, but she was scared out of her wits! (*Laughing*) It took two gendarmes to drag them out from under there!

AURE: All there was left to eat was roots. . . . We were as hungry as during the Dissidence,[9] much later . . .

Still, people managed to make up a song that went something like this: *"*Our mouth is rusty."* (*Laughing*) Our mouth is rusty! Caribbean people are too ready to laugh at their own hunger! (*Laughing, she sings the song "Bouch nou oxydé. . . ."*)

HERMANCE: I remember that Dissidence business. It was the reason I didn't see my last born for fifteen years. Xénio went off to Dominica, to join De Gaulle. He was . . . seventeen.

That morning his father had threatened him with a good licking on account of his insolence, and Xénio had run out the door laughing, all his teeth shining. Féfé said: "That kid's possessed by the devil!" I said: *"Dogs don't beget cats!* He's the spitting image of his father." Féfé said: "I'll bet you this evening I'll get him exorcised!"

Well, that evening there wasn't a child left to beat up! Xénio had gone. He'd enlisted into the Dissidence. I didn't find it out at once. It was Mme

---

9. The "Dissidence" is the Antillean name for the Resistance movement against Germany and against the German occupation of France during World War II. Admiral Robert represented the collaborationist Vichy government in Martinique during this period. *Resistance* in the Caribbean usually connotes local political activity against colonial powers.

Toussine, a fishmonger—her husband was a fisherman—who came to tell me
he'd got on an old gum tree canoe that left for St. Lucy.

AURE: For St. Lucy or for Dominica?

HERMANCE: I don't quite remember. . . . Probably Dominica, because I know
they sailed by St. Pierre. . . . The sea was rough. . . . Féfé screamed, he
stormed, *he yelled,* but the kid was gone, and we didn't seen him again for
fifteen years!

Those were the days of Admiral Robert. . . . September 1939 or 1940, I
think . . .

AURE: Some people used to say that Admiral Robert was good for Martinique!
They said he's the one who showed people how to work, because people didn't
know how to go about it anymore! But I say the Martinican didn't wait for
Monsieur Robert—*That Con Artist*—to figure out how to do things and
survive when nothing's left!

HERMANCE: We used seawater for our salt preserves. We made baskets and hats
with palm leaves, with pine straw. We sold things, made a little money. We
made shoe soles with car wheels, wheels made of rubber; *they called them
"Michelin soles.".* . . We made sandals with the leaves of a tree. . . . *What's it
called again?* . . . A tree with big leaves. . . . I can't remember the
name. . . . You cleaned the leaf, you beat it to extract the string and the
fiber, you boiled it and bleached it. It was used for a lot of things.

AURE: Then there were the ration cards.

HERMANCE: To get bread or salt you presented your card. We weren't used to that!

AURE: But there was a lot of hardship because many people didn't manage to get
all they needed to eat, especially in the towns!

HERMANCE: When I went to see my mother in the country, Toussine—she was the
neighbor—she often brought fried palm worms over. They were so good . . .

AURE: Nobody eats them anymore. . . . You marinated the caterpillars all night
in salt brine with lime, green onions, spicy Indian wood seed, *thyme* . . .

HERMANCE: And hot pepper. . . . The old folks knew how to fix them! Now a
coconut tree comes down, and it's full of caterpillars. People don't even
know. . . . They walk by without a glance. But they're even better than fish!

AURE: I'd say they're more delicate!

HERMANCE: We heated them up on a three-stone fire, in front of the house, over
logwood charcoal. . . . It smelled so good. (*Dreamily*) Sometimes Toussine
brought me fish. Cousin Sirop brought local vegetables or ground cassava,
and I would sew for them. We traded. When I sold a little dress it was in
order to get a ration card. But I kept on thinking: "My children are going to
die in a foreign place!"

(She hums a traditional Creole air, "Cé l'Alsace et la Lorraine":
  *For Alsace and Lorraine
  I said to my mother
  I'm off to be a soldier.
  De Gaulle called me.
  For Alsace and Lorraine
  I'm going to foreign lands.
  For Alsace and Lorraine
  I'm going but I won't come back.)*

AURE: Yes, oh my—children . . . one part bliss, one part pain! My belly was so
  big everybody thought I was going to deliver before term, or else have twins—
  my husband was one. I must say I was on the road from the hill to the village
  every day on horseback. At that time we lived on a very remote parcel of
  land—my husband, my little girl—who was two—and myself. We had a
  young maid with us who helped me around the house. And there was also this
  matronly friend of mine who'd come over. But she soon started to find the
  days long and complained: "I've been here eight days and this girl, this sister,
  is still not giving birth! August 15 is just around the corner and I have to go
  home to work on my daughters' outfits for the procession of the Holy Virgin."
  So she left, and I was by myself with the little maid.

  Benoît used to leave very early for the distillery, between four and five. . . .
  On the morning the baby came, when I got up, I had a kind of dizzy spell, and
  the labor pains set in immediately. I sent the servant off to fetch my husband,
  who was checking his stills. When she arrived at the distillery Benoît was
  standing on the scaffolding overlooking the coals. The fire for the still was
  ready. He took fright and ran like a madman down the slope to the house.
  When he reached our bedroom he stood transfixed on the doorstep. My two-
  year-old was crying, seeing me in pain. I had set myself down on a folding
  chair covered with clean old cloths—in order to prevent infection—and I was
  clinging to the two armrests. . . . The baby was very big, very cute, with a lot
  of black hair. My husband stood there, as though petrified on the doorstep.
  You would have thought he was about to collapse. He finally managed to find
  the strength to mutter: "By herself, all by herself like that. . . ." I replied: "I
  am not by myself, Benoît. I am with my children!"

HERMANCE: For me it was a Monday. It'd been raining since five in the morning.
  I got up with a backache! The day before I'd had to finish the dress Sansand's
  godmother was to wear for the christening. It was a blue dress with pleats and
  an elbow-length cape. I'd sewn flowers and silk ribbons on everything.

The children left for school, except for Ti-Ferdinand, who was too small. Somebody came by for the lady's dress.

When the rain stopped I let the child go out for a while. He was wearing some old underwear. He was an easy kid. He'd just stay there, playing with the rocks and the grass. He would stare at the sea and say, "Schushsh . . . schushsh." I stayed inside to wash the dishes in the tub. I didn't take long, I can guarantee that! I could hear the child playing by the door as usual. I started to prepare something to eat. But I couldn't hear the child anymore. I called out: "Féfé, Féfé." But the child had disappeared. I looked and looked all around the house and the neighborhood. No one had seen him. I panicked. I told my neighbor: "Go get my husband, because if bad luck has hit us. . . ." The children came home from school. Everybody started looking for him. The younger ones began to cry. And, then, it was his father who found him, in the cistern. We'd looked for him all over the place, and he was right there, behind the house. But we couldn't see him. You had to climb on the window ledge to see inside the cistern. How did that child have the strength to do it? I was never able to understand!

Ferdinand got the child out. I laid him down on my bed. I rubbed him all over with camphor. But the Good Lord didn't want him to live. Ferdinand was sobbing. He was saying: "No, no, don't do that, don't do that." And you know he wasn't speaking to me!

Well, that's how the child died. He was my fifth.

AURE: Benoît had always had a weak heart. So, I used to apply ether pads when he had an attack. At times he also had a fever and shook. Then I would lie down by his side and warm him up, holding him tight. It probably was malaria. Now they could control it, but in those days medicine wasn't available like now. Penicillin hadn't come around yet. . . . He was a very handsome man, but he always had a weak constitution. He always thought he would die young, and it made him sad, especially on account of me and the children.

Benoît often liked to sleep in the little room that looked out on the sunrise. It was the coolest in the house. That evening we were in bed. I'd fallen asleep. . . . He got up, opened the window to enjoy the cool air. His chest was bare. It'd been raining, and the palms of a great tree just in front of the window poured a shower of water on his chest. I woke up. I told him: "Heavens, Benoît, what on earth are you doing up? Do you want to catch your death?"

He said: "Come on, don't worry. . . . It's nice and cool. . . ." I forced him to come back to bed, but it was too late. Pleurisy had infected his chest. . . .

I started expecting the worst when he asked to see the children, who were in boarding school in town. Yes, he knew he was dying! He kissed them very hard, and me, too. He kissed me very hard. He was trying to speak, but he was unable. . . . His chest was rumbling: Rrrrrr, Rrrrrr! You could tell something was disturbing him in there. I tried to help him, clear him out, and I put my finger in his mouth. My God, he clenched and clenched. . . . We had to pry his jaws open to free my finger.

I said to his friend, Monsieur Vermont, the income tax agent, who was there: "Help me turn him over so I can apply the suction cups!" And he said: "Are you sure? Wait a minute. Let him rest. Just a minute. . . ." And Benoît was gone. He went away the second I said: "Help me turn him over so I can apply the suction cups!" So, I was left on my own, with the children. I was thirty-nine.

HERMANCE: I never was the kind of woman you push around. But Ferdinand did anyway! *A man's a man . . . , right? But he had to hear me stuff his ears, you better believe it! So, one day he went all the way to France with his mistress, an old *pale-skinned negress he had picked up. I asked him: *"Why aren't you taking me?"* He replied just like that: "Rig up a nutshell and follow me if you can!" He really shamed me!

He went: he stayed six months in France with that woman. And then Monsieur comes home, rolling his hips, proud as a peacock, to unwind his string of tales. He tells me: *I spent so much money, Hermance, you should have been there. . . . The French people said all the time:* "Whoa! Doesn't that nig-german look like a million!" And he was so delighted with himself. *He was simply on top of the world.* "Doesn't that niggerman look like a million!" (*Tchiip*) While Monsieur looks like a million in France, I work. I work to feed my children. *Day after day it's me who works!*

When he returned he brought back a little money. I didn't even open my mouth to speak to him. I took the money from his hand, and I spent it all to buy things for my kids!

One day, *I remember, Mariette was real little, poor kid. . . .* She was five, maybe six. She comes home and says: "Mama, I saw Daddy's hat in God-mother's sitting-room." She'd just spent three days at her godmother's house. Good god! My blood turned. I started running. My own friend! My daugh-ter's godmother! She had held my child, and *now she was doing it with Ferdinand!* And he was leaving his hat right there, so the child would see it and could come and tell me! Well! I trounced her good and clean, you should have seen it! *I let her have it!* Ferdinand got it, too! He didn't like to hit people, but that day *he was on the receiving end*. God be my witness! . . . It's only toward the last that Monsieur settled down. Old age brings wisdom.

AURE: With Benoît I always got along very well. . . . Only one time. . . . What was it about? I can't even remember. His voice rose. He banged on the table. I turned around in shock. I didn't expect anything like that. I simply looked at him. He understood. Do you know he even apologized! I'm told that seems normal to other women. Well, that's their problem! I, for one, have never understood why the woman should be more submissive than the man. When we discussed things like that before getting married, people our age—boys and girls—didn't agree. But Benoît always sided with me. . . . He was a very gentle, amenable man, even playful.

Before our marriage Benoît had a concubine. He even had a child by her. He liked the child and looked after him. . . . So, my parents, before giving their consent, asked him what he intended to do about it. Benoît declared that he had never promised to marry the person and that, above all, he would not allow her to make trouble for me . . .

So, then he offered to pay her way either to Cayenne or to Panama City, where people were going to dig the Canal. . . . She left. . . . She only made some sour references to those educated young mulatto ladies whom men preferred to marry . . .

HERMANCE: Monsieur lost the use of his legs. . . . He always had a weakness in them, and then, little by little, they started going . . .

One day he began not walking so good, and another day he had trouble standing up. Then, finally, he stayed down. Monsieur was so vain, so proud! He didn't want to go out in the street anymore, after being so dashing! He didn't want to be seen limping along or in a wheelchair. So, Monsieur got himself set up on the third floor, and he never descended again—ever! I'm the one who brought him his food. He didn't want to come down, not even to the dining room. He stayed on the third floor, paralyzed, for a long time—fifteen years, I think. *And then one day he died! And here I am!* He was really a burden to me, paralyzed as he was. I picked on him, too, of course . . . he was such a braggart. But, then, Féfé was just like all men, neither better nor worse! One day I was in the sewing room. I tell my friend Alcinda: "Alcinda, not so loud, Féfé's in the next room, and he's got a sharp ear. . . . Alcinda, where are we going to put Féfé when he's dead? Because the concession's so full, the tenants are going on a rent strike." Alcinda replies: "We got to throw out the old to accommodate the young!" So, I tell her: "Not in my lifetime, sister! As long as I live, no kin of mine will sleep outdoors." And we laughed. . . . And that braggart Féfé started knocking on the shutter of the next room with his cane. "Hermancia, my girl, don't you bury me yet! I'm still here!" My oh my, I can hear him now. (*She hits the floor with her cane.*) "Hermancia, **I'm still here!*" (*She laughs.*)

AURE: (*Laughing*) Oh, marriage . . . (*Dreamily*) Do you remember the old rules? For her wedding the young woman provided the bedroom furnishings and the young man those of the drawing room . . .

My wedding dress . . . I can see it: made entirely of French cambric. You can't find those fabrics anymore. It had braiding at the hem and very fine nun pleats on the bodice. I embroidered it all by myself. Certain people advised me against it, saying it brought bad luck: a girl shouldn't make her own wedding gown. But I didn't take it into account. Disaster comes when it wants, don't you think?

HERMANCE: I wore a beige crepe dress and a hat. And Ferdinand had a navy blue frock coat, with two tails—and a vest I probably still have in the house, if nobody stole it from me!

AURE: We had this wonderful ride in the country the day of my wedding. More than twenty horsemen. I mounted Princess, my white mare . . . a beautiful animal! All the men wore what we called a cod-tail jacket and top hats. There was a formal dinner, with a whole lamb as well as cutlets, stuffed crabs, coconut pastries . . . so many good things. . . . A lot of speeches, compliments . . . in French, of course. . . . And all of a sudden, in the middle of a speech, my grandfather gets up and says: **"They're speaking French. I don't speak French!* So, goodbye, lady bride." And he leaves! He could have waited, really! I was so embarrassed! . . . At the end of the day Benoît and I left in a Tilbury to go to La Poterie, where I'd been appointed schoolteacher. I was married on the 24th of September 1914.

HERMANCE: I wanted to get married, but to a man who knew how to talk to me: after all, the man makes the woman, the woman makes the man! Before I settled down with Ferdinand there was this gentleman after me who wanted to get married. He had no confidence. He didn't come to talk to me first. He went straight to my mother. She's the one who told me: "You don't know it, Cia, dear. This gentleman is proposing to you." I wasn't at all happy. I said to Mama, "Aren't I old enough to speak to the gentleman by myself?"

Mama Da told him: "I'm not the one who speaks for my daughter, Sir, you must speak to her yourself."

That man really looked like **a wind bag.* So, Monsieur comes to see me, very uneasy, on the way back from church. When he started to talk I thought he was going to faint, like a woman in labor. He says he "likes to look at me, do I want him for a husband?" I asked: "Do you smoke?"—because I knew he smoked plenty. Someone told me. (*Gleefully*) He said: "Yes." I said: "I'll never settle down with a man who smokes." . . . He was pretty uncomfortable! He said: "It's hard to stop just for a wedding." And I replied: "But that's the way it is!" *Poor devil. (*Laughing*) He was a little afraid, too!

And then the next Saturday he comes to call at my mother's house. And he talks . . . a little bit. I answer. Mama answers and . . . I don't hear another word. I look: Monsieur's seated there—asleep! (*Mimicking him*) He's full of rum! I told Mama: "Get this fellow out of here. He's loaded!" I was so mad! My mother said: "Come on Hermance! My, you're sure rough on him! He went out with his friends and drank too much! That sort of thing is forgivable, isn't it?" I said: "If I have to forgive before my marriage, I'll spend my whole life forgiving!" And I've always said it: "One time—that's enough for me. Twice—it's already too many!"

AURE: (*Deep in her previous story*) . . . I had that mare my father gave me . . . Princess . . . a beautiful, white hackney mare, with a glossy coat, as gentle as a lamb but fast as lightning. She'd only listen to me. Nobody else could ride her. Every morning I heard the school bells ring to announce the start of class. There were two bells: the first was a warning bell, the second to form class ranks. I always had a thousand things to do myself before going to school.

At the first bell I mounted Princess. You should have seen her fly downhill: dust carried her along. I rode her sidesaddle. I would lean over her neck and whisper into her ear: "Forward girl, catch time for me!" And she dashed like a white arrow. Her hooves threw sparks when they hit the rocks in the trail. . . . The peasants we passed were quick to step aside. They crossed themselves as we went by: "The schoolteacher will break her neck!" But I knew I wasn't in danger: I had the animal well in hand, and she knew better than anybody what her business was. God, how I loved that horse! (*Dreaming for a while*)

One day I came home from school to find my mother on my veranda, all decked out in black, her head scarf, too, and looking real gloomy, even angry. I said to her: "Well, now, mother? What's the matter? Is there a death in the family?" She glared at me and answered: "Mourning for you is what we'll soon be doing, your mother who conceived you, the husband you married, and the children you brought into this world! What's the idea of thundering down the hill, your skirts flying, on that infernal animal? Are you trying to outrace death, daughter, or are you going to wait for him to find you?"

(*Laughing*) I don't usually brag, but the truth is, I was a very good horsewoman! . . . Oh, Princess! . . .

(*Smiles and nods*)

HERMANCE: As for dying! Who likes the idea of dying? And who gives it a thought either?

Dying, that's your last home: two planks underneath, two on top, and two on the sides. It's the only cabin definitely yours. The only one you're able to buy . . .

Young people are always caught up with the idea of dying. Age will teach them to wait. You've got to allow time for time to end life.

Someone said . . . maybe the Bible . . . "Life is a valley of tears." But I say: "No!" A valley is a hollow, and life's like a hill. You have to climb up. The end is when you get to the top of the hill. You say: "I'm here, I got here all by myself!"

I don't buy those stories about falling into a hole! The higher you climb, the taller you get—and so, too, the shadow that's followed you since the day you were born keeps on growing. It's just a matter of cause and effect.

And all this to say that death is not a good topic for conversation. . . . Those who like to talk to say nothing will babble this and that about it. But it's all hot air.

AURE: Life is nonsense, Hermance. Nothing but nonsense! And if there's anything more nonsensical than that nonsense, it's death, my dear. Yes, indeed, death itself! Sometimes the young even die before the old! My mother used to say: "Even God makes mistakes on occasion!" And that's not blasphemy, Hermance! That's only a complaint for the sake of justice. Because it's behind justice that we have to walk. Only behind justice, yes, indeed. (*She sinks into deep day-dreaming.*)

HERMANCE: My big sister, she lost her son during the last war. Gabriel, that was his name. He died in France, I believe, or some nearby country. They brought back his body in a sealed coffin. I remember the funeral clearly. . . . The boy hadn't reached thirty yet. . . . All he thought about was soccer. His club—like a whole family for him—was the Golden Star.

(*She hums the anthem of the Golden Star: "Etoile d'or, étoile de mes rêves"* [*Golden Star, Star of My Dreams*].)

My big sister cried over that child long and hard—until her own death.

Every Sunday of the forty years she lived after her son died she ate her lunch at his graveside. And, while she was eating, she'd tell him about the soccer game she'd watched on his behalf the day before: "The goalie jumped up in the air and blocked the ball with his chest, and all the fellows rose like one man, and you heard a single 'Yehhhh!' And when there was the free kick, not a single fly could have flown across the stadium. The crowd stopped breathing. Marcius stood there, his eyes closed. Then he dashed forward and kicked. My God! A kick like that! I said: 'Jesus! Please don't let the goalie take it on his heart! Because he'll be off like a hummingbird if the ball touches his body.' I prayed awful good, I can tell you! Because the ball passed clear above his head . . . and the players of the Colonial Club, you should have heard the roars, like savages! Gabin, my son, I tell you, you'd have been ashamed of them!"

(*Pause*)

Society, naturally, said my big sister Alicia was crazy, that her son's death had killed her common sense. But I say: "Not so! You can talk to the dead. Even if they don't hear, they know. . . ."

(*She hums a few bars of a plantive léroz: "Dodo eh, dodo man ka alé"* [*Sweetheart, I'm Going Away*].)

AURE: Death isn't always a matter of destiny. Sometimes men give fate a real boost.

I've never forgotten the day Desétages was assassinated, in 1935—the law enforcement agents were responsible.[10] My husband and young brother were Socialists. They'd gone to watch the elections in Ducos, where everybody expected some trouble. I was horribly worried! I couldn't wait any longer, and so I decided to try and get information on what was going on there. I rode my horse down to Rivière-Salée, and I telephoned to the post office in Ducos— which was inside the Town Hall. All I said was "Hello . . ." and I heard the Ducos post office operator scream: "They're dead! They're murdered!"

I thought my husband and brother were in the lot. I wanted to go down to Ducos. I could only think about riding into town, but I didn't budge. A mother's place is with her children. I waited, and waited . . . and they came back.

That same morning Leymeriste had been killed, the wealthy white man who owned the Diamant Distillery . . .

It happened the night they counted the votes for the local elections. Mayor Desétages was drinking a punch with one of his Socialist friends, a black man who lived across from Town Hall. They heard a great racket in the street. Everybody knew that the gendarmes as well as the army were posted in front of Town Hall. In those days there were no black gendarmes. Every time there was an election, a great deployment of police was sent out to contain the masses. Revolt was rumbling, but people were afraid of guns. The day after

---

10. Desétages was a member of one of the most important Martinican families. His assassination in 1930 led to a series of popular uprisings, which have remained very important to the political memory of the Martinican Left.

elections the radio always announced: "The elections took place without incident!" Without incident, my foot!

(*She shrugs her shoulders.*)

In those days people's brains were not as nimble as now!

When Desétages heard the agitation in the street, he was sitting inside with his friend. They got up, walked to the veranda to see what was going on, and they got showered with bullets. They were killed. They were executed!

The gendarmes who killed the mayor and his friend went on vacation to France the next day. They were never seen again. They were never prosecuted!

(*Pause*)

That's the way it was!

(*Pause*)

Much much later Desétages's son, who was a child at the time his father was assassinated, took his revenge. He boarded a ship leaving for France and shot at the governor, who was also boarding. He missed. He did time, but he showed everybody he hadn't forgotten. (*We hear a few bars of a Creole song from that period: "Ancinelle lévé . . ." [Ancinelle, Get Up!].*)

HERMANCE: At that time I lived up north, in Basse-Pointe. . . . All day long, and especially all night, you could hear the rollers crash on the pier. At first I couldn't get to sleep, and then, when we went to Fort-de-France, I missed the sound of the waves! I really did.

In Basse-Pointe we used to go and wait for the fishermen to return, to get our fish fresh, just before the evening dew set down. We watched the sea, and we could see—behind the keys—the gum tree canoes negotiating the waterway, with their square sails. When the sea was rough the foam hid the key, and you had to know your business pretty well in order not to lose your skiff and your life with it.

One day the canoe of that little devil, Monsieur Tully's son, crashed on the reef, with the sailor and his mate. . . . In fact, it was the first time he'd been out!

On the pier the women fell to their knees. The fishermen on the other boats returning from Miquelon said they'd yelled to the boy: "Ready about! Draw the sail to the wind!" But the boy was already panicked: he didn't hear anything! His shell hit the reef straight on and split—swoosh—right down the middle, like a scarf you tear in two!

Well, then, by the grace of Almighty God, the young men were saved! They rode the billows with their bodies, just like the kids at Basse-Pointe on their coconut floating boards. A true miracle!

AURE: I remember an outing we took one Easter Sunday with the whole family and some of our in-laws. I was twelve, I think. . . . It was Easter day. . . . We left early, at six that morning, to go to where there were those stones carved by the ancients. It wasn't such a smart idea: the path had been buried under a landslide, and we had to leave the horses there, tethered securely, and continue on foot to the beach.

But it was truly a splendid day. The sky was pure, without clouds—that's pretty rare in our parts! The sea was like a lake. It sparkled.

When we got there I helped my mother unpack the food. The little ones were already playing around in the water . . .

I didn't swim much. I didn't have the appropriate attire, and then I was the eldest . . .

But it was Easter Sunday, and so we were expected to cleanse ourselves. I'd worn a white cotton dress, heavily starched and quite stiff, and I entered the water. It was warm, so clear you could see the bottom. After that we ate the traditional meal: my mother had prepared a heavenly cassava and crab dish. That was the reason why the children had been scurrying and chasing crabs for three solid weeks. Mama had purged them for a long time, feeding them mangoes, rich grass, hot peppers. . . . I haven't tasted such flavorful crabs since!

After that we settled in the shade, under some sea grape trees, and we sang love songs in French, as sappy as they come.

(*Humming a few bars:*
Madidina is not a girl . . .
But that is what they called . . .
In the old days, that sweet country,
The flower of the Antilles,
Martinique, where only love rules . . .)
(*She laughs softly.*)

Five o'clock came round, and we had to go home. Night falls so abruptly in our parts. When we got close enough to see the house, the hills were already beginning to turn blue, and the ground steamed. . . . Yes, indeed, it was a magnificent day . . .

HERMANCE: I don't really like the flat seas you have in the south. What's there to see? When I was little and went into Lorrain I watched the boys who had permission to jump the rollers. I wanted so bad to do like them! My mother would never have let me! She said girls had to keep their bodies straight up!

The boys would dive under the waves. You lost sight of them, as though they'd drowned, and then they reappeared on the other side, and they laughed. . . . They laughed. . . . The sea is dangerous there, especially near the Trou au Chien!

One time there was a kind of giant surge. It came with the bad weather. They call it a tidal wave. I saw the wave, high as a house, racing toward the village. I told myself: "Well, my dear, there'll be no village left down there tonight!" The wave wrecked all the boats, but, by the grace of God, it didn't kill anybody that day! The sea, for us northerners, means the ocean. It's like a horse: beautiful to watch, proud, but perverse, too!

AURE: It's getting late, Hermance!

HERMANCE: Hmm . . . hmm. . . .

AURE: Surely, the party will end soon.

HERMANCE: Of course not! They'll be at it till six in the morning, my dear! (*Wearily*) I'll call Joseph . . . (*Calling out softly*) Joseph!

AURE: Here he comes. Let's go, dear sister.

HERMANCE: No, dear sister, let's wait for him here. Now it's their duty to watch after us.

(*As the last few words are spoken, the last bit of music—perhaps "Woy Madiana," a traditional closing for Caribbean balls—dies down slowly, as do the lights. The women continue to hum the tune: one rubs her leg; the other massages her hands. They freeze, and only their faces remain circled by two luminous halos, which will go out abruptly and simultaneously. The only sounds to be heard in the dark are those of the Caribbean night. These take over the stage and the theater.*

Then, suddenly, silence.)

Antonine Maillet

ANTONINE MAILLET (B. 1930), novelist, playwright, and essayist, likes to speak of herself as a product of her rough coastal land, Acadia (or New Brunswick, Canada). She claims that her mentality and even the color of her eyes have been determined not only by her ancestors but also by the sea. Although she travels frequently and has lived in Montreal as a university professor, she is identified as *the* Acadian writer of her generation.

With her novel *Pélagie-la-Charette* (Pélagie, 1979) Maillet brought her region, its history of uprooted people, and its vivacious dialect to the forefront of literary attention in Quebec. By winning for this work the prestigious Goncourt Prize— the first of many awards—she garnered not only French but also international acclaim for her portraits of a people who, chased from northwestern Canada by King George at the end of the eighteenth century, returned one hundred years later to reclaim what had always been their psychological home. Her broad humor, her interest in the quotidian, her creation of a contemporary mythology—traits that demonstrate her continued affection for Rabelais and his giants—make her *Pélagie-la-Charette* the obverse of Longfellow's sentimental *Evangeline*. The greatest of Maillet's epic heroines, Pélagie joyously leads her troops back to their promised land with a combination of bravado, cunning, and guts.

These same qualities are present in the characterization of La Sagouine, the eponymous heroine of Maillet's best-known play of the dozen she has written to date. *La Sagouine* (The Charwoman, 1971) is the most resonant of Maillet's several dramatic monologues, which include *Evangéline Deusse* (1975), a parodic treatment of Longfellow's heroine, and *Gapi* (1976), the monologue of La Sagouine's man. *La Sagouine's* sixteen segments range from religious meditations to a recitation of the census, from the marvelous to the trite. The seventy-two-year-old La Sagouine speaks to her bucket of "troubled water" and, mordant critic of life, manages to effect a reconciliation with the inevitability of death. Having spent her time

This photograph introduces the remarkable Canadian actress Viola Léger (Avignon Theater Festival, 1978) in the role of Antonine Maillet's La Sagouine, the eponymous character from Maillet's 1971 dramatic monologue *The Charwoman*. The mythic Charwoman, who reappears as a central character in *The Rabble* (1973), represents for Maillet the enduring vitality and cleverness of the Acadian people. (Photo by Marc Enguerand.)

cleaning up other people's messes, she has no doubts about a social hierarchy based on material possessions. Her extraordinary will and awareness of her own distinctive identity vanquish despair and create of her—to borrow a term from Maya Angelou—a modern "she-roe."

La Sagouine, like several characters in Maillet's novels and plays, returns in other dramatic pieces, for example, in *Gapi et Sullivan* (1973) and *Les Crasseux* (The Rabble), versions 1 (1973) and 2 (1974). This technique establishes an interlocking theatrical fresco of the lives of simple Acadian people, poor, marginalized, but also feisty and fun—seafarers and lighthouse keepers, cleaning women and accordion players. Maillet thus builds a mythic structure for a people dispersed, regrouped, and economically oppressed. She keeps alive throughout her work and therefore valorizes their special language—the French of sixteenth-century Normandy brought to North America by Champlain's crew of sailors and adventurers.

The Rabble, written in 1965–66, was first published in the journal *Théâtre Vivant* 5 (1968) and later, in 1973, by Léméac.[1] Of all the plays in this anthology *The Rabble* is ostensibly the least "feminist" in terms of intent. It is also the most traditional in terms of structure. Maillet, unlike other authors included in this volume, questions neither representation nor image-making systems. She does not use Brechtian alienation devices, nor does she introduce forbidden themes. She is interested, however, in building mythology in the face of an absence. And in the richness of her particular struggle a parallel with the women's movement begins to emerge. Maillet's play make obvious the connection between a colonized class and women's situation of subordination.

The Rabble is concerned with the class inequalities of rural French-speaking Canada. In Maillet's play the Acadians are back home after their forced wanderings but are not comfortable there either. They are now dominated by those "standard" French speakers who have also developed into the mercantile and professional class of Acadia.[2] These are the Uptowners, who live on the right side of the tracks and who are determined to maintain, as flimsy as they are, their position of superiority and their feeling of worth. On the other side are the Folks from Across the Tracks: fishermen, itinerant musicians, cleaning ladies, and ragpickers—people who make do with the little they have. People, too, who have learned to distrust the Uptown folks while, at the same time, kowtowing to them. Of the Uptown crowd only the character of the Doctor, enlightened, one surmises, by enough contact with death, seems to understand that human beings are human beings whether or not they are born on the "right side of the tracks."

The Folks from Across the Tracks manage to move into the Uptown world after a series of skirmishes in the "war" waged between the two groups in the course of the play. They sacrifice to this end Punkin, a victim of the reigning ideology, which suggests that a man is a man only if he owns things. Deprived of his chance to possess a TV, which symbolizes "worth," and thus stripped of what he takes to be the only way of earning the love of a girl from the other side, Punkin kills himself. In this Romeo and Juliet subplot Punkin becomes the victim of the inability to see a way out of materialism.

There are many potential lessons in the play: that colonized peoples, both within cultures and from different cultures, are all exploited in the same way by those who purport to be the "decent folk" with the "true values." This is what Duke, war veteran and hero, learns in service to England when he meets other former colonials. The most obvious moral is that in union there is strength. Maillet presents a collective hero in her play. The Folks from Across the Tracks may have a leader (King Moose), but it is the collective thinking through of their situation and their collective action that brings them victory in the end. They stand like one at critical moments of the play. (And the syntax of Acadian performs this fusion of one with the multiple because it allows plural verb endings with singular subjects or first-person subjects with plural verbs.) The Folks from Across the Tracks learn from one another, whereas the Uptown Folks remain resolutely closed-minded and individualistic.

Within this world of slipping boundaries the "intelligence agent" and most striking character, the one who guides the collective toward what they must do, is again La Sagouine, the charwoman, the humblest of the humble, whose name ironically means "unkempt." It is she, in fact, who has spent her life on her knees in service to other people, keeping their houses in order, while her own daughter has become a whore. Yet when she raises her mop it becomes the staff that will goad her people into action. La Sagouine is emblematic of the strength and courage of people who have had to fight against marginality all their lives.

The play's struggle, then, does not pit men against women. Indeed, the arch villain of the piece is the Mayoress, the most intelligent but also the most ruthless of the Uptown schemers. Rather, the play confronts the haves with the have-nots. This encourages the audience to think about the ways in which material conditions, as well as gender identification, determine possibilities in life. It also clarifies how the possession of a particular language and culture is necessary to accede to certain levels of power.

Maillet conveys all this and the specificity of the lives of the seacoaster Acadians in a series of processional vignettes, some of which are meant to be mimed. She juxtaposes scenes from Uptown with those from Across the Tracks. The "Folks" actions and moods are also always reinforced by accordion and guitar music, which is their "other" language—a subversive language of music and dance that also serves to entice the Uptowners.

The somewhat happy ending—the Folks are not forced to leave their land again—does not provide an easy out. Punkin is dead, and Jugs, the whore, is back to selling her wares to the recently arrived seamen. Prostitution, Maillet seems to caution, takes many forms. But at the play's end, in the community of equal men and women that has won at least one battle, there is a form of hope. La Sagouine, aged beyond sex, asserts her strength and independence without denying her allegiance to men. Maillet thus displaces the whore-virgin dyad and establishes as her central female figure an experienced and conquering mature woman.

NOTES

1. The first reading of this play took place on 21 July 1968 at the Théâtre de Quat-Sous in Montreal, under the sponsorship of the Centre d'Essai des Auteurs Dramatiques.

2. Antonine Maillet's language for the Folks from Across the Tracks is "Acadian": that is, she writes her dialogue as the people of Acadia speak, taking into consideration their characteristic accent in French and the peculiarities, both grammatical and lexical, of their dialect. In our translation we have suggested the unusual constructions and the rich imagery based on the people's ties to their northern seascapes, the Catholic church, and their particular history of displacement. We have not attempted to adapt the play to a specific stateside setting, such as Appalachia or the rural South. Comparisons with such settings, however, are inevitable, especially where a social hierarchy is strongly marked by language usage. We hope that, in reading or producing this play, the reader/director/actor will use his or her imagination to reconstruct an accent and a pace that will help situate the characters in an environment not yet touched by high-tech jargon and standard TV intonation.

Antonine Maillet

The Rabble

Characters

THE UPTOWN PEOPLE

THE MAYORESS, 45 years old
THE BARBER, 40
THE SHOPKEEPER, 50
THE DOCTOR, 60
THE HATMAKER—a prude, 50
THE YOUNG LADY—THE SHOPKEEPER's daughter, 18
THE PLAYBOY—THE BARBER's son, 20

THE FOLKS FROM ACROSS THE TRACKS

KING MOOSE—the leader, 70 years old
MIKEARCANGEL—his general, 45
DUKE—KING MOOSE's son, the hero, 20
LA SAGOUINE—a charwoman, their intelligence agent
THE SAINT—a rag lady, 50
PUNKIN—THE SAINT's son, the victim, 19
JUGS—LA SAGOUINE's daughter, a whore, 19
FIRST LAY-ABOUT—a guitar player, 30
SECOND LAY-ABOUT—an accordian player, 35
FIRST SEAMAN, SECOND SEAMAN, THIRD SEAMAN

The action is set in Acadia in northeastern Canada. We are in a gently sloping coastal village whose social system is symbolized by the railroad tracks that divide the village in two. The time is here and now or any time.

Set

UPTOWN

The Barbershop—a barber's stand and chair
The General Store—a counter, a few barrels full of nails and molasses
A swing hanging from a tree
The fronts of two or three houses or doorsteps

ACROSS THE TRACKS

A tree stump shaped like a throne in front of a cabin
Three dories at sea
A fence between the two neighborhoods
A few crosses in a graveyard

All the props should be mobile in order to disappear or reappear in the various
scenes.

PROLOGUE

*The Uptown people parade by; eventually, only their silhouetttes are visible. The voice
of the* MAYORESS *in the distance: fragments of her discourse punctuate the conversation
of the Folks from Across the Tracks, who are leaning on the fence in the foreground. A
few bars on the guitar and the accordion groaning.*

MAYORESS: (*Sound of her voice in the distance, then*) . . . and as for you men!

PUNKIN: What about us, huh? Ain't we men, too?

LA SAGOUINE: We ain't men. We're Folks from Across the Tracks! Men are from
    Uptown.

KING MOOSE: I'm a man. And we're all men—men from Across the Tracks!

MAYORESS: . . . happiness . . .

PUNKIN: Happiness, the fine life, ain't for everybody.

LA SAGOUINE: Not for empty-bellies, not for the jobless . . .

MIKEARCANGEL: Happiness is for the guys who sell beer. They sell and we buy,
    and then we swell and they wait. And you know, they're waitin' for the day
    there won't be any more beer. "Now we got 'em," they'll say. "Get out them
    empty glasses." And they'll fill 'em up with shoe polish. . . . And we'll pay
    and we'll croak, in the name of the Father and of the Son . . .

SAINT: Amen.

MAYORESS: . . . morality . . .

FIRST LAY-ABOUT: Dum dadee dumdadee dum . . .

MAYORESS: . . . public duty . . .

SECOND LAY-ABOUT: Public like Jugs.

(*The men laugh, and the women are indignant.* JUGS *surrounds herself with her sense of dignity.*)

PUNKIN: The fine life ain't for everybody. Motorbikes and TV sets ain't for everyone.

LA SAGOUINE: Well, what I know is, TV suits me just fine. I set myself up in front of them beautiful people with my feet propped on one of them little plush things, and I take it all in! I look at them picture-frame types, them announcers . . . by golly, they have some announcers in there! When they whisper in your ear about brushin' your teeth with that toothpaste, well, I can feel the toothpaste runnin' right down the middle of my back. Some fine announcers—them fellas! You can't go around sayin' La Sagouine don't know the difference between one of them announcers and MikeArcangel.

MIKEARCANGEL: Oh yeah? but tell me, La Sagouine, ain't you seein' 'em on all fours? You're watchin' while you're scrubbin' the wood floors at the Doc's!

LA SAGOUINE: So . . . you can see 'em better with your nose right on 'em.

MAYORESS: All of us, whoever we may be, all for one, one for all . . .

FIRST LAY-ABOUT: (*Noncommittally*) Hurrah, hurrah, hurrah.

MAYORESS: We shall build . . .

MIKEARCANGEL: That's right.

MAYORESS: . . . shall embellish . . .

LA SAGOUINE: You bet.

MAYORESS: . . . salvage . . .

SAINT: Not a minute too soon!

MAYORESS: . . . prosperity, fraternity, propriety . . .

KING MOOSE: And Paradise at the end of the road.

(THE SAINT *crosses herself. Lights dim.*)

ACT I

SCENE I

Mime scene far upstage. The general store. Two LAY-ABOUTS *sitting on barrels. They play a few notes on the guitar or accordion.* THE SHOPKEEPER *is at his bookkeeping, behind*

the counter. THE HATMAKER *walks in and looks for the item she needs.* THE SHOP-
KEEPER *presents various sorts of lace to her. At every note of music she glances disapprov-
ingly toward the* LAY-ABOUTS. *Their presence clearly offends her. Finally, when they
start whistling, she storms out.* THE SHOPKEEPER *gesticulates in front of* THE LAY-
ABOUTS *to impress on them that they must leave. They accept this in the end and shuffle
off while playing their instruments.* THE HATMAKER *reenters, escorted by* THE
MAYORESS. THE SHOPKEEPER *cannot apologize enough. He eats humble pie. The
haughty* MAYORESS *has the upper hand. Enter* MIKEARCANGEL *and* PUNKIN, *followed
by* THE LAY-ABOUTS. *All of them sit down on barrels and observe the Uptowners.* THE
SHOPKEEPER *looks dismayed.* THE MAYORESS *and* THE HATMAKER, *having reached
the heights of indignation, exit. On her way out* THE MAYORESS *stops downstage center
and addresses* THE SHOPKEEPER *and the assembly in general.*

MAYORESS: We are respectable people up here. Ladies of our class do not tolerate
smut and boorishness. Maybe the world is sliding into licentiousness, but
allow some of us to resist the trend. Make up your mind, Shopkeeper; either
you reserve your sales counter for the decent people who buy your silk lace, or
you open it up to the rabble of the entire region who will walk off with your
tobacco pouches hidden under their shirts.

(*The women exit. Notes from the guitar. Then the four men stand up and exit in turn. On
the way out,* MIKEARCANGEL *stops at the counter.*)

MIKEARCANGEL: A tobacco pouch, Shopkeeper . . .

(*Lights dim.*)

SCENE 2

Across the Tracks in front of KING MOOSE'*s cabin: he is sitting on his "throne."*
MIKEARCANGEL *and* PUNKIN *enter, followed by* THE LAY-ABOUTS. *They remain
solemn and speechless. After a while* LA SAGOUINE *arrives.*

LA SAGOUINE: Well?

MIKEARCANGEL: Well, that's the way it went. We was sittin', all four of us,
Punkin and me and them Lay-abouts, comfy like—with our asses parked on
nail barrels. The Shopkeeper had told us we was all right sittin' there, and I
believed him. So, we stayed. He told us, "Come any time you feel like it." So,
we feel like it; and we wasn't gonna make a fuss, if you know what I mean, and
so we don't move our behinds from on top of the nails. But man oh man, the
bugger takes it into his head to throw us out! "My curtain lace," he keeps on
whinin', "my Paris curtains!" And he wrings his hands and shakes his head; he
looks like he's havin' a fit, you know . . . that Saint What's His Name's dance?

FIRST LAY-ABOUT: Saint What's His Name? . . .

SECOND LAY-ABOUT: And them women . . .

MIKEARCANGEL: Them women rolls in: The Hatmaker and the Mayoress. Should've seen the grinnin' and the smirkin', but when they see us they go stiff like a board.

SECOND LAY-ABOUT: Like *two* boards!

MIKEARCANGEL: And then all hell breaks loose. First just a little crackle: ptt ptt ptt . . . then a real blast, a giant bonfire: psh psh psh! In no time the whole place feels like it's burnin' up: pt pt pt . . . psh psh pshewsh! We opened our eyes, and there was nothin' left but me and the Lay-abouts and Punkin—and that Shopkeeper doin' his Saint What's His Name's dance again.

FIRST LAY-ABOUT: And that was the end of it.

LA SAGOUINE: It ain't over.

KING MOOSE: It'll happen again. You know it!

LA SAGOUINE: First we got to worry about the Mayoress, then the Hatmaker, and then the Barber, and now the Shopkeeper . . .

SECOND LAY-ABOUT: And all them sweet Uptown gals.

MIKEARCANGEL: Hands off them nice gals! We fellas'll take care of the hatmakers and barbers, but the gals is Punkin's job!

(*Goaded,* PUNKIN *jumps on* MIKEARCANGEL. THE LAY-ABOUTS *laugh and pull them apart.*)

KING MOOSE: Hey, no fightin' here now! The sun's not even set!

MIKEARCANGEL: That really stung him, huh? Maybe I said somethin' too close for comfort?

KING MOOSE: In this day and age anythin' a man can get into his head he can stuff into his gut.

MIKEARCANGEL: Yeah, but who says a man still has guts if he's lookin' around Uptown?

KING MOOSE: Come on, man. . . . Give the fella his chance. I remember when you had yours. Right here—on this side of the tracks.

MIKEARCANGEL: You said it, King: on this side of the tracks. I walk on my own shit pile, not anybody else's!

PUNKIN: OK, but the shit over there doesn't stink as much.

MIKEARCANGEL: Sure it does, when you have to swallow it!

LA SAGOUINE: I want to know more about this. I'm gonna find out what the Uptown people have in mind. Are we gonna let them salesmen and shopkeepers push us around like that? I'll find out the long and the short of it!

FIRST LAY-ABOUT: Likelier long than short, I'd say. . . . There's war in the air. When a battle's brewin' the first ones to smell the armies on the move are the whores. Looks like Jugs's got a whiff of somethin'.

(JUGS *enters*.)

SECOND LAY-ABOUT: Well I guess it's not war yet. Jugs's sniffed out a ship.
(*A foghorn in the distance*.)

FIRST LAY-ABOUT: Ha! Jugs heard the tooter before it got to toot.

(JUGS *looks at him scornfully and moves away toward the pier.* THE LAY-ABOUTS *play,*
"Il était un petit navire.")[1]

KING MOOSE: Maybe Duke'll come home pretty soon.

LAY-ABOUT: Duke, yeah, sure, Duke . . .

(LA SAGOUINE *exits in the opposite direction from* JUGS.)

LA SAGOUINE: I'm gonna find out the long and the short of it.

SCENE 3

(LA SAGOUINE *walks by "armed" in her usual style, scrutinizing the passersby from*
Uptown. Then she turns around and follows them.)

LA SAGOUINE: You got to know how to land right in the middle of the general
    staff's hindquarters.

SCENE 4

Far upstage—mime: the barbershop. THE BARBER *is trimming* THE DOCTOR's *beard.*
THE BARBER *gestures a lot, holding a brush or a pair of scissors. Gradually, we hear him*
producing sounds, a sort of continuous chatter without distinguishable words . . .

DOCTOR: Shave it rather close, please.

(THE BARBER *resumes his chatterbox act. Then he pushes the swivel chair to the front of*
the stage, where he can be understood clearly.)

BARBER: You've got to nip it in the bud before it spreads, I tell you. The future's
    in the pruning. (LA SAGOUINE *enters with her "weapons."*) What do you want,
    Sagouine?

LA SAGOUINE: I've come to lather up your floor. You do your job. I'll do mine.

BARBER: Not right now, you won't! Not with a customer right here in my
    chair . . .

LA SAGOUINE: You take 'em when they come, right? That's what I do, too.

BARBER: I'll do the Doctor's beard when he pleases, woman, and you'll do my
    floor when *I* please!

---

1. "Il était un petit navire" is a children's song whose moral might be understood as "wandering off
to sea can be the end of you."

LA SAGOUINE: When it pleases your wife, the Barbaress! She ordered me to clean up this place!

(LA SAGOUINE, *on all fours, gets on with the job. Throughout the following scene she switches cleaning tools at the same time that* THE BARBER *switches his barbering tools, marking a parallel between shampoo and wood soap, shaving brush and scrub brush, towel and rags. With her brush she underscores the tempo of the conversation.*)

BARBER: As I was saying, society must be saved: the country, the whole world, and . . . the Uptown district.

DOCTOR: Saved from what?

BARBER: Don't you realize? It begins with a little tiff at the sales counter, and you end up with a revolution. It's not too soon to move in the artillery, I tell you.

(LA SAGOUINE *looks up.*)

DOCTOR: Look, here comes our Mayoress.

(THE MAYORESS *enters.*)

BARBER: Well, good day to you, Madam.

MAYORESS: Hello, dear Doctor.

DOCTOR: My respects, Madam.

MAYORESS: (*To* THE BARBER) I need a word with you, my friend.

BARBER: I'm all yours, Madam.

MAYORESS: No, no need to keep the Doctor waiting. Actually, what I have to tell you I can say right here. It has to do with your son, the "professional playboy." You musn't let him create a scandal in our town. I simply will not tolerate it. The whole region knows us as a clean, healthy, and dignified community. We live an orderly life. We respect good morals and traditions. Tell your son to sow his wild oats somewhere else.

BARBER: He usually goes Across the Tracks.

MAYORESS: Across the Tracks! But that's next door! Don't forget that, between those people and Uptown, the only thing that stands in the way is a little fence. And they've learned very quickly to jump it. Those people invade us on a daily basis. They clutter up our sidewalks. They spot my desktop with their mackinaws. And they overrun our church benches with their fur caps. We'll end up drowned and buried in their dirt.

BARBER: That's what I was telling the Doctor. We absolutely must take action at once. We must save our society. It's none too soon to work out a strategy, ladies and gentlemen.

DOCTOR: You can't pitch men against one another. War never brings about anything good.

MAYORESS: It would be something good and permanent if it would rid us of the riffraff we have around here.

(*As they exit,* LA SAGOUINE *wrings her rag as if it were a neck.*)

LA SAGOUINE: Arrgh!

(*Lights out.*)

SCENE 5

PUNKIN *leaning against a tree; he gazes upon an empty swing. Then* THE YOUNG LADY *enters and sits on it.* THE PLAYBOY *enters. It's a moonlit night.*

PLAYBOY: Hello, silky hair and pretty face! Have you come to heal your heartache in the swing?

YOUNG LADY: Be quiet! You're just a mean, stupid boy. You don't know a thing about love or heartaches. How can you talk about them?

PLAYBOY: I don't know a thing about love? But that's what I live for! As for heartaches, my sweet, if only you knew the heartaches I've caused!

YOUNG LADY: That's the business you're in, all right, you monster. Go away, you make me sick!

PLAYBOY: But what are you doing here in the moonlight? You must be waiting for someone.

YOUNG LADY: Yes . . . and you think you're "someone," don't you! But you're just some *thing,* a kind of Don Juan. Any girl is good enough for you. You demean and degrade yourself. What I want is a man who looks up to the stars to see me.

PLAYBOY: The stars?

YOUNG LADY: Yes, the stars . . .

PLAYBOY: Yesss, the staaahs . . . ! You have a way of saying it . . . ! I can see stars in the eyes of all the girls. . . . I put them there. Can you see the end of the Big Dipper? There's nothing there, it's perfectly empty, but, if you keep looking at that little empty area, you'll see something. (*She joins in his game.*) Look, keep looking at the same spot. Aren't you beginning to feel dizzy? Do you see the tiny light that vibrates like a brand new blade of grass. Can you see it? It takes shape and pierces the sky, just a dot. One more star, and I've scored a point. That's how I light up the stars in the hearts of pretty girls. (*She stiffens up.*) There are as many hearts in love with me in this town as stars in the sky. Ah! what a wonderful thing love is! So long, lovely one with the soft hands.

YOUNG LADY: Goodbye, you devil. Ohh! What an ugly grin for someone whose business is love.

(*Seeing that she is alone,* PUNKIN *moves closer, shyly. She notices him, hesitates, sighs, and walks away reluctantly. Very disappointed, he returns to the tree. He will be patient. . . . Lights dim and go out.*)

SCENE 6

(*It is morning.* KING MOOSE's *cabin.* KING MOOSE, MIKEARCANGEL, PUNKIN, LA SAGOUINE.)

KING MOOSE: (*Gazing at the horizon*) He shouldn't be much longer.

PUNKIN: What if he's so different we don't recognize him?

LA SAGOUINE: Yeah, wars sure turn fellas around. You can't trust 'em. I've seen a few worn-out soldiers in my time. I didn't know 'em when they came back. Their jaws are hangin' open, teeth missin' in combat, their skin's turned green. They got bags under their eyes, and they're pierced through from port to starboard by some cannonball. Filthy wars! Can't trust 'em.

MIKEARCANGEL: But ain't it wars that brought La Sagouine all her men?

LA SAGOUINE: All her men, why, all they brought me was one, and I took him just the way all women take men when they serve their country.

KING MOOSE: Don't pay him no mind, La Sagouine. The priests say there was one in the Scriptures who took seven men . . . and she was called something like you . . . the Samaragouine.

PUNKIN: Maybe he'll be different.

LA SAGOUINE: Different for sure. He'll be different as sure as I'm the daughter of Jos son of Pit son of Boy son of Thomas Picoté.

MIKEARCANGEL: It ain't as sure as all that.

LA SAGOUINE: What? Ain't I the daughter of Jos of Pit?

MIKEARCANGEL: He'll probably look real healthy.

(LAY-ABOUTS *enter, carrying* DUKE *triumphantly on their shoulders. Military music.*)

FIRST LAY-ABOUT: The war's over!

SECOND LAY-ABOUT: No more wars. Duke did in all the sergeants!

(*Cheers and hurrahs*)

LA SAGOUINE: Look at your old man, Duke! Your war's made his hair turn white, ain't it somethin'? But you ain't gone to waste! I wonder what wars are all about these days! A man comes back from the other side like he's been to a weddin'. He ain't missin' a leg, a stump of tooth, or even a single hair. War ain't what it used to be . . .

(*Bottles appear as if by magic.*)

KING MOOSE: Son of a gun, you've grown so big, Duke!

DUKE: Son of a gun, Pop, war ain't a funeral!

PUNKIN: Same old Duke.

MIKEARCANGEL: You still aim straight, I hope.

DUKE: You bet I do! I shot straight into the hearts of three charming tarts—brown-skinned. They call them *"marchionesses"* over there. They're better dressed than our own gals, and they move and walk like queens. But for all that they don't age any better . . .

LA SAGOUINE: Fancy ladies!

FIRST LAY-ABOUT: Tell us about 'em!

DUKE: Naw, they're not describable. You got to see 'em. They stay in these castles at the far ends of parks. They take you in because the government forces them, and they say, "Yes, sah." Then they invite you to come back because you came a long way and they've got brothers in the war, just like you, and they tell you, "Of course, ma deah." And then they crawl at your feet and cling to you and whimper and cry and tell you . . . well, they tell you real nice things.

LA SAGOUINE: When my man up and left for the first big war, I got up bright and early and went to the window and shouted after him—it's as clear as yesterday—I shouted: "Elouèze, my chéri, when you're on the Other Side, I'd be obliged if you'd send me that song: 'It's a Long Way to Tipperary.' " Never saw him again.

MIKEARCANGEL: But you've seen others, you can't have everything.

(THE DOCTOR *enters. He casts a pall on the celebration, but gradually the tension lifts.*)

DOCTOR: I heard you had some news, King.

KING MOOSE: I do, indeed. It's news all right.

DOCTOR: We heard you were back, Duke, all sound and hearty. For a while, you know, we sort of lost hope of seeing you again.

DUKE: You see, Doc, I climbed up the apple tree to Paradise, and I didn't want to climb back down.

DOCTOR: Who would have guessed the devil was hiding out in England these days? We should send MikeArcangel over there.

(*Laughs. Someone pours a drink for* THE DOCTOR.)

MIKEARCANGEL: MikeArangel is past the age to do battle with them *marchionesses*. When he fights, it's with men.

DOCTOR: My, there's a real general for you! Well I just came by to say hello to Duke who saved our country for us. You owed it to us, Duke, to your father and me. Do you remember how the two of us saved your life the day your mother thought you were ready to be shown to the world? You better not forget it!

DUKE: I'll remember it all right—all my life, Doc. It was a real cold mornin'.

KING MOOSE: Son of a gun, anybody'd think he did remember it!

DOCTOR: Well then, good day to you all.

KING MOOSE: Be seein' you, Doc!

ALL TOGETHER: See you later!

(*On his way out* THE DOCTOR *passes* THE SAINT, *who is coming home.*)

SAINT: It looks like we're havin' visitors from the silk stockin' district, my! I wonder, is somebody about to give us orders? . . . Why, ain't this the Duke of King Moose right here before my eyes?

DUKE: Well, if it ain't the Saint! Come here, Woman! This'll be the first time in four years I hold a Saint in my arms.

SAINT: You let me go, you big oaf. I guess even the war ain't enough to straighten you out!

LA SAGOUINE: Just what do you do in a war these days?

DUKE: War? I kill them; they kill me; we kill left and right and everywhere.

LA SAGOUINE: War sure ain't what it used to be.

KING MOOSE: Duke, my boy, I got to tell you there's a little bit of trouble brewin' around here just now.

LA SAGOUINE: You listen to your pop, Duke; he'll tell you all about it.

KING MOOSE: It started over nothin'—a barrel of nails.

LA SAGOUINE: But it soon got bigger, and them Uptown women and our own men were fightin' over lace and tobacco; then, as sure as I'm standin' here, the whole Uptown met in the barbershop. . . . I saw 'em with my own eyes. And the Barber tells 'em that they got to make a move, and the Mayoress tells 'em that we're draggin' our boots on their sidewalks and droppin' our loads in their church.

ALL TOGETHER: Oh!

(*Murmurs ripple through the gathering.*)

KING MOOSE: You listen; listen good!

MIKEARCANGEL: Hush! Close your traps!

KING MOOSE: Is there anybody here who'd go and crap in the church?

SAINT: There was Jug's kid who couldn't hold it on New Year's Day when the priest was blessin' the congregation.

LA SAGOUINE: But he's a baby; he ain't even two years old yet.

MIKEARCANGEL: They just said that to make fun of us.

SAINT: To hurt our feelin's.

LA SAGOUINE: To steal our land.

MIKEARCANGEL: Just let 'em try! I ain't sellin' them three clover leaves.

KING MOOSE: They could go and take it without buyin' it from us; the land don't belong to anybody.

MIKEARCANGEL: What're you talkin' about? . . . It don't belong to anybody? Didn't you get your land from your poppa?

KING MOOSE: Of course, but my poppa never paid anythin' for it. One fine evenin', when he set up house with his woman, he just had to find a little nook for lyin' down in, right? . . . So, he pitched his cabin by the waterside, where nobody was likely to come and chase him away, at least not that night. Well, I'm still here.

LA SAGOUINE: Not paid? You don't know anythin'. My father, Jos son of Pit, brought 'em barrels of beer he brewed himself in a cellar he dug out with his own two hands; and his poppa, Pit of Boy, gave 'em smelt every winter the good Lord sent, sweet or stormy; as for his dear deceased—bless his soul—grandaddy, Boy son of Tom Picoté, he just offered 'em a few good kicks in the rear when those riffraff were cocky enough to say he didn't own his land. That's how the little acre came down to us—from Tom to Boy to Jos to me—La Sagouine. And that's how I'll hand it down to Jugs when I come to my own end.

FIRST LAY-ABOUT: Yeah, but are you sure Jugs'll be around when that happens? Looks like her future is elsewhere.

(JUGS *walks by, escorted by a sailor.*)

SAINT: Ho! (*She crosses herself.*)

KING MOOSE: A girl's future is in front of her.

MIKEARCANGEL: Like Duke, huh, always higher?

DUKE: A man's future is upward bound!

LA SAGOUINE: Come on home to your mother, Jugs! You hear me, you good-for-nothin'! Come over here where you belong, with your folks. . . . It's enough to break my heart, sink it like a cemetery in a churned-up sea.

LAY-ABOUTS: (*Singing*) The sea's her turf . . . la la la la.

SAINT: I'm off, if you'll excuse me, folks. I have business Uptown; the good Lord comes first. (*She exits.*)

LA SAGOUINE: (*Bursting into laughter*) The Saint's got business Uptown. She's gonna sell the good Lord for a pair of First Communion trousers!

(*Lights dim.*)

SCENE 7

Uptown: THE SAINT, THE MAYORESS, *then* THE HATMAKER. THE SAINT *is banging on door after door.*

SAINT: Good day to you, ma'am. For the love of God, would you happen to have a pair of old trousers in your castaways to help a poor soul?

MAYORESS: Why, now, who is it for this time?

SAINT: Punkin's havin' his First Communion.

MAYORESS: His First Communion! But he's big enough to have reached his Confirmation at least! That child makes his First Communion every year, doesn't he? Is there no end to this? At his age . . . (*She walks away.*)

SAINT: (*At the top of her voice*) I'd be obliged if you chose some medium big ones. Poor Punkin. He don't look too good. Like his poppa, he is. When you're not fed proper, you know. . . . Like our priest says, "The Good Lord comes first."

MAYORESS: (*Returning*) Here and be done with it. But a First Communion at his age . . .

SAINT: The good Lord'll return the gift, just you wait . . .

MAYORESS: For pity's sake, I hope not. I don't want to see these things again!

SAINT: (*Alone*) Hmmm. . . . Hardly good enough for fishin'. (*She knocks on* THE HATMAKER's *door.*) It's for Punkin. He's bein' confirmed.

HATMAKER: Confirmed? But the Bishop isn't coming this year; surely I would have heard if anyone had.

SAINT: Well, it's for catachizen . . . before Confirmation, the children go through catechizen . . . and the Bishop, the Scriptures say, turns up like a thief when you don't expect him.

HATMAKER: Ahh! You people never give up, do you? (*She disappears.*)

SAINT: (*Shouting*) A parka and a shirt! Times are real hard—you can't call it livin' for us poor folks.

HATMAKER: Here, and take this shoe, too. It's brand new. It's really a shame, but I just can't find the other one. But it *is* a top-quality, absolutely brand-new shoe. (*She exits.*)

SAINT: (*Alone*) Oh, fine! Now I suppose I should get one of my legs chopped off so I can wear the Hatmaker's brand new patent leather shoe!

(*Lights out.*)

SCENE 8

Uptown: PUNKIN *and* THE YOUNG LADY. *Then* THE PLAYBOY.

YOUNG LADY: (*In the swing*) Are you by yourself?

PUNKIN: (*Moves closer, bashfully*) Yeah, I was just passin' by. . . . I felt like stoppin' here. It's so peaceful under the tree.

YOUNG LADY: It's an aspen. My grandfather planted it the day I was born.

PUNKIN: It must have been a real beautiful day.

YOUNG LADY: I was told it was daybreak. I was born with the sun. That must be why I often dream that someone is carrying me off beyond the clouds. Do you have dreams, too?

PUNKIN: I dream that it's winter and I'm ice-fishin', or it's summer and I'm fishin' from a dory. I sell my catch and make a lot of money, then I buy a house, a great big house with fireplaces.

YOUNG LADY: (*Faltering*) A house? But what for?

PUNKIN: For puttin' my TV set in.

YOUNG LADY: Do you have a TV set, Punkin?

PUNKIN: In my dream I also buy a TV. But it takes a lot of money, a lot of fishin', and a lot of winters on the ice.

YOUNG LADY: Why do you want a TV so badly?

PUNKIN: A TV set goes with Uptown ways of livin'. A man can't get married without a TV. (*Pause*) Duke's back. Hasn't changed a bit. He's gonna stop 'em, Duke. He's gonna stop them Uptown folks from takin' our lands because we didn't pay for 'em.

YOUNG LADY: What lands?

PUNKIN: I don't know where I'll be goin', myself. It'll take lots more fishin', summers and winters, before I can settle down. A man without a house and a TV can't get himself a woman.

(THE PLAYBOY *enters, whistling.*)

PLAYBOY: Oh, what a lovely sight through the trees! The picture of youth! Ah ha! Some ladies real highbrow at night are awful generous in the morning. They want to look nowhere but upward and far away at the stars, but suddenly they condescend to set their eyes on lowly pumpkins. Ha! Ha! Ha!

YOUNG LADY: Go away, you brat!

PLAYBOY: The Barber's son at your service.

YOUNG LADY: You're certainly not in a position to preach good conduct, you . . .

(PUNKIN *walks away.*)

PLAYBOY: Oh, but look! He's leaving already! A shanty coward—likes to show off for the ladies but runs away from the men.

YOUNG LADY: You're not a man! You're a stupid loudmouth who tries to scare away the . . .

PLAYBOY: The birds?

YOUNG LADY: You're just like the rest of them. They want to take and own everything, even their lands.

PLAYBOY: Who cares about their lands?

YOUNG LADY: All of Uptown. They want to take the lands from those poor people who've never paid for them.

PLAYBOY: Never paid for them?

(*Lights out.*)

SCENE 9

One side of the stage is lit. A few gestures are enough for THE PLAYBOY *to tell the whole story to his father.* THE BARBER *puts a finger to his mouth and orders his son to keep the secret. He hurries off, and the lights go down. The other side of the stage lights up.* THE BARBER *stands on an overturned barrel and addresses the Uptown crowd with forceful gestures.* THE MAYORESS *enters, pushes him off the barrel, climbs on it herself, and addresses the crowd in turn.*

MAYORESS: It's time to take action. We must organize, assign tasks and charge ahead. The war is on!

DOCTOR: You could see it coming.

ALL: The war is on. . . . It's on!

(*Lights out.*)

SCENE 10

Across the tracks: KING MOOSE's *cabin.* KING MOOSE *and* MIKEARCANGEL *are playing cards.* DUKE *enters.*

DUKE: They want war! (KING MOOSE *and* MIKEARCANGEL *jump up, dropping their cards.*) So . . . that's it. The cards are dealt. There's no turnin' back anymore.

(LA SAGOUINE *and* THE LAY-ABOUTS *enter.*)

KING MOOSE: What's goin' on?

LA SAGOUINE: Nothin's goin' on. Everything's stalled, stuck!

MIKEARCANGEL: What?

LA SAGOUINE: Blocked, braked, bogged down. They've kicked me out.

KING MOOSE: You?

LA SAGOUINE: Yeah, me, me right here in front of you—mind, body, and soul!

FIRST LAY-ABOUT: You're forgettin' your guts!

(THE SAINT *arrives with* PUNKIN.)

SAINT: I swear, they'll never catch me again.

MIKEARCANGEL: Doin' what?

SAINT: Buyin' their rags. The Hatmaker slammed her door in my face!

MIKEARCANGEL: Old biddy!

DUKE: Well, that's it, then; that's how it starts.

PUNKIN: What starts?

DUKE: The war, boy. We'll be makin' a soldier out of you yet! And I'm gonna be your teacher. I'll show you how to eye a *marchioness* at the far end of a park. It's gonna be a pretty war for us.

SAINT: You can't send Punkin to war!

PUNKIN: I don't want any *marchioness!*

DUKE: Well, call 'em what you want.

LA SAGOUINE: Let's not waste time here.

MIKEARCANGEL: We've got to get goin'.

KING MOOSE: Just hold on a second! First, I want to know where this story got its start?

ALL: I was there . . . I know. It's them Uptown folks. It's all started on them barrels, [etc.].

KING MOOSE: Quiet! What kind of barbarians are we? I can't think in this racket. You'll speak in turn, one by one.

(*Quiet*)

MIKEARCANGEL: I think, King, with all due respect, it's time to move our asses. There ain't a second to waste. While we're down here screwin' off on our stumps, the Barber's on top of his barrel stirrin' up trouble. Some folks say that the Shopkeeper won't sell molasses anymore to us folks.

KING MOOSE: We gotta tend to that for sure.

MIKEARCANGEL: Come on now, shake a leg!

LA SAGOUINE: Yeah, we've got to shake it! Like they shook me—right up and out of their door!

SAINT: Threw me out, too!

DUKE: Listen, you have to understand. . . . They want to buy our land.

LA SAGOUINE: Yeah, buy it *from the government.*

ALL: The government?

LA SAGOUINE: Hey, what do you think La Sagouine does when she's scrubbin'?

SECOND LAY-ABOUT: Scrubbin' and more scrubbin'.

LA SAGOUINE: Naw, she opens her ears wide, and she listens.

SAINT: (*Lamenting*) Then what's the point of goin' out and electin' in elections and gettin' stuck with a government that sells our lands to them Uptown scum!

(*Murmurs through the crowd*)

MIKEARCANGEL: Listen, listen to me! King Moose, everybody, hear me out! When the Uptown folks have fleas, we're the ones who itch. It ain't too soon to worry about this. We got to get together; we got to pull up our bootstraps and get goin'.

LAY-ABOUTS: We can't wait anymore. Let's go!

ALL: Yeah! Let's go.

LA SAGOUINE: (*To herself*) And you, La Sagouine, let's find out the latest!

(*Lights dim.*)

Scene 11

JUGS *escorted by a sailor; she strolls past* THE YOUNG LADY *on the swing. Highbrow scorn of the Uptown lady, imperial disdain from the Shantytown girl.*

SCENE 12

Near the fence between the two communities: All the Uptown people are there. THE MAYORESS *stands apart, lost in thought.*

BARBER: (*Gesticulating wildly*) Yes indeed . . . war, yes . . . war is like that. Yes sir!

HATMAKER: Let's get it over with!

PLAYBOY: Yeah, let's really knock them for a loop!

HATMAKER: They have to go.

BARBER: The problem is how.

HATMAKER: Well, in carts, for Heaven's sake!

DOCTOR: (*Ironically*) Why not? Exile to Louisiana. That's not new.

BARBER: Come on, Doctor, think of public health.

HATMAKER: Think of morals! Think of the children!

DOCTOR: Which children?

HATMAKER: (*Angry*) Uh . . . everyone's children.

DOCTOR: What about their children, huh? Shouldn't we think about them?

BARBER: My dear Doctor, really you're overdoing it you know.

HATMAKER: You're getting . . . soft.

BARBER: You have an overwrought conscience.

HATMAKER: And what drives us all if not our conscience? Our awareness of our true duties toward the church . . .

BARBER: The country . . .

PLAYBOY: Our young people . . .

HATMAKER: The *decent* people . . .

DOCTOR: You mean . . . ourselves?

ALL: (*Scandalized*) Oh!

MAYORESS: The Doctor is right! Not so fast. These people are human, like us. We can't yoke them like beasts of burden.

BARBER: Madam who's talking of beasts?

PLAYBOY: All we talked about was carts.

MAYORESS: No, that's exactly the wrong way to go about it. Let's be methodical. What is it we want, exactly?

ALL: To see them off . . . clean up the town . . . save our children . . .

MAYORESS: Enough! Enough! Are we Shantytown rabble to create such an uproar?

BARBER: We want to save ourselves and save them.

MAYORESS: All right. So, their departure is our salvation, and their salvation is settling down somewhere, finding their own harbor.

ALL: Right, that's right.

PLAYBOY: (*Ironically*) You can't drown them, you know.

MAYORESS: Then we must find a new social environment for them, a safer economic system.

SHOPKEEPER: (*Grinning*) Ah!

BARBER: Now we've hit on it, ladies and gentlemen . . .

HATMAKER: Let's scatter them!

SHOPKEEPER: Then what happens to us? How are we supposed to live?

MAYORESS: Morally speaking, they'd be more easily cured if they were separated from one another. Their vices are contagious.

BARBER: How do we get them out of here, though?

PLAYBOY: We could set fire to their cabins.

MAYORESS: We could buy their land.

SHOPKEEPER: They won't sell.

MAYORESS: Of course, they won't sell. But what if the land, in fact, belonged to the government?

ALL: The government?

BARBER: Ladies and gentlemen, let us refer this to the government.

SHOPKEEPER: Who will be the buyer?

MAYORESS: The government will sell to the community.

HATMAKER: To build some charitable facility.

DOCTOR: A home conceived to give shelter to the poor on the very land of the poor we're about to chase away. How clever . . .

MAYORESS: The rabble from Across the Tracks are not really poor people, Doctor. They're just poorly brought up.

BARBER: Ungrateful.

HATMAKER: Vicious.

BARBER: Drunkards, foul-mouthed riffraff.

PLAYBOY: Dissipated individuals.

DOCTOR: Quadrille dancers, guitar players, and accordionists. Do you think all that makes them truly different from us? If you took a closer look, you'd probably find Uptown people who enjoy their beer, their girls, and their songs.

HATMAKER: But that's precisely the danger, Doctor. One must flee from vice while there's still time.

DOCTOR: Except that in this case we're not planning to flee from it but to chase it away.

BARBER: Comes to the same thing, really.

DOCTOR: Oh . . . of course.

HATMAKER: You're so stubborn.

BARBER: You don't want to collaborate with us, and you hamper the path of progress.

MAYORESS: No, no, no! The Doctor is right. Let's work it all out in justice and fairness. We don't want anything on our conscience. We won't chase them away; we'll make them a better offer.

ALL: Ah!

MAYORESS: Let's find them free land in the outlying villages, nice plots on the edge of the forest or right on the water.

SHOPKEEPER: I say the closer villages, so they can come back to do business if they feel like it.

HATMAKER: Heavens no! We don't want to see them again. Send them off to Saint-Hilaire.

BARBER: To La Pirogue.

PLAYBOY: Why not Bermuda?

MAYORESS: Everyone his fair share.

DOCTOR: And what, then, is *our* share?

MAYORESS: We have been earning it for centuries.

BARBER: And when they are satisfied and have agreed . . .

HATMAKER: We'll quickly buy their lands before it occurs to them they want to come back.

SHOPKEEPER: But who will pay for the land?

BARBER: Everybody.

MAYORESS: Nobody. It will be the community's money. We'll have a fund-raising fair, with a big dinner and a big raffle.

BARBER: What will the first prize be?

HATMAKER: A statue of the Holy Virgin.

SHOPKEEPER: No, a TV set. I have a very good brand name in stock. You can have one—for a nominal price, just to be on the safe side with the authorities.

MAYORESS: And we'll draw the first prize during the dinner . . . an oyster dinner.

SHOPKEEPER: Oysters? Wonderful idea!

HATMAKER: It'll be delightful! An oyster dinner!

ALL: An oyster dinner . . . oysters, oysters . . .

(LA SAGOUINE *walks by with her "weapons."*)

BARBER: Oh no! Not that woman again!
(*Lights out.*)

SCENE 13

At sea: MIKEARCANGEL *and* DUKE *are raking oysters from a rowboat. Further out* PUNKIN *is fishing alone from a raft. At the far side of the stage* THE LAY-ABOUTS *sing and play music on their dory.*

MIKEARCANGEL: Maybe they beat us and rob us, but I'll be a monkey's uncle if they laugh at us.

DUKE: They're not goin' to beat or rob me. As for laughin' . . . that's something you can pay back in kind.

MIKEARCANGEL: No, you can't. All them "Goddammits" and "Go to the devils" from down here, they just don't register Uptown. You can grin at 'em all you want; they just think you're born with a twisted mouth. A fella from our side, he don't have the chance to let 'em know what he's got in his pants.

DUKE: No chance?

MIKEARCANGEL: Well, maybe one: oysters.

DUKE: Oysters can't talk!

MIKEARCANGEL: They talk. . . . They'll talk on Sunday.

DUKE: Well, I've got other kinds of talk to give 'em. I'm gonna tell 'em a whole different way.

MIKEARCANGEL: Don't! This is the only way, the only one that'll work. We fish for the oysters for the Uptown citizens' big dinner. And, while them good Uptown citizens are eatin' our oysters, us poor folk . . .

DUKE: . . . buy all the Uptown raffle tickets. . . . (*Peals of laughter*) Hey Punkin! (LAY-ABOUTS' *song and music.* DUKE *jumps aboard* PUNKIN'S *raft.*) Bring it in, bring it in, boy. A lot of bucks buys a lot of tickets. And the sucker who tries to stand between you and that TV set, why he'll be pushed right up against the old wall! Hey, you got quite a catch there! You got enough fish to buy out the entire raffle.

PUNKIN: A man's not a man if he doesn't have a house and a TV set. He's nothin' but a Shantytown bum.

DUKE: What are you sayin'? A man *is a man*, Punkin, from Uptown or from Across the Tracks. I learned that overseas. Over there, too, they tried to pull that sort of shit on us. If you listened to 'em, not everybody was somebody. Well, sure, some walked this way, and some walked that way, but, let me tell you, the night the bombs started burstin' over our heads, that night, Punkin boy, we all ran exactly the same. . . . We was all men and only men, panickin' on the ground. There was none of that Uptown–Across the Tracks crap.

PUNKIN: It's not bombs I'm afraid of!

DUKE: You're afraid of the weapons under skirts and petticoats. But it ain't more dangerous. A pretty girl's like a bomb. She makes men run. But they all run the same, Uptown and us fellas, all of us.

PUNKIN: Yeah, but the Uptown fellas catch 'em!

DUKE: You just run faster! Listen, Punkin, the Shopkeeper's daughter is what's eatin' you, right? Sure, she's a sweet little thing. But she's only a girl, just the same. You're a good solid fella!

PUNKIN: I don't have anythin'.

DUKE: All I had in England was my private's helmet and an army jacket. That's all, plus a brain full of stories. All these years we've been watchin' the Uptown folks, so we've got a pretty good idea of what it's like—the pretty world behind the shutters. You walk by at night, under the windows, and you stop, and your head starts spinnin' in front of all those yellow lights. You see fluffy sofas, and those little tables on wheels, fancy lamps, and a log burnin' in the fireplace, and a lady in a white dress who's rollin' her shoulders over a piano. That's Heaven all right; but you know, Punkin, it's only your own, poor folks' Heaven, because Paradise is really up there (*points to the sky*) or in here (*taps his forehead*). The day I entered their world, when I walked to the far end of their park, well (*gesture: "Heaven"*) psht . . . busted! To see Heaven you have to look at it under yellow lights through a windowpane.

PUNKIN: I have to make it to the other side.

DUKE: Just call out to her! Get her to come over to this side!

PUNKIN: I'll make it, or I'll break their damn windows.

DUKE: You'll break your head, I tell you, and we'll end up buryin' Punkin.

(DUKE *returns to* MIKEARCANGEL. *Music from* THE LAY-ABOUTS.)

PUNKIN: Buryin' Punkin . . .

DUKE: (*In the distance*) Yeah, buryin' Punkin!

PUNKIN: To cancel or not to cancel, that's the big question. Whether it's best for a Shantytown hooligan to drag his misery of a life between his cabin and his boat or to put an end to it by lowerin' himself between the two. To cancel. To be done with it. Once and for all. One Punkin off the face of the Earth. To cancel, to sink, maybe to dream . . . hey . . . dreams. Forever through the other life—to dream at the bottom. What would a fella find there? Oysters? What then? No one can know. That's how come you cling to your boat. Because nobody knows what's waitin' at the bottom of the sea. Otherwise, who would stand bein' swindled by an Uptown bugger or bein' beaten up and called names or hearin' 'em whistle at your gal? It's only because the water's chilly and he's got a chicken's heart that a fella clings to his boat.

(PUNKIN *resumes his fishing. Music from* THE LAY-ABOUTS. *Lights dim.*)

SCENE 14

Two counters on each side of the stage. At one THE SAINT *is selling clothes to the Folks from Across the Tracks,* THE LAY-ABOUTS, *and the sailors; at the other,* KING MOOSE, *assisted by* MIKEARCANGEL *and* DUKE, *is selling oysters to the Uptowners. We see* THE SHOPKEEPER *and his daughter.*

SHOPKEEPER: A hundred dollars!

DUKE: Three hundred.

SHOPKEEPER: A hundred and twenty-five!

MIKEARCANGEL: Two hundred and fifty!

SHOPKEEPER: A hundred and sixty!

KING MOOSE: Two hundred!

SHOPKEEPER: A hundred and eighty!

(PUNKIN *enters. He is carrying a big basket full of oysters. He sees the* YOUNG LADY.)

SAINT: Who wants two real good parkas almost like new? Three cloth caps and one fur one! A brand new shoe—never worn!

(PUNKIN *draws close to* THE YOUNG LADY *and shows her his basket.*)

PUNKIN: It's for the TV set.

(*Lights dim.*)

SCENE 15

The general store. THE SHOPKEEPER *is selling oysters to* THE MAYORESS *and* THE HATMAKER.

MAYORESS: Three hundred dollars!

SHOPKEEPER: Five hundred!

HATMAKER: Heavens! . . . Four hundred!

SHOPKEEPER: Four hundred and eighty!

THE TWO WOMEN: (*Look at each other, then:*) Four sixty!

SHOPKEEPER: You can have them for four hundred and sixty dollars.

MAYORESS: Four hundred and sixty! Why, it's almost the entire profit from the raffle!

HATMAKER: But don't forget the "profits" from the oyster dinner . . .

(THE MAYORESS *smiles. Lights dim.*)

SCENE 16

THE YOUNG LADY *is swinging on her swing.* JUGS *walks by escorted by two sailors.* THE PLAYBOY *speeds across the stage shouting: "Tickets for a TV set, tickets. . . ." We see* PUNKIN *in the distance. Lights dim.*

SCENE 17

Upstage: A big oyster dinner party with Uptown people sitting at a long table. THE BARBER *drinks a toast to the company.* THE SHOPKEEPER *unveils an enormous TV set: stirrings of the crowd. One by one, to the great dismay of the Uptown diners, the Folks from Across the Tracks enter.* THE MAYORESS *stands up and stalks offstage, followed by all the Uptown people except* THE DOCTOR. *He approaches and spins the Wheel of Fortune.*

DOCTOR: Number 347!

PUNKIN: (*Shyly*) Me . . . Why, yeah, it's me . . .

ALL: Punkin! The TV set's for Punkin. Hurrah! Hurrah!

(*Cheers. They sit down at the dinner table and start eating oysters.*)

MIKEARCANGEL: (*In the* BARBER's *place*) Well, I'll be damned! The Uptown folks buy oysters from us Folks from Across the Tracks, and we folks from Across the Tracks . . .

DUKE: Carry off the TV set!

(LAY-ABOUTS' *music*)

DOCTOR: Be careful though! They're the ones with the money.

(MIKEARCANGEL *suddenly looks worried.*)

DUKE: To the devil with their money. We're feastin' for free!

LA SAGOUINE: Money that don't buy a feast ain't real money.

ALL: The war is *over!* We won it!

KING MOOSE: Well, son of a gun!

(PUNKIN, *ecstatically happy, contemplates his trophy.*)

(*Curtains close.*)

ACT 2

SCENE 1

Pantomime at the far side of the stage: THE BARBER's *shop.* THE MAYORESS *enters with* THE HATMAKER. *Their gestures indicate weariness and disappointment.* THE SHOPKEEPER *then enters with the money satchel. All grow excited when he starts counting the money.* LA SAGOUINE *passes downstage. They cross down to her. They stare at one another.* LA SAGOUINE *sees the money.*

LA SAGOUINE: Some people got the money, some people got the picnic. . . . Nobody got everythin'.

MAYORESS: A big party is quickly gone and forgotten, but money stays with you forever, La Sagouine.

BARBER: Like the poet says: money is gold!

LA SAGOUINE: My poppa—bless his soul—he liked to say a buck that don't buy you fun ain't an honest buck.

HATMAKER: You can *have* all the parties like this last one!

LA SAGOUINE: Likewise, you just sit on that money for all I care!

MAYORESS: We'll put it to good use, don't you worry!

BARBER: Very intelligent use.

HATMAKER: Very profitable use.

MAYORESS: One can, for instance, buy certain lands from the government, and when that is done the people who had taken them illegally will have to go and have fun somewhere else.

HATMAKER: To Sapin-Court, to Saint-Hilare.

BARBER: To La Pirogue.

LA SAGOUINE: (*Shocked*) Oh! What are you sayin'?

MAYORESS: We won't put up with anymore of your abuse.

HATMAKER: It's lasted long enough.

MAYORESS: Everyone must have his day, La Sagouine.

HATMAKER: Everyone his oyster dinner. I haven't even digested mine yet!

LA SAGOUINE: Oh my! Oh my!

(*They push her off.*)

BARBER: Well, it's done.

HATMAKER: You can't say after that dinner they're just "ordinary poor."

MAYORESS: Come on, let's get down to business.

(*Lights dim.*)

(*Lights up. Across the Tracks:* PUNKIN *is busy installing a TV antenna. Everybody is singing, dancing, and helping fix up the cabin. Music.* LA SAGOUINE *storms in.*)

LA SAGOUINE: Un huh!

ALL: What?

LA SAGOUINE: To Saint-Hilaire and Sapin-Court. And La Pirogue, too. Ever heard of it? La Pirogue? Ain't it bad and shameful enough to live here Across the Tracks?

MIKEARCANGEL: What's goin' on in La Pirogue?

LA SAGOUINE: MikeArcangel, just like everybody here, you'll be movin' on to La

Pirogue. You think you're as good as the pope with that TV set. Well, I'm tellin' you that soon you're gonna have to drag your darlin' TV onto a boat, that's what!

KING MOOSE: What the devil is that woman sayin'?

LA SAGOUINE: The woman is sayin' that we might as well sneak out without trouble right now because them charitable, kind-hearted Uptown folks want to put us away like orphans.

MIKEARCANGEL: And how do they figure they'll do that? (*Straightening up*)

LA SAGOUINE: With money, your honor, sir, just plain old money. You do everythin' with money; you even make orphans.

(*They are crushed.*)

SAINT: Oh no! Not runnin' away again? It ain't even ten years since I had to move on when the house burned down! We had to run off to the river. We was in a little flat boat: Punkin, my man and me. We was sort of like the Holy Family.

KING MOOSE: This has to be stopped!

MIKEARCANGEL: We got to keep 'em from buyin' our lands.

PUNKIN: But how are we gonna do that?

DUKE: Make 'em spend their money.

ALL: Yeah . . . sure . . .

DUKE: Of course! It's just as easy to spend money as to make it.

FIRST LAY-ABOUT: You spend it on dancin'.

SECOND LAY-ABOUT: You spend it on booze.

DUKE: You spend it on gals.

LA SAGOUINE: You spend it on oysters.

MIKEARCANGEL: You spend it on a TV set.

PUNKIN: No . . . not . . .

MIKEARCANGEL: I'm gonna throw 'em a party shanty style. How about a raffle for a spanking new TV?

PUNKIN: But it's my TV.

SAINT: Yeah, it's Punkin's TV.

KING MOOSE: That's true. He won it.

MIKEARCANGEL: Sure, but it's our money that done it. It's 'cause us poor folks bought all them raffle tickets that the first prize tumbled downhill to us. And it was just mother luck that it rolled into Punkin's lap.

LA SAGOUINE: Punkin, you know if you want to catch people, you have to offer bait.

DUKE: So, we put together a big shindig with music and quadrilles and beer.

FIRST LAY-ABOUT: And we all do our best to attract 'em.

SECOND LAY-ABOUT: Even Jugs'll do her civic duty.

FIRST LAY-ABOUT: We'll all give ourselves to it, body and soul!

(*Laughs.* THE SAINT *crosses herself.*)

KING MOOSE: We got to get that money back from 'em.

MIKEARCANGEL: We got to save our homes.

LA SAGOUINE: Even if it means losin' the TV set.

DUKE: (*Apart to* PUNKIN) Don't worry, Punkin, the best gals from Uptown'll most likely come to our party.

LA SAGOUINE: I'm gonna make her spit them oysters out, Her Highness Hatmaker . . . her with them two little oysters sittin' on her fat little stomach!

(*Lights out.*)

SCENE 2

PUNKIN *and* THE YOUNG LADY *are deep in conversation by the tree.*

PUNKIN: So that's the end of it. They're gonna take it back from me, and here I was gonna go fishin' all fall and winter long, and in the spring I was gonna build myself a house with a fireplace. And I was gonna put it inside.

YOUNG LADY: Why do you have to have a TV inside your house?

PUNKIN: To be a man like other men.

YOUNG LADY: A man isn't a man for that reason. It's not what he has in his house that counts . . . it's what his heart holds.

PUNKIN: But you can't know what I have in my heart.

YOUNG LADY: (*Bashfully*) No . . .

PUNKIN: A TV set.

YOUNG LADY: (*Disappointed*) You could have something else. I don't know but . . . some people have other things there . . .

PUNKIN: Yeah . . . other things. . . . More hollow, though. A fisherman, you know, puts a worm at the end of his line. But he's not fishin' for worms, right? Worms are bait. The fella who gets his bait whisked away from him before he throws his line in, well, he can't catch anythin'.

YOUNG LADY: Yes, but perhaps if fish could talk they would tell you they don't give a hoot about your worms; that the river is full of them; that they're not drawn to the line by that. They'd tell you that the line opens a tiny luminous path through the water, it shines like a shooting star, and it leads somewhere into an unknown mysterious world.

PUNKIN: (*Touched, moving closer*) I don't understand what you're sayin', but I feel so happy . . . so happy . . .

(THE PLAYBOY *and* DUKE *can be seen on either side of the stage, defying each other and watching over the couple.*)

(*Lights dim.*)

SCENE 3

LA SAGOUINE *and* THE SAINT *are walking in opposite directions. They stop at different houses to announce the raffle and collect donations.*

LA SAGOUINE: (*At the* SHOPKEEPER'*s*) Good Day, Mister. The sky's gettin' cloudy, and King Moose is sendin' word that there's to be a little party in our part of the world, just a little get-together to limber up. There'll be songs and accordions. And have you heard that Punkin wants to sell his TV set? Times ain't easy, you see. So we're havin' a little raffle. (*She walks away.*)

SHOPKEEPER: Music and a raffle. Hmmmm. . . . They need money. It wouldn't be a bad idea to get the TV back. I could sell it again . . . eh heh!

LA SAGOUINE: (*Cheerfully*) Well, hello there, Mister Barber. Nice day today, ain't it? How about a party with accordions and rigadoons and maybe beer and beans?

BARBER: Who on earth do you think we are?

LA SAGOUINE: (*Walking away*) Just the same as everybody else: pigs!

BARBER: (*Seduced*) Hmmm, my, my . . . beer and rigadoons . . . hmmm. . . . Life can certainly steer a body hither and yon, can't it?

SAINT: Greetings, Your Grace. Do you happen to have a suit for Punkin, who's gettin' married soon?

MAYORESS: Is that possible? Punkin getting married? A young man of the parish who can't even dress himself properly . . . and now he wants to start a family? Do you realize what you're saying? Marriage—marriage is not a picnic you know! Marriages generate society. Of course, you people can't understand that. All you can think of is pleasure. But marriage is an entirely different business. . . . Ah! You can't talk sense to them. (*She disappears.*)

SAINT: (*Having spotted* LA SAGOUINE) Look at her washin' and scrubbin', peddlin' her trade from door to door.

LA SAGOUINE: (*Having spotted* THE SAINT) Beggin' her way from door to door; almost makes me sick! (*She walks away.*)

MAYORESS: (*Returning*) Here! I hope he'll be married quickly so we'll be done with it. At least he'll be over his First Communion! (*She disappears.*)

SAINT: (*Walking away*) My thanks to you, Your Gracious Lady.

LA SAGOUINE: Good Day, Madam. I was walkin' past your house just by chance, you might say, and I thought you'd like to know we was havin' a little party, just like the other day. Well, no oysters, of course, we're just poor folks down there. Like I was tellin' the Shopkeeper, it's just a get-together to return your hospitality.

HATMAKER: Oh? What cheek!

SAINT: Hello, Mister Barber! Have you, by chance, an old hat to wear to a wedding?

BARBER: I, of course, wear new hats to weddings.

SAINT: It's for Punkin's wedding. He needs some headgear.

BARBER: Punkin! It's not *on* his head that he needs something. He's getting married, is he? So that's what this party is all about! Married to whom?

SAINT: That's his secret. But I tell you it ain't trash. My son don't get married too often, but when he does take the trouble. . . . If you want to know, it's a gal from Uptown.

BARBER: From Uptown?

(*All heads pop out as if summoned by the call of a gong.*)

MAYORESS: From Uptown!

SHOPKEEPER: From Uptown!

HATMAKER: From Uptown!

ALL: (*Coming together*) From Uptown!

BARBER: Did you hear that?

HATMAKER: Heavens! Where are we heading?

MAYORESS: This cannot happen. No, no, no, a thousand times no!

(*All the Uptown people are gathered together, except* THE YOUNG LADY. *They gesture and talk in impenetrable jargon.* THE PLAYBOY *arrives and is questioned immediately. It takes coaxing before he will speak. When he does* THE SHOPKEEPER *clutches his head in his hands. They all point an accusing finger at him.* THE SHOPKEEPER *runs to the front of the stage and screams, "My daughter!"*)

ALL: Oh! God! Is this possible! She must be mad! Where are we heading? It can't happen to us!

PLAYBOY: A boy so young with a big TV set, it gives you ideas.

HATMAKER: It does! I've always thought so. These things are just not good for them. Give them an inch, they'll take a mile.

PLAYBOY: They'll take the whole highway and more!

MAYORESS: We *must* retrieve our raffle prize. Televisions, radios, movies, all that gives them ideas. Progress is much too dangerous a weapon in their hands.

BARBER: One man's prize is another man's burden. You can't let children play with matches.

MAYORESS: We must get that set back.

BARBER: Then, let's go to their party.

HATMAKER: Their party! The Ball Across the Tracks! Gobbling down pork and beans from a pot dripping with molasses. The thought of it turns my stomach.

BARBER: You have to choose, my dear, between eating their beans or seeing our daughters seduced by their TV sets.

SHOPKEEPER: Let's go to their party.

HATMAKER: That's where we'll lose our children to them! Their morals lead to the worst possible kind of debauchery.

SHOPKEEPER: This party is not for our children but for us. Let's go. We simply must outwit them.

BARBER: For a change, the cats *won't* be away when the mice play!

MAYORESS: We'll go to their party, and we'll carry that TV set home with us.

PLAYBOY: (*Apart*) And their wine, women, and songs.

(*Lights dim.*)

SCENE 4

Across the tracks: the party is on but offstage. Music of guitars and accordions, sounds of songs, laughter, and dancing. Uptown people walk across the back of the stage to go to the party. PUNKIN *is alone downstage, watching the party from a distance. Occasionally, someone walks toward him then exits.*

PUNKIN: (*Ecstatic*) She's comin'. She doesn't know it, but the party's for her. Yeah, just for her. King Moose thinks he's givin' a party for the town, and MikeArcangel thinks he's savin' our land, and La Sagouine thinks she's gettin' the Hatmaker to throw up her oysters, and Jugs, well, Jugs . . . nobody knows, I'm sure. But the party's really for her. Why else do they reckon I would've let the TV go? I needed it for her. But she said a line doesn't need bait, that fish love to watch shootin' stars. The devil take it! I don't care right now about their TV so long as she comes.

(LAY-ABOUTS *appear. They're ready to drink.*)

FIRST LAY-ABOUT: Hey, Punkin! Everything's ready!

SECOND LAY-ABOUT: You're the only one missin'. Everybody's showin' up.

(*They disappear. The Uptown people can be seen crossing upstage to go to the party.*)

PUNKIN: I'll walk with her. They'll see who I am. She'll be wearin' her white dress. I'll tell her I don't need my TV anymore and that I'm gonna build a house with a fireplace. And I'll build it up there, where they live.

(DUKE *appears.*)

DUKE: Come on, Punkin. They're tunin' the violins. This isn't the time to hang around here. You should see La Sagouine—she's turnin' around the Hatmaker like a wildcat. She'll have her spittin' out those oysters before the night sets in. Ha! Ha! Ha! (DUKE *exits.*)

PUNKIN: (*Disturbed*) There's a whole lot of people there already. And the Mayor's losin' her voice, thanking 'em. But the Shopkeeper's not here yet. So she'll be comin' with her father. That's it! She *will* come. Because she said, if a fish

could talk, it'd tell the fisherman he doesn't need bait. The line draws a little
path in the water. . . . I don't quite know how . . . among the stars.

(JUGS *enters with* THE PLAYBOY. *They don't see* PUNKIN.)

PLAYBOY: Come on, sweetheart! You can't run away like that. It's not nice. You
have such wonderful eyes, so large and wet, and lovely round hips, too. The
Uptown gals are fence pickets compared to a gorgeous feline like you. Come
on, let's go Uptown.

(*He tries to take her in his arms. She runs away from him, and he runs after her.*)

PUNKIN: (*More and more disturbed*) She's gonna come. . . . She's gonna come
with the Shopkeeper. . . . The Shopkeeper'll be closin' his shop any minute.
They'll be comin'. . . . They're gettin' the Wheel of Fortune ready. They're
gonna draw the ticket for the TV set. (THE SHOPKEEPER *walks across the stage.*)
There he is. But he's alone. Maybe she's not comin'. (*Shouting: the first prize is
drawn.* THE SHOPKEEPER *wins.*) She's not comin'. It's all over. (*The TV is
paraded across the stage. Congratulations to* THE SHOPKEEPER.) It's over. She's
not comin'. (*The party winds down, with the Folks from Across the Tracks spilling
onto the stage.* PUNKIN *walks away. Lights dim.*)

SCENE 5

JUGS, *flanked by two sailors, strolls past* THE YOUNG LADY, *who is sobbing.*

SCENE 6

By the sea

PUNKIN: The water's warm at the bottom of the sea. There's oysters and tiny fish
like shootin' stars and maybe great big glass houses with yellow lights. A
fella'd love to spend his lifetime there, his whole entire life. The sea's warm at
the bottom of the water.

(*Lights dim.*)

SCENE 7

Across the Tracks: KING MOOSE, MIKEARCANGEL, *and* LA SAGOUINE *are counting
money. A bit later* THE DOCTOR *and the other folks from Across the Tracks enter.*

LA SAGOUINE: Well, for a party, that sure was a party! I'm not one to eat
oysters, but you can't say I don't know how to kick up my heels and look the
bottom of a bottle in the eye.

MIKEARCANGEL: . . . Thirty-eight, thirty-nine, forty . . .

LA SAGOUINE: And didn't you see that fancy speechmaker, that Barber, who's always stuffin' them big vocabulary words down his throat, he's gone and lost his taste for speeches, that old Barber! He's as drunk and out as my defunct poppa, when he was alive.

MIKEARCANGEL: . . . Sixty-five, seventy . . .

LA SAGOUINE: And that Hatmaker doin' her VIP performance as if the world had invented parties just so she could stick her big goosey beak up in the air. And then that Shopkeeper, who chose his time just like a real do-business fella. He made one of them entrances, "Here I am—God—" right when that old Wheel of Fortune was turnin' the TV around. You might as well say we plopped that fortune right in the lap of our old Shopkeeper.

MIKEARCANGEL: So, let him take it with him, his pretty prize. And we keep the money.

LA SAGOUINE: And I keep my land. Yeah! A plump little piece of Earth that smells like cookin' fat and manure. I saw that Hatmaker holdin' her nose when she bent her spine to pick up that silk kerchief. Oh, là là, does she think she's deliverin' gold and pearls into her hankie? Would I be less snotty if I had a silk nose rag? The beans and rice I eat—just like the ones the Hatmaker eats and all them others, too—grow on land stinkin' with manure. On land that don't bother with manure, you get crab grasses and thistles. And they go and hold their nose over here? But then why do they want to grab our land from us?

KING MOOSE: So, they can rub it and shine it and make it all clean and nice like a baby's hiney.

LA SAGOUINE: Well, I tell you, I'd worry about a baby's hiney that stayed clean for too long. And I'd make him take some castor oil, the little fella, to fix up his insides.

(THE SAINT *enters. She is screaming.*)

SAINT: Punkin! Punkin! They've gone and drowned him on me.

LA SAGOUINE: Holy Mother of God!

(*A whole procession enters:* THE LAY-ABOUTS *carrying* PUNKIN *on a stretcher,* JUGS *crying,* DUKE, *then* THE DOCTOR.)

KING MOOSE: (*Solemn*) Should have been expectin' this would happen one day. Who did it?

DOCTOR: Himself, King Moose. He did it all by himself.

MIKEARCANGEL: All by himself? You believe, do you, that's a thing a fella would do all by himself? No! I tell you, no! . . . Not that! A twenty-year-old fella that'd throw himself in the river, that's because there ain't a friggin' piece of land for him to put his feet on. The ones who kept him from a piece of land, they're the ones that pushed him off the edge.

LA SAGOUINE: And the ones who stole his TV from him, that gave him a kick in the shins.

DUKE: And the ones who went and took his gal from him—they're the ones who threw him in the water.

KING MOOSE: Don't worry Punkin. I'm on your side. We all are. And I still feel strong as an ox. Goddamit to Hell! You liked those TV's and those Uptown gals maybe too much, but you were a worthy fella who knew how to rake up them oysters and clams with the best of 'em. You should've waited just a bit longer, boy. And you would've had your own cabin to put your own woman in. But don't worry right now. The rest of us are still alive, and I promise you a piece of land. You'll get your own.

MIKEARCANGEL: Yeah, you said it, a piece of land for Punkin.

EVERYBODY: (*Angry*) Land for Punkin!

(*Each one picks up a shovel, a pitchfork, or a club and follows* MIKEARCANGEL. LA SAGOUINE *slips back and bends over* PUNKIN's *body*.)

LA SAGOUINE: And then you'll see Punkin, we'll send you straight off to Paradise.

(*Lights dim.*)

SCENE 8

Uptown: Everybody is silent and tense. THE MAYORESS *is pacing.*

BARBER: (*Very upset*) Yes . . . but then what do we do? Tell me that? Afterward? As far as I'm concerned, it's facts that are important. All this taking the law into one's own hands and the strongest man wins is fine in theory. But all our strength combined won't keep them from closing in.

HATMAKER: Vandals!

SHOPKEEPER: We should offer them our condolences.

DOCTOR: We should give them justice.

MAYORESS: Justice! And how exactly were we unjust to them?

DOCTOR: A man is dead.

MAYORESS: Dear Doctor, a man killed himself.

DOCTOR: Out of despair, Madam. Punkin, a twenty-year-old man, didn't even have a little corner of land to put his feet on. He walked straight into the sea because that was the only place worth anything that was left to him. The sea, like death, still belongs to everybody in our democracy.

(*In the distance we hear the Folks from Across the Tracks yelling.*)

BARBER: They're getting closer.

MAYORESS: Go ask them what they want.

BARBER: Oh! My voice will never carry over all their commotion.

MAYORESS: (*To* THE SHOPKEEPER) You do it. (THE SHOPKEEPER *exits.*) Can you still talk about democracy and justice when a hoard of anarchists is approaching to pillage our homes?

DOCTOR: And isn't it, in fact, their homes that we're trying to take away from them?

MAYORESS: But legally, Doctor.

DOCTOR: That's a mighty big word, that one, Madam, in the hands of people who only know the letter of the law.

SHOPKEEPER: (*Entering*) They demand a plot for Punkin.

HATMAKER: Up here?

MAYORESS: Punkin is dead. May he rest in peace. Give them their cemetery plot.

SHOPKEEPER: To be completely within the law about it, let's sell it to them for a dollar.

DOCTOR: (*Taking out his wallet*) Here.

PLAYBOY: Punkin is dead! Long live Punkin!

DOCTOR: (*Alone*) You've won, Punkin, but it cost you your life.

(*Lights dim.*)

SCENE 9

The cemetery. THE DOCTOR *at first is alone at the foot of an immense cross. Then the Folks from Across the Tracks arrive in a procession, humming a funeral march and carrying* PUNKIN'S *coffin. The People from Uptown arrive from the opposite direction. The two groups stop on opposite sides of the cross. Then* THE DOCTOR *throws the first shovelful of dirt into the grave. He hands the shovel to* KING MOOSE, *who throws in a shovelful. Then* THE DOCTOR *passes the shovel to* THE MAYORESS. *At last the shovel is passed back and forth from an Uptown hand to the hand of a person from Across the Tracks without need of* THE DOCTOR'S *mediation. When they have finished the two groups have merged into one; all their heads are bent over the coffin.*

SCENE 10

THE MAYORESS *and* THE SHOPKEEPER

MAYORESS: Even dead, these people make me nervous.

SHOPKEEPER: What's there to fear from a poor buried dreamer?

MAYORESS: Buried on our doorstep! What if it gives them ideas?

SHOPKEEPER: You mean they'll all want to be buried up here?

MAYORESS: It sends shivers up my spine to think that our lands have been violated by a dead man, and a suicide at that!

SHOPKEEPER: They're the least dangerous ones.

MAYORESS: You're talking like a man. But a woman has her intuitions. (*Silence*)
    They've got to go.

SHOPKEEPER: You're forgetting that we don't have a bankroll anymore.

MAYORESS: No, but we do have ideas. For a businessman you're not very clever.
    Leave the business to the Shopkeeper and the legal subtleties to the Mayor.
    How much did they pay for the plot where they buried Punkin?

SHOPKEEPER: A dollar. The Doctor paid it. (THE MAYORESS *smiles enigmatically.*
    Finally, THE SHOPKEEPER *understands.*)

MAYORESS: A dollar. . . .

(*Lights dim.*)

SCENE 11

LA SAGOUINE *passes, armed as usual. She is muttering to herself. She arrives at* KING
MOOSE'*s cabin.*

LA SAGOUINE: (*Alone*) Something's stinkin' around here. There's some nastiness
    in the air. Got to warn King Moose. The Mayoress has a queer look in her
    eyes, the Barber is whistlin', the Shopkeeper is talkin' to himself, "eh heh,"
    and the Hatmaker is breakin' wind for all the world to hear. Got to warn
    King Moose. (*At* KING MOOSE'*s cabin.*) Something's cookin', something
    crooked, King Moose, we've got to watch out, it don't smell good at all.

KING MOOSE: Where abouts?

LA SAGOUINE: Up there.

(DUKE *enters like a whirlwind.*)

DUKE: They bought the land. Bought it from the government.

(*All the others enter.*)

MIKEARCANGEL: It ain't possible. I made 'em spend all their money.

ALL: Ain't possible.

(*Murmurings*)

DUKE: The land didn't belong to anybody—that way they could get it for a buck.

(*They're all dumbfounded. Lights dim.*)

SCENE 12

The Barbershop: Everyone from Uptown is there.

BARBER: A dollar! And the land is ours! We won! The war is won!

DOCTOR: All the same, they have the money now. Don't count your chickens just yet.

(THE MAYORESS *grows solemn.*)

HATMAKER: Shame on you—you're just a harbinger of unhappiness. Rejoice with us instead, Doctor! They're off to Saint Hilare and La Pirogue.

BARBER: And we're saved!

SHOPKEEPER: Eh heh! (*He pats the television.*)

(*Curtains down.*)

ACT 3

SCENE 1

Across the Tracks: The Folks enter, one after the other, tired, discouraged. A long silence in which each one appears to be bidding farewell to his cabin and his land.

MIKEARCANGEL: Lost: our land, our television, our boy. Won: a bankroll.

KING MOOSE: We ain't in such good shape.

MIKEARCANGEL: Where are we gonna go with that? Money, but no house, no land, where does that take us?

LA SAGOUINE: To the river.

KING MOOSE: None of that talk, La Sagouine. You've got to respect the dead.

MIKEARCANGEL: Just the same, there's got to be some place, some way, to spend that money.

SAINT: And what about some masses for our dead? God comes first.

LA SAGOUINE: Let's buy each of us a little piece of land.

KING MOOSE: Where abouts?

LA SAGOUINE: In the cemetery to put to rest our poor old bones.

DUKE: Money—what did we do the last time with our money? Where did it get us?

SECOND LAY-ABOUT: It got us parties!

FIRST LAY-ABOUT: Oyster parties and beer parties.

DUKE: And every time we had a party it was a big success.

KING MOOSE: For who?

DUKE: Why, for us, of course. The first one, we ate oysters and won a TV. The second we drank beer and walked away with the money. And what did it cost us? Nothin', except a couple of days scratchin' the bottom of the bay.

LA SAGOUINE: And that didn't kill you.

KING MOOSE: Parties—those are Uptown folks' ideas. They ain't for us down here.

MIKEARCANGEL: And what are we gonna celebrate this time? I ain't so keen on celebratin' the victory that robbed us of our land.

KING MOOSE: Well, how about that? What are you thinkin' about? It so happens that we don't need a reason for a party. Those are the Mayoress and the Barber's fancy manners. We celebrate because we celebrate. How about a party for the Doc?

SAINT: Sure, why not, let's celebrate the Doc.

DUKE: He practically saved Punkin. Son of a gun, he sure pumped a lot of water out of his gut!

LA SAGOUINE: And, even more important, when we were buryin' Punkin, the Doc sure said some beautiful things about him.

MIKEARCANGEL: But the Doc's a fella from Uptown.

KING MOOSE: No, he ain't an Uptown man.

MIKEARCANGEL: And just where is he from, according to you?

KING MOOSE: The Doctor! He sits on the fence, because there's sick folks on either side.

(*Lights dim.*)

SCENE 2

JUGS—*followed by* THE PLAYBOY—*passes by. They mime a flirtation.* DUKE *catches sight of it.* THE PLAYBOY *takes off in a hurry.*

SCENE 3

THE DOCTOR's: *the Folks from Across the Tracks arrive on tiptoe guided by* MIKEARCANGEL.

MIKEARCANGEL: Shut your traps! By golly! If you want this to be a surprise, I better take care of things. Then we'll have a real surprise! Everybody, hide! Get behind the tables and chairs! (*Noise of glass breaking.*) Hey! What's goin' on in the kitchen?

SAINT: It's La Sagouine. She put her foot through the wrong window, the one that was shut.

MIKEARCANGEL: That ain't the way to go about things! Sure ain't. When I said, "Come in through the window," I don't mean stick your feet through the glass!

FIRST LAY-ABOUT: Wasn't her feet—it was her mop.

(LA SAGOUINE *enters, armed as usual.*)

MIKEARCANGEL: What's the idea of draggin' that mop all around with you?

LA SAGOUINE: And just who do you think's gonna pick up the pieces after this party?

SAINT: And you know they'll be plenty of pieces when you go around smashin' windows.

DUKE: Gotta change the glass before the Doc gets here.

MIKEARCANGEL: Uh . . . a pane of glass, where do you find that kind of thin'?

SAINT: I see one.

LA SAGOUINE: That ain't a pane of glass—that's a meer. You'd think she'd never seen anythin'.

MIKEARCANGEL: It'll do the trick in the meantime. That way maybe he won't notice anythin' till we find the real thin'.

(THE LAY-ABOUTS, *led by* THE SAINT, *carry the mirror off.*)

LA SAGOUINE: If this sure ain't an idea of MikeArcangel to throw a party for the Doc in his own house!

MIKEARCANGEL: I wasn't about to throw it in our cabins. So, we're all profitin' from the fact that he's out makin' his deliveries. No time to lose. He'll be back soon as the lady . . .

DUKE: Here he comes!

LA SAGOUINE: Hide!

MIKEARCANGEL: Yeah, hide! When I stick up my head, you all shout together.

(*They hide. Spot on the tip of* LA SAGOUINE's *mop sticking up from behind a chair.*)

EVERYONE: Surprise!

SAINT: Here's to your party!

(*We hear the sound of glass breaking, then* KING MOOSE *enters.*)

KING MOOSE: Who's the bugger who came after me and made faces in the window? He got my fist so good on his mug that he fell to pieces, and the window did, too!

SAINT: Oh no! The meer!

LA SAGOUINE: King Moose, that wasn't a window, that was a meer. You went and put your fist in your own beard while I was shoutin' surprise at the Doc.

DUKE: They all took you for the Doc!

KING MOOSE: Hey! A doc? Why I don't even know how to say *tranquillisant* in English.

LA SAGOUINE: That's *transkillers.* I heard the Hatmaker say it.

(*During all this scene they pass a bottle around.*)

MIKEARCANGEL: Ain't he got another meer somewhere to plug up the hole?

LA SAGOUINE: We're not about to break all his windows! Use some rags. (THE LAY-ABOUTS *tear the drapes down.*) Hey! Don't tear up them curtains! (*Too late—they've been turned into rags.*)

DUKE: Hurrah! I just found the treasure chest. (*He enters, loaded down with beer bottles.*)

KING MOOSE: What do you have there?

DUKE: Can't you recognize 'em, Pop? It's not like you've never seen 'em before.

MIKEARCANGEL: Where'd you get 'em?

DUKE: Off some real hard ice in a big white box.

LA SAGOUINE: A frigerator, that's what it was.

KING MOOSE: And that belongs to the Doc. Keep your hands off his stuff.

LAY-ABOUTS: Oh . . .

DUKE: But it's a treat for all of us! A man don't drink alone. That ain't Christian. He offers a round to his guests. And I'm a guest!

KING MOOSE: Well . . . maybe you got a point.

MIKEARCANGEL: No, he don't. Because I wasn't invited. I came by myself. I'll only be invited when the Doc gets back.

LA SAGOUINE: And maybe he'll get back real late. Them deliveries, you can't trust 'em. Nobody but the Saint gets 'em over with fast. She puts a St. Jude medal on your belly, and it's over before . . .

DUKE: Let's all have a little drink, and then we'll explain things to the Doc.

FIRST LAY-ABOUT: Sure, tell him we couldn't wait, and then we'll explain things to the Doc.

KING MOOSE: I'll drink to his health in that case! Raise your bottles everybody to the Doc, who took good care of Punkin when he died, who said pretty words on his grave, and who's a real good fella, a real good fella.

SAINT: (*Crossing herself*) In the name of the Son and the Holy Spirit.

(*They drink, play music, sing ballads. Once in a while they knock over a chair or a table. They're finally all spread out in the room, quite drunk. It grows quiet. All that can be heard is* MIKEARCANGEL.)

MIKEARCANGEL: (*Drunk*) A good egg, that Doc, a real good egg. Yeah . . . one great egg. A town that can make a man like the doc . . . a town . . . yeah . . . a swell egg, the Doc's town . . . maybe he's a fella from Uptown, but . . . but he ain't really a fella from up there. No, sir . . . he's a fella on the fence.

(THE DOCTOR *enters and sees what's going on. He lifts up his arms in despair.*)

DOCTOR: What's gotten into them?

MIKEARCANGEL: (*Belches*) Doc . . . you good egg, Doc . . . you fine egg. . . . Surprise! . . .

(*Lights dim.*)

SCENE 4

THE SAINT *is knocking at* THE HATMAKER's *door begging clothes again.*

HATMAKER: What do you want this time?

SAINT: I've come for a black dress. The priests say we got to be in mournin'.

HATMAKER: Yes . . . of course. . . . I'll go and see if I have something.

SAINT: (*Alone*) She knows she killed him. That bitch—she never wanted him to marry an Uptown gal, but you just wait, Punkin, we'll have our revenge. (THE HATMAKER *returns.*) Thank you. Thank you so much. That sure looks like a fine dress. Guess it might even go to a weddin'? You never know.

HATMAKER: A wedding?

SAINT: Oh! Not me! I ain't goin' to a weddin' with my boy under the ground! But I might lend it to La Sagouine if there's a weddin' Across the Tracks.

HATMAKER: But who Across the Tracks?

SAINT: These past few days Duke's been seein' the Barber's boy hangin' around, with that look. . . . But that ain't the sort of thin' that gets repeated among respectable women.

HATMAKER: The Barber's son? But with whom?

SAINT: (*Confidentially*) Jugs.

(*Her news produces the desired effect.* THE SAINT *can walk away satisfied. Immediately after,* THE HATMAKER *rushes to* THE MAYORESS'*s. Everyone from Uptown gathers there. They are bursting with excitement. All that can be heard are panicked voices. Everybody is talking and gesturing at once.* THE BARBER *tries to defend himself, but everyone jumps on him. Then* THE MAYORESS *moves away and walks downstage. The others follow, one by one.*)

MAYORESS: We have to work fast. First, let's stop this marriage. Then, we must begin to move them out. I will not be able to sleep as long as I know they're there. We have the right to expropriate them. Signed and sealed by the Ministry. The land is ours. What are we waiting for now?

SHOPKEEPER: It's because we can't make them move. We agreed to find housing for them, not too far from town.

HATMAKER: As far away as possible.

BARBER: We're still waiting to hear from Sapin-Court and La Pirogue.

SHOPKEEPER: May I remind you that they still have a large sum of our money in their possession?

MAYORESS: Let them keep the money and hang themselves with it!

SHOPKEEPER: Watch out, I tell you. Once the poor have money it's just not safe! They aren't poor anymore. They can get out of hand.

MAYORESS: You aren't suggesting that we steal it, are you?

SHOPKEEPER: (*Taking exception*) Madam!

HATMAKER: Well! Look at that, the word scandalizes him!

MAYORESS: So?

SHOPKEEPER: So. . . . eh heh . . . the TV set—what if we sold it back to them?

MAYORESS: Never. You've already seen what they'll do with a TV set. Once they own something they think they have the right to marry our daughters!

SHOPKEEPER: But with nothing they come around to marrying our sons!

MAYORESS: My good barber, it's up to you to stop it.

SHOPKEEPER: If we had a little money, we could easily convince La Pirogue to make room for them.

MAYORESS: (*Gathering herself up*) Someone should approach Duke, King Moose's son. That one will be tempted by a TV.

SHOPKEEPER: Eh heh . . .

(*Lights dim.*)

SCENE 5

MIKEARCANGEL *and* THE DOCTOR

MIKEARCANGEL: (*Timidly*) Doc, I have a few bucks that I won at the lottery. I have what it takes to pay for your meer, and your rum, and them chair legs. . . . (THE DOCTOR *maintains a stony silence.*) And then I want you to know . . . you see, I didn't break into your house, but, it's just that I know you're on our side, and I thought I'd pay back your kindness. (*Silence*) I meant to honor you. (*Silence*) Yeah, you see, when I decided to do that, La Sagouine says, "Let's throw the party some night when he's out stalkin' the bears—if you know what I mean—and then we can manage a real good surprise." Well, so you went and stalked the bears all night, and we waited on you till morning. . . . I'm real sorry for the mess 'cause of our drinkin' a little. I want to pay you for it. (*Silence, then* MIKEARCANGEL *takes off his jacket and approaches* THE DOCTOR.) Between men, Doc, there ain't but one way to settle up if you refuse my money. Go ahead! Put your fist into my mug. I guarantee my jaw can take it. Go on!

(THE DOCTOR *makes a fist and is about to throw a punch, but he stops because his opponent refuses to defend himself.*)

DOCTOR: I don't hit posts. I hit men. Go to the devil!

MIKEARCANGEL: So MikeArcangel ain't a man! (*He rolls up his sleeves.*) Come on and prove it!

(*He puts up his fists.* THE DOCTOR *slugs him.*)

DOCTOR: What a jaw!

MIKEARCANGEL: Now we're OK, Doc. I think we're even. The Uptown folks have paid their debt.

DOCTOR: Even steven. (*They shake hands.* MIKEARCANGEL *starts to walk away.*) Hey, MikeArcangel, you might need your money. . . . You know there's a certain piece of land for sale, not far from where you live. It belongs to a friend of mine from the States . . .

(*Lights dim.*)

SCENE 6

Across the Tracks. KING MOOSE *and* DUKE.

DUKE: Pop, do you think this war between us and the Uptown folks can go on much longer?

KING MOOSE: Just what's eatin' you, boy? Your poppa can see something's goin' on by the way your ears are flappin'. Might as well spit it out right away. Duke, what's on your mind?

DUKE: Well . . . not much. Only it's about that TV that's right at this minute in their hands.

KING MOOSE: Let 'em keep their machinery! It only makes trouble, that kind of thing.

DUKE: Except it's Punkin's TV, and I was thinkin' that it's shameful to allow 'em to keep the property of a dead man.

KING MOOSE: But it all came out even. We got their money.

DUKE: And what're you gonna do with it? Money is made to be spent on beautiful things.

KING MOOSE: Sure, true enough, but you never know about rainy weather. I'll be spendin' it then, all right.

DUKE: Well, I ain't one of them Uptown folks hidin' money away in a bank. Down here we know what to do with money and just what it's worth.

KING MOOSE: Sounds like you learned something over there.

DUKE: Naw, I learned that right here, on this old stump.

KING MOOSE: (*Smiling and proud*) Like father like son.

DUKE: Son of a gun, you bet!

KING MOOSE: What is everybody gonna say when you come rollin' in here with it?

DUKE: They're gonna say, King Moose is BOSS here. And they won't say anything else.

KING MOOSE: (*Giving* DUKE *the money*) Maybe they'll say, "Son of a gun." (*They laugh.* DUKE *exits.*) That Duke, if he ain't something! (MIKEARCANGEL *enters.*)

KING MOOSE: What's the matter? You look like you've seen a ghost? (*The others enter.*)

LA SAGOUINE: What's this news you're bringin' us, Arcangel?

MIKEARCANGEL: I'm bringin' you salvation. So, prepare yourselves. The Uptown folks are gettin' ready to kick us out with the government's blessing.

LA SAGOUINE: And you're speakin' about salvation?

KING MOOSE: Hush up! Be quiet! Let him speak!

MIKEARCANGEL: We've got to move. 'Cause they intend to send us off to La Pirogue and Sapin-Court.

ALL: No they ain't. I ain't budgin' from here. They're gonna have to carry me.

KING MOOSE: Shut your traps! We've got to listen to MikeArcangel!

MIKEARCANGEL: But . . . the Doc offered us some land right next door. It belongs to one of his acquaintances from the States, a rich fella who'll sell it to us if we want it.

ALL: Of course, we want it! . . . Let's buy it. . . . We've got money. Get it out!

KING MOOSE: (*Worried*) Not so quick; take it easy . . .

MIKEARCANGEL: What's the matter, King Moose?

(*Silence*)

KING MOOSE: I don't have the money anymore.

MIKEARCANGEL: What? (DUKE *enters with the TV set in a wheelbarrow.*) Oh? So that's it! That's how we're gonna end up—out in the cold with that machine under our arms. King Moose, you let your boy get carried away with them Uptown ideas. Well, I tell you, we just lost our most beautiful chance to set ourselves up on a good piece of land. Now we can just rot on our manure piles, like Saint Job.

(*They are crestfallen. Lights dim.*)

SCENE 7

JUGS *crosses in front of* THE YOUNG LADY *seated on her swing.* THE PLAYBOY *joins* JUGS, *and they walk off together.* THE BARBER *crosses in a hurry, looking for his son.* DUKE *enters and stops in front of* THE YOUNG LADY, *then he wanders off whistling. She gets up, hesitates, then follows him.* THE BARBER *reappears, still looking for his son.*

SCENE 8

Across the Tracks. THE MAYORESS *and* THE BARBER *stand before* KING MOOSE *and* MIKEARCANGEL. *All the others, both Uptowners and the Folks from Across the Tracks, keep their distance and wait. Solemn atmosphere.*

MAYORESS: King Moose, you know that you're occupying land belonging to the Commune—and that the Commune has voted a construction project on this site. We intend to build public gardens in order to beautify our town and provide a playground for the children. I have in my hand the expulsion notice that we just received from the Housing Ministry.

BARBER: In good and proper form.

KING MOOSE: (*Who takes the piece of paper and hands it to* MIKEARCANGEL.) Take your foot off my stump, Barber. Read that MikeArcangel. . . . And tell us if it's legal.

MIKEARCANGEL: (*Reading between his teeth, then:*) Rotten government!

MAYORESS: The towns of Sapin-Court and La Pirogue are ready to give you an allotment.

LA SAGOUINE: This stinks . . . La Pirogue. . . . Allotments!

SAINT: In the middle of the woods!

MAYORESS: Do you wish to say something?

KING MOOSE: I'd like to say that you all look pretty ugly. But it don't matter. Everybody has his day, Madam Mayoress. Today you chase us off our land, you tear down our cabins, you deport us. OK. I'll leave. I was happy here. We're gonna be happy somewhere else. Maybe even one day we're gonna be as well off as you folks. Today, I'm the poor one, but tomorrow, who knows? Because God said there'll always be poor folks. So, everybody gets a turn, right, Madam Mayoress? (*To the others*) And the rest of you, pick up your things and leave—out of your own free will. Nobody's gonna say among our children and their children that we were kicked out.

(*They put their bags, etc., on their carts.*)

SAINT: So, I guess we look like the Holy Family one more time.

(DUKE *bursts in.*)

DUKE: Hey! Hold on! Wait a minute!

MIKEARCANGEL: King Moose, it looks like the winds are changin'.

DUKE: Here's our permit, signed by the government. I found some land Uptown, right behind the barbershop, land that don't belong to anyone.

MIKEARCANGEL: Too late, soldier.

KING MOOSE: We don't have anything to pay with, Duke. Got to leave.

DUKE: But I already paid for it . . . one whole buck! I bought the land for a buck. It's the same government for everyone.

(*The Folks from Across the Tracks are open-mouthed with astonishment, then they explode with joy.*)

KING MOOSE: When you deal with foxes all the time, you can't help but get hairy.

LA SAGOUINE: And people that play with mooses end up on the rack.

(*Everyone, except the Uptown people, laughs.* JUGS, *flanked by three sailors, enters. Lights dim.*)

Procession of the Folks from Across the Tracks, who are moving Uptown. The Uptown folks, leaning against the fence, watch the activity, muttering among themselves. KING MOOSE *leads the way, yelling, "Get along now, folks!"* DUKE *and* MIKEARCANGEL, *carrying the cabin, follow; then come* JUGS, THE SAINT, *and the two* LAY-ABOUTS *carrying the TV set. Finally, at the end,* LA SAGOUINE *closes rank with the antenna. The cabin is set up. The TV installed inside (not without difficulty), and* LA SAGOUINE *plants the antenna on the roof, while everyone holds their breath. The operation a success; they all sigh, "Ahhhh."* THE DOCTOR *stands to the side near* PUNKIN'*s grave. The* LAY-ABOUTS *play their music. Curtain closes.*

Denise Boucher

DENISE BOUCHER (B. 1935) has been a journalist, poet, lyricist, scriptwriter, and playwright. Throughout her life and her many activities she has never stopped militating for cultural autonomy for Quebec and for women's liberation. Based in Montreal, she also writes a popular television detective series for Canadian television. She is, furthermore, a central figure in the Quebec Writers' Union. Among her most appreciated theater pieces are the rock opera *Rose Ross* (1983) and the musical review *Gémeaux Croisées* (Matched Twins), which was performed by Québécois singer Pauline Julien and by Anne Sylvestre, Julien's French counterpart. Adapted and directed by French director Viviane Théophilidès, this piece toured France as well as Quebec to overflowing houses in 1987.

The circumstances surrounding the production of *When Faeries Thirst,* her 1978 piece that attacks the symbolic structure underpinning the importance of the Virgin Mary, tell one rather captivating tale of how the feminist movement has wreaked havoc upon the social and political status quo in Quebec. The trouble began in the spring of 1978, when the Greater Montreal Arts Council, which helps subsidize the Théâtre du Nouveau Monde—the premier theater of Montreal and producing agent for *When Faeries Thirst*—finally read the plays, which were to be part of the 1978–79 season. Certain members of the council were so shocked by the virulent attack against the Catholic church in Boucher's play that they withdrew $15,000 from the grant they had already allocated for a fall production.

The Théâtre du Nouveau Monde's director called for a public explanation, accused the Arts Council of censorship, and rallied Québécois theater professionals, other artists, and intellectuals to participate in a series of protests. UNESCO's International Theater Institute joined forces and sent its own petition to the Arts Council. This was later supported by an open letter from forty-three French intellectuals.

The Arts Council was consequently forced to clarify its position. Its chair,

Louisette Dussault plays "The Statue" (paradoxically Virgin and Mother) in the controversial and rollicking 1978 production of Denise Boucher's *When Faeries Thirst* at Le Théâtre du Nouveau Monde in Montreal.

outraged and frightened, indicated how anxious he was about the play's content by pronouncing it "dirty." On the other hand, another member quit the conservative arts body to stress her belief in free speech.

The Théâtre du Nouveau Monde went ahead with the production in November 1978,[1] prompting the archbishop of Montreal to encourage a boycott. Fanatic Christians worrying about chastisements from heaven picketed the theater and furious Catholic groups even succeeded in pressuring a judge to call for a temporary injunction of the play's publication. Public response to this zealotry was extraordinarily gratifying for Boucher, her production team, the three actresses who created the play, and the Théâtre du Nouveau Monde itself. There were two months of standing ovations, eventually three printings of the play, and two reprises of the production—one on the occasion of Pope Jean Paul's visit in 1984. The latter performance provided a rallying point for discussions of abortion rights, divorce, and contraception.

That this very funny, ultimately optimistic, cabaret-style piece could be responsible for such a fracas speaks to the terrible impact that certain traditional images still have on Québécois culture. It also highlights the ongoing contemporary strength of the religious hierarchy. Indeed, set designer Marie-Josée Lanoix lost no chance to reinforce visually the critique of this impact by overarching the performance space with a giant rosary and enclosing the "Virgin Mary" in a sky-blue plaster cast, the likeness of which in smaller format can be found in every Catholic church in Canada.

In discussing the writing of this play, Boucher likens herself and the actresses who performed it to witches—the Celtic witches (or faeries) who kept on dancing, according to French historian Michelet, even after Christ and his disciples first appeared. Boucher believes that, especially in a Catholic-dominated society such as that of Quebec, women have been alienated from their bodies and their desire. They have been taught to aspire to a metaphorical virginity—either that of the fashion model or the sexless mother. Their only alternative is the role of the prostitute. In the case of either of these two archetypes, virgin or whore, women are set up for the benefit of men and male-dominated institutions. According to Boucher, the Virgin Mary is the key representational figure of this oppression, the major cultural sign of male domination.

Thus, in *When Faeries Thirst* Boucher set out to exorcise defiantly and with great verve her feminist-configured devil and to propose through the strategy of female bonding a new means of arriving at self-confidence and self-awareness. Three characters—an animated statue of the Virgin Mary; the "Virgin" Mary, an abused housewife and mother; and Mary Magdalen, the "fallen" woman—all three confined in their separate shells and all three projections of masculine fear,

gradually talk themselves out of the images and expectations that have impris-
oned them. They also play out scenes of brutality toward women: for example,
emotional abuse by husbands or physical rape and the ensuing psychological rape
perpetrated and abetted by the medical, legal, and religious establishments.

The characters come slowly to an appreciation of one another's strengths.
And, as their consciousnesss is raised, so is the public's—in an affirmation of
positive female energy and support. Indeed, by the end of the play, and in a
resolutely Brechtian gesture, Mary and Magdalen have rejected the objects that
have symbolically bound them. Mary drops her apron and Magdalen her high-
heeled boots. Apron and boots hit the stage with the exaggerated and resounding
crash of finality.

As the Virgin's encasement ascends into the flies, a "newly born" woman
remains behind, standing on the carcass of what at play's end clearly appears as a
harmless and silly snake. No thing and no one will tell this new woman what to
do or whom to desire. No "representation" will keep her from grasping for
something else. She is ready to imagine a new configuration, with a "new man,"
too. Not merely a birthing, the ending can also be read as a healing process: the
collective character acknowledges all parts of herself, thus refusing a societally
induced schizophrenia.

A double consciousness is at work in the production, for the actresses can and
do step out of their separate realms to enter a neutral space in which, no longer
characters, they comment on the situation through songs ranging from melancholic ballads to raunchy rock and roll tunes. By this technique Boucher suggests
that the witches are always already present, just under the surface of every woman
and waiting to be free of representation. Thirsty for their own voices and their
own authenticity, women have only to start to sing.

NOTE

1. This play was first performed in the fall of 1978 in Montreal at the Théâtre du
Nouveau Monde in a mise-en-scène by Jean-Luc Bastien, with Sophie Clément as
Magdalen, Michèle Magny as Mary, and Louisette Dussault as the Statue.

Denise Boucher

When Faeries Thirst

Characters

A STATUE OF THE VIRGIN MARY

THE VIRGIN MARY

MARY MAGDALEN

Each character is in her own separate space. At the beginning of the play the actress who performs the role of the Statue is positioned within a large sculpted statue of the Virgin. A neutral space should also be designated downstage.

THE STATUE OF THE VIRGIN: I am a desert that reproduces itself grain by grain.

MARY: I am lost.

> Can I trade myself in for another?
>
> Can I find myself somewhere else?

MAGDALEN: I am thick and clotted. Life has paralyzed me.

ALL THREE: (*As if a Gregorian chant*)

> So So So So
>
> So So So So
>
> So-oh we are.
>
> So So So So
>
> So So So So
>
> So-oh we are.

THE STATUE OF THE VIRGIN: I am what is delectable in denial.

MARY: I am the icing on the cake of your sociological samplings.

MAGDALEN: I am disgusting.

THE STATUE OF THE VIRGIN: What weighs on me so?

MARY: I'm sick of taking valium.

MAGDALEN: I'm hungover from yesterday's drunk.

MARY: Who am I to be as if I had never been?

MAGDALEN: On the stove the coffee grumbles like someone's guts.

MARY: Do you hear the song of the worn pots and pans?

THE STATUE OF THE VIRGIN: The drapes of the temple snap like old damp sheets. (*Silence*) The air is heavy tonight.

MARY: My name is Mary. They glorify my maternity, yet they cannot stand me.

MAGDALEN: I am "the one with the heart of gold." Or so they say. Them. But who makes an effort to be loved by me?

THE STATUE OF THE VIRGIN: I am a desert that reproduces itself grain by grain. Day after day.

MARY: I guess I'm going to take some valium.

MAGDALEN: I'm fed up with booze.

MARY: It's always the same. Nothing ever changes. Me—I thought I'd do better than my mother.

THE STATUE OF THE VIRGIN: Who's that—me?

MARY: I didn't get much farther than her.

MAGDALEN: So what do you want to change? Us—maybe?

MARY: (*Laughing*) And, lo, we saw the victim begin to transform herself.

(*They leave their respective spaces and advance toward the neutral space.*)

ALL THREE: A SONG OF WANDERING

> If the words of this song
> Seem sad and bitter
> If our voices, disillusioned,
> Speak of losses and defeats
> Take pity on us.
> Take pity on yourselves.
>
> Truth is in exile.
> Distant beauty in peril.
> Love is gravely ill
> And we are looking . . .
> For our bodies, our hearts, our minds.
>
> Here we are, half-alive
> Women silenced, women battered,
> Alienated and outraged,
> All burned-out passion; sweet
> Penelopes awaiting a voyager.
>
> Our panicked lovers pale.
> Mothers, estranged from their bodies

Have deprived us of our treasures.
Our hands take their fill of emptiness
While waves die for nothing on our breasts.

If the words of this song
Seem sad and bitter
If our voices, disillusioned,
Speak of losses and defeats
Take pity on us.
Take pity on yourselves.

We are strong women
Crazy, demented, foreign.
What are we doing on this
Violent and scandalous earth?
Can we change destiny?

MAGDALEN: (*Speaking*)

We appeal to you, Jane
To you Mary, to you Louise
To you Theresa, to you Julie
To you Pierrette, to you Aline
To you Justine, and to you Robert.

MARY: (*Speaking*)

We appeal to you, Jocelyn
To you Francine, to you Michele
To you Madeleine, to you Agatha
To you Josephine, to you Marielle
To you Sophie, and to you Arthur.

THE STATUE OF THE VIRGIN: (*Speaking*)

We appeal to you Simone
To you Colette, to you Cecilia
To you Jeanine, to you Pauline
To you Joan of Arc, to you Rachelle
To you Yvonne, and to you Josh.

If the words of this song
Seem fragile and yearning
If our voices, hopeful,
Speak of quests and of prayers

Take care of us.

Take care of yourselves.

(*Each goes back to her own space.*)

THE STATUE OF THE VIRGIN: Once upon a time there was a day. That's today, and I'm starting to see the Angelus in a new light.

MARY: My house is clean, clean, clean. My name is Mary. I buy things. You've run into me in shopping centers.

MAGDALEN: I'm throwing all that sperm out the window. (*Silence*)

"I'm sorry, your three minutes are over." (*Silence*)

My lusty blood drips from your children forever. Pitiful Fatherland.

THE STATUE OF THE VIRGIN: As I said to Saint Fatima: "Pity Canada and the West!"[1]

MAGDALEN: "I'm sorry, your three minutes are over."

MARY: They sell beautiful bathing suits in shopping centers. Miniscule bikinis. I'd never be alone on the beach. I'm too afraid. The waves roll toward me. They want to talk. I never want to be alone on the beach. I'm too afraid. The waves could gather me up in their folds and take me where I never want to go. I'm only a servant.

THE STATUE OF THE VIRGIN: Whose servant?

MARY: I listen to my transistor radio. In the winter I go to Florida with my husband. He plays golf.

THE STATUE OF THE VIRGIN: (*Singing*) "Some day my prince will come."

MAGDALEN: In reform school they told me: "Mary-Magdalen, make a
                  woman of yourself."

I never knew what that meant. (*Silence*)

I am the shit-colored river of great disasters.

Dried coffee in the bottom of a cup that no one has ever
        washed.

I am a hole. I am a great hole. A great hole where they
        stash their money.

A great hole encased in a round enclosed in a circle which
        squeezes my head.

---

1. "Saint Fatima" is a popular misconception, associating the appearance of the Virgin Mary to a young girl in Portugal in the early twentieth century with the site, the town of Fatima, where the vision occurred. The Portuguese vision supposedly revealed a great secret, to which only the pope has access.

> I don't see the hole.
> There are days when I want to believe in love.
> In reform school, before they let me out, they decided to cure me.
> The shrink wanted to sleep with me.
> That seemed kind of funny for a voyeur.
> "OK," I says to him, "you can have my pussy for a thousand bucks a shot."
> He thought I was too serious. He told me I was "irredeemable."
> He didn't want to see me anymore.
> And that's how I took up a life of pleasure.

THE STATUE OF THE VIRGIN: Whose pleasure?

MAGDALEN: There are days when something in me wants to believe in love.

THE STATUE OF THE VIRGIN: (*Singing*) "Some day my prince will come."

MARY: When I was twelve what didn't I want? Adolescence is a sickness. It's better not to remember it. The fewer things I want, the more adult I'll be. Don't worry about me. I think I don't want one single thing anymore, except what I'm supposed to. As far as what's new, what I want now are the laundry detergents that make your wash even whiter and cleaner. Dish-washing liquid that keeps your hands soft. Like you didn't even do dishes. What more could I ask? And, as far as husbands are concerned, there are worse ones than mine. And, anyway, what good are husbands?

MARY: (*Singing in the neutral space*)
> My father gave me a man to wed.
> Boom daddy boom daddy barbary
> But he gave me one so poorly fed
> Spiritum sanctum oh daddy
>
> That soon I lost him in my bed.
> Boom daddy boom daddy barbary
> Here Kitty. Here Kitty. Here's a mouse.
> Here Kitty, Here Kitty.
> Why it's my spouse!
> Spiritum sanctum oh daddy
> Boom daddy boom daddy barbary

(MARY *stays in the neutral space.*)

THE STATUE OF THE VIRGIN: (*In place of a rosary she fingers a large metal chain.*)

I—I am an image. I am a patient.

My two feet are anchored in plaster.

I am the queen of nothingness. I am the door to nowhere.

I am the celibate marriage of priests.

I am the unshorn white sheep.

I am the wishing star of the bitter.

I am a bleached-out ideal.

I am the mirror of injustice. I am the heart of slavery.

I am a sacred urn, lost forever.

I am the obscurity of ignorance.

I am the passionless, profitless waste of all women.

I am the shelter of imbeciles. I am the refuge of the useless.

I am the tool of the impotent.

I am the rotted symbol of rotten abnegation.

I am a silence that is more oppressing and more oppressive than any words.

I am the imagined image. I am she who has no body.

I am she who never bleeds.

MARY: (*Singing to the "Pont de l'île" by Félix Leclerc*)[2]

"He barely touched my mouth

Like the wind, the lying wind . . ."

(MARY *returns to her space.*)

THE STATUE OF THE VIRGIN:

They gave me a bird for a husband.

They deprived me of my son century after century.

They gave him a celibate father, jealous and immortal.

They carved me out of marble and made me crush the serpent with my
   weight.

I am a perfect alibi for the absence of desire.

They gave me a bird for a husband.

They carved me out of marble and made me crush the serpent with my
   weight.

(*Silence*)

No one destroys the image.

They recreate me ceaselessly.

---

2. Félix Leclerc, one of Quebec's most famous singer-songwriters, composes nostalgic and tender ballads, many of which take as their inspiration the Laurentian island on which the first French colonizers settled and on which Leclerc has built a home.

Who will disfigure me?

Do I not have somewhere a daughter who will deliver me?

Who will free me from virginity?

(*The "rosary" slips from* THE STATUE OF THE VIRGIN's *hands and makes a tremendous racket, all out of proportion to what it should sound like.*)

MAGDALEN: A speechless woman doesn't speak. And yet I hear sounds.

THE STATUE OF THE VIRGIN: In the name of the phallus, the father and
the son.

Brr. The wind is raw. It's damp in this
statue.

I'm stuck up in a tree. With nests.

I watch myself watching myself being Eve.

I watch myself watching him being Adam.

I watch myself watching what never
existed.

I watch myself watching his Adam's apple,
which rises and falls more and more
quickly as he hears me speaking.

MARY: There's a song in my throat.

There's a frog in my throat that is nibbling at my song.

There's an idea in my head.

There's a hierarchy in my head that is devouring my idea.

MAGDALEN: (*While walking toward the neutral space*)

There's a shell around my heart, which keeps me from singing.

There's rubbish around my feet, which keeps me from dancing to my—

FREEDOM.

BECAUSE . . .

THE STATUE OF THE VIRGIN: To speak you have to climb down from the tree.

MAGDALEN: (*Raunchy, with a "down-home" accent*)

MAGDALEN'S SONG

The boys don't look at me no more.

I've lost some twenty pounds.

My ma don't write to me no more.

I'm drinkin' the hair of the hounds.

My girlfriends are all married now.

But me I never could do it.

Never dreamt a white dress anyhow.
Rather pack my old jeans with my suet.

I didn't want to have no kids.
I never told my honeys.
All them abortions I had did
Is a secret between me and other rummies.

Sure, there's a man to fill my bed.
I'll find him before I'm wore out.
If I don't drink till I am dead
I'll die from marriage no doubt.

I might find a guy in the city.
It's jumpin' with all kinds of men.
A fur'ner'd make life pretty
And be better than the county pen.

Yeah, it'd be sweet to be called "Ma"
With a husband at the door.
But I can't go on dreamin' now
Cuz I'm jist a hard-drinkin' whore.

THE STATUE OF THE VIRGIN: To speak you have to climb down from the tree.
(MAGDALEN *goes back to her space. She and* MARY *chat with each other as if on facing balconies.*)

MAGDALEN: Oh God, you're all alone too. How about a drink? Come on and have a beer with me.

MARY: Thanks, but I can't. I can't mix alcohol with my valium.

MAGDALEN: So I'll drink alone. I'm used to it. I do it all the time. I'm not taking any customers today. No reason to hide it from you. Anyway, I suppose you know what I've been up to. I'm tired today. Sort of depressed. It gets to me a couple of times a year. Usually, I'm able to push it out of my mind. But sometimes it pops back up, all by itself, like a drowned person. Maybe it's my period. And when I've got the curse . . . Christ . . .

THE STATUE OF THE VIRGIN: (*Sounding like a television commercial*) Now on those days, ladies, thanks to Tantax, feel free. Ride horses, play tennis, go swimming. Tantax is discreet. Tantax protects. Tantax gives you complete freedom of movement. On *those* days, use Tantax. Be modern. Be free. Be "tantax."

MAGDALEN: Don't know if you're like me "on those days," . . . but they'll never make me believe that their tampon works like a dose of vitamins and Geritol. When I get my period I'm bloated, I'm constipated, I'm depressed. It's simple. I want to lock myself up in my room and shut the blinds. What about you?

MARY: Oh, it's the same with me. I always know when it's coming. I feel heavy. Then, I always get a big pimple on my face, right here. When I get my period I don't leave the house.

MAGDALEN: Even without it you don't seem to go out very . . . very often. It seems like you're always in.

MARY: Oh, sometimes I do. But just to go shopping. When I can't stand being by myself. The thing is—I go out when I catch myself blabbing and nobody else is here. Yesterday, for example, I caught myself talking to my toaster.

MAGDALEN: (*Laughing*) "My dear toaster, if I speak to you this morning, it's to tell you . . ." (*Laughter*)

MARY: I guess you're always in a good mood.

MAGDALEN: Well I'm pretty good-natured.

MARY: You always look nice. I've noticed. You have all kinds of terrific boots.

MAGDALEN: Sure, I have a ton of boots—leather ones and vinyl ones, too. All the colors. And high ones, especially. Did you notice that? They're sexier than shoes. I don't know why. . . . But I'll drink to that. You, now, I think you're sort of fragile.

MARY: But my health is real good. I guess it's boredom that makes me look that way. I think I'm more bored all the time. When the housework is done. . . . TV tempts me less and less. Even the love stories. I don't know what to do with myself.

THE STATUE OF THE VIRGIN: They said that flesh was a sin against the soul. But they locked me up in the meatiest part of the apple.

(*All going toward the neutral space*)

MARY: Between the stove and the refrigerator
  Between the refrigerator and the stove
  I wait for you and I take my pill.
  I take my pill between the stove and the refrigerator.
  And I wait
  Between the refrigerator and the stove.
  Between the stove and the refrigerator
  I wait for you, and I take my pill.
  The walls close in on me
  And I take my pill.

(*Silence*)

It's strange. I've had two kids, and it seems like nobody's even touched my body. Why shouldn't a mother have an orgasm? What button do I have to press to come?

THE STATUE OF THE VIRGIN: Poor little girl. Perhaps you have come. Maybe you've forgotten it. Mental institutions are full of women who think they're me. They've forgotten what they are. You've seen too many pictures and statues of me. Too much blackmail, too many threats, too many promises have stuck you with my image. . . . I have to get out of here.

MAGDALEN: (*In the neutral space*)

I made love at such and such an hour in such and such a place with Don Juan.

I made love at such and such an hour in such and such a place with Casanova.

I made love at such and such an hour in such and such a place with Abelard.

I made love at such and such an hour in such and such a place with the Phantom.

I made love at such and such an hour in such and such a place with the Great Satyr.

I made love at such and such an hour in such and such a place with Tarzan.

And, if I'm not a virgin anymore, I still like the taste of virginity.

(*Singing*) "Blue moon, it's not fair to be alone."

I understand Marilyn Monroe . . .

I'm like her. Hungering after beauty.

Hungering after anything to make me seductive.

I desire to be beautiful. I want to be desirable.

And, at the same time, I must be unobtainable.

I'd like people to find me transparent.

Virginal. So virginal.

Like a nun with a pale face and soft little hands.

As in a convent . . . protected from the world and its filth.

I tried to abstain from all corporal desires.

I want to be thin, just a wisp. I want to be mere skin and bones, deprived of all flesh.

I want to have the smallest possible body.

I have never been frail and fragile and translucent enough.

I have always had too much body.

And I like cheesecake.

Too much body for their sex and their hands, which ceaselessly demand and push.

I have myself known their desires. Yes, desired *like* them without ever obtaining what I wanted.

And I've been a whore. Tramp. Prostitute. Tart.

I have sunk into their madness without ever exploring the depths of my own.

I have been waiting a long time.

(*Each character in her own space.*)

THE STATUE OF THE VIRGIN: Wait.

MARY: Wait.

MAGDALEN: Wait.

THE STATUE OF THE VIRGIN: Speak to yourself.

MARY: Wait for nothing.

MAGDALEN: Love no one.

THE STATUE OF THE VIRGIN: Speak.

MARY: Sing.

MAGDALEN: Dance.

THE STATUE OF THE VIRGIN: Love.

MARY: Gaiety.

MAGDALEN: Freedom.

THE STATUE OF THE VIRGIN: Wait.

MARY: Be bored.

MAGDALEN: Cry.

THE STATUE OF THE VIRGIN: Because.

(*Silence*)

MARY: Who am I?

MAGDALEN: Who am I?

(*All three put on straitjackets while walking to the neutral space.*)

ALL THREE: THE SONG OF IFS

THE STATUE OF THE VIRGIN: Let's say that I were the most beautiful woman in the world.

MAGDALEN: What if I were the most delicate?

MARY: Let's say that I were a woman who never grew old.

THE STATUE OF THE VIRGIN: What if my hair were blond?

MARY: Let's say that I didn't remind anyone of my mother.

MAGDALEN: What if I had the long thighs of a nymph?

Let's say I were an extraordinarily passionate wife.

THE STATUE OF THE VIRGIN:

What if I seemed like everyone's sister?

Let's say that I were the perfect comrade.

What if I were not Angela Davis.

Let's say that I were not a rose.

ALL THREE: What if I weren't a pain in the neck?

MAGDALEN: Let's say that I were the most docile of all.

MARY: What if I were as shining as the Holy Virgin?

MAGDALEN: Let's say that I became your favorite mattress.

ALL THREE: Let's say
          What if
          Let's say
          Suppose that

(*Going back to their separate spaces*)

MARY: Do you think that would bring me luck?

MAGDALEN: Do you think that would bring me luck?

THE STATUE OF THE VIRGIN: Do you think that would bring me luck?

ALL THREE: Let's say
          What if
          Let's say
          Suppose that

MARY: Do you think the doctor would give me some time off?

MAGDALEN: Do you think the doctor would give me some time off?

THE STATUE OF THE VIRGIN: Do you think the doctor would give me some time off?

MAGDALEN: They'd all say that you're crazy.

MARY: They all say that I'm crazy. I'm not crazy. No, I'm not crazy. Of course, I'm not crazy. Not crazy. I'm not crazy. Of course. Of course, I'm not crazy. Good God, I'm not crazy. I'm not crazy. There's nothing crazy about me. They'll see there's nothing crazy about me.

THE STATUE OF THE VIRGIN: They all say I'm a saint. I'm not a saint. No, I'm not a saint. Of course, I'm not a saint. Not a saint. I'm not a saint. Of course. Of course, I'm not a saint. Good God, I'm not a saint. I'm not a saint. I'm nothing like a saint. They'll see there's nothing like a saint about me.

MAGDALEN: They all say I'm hysterical. I'm not hysterical. No, I'm not hysterical. Of course, I'm not hysterical. Not hysterical. Of course. Of course. Of course, I'm not hysterical. Good God, I'm not hysterical. There's nothing hysterical about me. They'll see there's nothing hysterical about me.

MARY: But I'm afraid.

(*All three slowly walking toward the neutral space, reciting as if a children's counting-out rhyme.*)

THE STATUE OF THE VIRGIN: Afraid.

MARY: Afraid of being crazy.

MAGDALEN: Afraid to be alone.

MARY: Afraid of being ugly.

MAGDALEN: Afraid of being fat.

THE STATUE OF THE VIRGIN: Afraid of knowing too much.

MARY: Afraid to touch myself.

MAGDALEN: Afraid of laughing too much.

MARY: Afraid of crying.

THE STATUE OF THE VIRGIN: Afraid to speak.

MARY: Afraid of being laughed at.

MAGDALEN: Afraid of being a bitch.

MARY: Afraid of being frigid.

MAGDALEN: Afraid to come.

MARY: Afraid not to come.

MAGDALEN: Afraid of being free.

MARY: Afraid of him.

THE STATUE OF THE VIRGIN: Afraid of mice.

THE STATUE OF THE VIRGIN: Afraid.

MARY: Fear.

MAGDALEN: Dread.

THE STATUE OF THE VIRGIN: Terror.

(*Back to their spaces*)

MARY: Let's talk, talk, talk. Words.

  Hymns. Songs. Dances. Laughter. Tears.

  Let's tear down the walls of silence.

THE STATUE OF THE VIRGIN: We'll break open the words that imprison us. Evil by evil. Guilt by guilt. Fear by fear.

MAGDALEN: Fear. Terror. Fright. Apprehension. Dread. Panic.

MARY: Fear makes us panic. Blows us up. Slips under our bones.

THE STATUE OF THE VIRGIN: Don't scare me.

MARY: Don't upset me.

MAGDALEN: Don't bother me anymore.

MARY: Why, Grandmother, what a big mouth you have!

THE STATUE OF THE VIRGIN: (*With the deep laughing voice of Santa Claus*) Ho! Ho! Ho! It's better to eat you with, my children.

MARY AND MAGDALEN: (*While running toward the neutral space*) Mama, I'm afraid.

MARY: THE SONG OF FATHER CHRISTMAS

When you come down
My long chimney
Without knocking
At the door
Father Christmas
There's no present
From your big pouch
For me.

You see I'm not made
Like an inflatable doll.
But Father Christmas
Doesn't understand.

Your good witch
From the northern heavens
Is freezing outside
All alone.
Why? Why?

The snow
Falls white
Unloved
Poorly received
Oh the anguish

The distress
Of a spirit
Forgotten and lost.

When you come down
My long chimney
Without knocking
At the door
Father Christmas

There's no present
From your big pouch
For me.

I didn't leave
No, I didn't leave
Just the same
Just the same
I thought
That some children
Would put us back together again.
Some beautiful little ones
Would turn us back into friends.
Why? Why?

You bore me.
I bore myself.
Our love story
Bores me too.

Your good witch
Is freezing outside
In anguish
All alone
All alone.
I believed in Father Christmas.

(MARY *starts to cry. She has been beaten up and is doubled over with pain.*)

MAGDALEN: My God, Mary, what happened to you?

MARY: He beat me. He came home drunk this morning. He wanted his breakfast
right away.

(THE STATUE OF THE VIRGIN *and* MAGDALEN *both play the husband.*)

THE STATUE OF THE VIRGIN: Fat slob.

MAGDALEN: The toast is burning.

THE STATUE OF THE VIRGIN: Jerk.

MAGDALEN: You can't do anything right.

MARY: I waited up all night for you.

THE STATUE OF THE VIRGIN: You know how much your burned toast costs me
per year?

MARY: I couldn't get to sleep.

MAGDALEN: Have you had a look at yourself lately?

MARY: Marcel, Marcel.

THE STATUE OF THE VIRGIN: I see you shaved under your arms with my razor again. You crazy bitch.

MARY: Marcel, Marcel.

MAGDALEN: Is breakfast coming or what? Bring me a beer while I wait. And some tomato juice.

MARY: Yes, yes, Marcel.

THE STATUE OF THE VIRGIN: Stop your wailing and bring me what I asked for.

MAGDALEN: I worked all night with the big shots to get this contract and look at the thanks I get from you.

MARY: Marcel, Marcel. Can't you talk decent to me? Stop calling me names. It hurts.

MAGDALEN: I've had it with assholes like you.

THE STATUE OF THE VIRGIN: You support them, then, when you get home their eyes are red from bellyaching. Masochist. Bellyacher.

(*Sounds of a beating*)

MARY: Marcel, Marcel. No, Marcel.

MAGDALEN: I don't know what keeps me here. With a mess like you who's asking for it all the time. A real masochist. I could do nothing but that all the time if I wanted, and I could handle two just like you. Nah, not like you. Two pretty little pieces about eighteen years old. Who *like* sex besides everything else.

THE STATUE OF THE VIRGIN: Yeah, who *like* sex.

MAGDALEN: And then tonight, when I get home, you're going to complain that I hit you. Well, it's your fault. You're dying to get hit. You're real nuts. A long suffering bellyacher. You make me sick. Get lost, Bellyacher.

MARY: Marcel, Marcel.

I love you. You know it.

THE STATUE OF THE VIRGIN: Women have always loved bastards.

MAGDALEN: (*With* MARY) A man. A husband. A brute. Where's love in all that?

MAGDALEN: (*In her space*)

Love! That's their protection racket.

They're all pimps

"Have no fear, your man is here."

MAGDALEN: (*In her space*) And in his head? Nothing. It's just a depot for his precious prick.

THE STATUE OF THE VIRGIN: (*In her space*)

I am Immaculate in their conception.

I am rigidified in their obsession.

Men are afraid of what blossoms between their legs.

That's why they beat you. That's why they created me.

By the time they became afraid of the abyss, they had already invented God.

MARY: What am I doing staying here?

  Am I going to wait till he kills me?

  Maybe I don't know what to do for him.

  Maybe I never understood him.

  It's got to be my fault if I make him so mad. I have to watch
   out. I know he'd like more kids . . .

  Maybe it'd straighten us out.

MAGDALEN: Ask the Holy Mother what she thinks.

(THE STATUE OF THE VIRGIN *walks toward the neutral space. She sings.*)

THE STATUE OF THE VIRGIN: THE BALLAD OF THE BIRDS

When the blue jay passed by

Red roses in his beak

He filled me with promises:

He'd always be true to me

And teach me how

To love.

In his hands he'd bring me

The moon and the sun.

Refrain: Men don't own me.

  Women neither.

  Money doesn't matter.

  The Birds are my master.

When the dove flew

Over my bed

His shadow awakened me.

He charmed my ears and made my rose bloom:

"Don't be afraid, pretty.

Don't give up the ghost."

My belly swelled

And the bird flew away.

Refrain: Men don't own me.

  Women neither.

Money doesn't matter.
The birds are my master.

When the vultures hovered
My scream etched a cross in the air:
"He was sacrificed by judges.
Nailed by executioners
To the stake."
The crows' black flight
Tore the heavens.
And the raven's cry
Bloodied my life.

Refrain: Men don't own me.
          Women neither.
          Money doesn't matter.
          Birds are my master.

When the nightingale sings
(Are you getting my message?)
He sings the pain
Of having loved too much.
What is the use?
My lover left me.
And my little child's gone.
My daughter, are you listening?
Your mother wanders aimlessly.
Some sparrow drove her mad.

MARY: (*In her space, with two cradles, one pink, one blue*) Ugh! I feel just like a box of corn flakes.

And what if mama's little sweetheart opened up his box of corn flakes, maybe he'd find a little toy—maybe there'd be a baseball card inside? Mama's little darling. . . . Got a pretty mama. Got the prettiest mama in the whole world. He's so cute, mama's little sweetheart.

Mama's precious baby, is he a sweet little Jesus? Kootchy. Kootchy. When he's a big boy will he be his mama's friend? When he's a big boy will my little fellow be as strong as . . . as . . . as his mama? Or as Tarzan? Is he going to go sleepy-by again, sweet little fellow?

I feel like a lump of dough that just won't rise. And to think it's spring. I have no energy. It's sure not me that gets high on the joys of motherhood. I can't be normal. And I'm supposed to spend my life like this?

Once upon a time there was a very very strong little boy. One day when he was playing outside, a great wind tried to push him over. But the little boy was faster and stronger and more powerful than the wind. He fought for a long time against the wind. Then he started to run faster, faster, faster. He ran into his home and shut the door before the wind could slip in after him. And the strong little boy ran right into his mama's arms to tell her just how strong he had been.

I feel ridiculous. Useless. It's all stupid. That kid, even when he's asleep, uses up all the energy I've got. Ma, how did you do it?

(MAGDALEN *laughs softly.*)

MAGDALEN: (*In her space*) Once upon a time there was some pizza dough as light as a little girl spinning in the arms of an Italian gentleman who knew how to make the dough dance. The dough, like a little girl, took a great leap. And with that leap the little girl, carried away by a faster and faster rhythm, began to fly and managed to escape far far away up into the sky. To this day the Italian gentleman is still looking for his dough.

Would I have wanted a little baby
A pretty little girl
From that exquisite beau of my eighteenth year?
From. . . . Oh, yes.
If he had loved me longer.
Oh! I long to rock myself like a baby. Slowly.
Softly.
With the smell of baby's skin in my arms.
A little girl
Two little girls
And a little boy, too.
Three children. I would have liked to have had
Three children. Oh! I feel like rocking myself like a baby.
Tiny voices that say: "Mama."
"Mama, Rock a bye baby . . ."
Oh! I feel like rocking myself like a baby.
I'll rock all the little babies that I never had. (*Silence*)
When my cat has her kittens, in the box next to my bed,
It seems like all the stars start to mist.

(*Silence*)

A double scotch, if you please. This witch is thirsty.

THE STATUE OF THE VIRGIN: (*In her space*)

They disallowed all my children.

They tore them all away from me.

They made me virginal so they'd have a right to God.

MARY: My dear shrink, it's not my father that I'm looking for. I've found him. . . . I'm looking for my mother. My likeness. My other self. My mother, my foreign self. Who has separated us, Mama? You from me. You from yourself.

THE STATUE OF THE VIRGIN: You, me.

MARY: You.

THE STATUE OF THE VIRGIN: Me.

MARY: You, divided from yourself? And me from myself?

THE STATUE OF THE VIRGIN: Me, you.

MARY: Mama. You taught me to be clean, feminine, refined. And pure. Pure. What am I saying?—Sexless.

THE STATUE OF THE VIRGIN: Me?

MARY: I was fooled by your stories. I understand that you cried. You cried, and you learned *nothing* from your tears. All for virtue, Mama. . . . But what is their virtue? You told me: "You're always somebody's servant." Well, I don't want to be. I love my baby. But all day long, alone with him, Mama, I can't take it. I'm bored. Mama. I'm stifled. You had to put up with being subjected to men, but why did you teach me to subject myself, too? It doesn't make sense, Mama. There's something that you didn't tell me. You seemed to think you were the Holy Virgin, "Receptacle of all the world's pain." You loved priests. They robbed you of your body. Of your man. I'm looking for my mother. Mama, tell me which battle we lost to end up one day of less consequence than the rugs we walk on. Was there ever such a battle, Mama? You were made to love. They neutered you. Mama, what does a mother's language sound like? They told you what to speak. It was *their* language. They set it up so you'd only pass on what *they* wanted, what *they* believed in.

THE STATUE OF THE VIRGIN: They were the eunuchs of the prophet, the eunuchs of the flesh *and* of the spirit.

MARY: They deceived you, Mama. Their language doesn't belong to us. It doesn't give a name to what I'm looking for. It hides my identity. Everywhere I am haunted by that secret part of me. That part of you that was never given over to me. If I don't find you, Mama, how can I find me? I need the mother who is still inside you. Mama, I want to sleep in your arms again. I want to be close to you again.

To find the real voice of our true insides I'd peel myself like an orange. I want to throw away your policeman's skin. I want to remove my skin, layer by layer like an onion. Until I bathe in our common soul. Mama. Mama. Come look for me.

MAGDALEN: Mama, come look for your little girl.

THE STATUE OF THE VIRGIN: My poor little babies, my love children. . . . All those who wanted to be God—to be gods—emptied my insides and dried up the love that filled my arms, my hands, my thighs, my eyes, my breasts.

MAGDALEN: Cell

MARY: Fa-mi-ly

MAGDALEN: Home.

THE STATUE OF THE VIRGIN: Re-li-gi-on.

MAGDALEN: Cell

MARY, MAGDALEN, THE STATUE OF THE VIRGIN:

Our tears

Do not wear away

The bars of our prison cells.

We are the prisoners of a political system.

We—the mothers, the whores, and the saints

We are the prisoners of a political system

Just like women who murder their husbands.

MAGDALEN: It was me or him.

MARY: I bent for so long, I broke.

ALL THREE: We are the prisoners of a political system.

Our tears do not wear away the bars of our prison cells.

MAGDALEN: One day, the rabbit said to Alice: "Stop crying, or else you'll drown yourself in your tears."

MARY: If I wended my way up the course of each tear, what source would I come to? Hell! From one deluge to another, I've had enough. I don't want to go back anymore. I've had enough of those obstacles. I'm going to cancel that life.

MARY: (*Heading toward the neutral space, she turns toward* THE STATUE OF THE VIRGIN) Would you mind watching the children for a little bit?

THE STATUE OF THE VIRGIN: Oh no! You aren't going to do what your brothers did? Free yourselves at the expense of your mother.

ALL THREE: Wanted only my weaknesses to count so that I'd spend all my time worrying about them.

Sermonized: "Silence is golden." (That's how they keep the
  silent majority under their feet.)
Wanted me to shut up and stay that way so that I would
  listen to him, alone, forever.
Forced me to have the smile of a buddha, the head of a
  sphinx, and the glance of a virgin.
Demanded that I be Mona Lisa with her unchanging poker
  face.
Suggested I hide myself so that he'd feel like finding me.
  Where was the real me?
Forced me to play hide and seek: "I saw you."
"I saw you." Whose body harbors my being?
Persuaded me with the smile of a used car salesman that
  love was impossible.
Told me that my velvet eyes hid a vagina full of teeth and
  dead men.
—That took care of my beauty routine.—

Then, I bled each of my silences.
I sewed up the fissure. My walls grew back together.
I pulled my cord out of emptiness.
"Mr. Wolf, are you out there? Do you hear me? Ready or
  not, here I come!"

(MARY *leaves her space, removing her apron and dropping it on the stage. It makes a
tremendous noise like that of the rosary. Then she walks to the neutral space.*)

MARY: THE SONG OF PAID DUES
Refrain:

My dear husband
It's your turn to worry,
I've left
To see the world
Because here
It smells like nothingness.
I leave you
The two children.
Take care of them.

You covered
My life

With a long night.
I go away alone
Inhabited by sleep
To try and wake up.
I will cry out
My desires
In laughter—
Like delirium.

Refrain:

> My dear husband
> It's your turn to worry,
> I've left
> To see the world
> Because here
> It smells like nothingness.
> I leave you
> The two children.
> Take care of them.

And so I say good-bye
So long, old friend.
It serves no purpose to be angry.
I want to see the day
Rise on me
To nourish myself with myself
And with joy.
I no longer want
To look for death.

Refrain:

> My dear husband
> It's your turn to worry,
> I've left
> To see the world
> Because here
> It smells like nothingness.
> I leave you
> The two children.
> Take care of them.

While I'm gone
Seek warmth
And sweetness.
I will come back
Later. Later.
When I like myself
Enough. Enough.
When I like myself
Enough.
For the children.

THE STATUE OF THE VIRGIN: I had that same old dream last night. The sun was shining oh so brightly in the sky. And the sky was like all my insides put together. There were violets, laughing like to burst open. I kept telling them: "Keep quiet. Keep still. . . . My son is dead," while he was hitting me with his cross. All my daughters were crying. I kept telling them: "Keep quiet. Keep still." And they, too, were looking at me with nasty eyes. Then I tried to hide from the sun. I tried to find an egg to hide in. But there wasn't any anywhere. And I said to myself, "If this is going to change, I have to find an egg. A red egg." Has anybody seen an egg? A red egg? And not a single bird on the horizon . . .

(MARY *arrives at* MAGDALEN'*s space.*)

MARY: Magdalen, Magdalen,
Magdalen, I left him.
Just like that. Up and left.
And I didn't even get nerved up. At least not
Like I thought.
OK? Am I bothering you? Can I sit down? . . .
It's been a week.
Yeah, all alone. I rented a room in a boardinghouse at the St.
Louis Square.
I walked. Walked and walked. Thought. Then slept.
I don't even wonder what he thought.
I don't care. I only think about the kids.
I only think about the kids.
Maybe he'll find out that they're his kids, too.
I gave him his chance.
I don't want to go back. Uh uh, I won't go back.
It's really over.
The first day, know what I mean?

The first day was like I'd been alone all my life.

A big hole. Just walking, without an idea in my head.

I felt like a can of tomato soup.

I took up a little red space. That's all.

THE STATUE OF THE VIRGIN: They took away from me everything that was red, and they made red the color of shame.

MARY: Give me a little Scotch.

Not much.

It'll warm me up.

I ask myself what I did to deserve so many years with him.

Eight years is a long time.

Well now I guess I have an idea of what eternity's like.

Are you waiting for somebody?

You know, a sort of hindsight makes me scared for what would've happened to me in that house.

I was at the tobacco shop on the corner, looking at the racks of newspapers.

And all of a sudden I saw that I'd left so I wouldn't end up in *True Detective.*

Used to be, things seemed normal to me that don't make sense today.

Before I got married, when I was dating him, he told me if I left him, he'd kill me.

And me, like a fool, afraid of losing him, I told him if he left me, I'd kill myself.

Either way I was the only one who'd end up dead.

I'm not afraid of dying anymore. But it doesn't make me feel any better.

The kids are all I can think about now.

It's really eating me up. It seems like I'm out of the frying pan into the fire.

You know, one time after they had a big fight his mother said to me:

"Look, Mary, a mother always acts like a coward with her kid. She forgives everything.

But you, you don't have to be a coward."

When she told me that, it seemed like she was telling me to get out.

MAGDALEN: Me—my mother had nine kids.

I was the oldest.

And my father—well, when you don't have much
education, children, you have plenty of them.

That's all you know how to do . . .

My mother, when she was too tired,

When she couldn't take the house anymore or its meanness,

Or of dreaming that things would get better, she'd say:

"I'm sick of dreaming; I don't know what we're going to
do, where we'll end up."

Poor Mama. Then she'd go outdoors, pick up a brick from
somewhere, and throw it through a window.

Then she'd laugh. The police would come.

They'd take her to jail then to the hospital, with the other
crazy ladies.

To Saint John's of the Father.

My mother'd take a hot bath and go to bed.

Then she'd sleep. Wouldn't answer their questions.

Wouldn't take their pills. She slept. That's not crazy. Just
slept.

She was lucky; there was always an attendant who
understood her.

After a few days, she'd wake up. Better.

Say "OK, I'm cured. Give me a bus ticket.

I'm going home."

My father always signed for her. Mama, what a character!

(MARY *goes back to her space.*)

MARY: Blues. Infamous blues.

Blues. Blues. Blue blues.

Infamous blues. Family blues.

Family. Families. Infamies. Infamous

Blues.

Blues. The family made me black and blue.

Blues. Infamous blues.

Female. Infamous. Infamy. Family.

Female.

Female blues.

Blues. Female. Female. Infamy. Family.

Infamy.

Blues. Females.

Blues. A female blues.

A family blues. Blues.

Infamous blues.

Blues.

Little baby blues. My baby blues.

My baby blues. Female blues.

Blues. Infamous blue.

Blues. Blues. Blues. Blues.

Blues. Blues. Blues.

Infamous blues.

Female, play me a blues. A family blues.

MAGDALEN: Me, I'm not the kind of girl who collects mementos,

Boxes full of photos and love letters bound by a little pink ribbon.

Anyway, I've hardly got enough to matter.

All the same, there were a few: "Yours forever, if you want me . . ."

And I've kept two things.

My first Raggedy Ann doll.

I called her by my name. I called her Magdalen. "My pretty little Magdalen."

I also kept the first pair of sheets that I slept in for money.

That day I dechristened my doll and stuffed her in a box.

Then in another box, I stored those sheets. Covered with coal dust.

I kept them to give them back. To give them back to the first guy.

I tell myself I'll see him again someday and give them back.

Since he paid for them.

They belong to him, those lousy sheets.

I'm sure I'll see him again.

Give him back those sheets. I'd like to see his face when I do that.

THE STATUE OF THE VIRGIN: A SONG OF FRIENDSHIP

Tonight I visit my childhood friend;
Behind her house lies a silken field.

We'll count the stars on our fingers.
And relive for each other our women's secrets.

My heart offers blossoming peonies.
I'll bring some wine and cakes.
We won't fall asleep for two days
Enraptured by our own true love stories.

I remember the last time together.
I was only ten years old.
Since then, what lovers, what torments
What pleasures, what joys, what pain.

Will there be enough wine
To dissolve our sorrows?
To dress us in shared insanities
Rather than sleeping bonnets?

We won't play doctor
Though our hearts in truth are sick.
We must start up our lives again
Filled with friendship energy.

"Haven't you finished yet, you girls?"
"Shhh, or Mama will get mad."
All my soul is quivering—
No more mother, no more man.

It's forgotten bliss, it's madness.
Past and present power my inner space.
At once I'm ten and thirty-five.
Soon to set off for the future.
Tonight I visit my childhood friend.

MAGDALEN: (*In her space*) Since Mary's become my friend, I can't stop thinking
about things. . . . I understand what she means. And, then, she puts ideas in
my head. Sometimes I feel like chucking my customers out the door. It'd be
nice to open up a little business. Maybe a remnant shop. I'd like that—piles of

cloth. Silk. And velvet. And fine cotton. I could open it with Mary. I finally figured out I hate sex as much as a chocolate maker gets to hate chocolate.

(MAGDALEN *pours herself something to drink and immediately drinks down the whole glassful.*)

It's by naming what I need that I discover what I want.

"And I get something trotting in my head."

(*She starts to pour another drink, hesitates, then doesn't do it.*)

Usually, it's the second shot of Scotch that explodes my daydreams.

That's when I blast wide open my fictions. Like lightning.

And reality steps in. Men in and out of my bed. And never one who . . . who's . . . sensitive.

Nah, the ones who come here are looking for their share of Hell.

They have to have a demon.

So, they come to me for what I'm not. The world's a funny place.

When you get right down to it, what I am is a cop.

There are mama cops.

There are statue cops.

There are whore cops.

We're the guardians of the moral code of their society.

Usually, when I get to my fifth Scotch, I start to cry.

Then I drink another one. Then I wail less and less loud.

Then I fall asleep.

The next day I wake up, and I start trying to remember.

It always seems that just before falling asleep I'd understood something real important.

It'd all been real clear. But what was it?

It disappears out of my head without ever coming back.

Like a truth dream that you can't get a handle on.

What am I trying so hard not to know? I know it for a little while . . .

Maybe tonight I'll get there. I have a kind of feeling that it's right at the tip of my fingers.

I feel like a furious wind, in early June, in the country.

The kind that tears the flowers off the trees. I feel like a furious and necessary wind.

Talking with Mary helps a lot. I guess I'll go for a walk.

I guess I'll go for a long walk. I guess I'll go see her.

(MAGDALEN *picks up a pair of high boots and drops them on the stage. They make the same noise as the rosary and the apron.* MAGDALEN *leaves her space permanently.*)

(MARY *and* THE STATUE OF THE VIRGIN *play the rapist during the following scene. Catcalls and whistles in the beginning*)

MARY: You're just the kind of girl I was looking for tonight. Recognize me, "sweetheart?"

MAGDALEN: Sure, I recognize you, but tonight I don't feel like talking to anybody. Beside, I'm in a hurry. So long.

THE STATUE OF THE VIRGIN: You sure *seemed* to like me all right. You know, you're a pretty lady? Maybe not so young anymore but pretty all the same.

MAGDALEN: What's the matter? You don't understand English? *I want to be alone.*

MARY: What do you eat to get to be so pretty, anyway?

MAGDALEN: I eat the same things as you, mister, only I chew them—OK? I've had it. Let me by.

MARY: Why, what do you know, you're just as pretty when you're mad.

MAGDALEN: That's it! Leave me alone.

THE STATUE OF THE VIRGIN: Oh, come on. Don't you understand I want to fuck?

MARY: Don't you understand I want to fuck?

MAGDALEN: Oh no! You're not going to do that number. . . . Oh God! Oh no! (MAGDALEN *falls to the floor.*)

MAGDALEN: No! No! No! No! No! No! No!´

(MAGDALEN *seems to be fighting off a huge bird that has pinned her down. The Christian symbolism is important here.*)

THE STATUE OF THE VIRGIN: Cut it out. Stop pretending you're afraid. I know all about sluts like you.

MAGDALEN: Please, mister, let me go. Let me go. Let me go.

MARY: You know you're just as pretty. You're my type.

MAGDALEN: Please, mister, please. Go away. Go away before my husband gets here. He's going to kill you.

THE STATUE OF THE VIRGIN: It won't work. I know you haven't got a husband. I like it when you fight.

MAGDALEN: No! No! No!

THE STATUE OF THE VIRGIN: Jesus Christ, who the hell do you think you are to act like a scared virgin? I know you're going to like it.

MARY: Open up! Spread your legs. You'll see. Wide open. . . . Let me stick my beautiful dick right up there.

MAGDALEN: No!

THE STATUE OF THE VIRGIN: Come on, baby, wait'll you get my prick inside you. You'll see how good it is. The best in town. Don't worry, it's going to be

big enough for you, you pretty cunt. Open up, or I'll break your ass. I'm the
strongest one here.

MAGDALEN: No! No!

MARY: Open up. Yeah, and I'm going to have some of your milk while I'm at it.
For your big papa. You wouldn't refuse a drink to a thirsty man.

THE STATUE OF THE VIRGIN: You're going to see how I fit in you. Cut the
"delicate" crap. I know you're going to like it. You're made for it. Fucking
pretty cunt. God damn whore. Come. Shit. Come!

(MARY *and* THE STATUE OF THE VIRGIN *pant.* MAGDALEN *moans. The bird disappears. The actresses return to their places. Then silence.*)

MAGDALEN: THE SONG OF RAPE
When the moon opens out like a fan
I stay closed up behind my window.
In the evening I will not walk along Marianne Street
From the mountain to La Fontaine Park.
—I'm too afraid now of the dark.
I was raped.

MARY: There was a trial.
There was a judge.
There were lawyers.
There was the accused.

THE STATUE OF THE VIRGIN: It was a plumber.
It was a CPA.

MAGDALEN: It was a professor.
It was a musician.

THE STATUE OF THE VIRGIN: It was a psychiatrist.
It was a carpenter.

MAGDALEN: It was a reporter.
It was a sociologist.
It was a traveling salesman.
It was a gynecologist.

THE STATUE OF THE VIRGIN: He knew the patient and testified that he had
examined her two or three times in his office. On each of these occasions she
made obvious sexual advances.

MARY: There were criminologists there to query whether the accused in this case
did not feel like the real victim.

THE STATUE OF THE VIRGIN: Justice also called out its other vice squad: the
  medical establishment.

MARY: There were hundreds of women who came from all over to give moral
  support to the plaintiff.

MAGDALEN: I am single and I live alone.

> I used to be proud; now I am frightened.
>
> My God, why, I wonder, did that man need to hurt me?
>
> I was all alone on Marianne Street.
>
> He could have talked to me.
>
> I was raped.

MARY: There were the authorities who asked questions, who tormented,
  watched, spied, frisked, squeezed, and pursued; who opened their eyes wide
  then closed them in a knowing wink. Authorities who desire and stigmatize
  at the same time.

THE STATUE OF THE VIRGIN: It doesn't really bother them.

MARY: Raping a whore isn't rape.

THE STATUE OF THE VIRGIN: Temptation is the province of women.

MARY: She did everything to make it happen.

THE STATUE OF THE VIRGIN: Do you know what you are, Eve? You're the gates
  to Hell.

MARY: Snow White is a nymphomaniac.

THE STATUE OF THE VIRGIN: Raping a prostitute isn't rape.

MAGDALEN: I am a giving woman with a warm heart.

> Not even a skeptic would question it.
>
> How did I lose myself?
>
> On Marianne Street
>
> I lost my self-assurance.
>
> It fell in the fray.
>
> I caught fear.
>
> I was raped.

MARY: And there was all the masquerade. All the humiliation, all the misery of
  the violated woman.

THE STATUE OF THE VIRGIN: The judge thought he was being objective. The
  lawyers, too. None of them ever felt implicated. Even if the rape was admit-
  ted, what it really meant was never discussed. Nobody saw it could have been
  his mother, his daughter, or his wife. The patrimony remained intact. As if a
  woman's rape were only an offense against a man's property.

MARY: Then there was the defense lawyer, who asked how anyone could suspect
  the gynecologist, a man who knew women better than any of them.

THE STATUE OF THE VIRGIN: In the course of the trial the question that provoked the most interest and created the biggest stir and even made everybody forget all about the accused, the question that became THE QUESTION was: Did the plaintiff have an orgasm?

MARY: So, there was, all of a sudden, Authority no longer objecting to pleasure.

There was even, in a flash, all the strength of Authority riding on the promotion of pleasure.

There was a renaissance of orgasm.

There was an alliance of justice and medicine to reestablish the prostitute's right to come.

THE STATUE OF THE VIRGIN: Anywhere. Anytime. Anyway. A prick means orgasm. Everybody knows it.

MAGDALEN: Where did they learn to make us so afraid?

How did they become rapists,

And lose their softness

On Marianne Street?

They shut me up alone in my house,

With my fear

Pummeling my heart.

I was raped.

MARY: There was the end of the trial.

The rapist was let off.

It was like the end of a glorious summer.

In the transept, proud of themselves, the lawmen congratulated each other.

In the courtroom everyone stood up at the same time.

THE STATUE OF THE VIRGIN: You could almost say a flight of starlings suddenly deserting a wheat field. Satiated perhaps? Magdalen, the plaintiff-prostitute, screamed a single cry in the burning sun. It was still summer. But deep in the air golden shafts had flowered. And it was like the last day of every day of every summer that has been or will be.

MARY: There were women who left the courtroom strangled by sobs.

There were women who laughed at the fate of the violated whore.

There were women whose teeth clenched back violent shrieks.

There were women who simply cried softly.

There was a woman who, at the door, asked if rape were part of the pathology of sex or of political power.

There was no one to answer.

Answers came in their own sweet time.

There was a woman who acted as if she had never been raped.

MAGDALEN: Now night in the parks
On the boulevards
And in all the streets
Is forbidden to me by the rapists.
I no longer have the right to be alone
On Marianne Street.
Or to walk to drown my pain
Clear my head and forget
I was raped.

Your Honor . . .

THE STATUE OF THE VIRGIN: She screams out her rage.

(*The actress playing* THE STATUE OF THE VIRGIN *steps violently out of it through the abdominal cavity. Her words continue to be associated with* THE STATUE OF THE VIRGIN, *and she seems to speak in all directions at the same time.*)

I can't take it anymore. I can't take it anymore. I can't take it anymore. I can't take it anymore. I won't take it anymore. I won't take it anymore. I won't take it anymore. I won't take anymore of this horror. I won't take anymore of it. No more. No more.

You've just lost your hold.

Do you understand? There's always an end.

An end to all the CRAP.

(*She turns to face* THE STATUE OF THE VIRGIN.)

GO TO HELL!

(THE STATUE OF THE VIRGIN *is slowly lifted into the flies. At first a serpent follows the movement with its body, but then it falls back to the stage as* THE STATUE OF THE VIRGIN *disappears. The actress playing* THE STATUE OF THE VIRGIN *talks to the serpent.*)

THE STATUE OF THE VIRGIN: (*Laughing*)
What are you doing there?
Go away! Stop following me!
Get out of that hiding place!
We've seen all we want of you.
Learned all your tricks.
All the tricks of an old bachelor.

You belong with other ancient fuddy-
        duddys.
You denounced the Earth, you sick old
        disaster.
Your jealousy made people believe
I was a castrating mother.
Look for a future somewhere else!
I won't crush you anymore. And you won't
        hurt me.
Go crawl away! Take your place on Earth.
        It's a good one. When I was a little girl
        I played in the mud in my bare feet.
        What do you think of that, you
        hypocritical sinner?
All your old schizophrenic ambitions have
        been blown away.
Get going.
Nothing will be the same as before.
Imagine!

(She laughs. The snake disappears. MARY *and* MAGDALEN *step forward. They are laughing too.)*

THE STATUE OF THE VIRGIN: Imagine!

MAGDALEN: Imagine!

MARY: Imagine!

MAGDALEN: Pandemonium is about to strike!

MARY: Imagine!

THE STATUE OF THE VIRGIN: Imagine!

MAGDALEN: There are no directions for those who seek what no one's ever seen.

THE STATUE OF THE VIRGIN: Every echo of every folly reverberates under our skin.

MAGDALEN: *(Singing)* "Take my hand I'm a stranger in paradise."

MARY: What is this old dream of every living being to be, for at least one person in the world, the most important person in the world?

MAGDALEN: I don't know. I don't know what love is.
        I don't know what dignity is.
        But I know everything about contempt.

THE STATUE OF THE VIRGIN: Before talking to you, I had it out with
                the trees, the clouds, the moon, my
                plants.

And my cat.

I prepared myself.

So, listen carefully.

MAGDALEN: Because you're not going to tell me in what manner and what style battered women, torn women, cloistered women, prostituted women, are going to break open everything existing.

MARY: You will not tell me how senility sets in.

You will not tell me how grandmothers gray.

You will not tell me how sensuality dissipates.

You will not tell me how reason relives.

THE STATUE OF THE VIRGIN: You will no longer discourse on how my body should know rapture.

You will no longer deny the totality of me.

You will no longer take all the credit for my orgasms.

You will no longer name what is beautiful in me.

You will no longer dictate a single duty.

MAGDALEN: You will no longer tell me how youth hardens.

You will no longer tell me how lilacs bloom.

You will no longer tell me how peonies redden.

You will no longer tell me how rivers become muddied.

MARY: You will no longer tell me.

THE STATUE OF THE VIRGIN: You will no longer tell me.

MAGDALEN: You will no longer give the pitch nor set the beat.

MARY: Keep your advice to yourself

And think about it.

THE STATUE OF THE VIRGIN: And open your ears.

And weigh your words.

MAGDALEN: I will be waiting for you somewhere. There, where hearts etch their names on living bark and grow with the birch trees.

THE STATUE OF THE VIRGIN: I stand, fixed, in the midst of a path that radiates joy.

And I am the radiant flow.

MARY: I appeal to you, you knights in morose armor, you who've vowed to be male. I invite you to desert your hysterical virility. Deserters wanted! Iconoclasts wanted!

MAGDALEN: If you do not respond, who will confirm my womanhood, except other women?

THE STATUE OF THE VIRGIN: I make this appeal to myself, also,

Because the time for victims is over . . .

MARY: Because there has only been since the beginning of time . . .

MAGDALEN: Because there has only been since the beginning of time . . .

MARY: *One* interdiction.

MAGDALEN: *One* interdiction.

MARY: Lovers.

MAGDALEN: Lovers.

MAGDALEN: Imagine!

MARY: Imagine!

THE STATUE OF THE VIRGIN: And I am here before you

The new woman ready to be loved

Ready to love you, the new man.

I am here, a carnal woman.

With all my desires.

I am not only the purity of Sunday

morning in a big city.

I am not only the countryside divorced

from the flesh of farm animals.

I am here seven days a week

Upright, alive, before you.

Here to eradicate all inequalities.

I stretch across you like an orgasm that

invades every sinew.

I engrave on your skin each of my parts.

I will not again be lost in you and exiled

from myself.

Because my newborn form excites me.

It fires my breasts, my thighs.

I am here before you, standing,

Standing in my woman's form

Out of the sea, my Venus hair moist.

When, trembling, you contemplate your

own birth

Do not defile what I am.

I am here before you, standing.

                      With my Venus hair moist
                      I tremble too.

MAGDALEN: I will not again be lost in you and exiled from myself
            Because my newborn form excites me.
            It fires my breasts, my thighs.
            I am here before you, standing,
            Standing in my woman's form
            Out of the sea, my Venus hair moist.
            When, trembling, you contemplate your own birth
            Do not defile what I am.

THE STATUE OF THE VIRGIN: Imagine.

MARY: I engrave on your skin each of my parts.
        I will not again be lost in you and exiled from myself
        Because my newborn form excites me.
        It fires my breasts, my thighs.
        I am here before you, standing,
        Standing in my woman's form
        Out of the sea, my Venus hair moist.
        When, trembling, you contemplate your own birth
        Do not defile what I am.

THE STATUE OF THE VIRGIN: Imagine that I exult in living.

MARY: Imagine that I exult in living.

MAGDALEN: Imagine that I exult in living.

THE STATUE OF THE VIRGIN: And imagine that I will not die easy.

MARY: Imagine.

MAGDALEN: Imagine.

THE STATUE OF THE VIRGIN: Imagine.

Andrée Chedid

ANDRÉE CHEDID WAS BORN in Cairo in 1920 into a Lebanese family for whom French language and culture were a second psychological home. She has lived in Paris most of her adult life and since 1949 has published some thirteen volumes of poetry, nine novels, two collections of short stories, several essays, stories for children, and, from the late 1960s, seven plays. Her prize-winning poetry has been praised for its elliptical style, limpidity, lack of artifice, and generosity. Her poems abound in images of light and fire—metaphors for her confidence in the future—and in the pleasure of the transcendent quest. They also speak of fear, of the tragedy of Middle Eastern wars, and, in her latest volumes, for example, *Epreuves du vivant* (Proofs of the Living, 1983), of women in the act of creating themselves.

Her childhood memories of Egypt, with its burning sun, resplendent desert, and centuries of rich history, often provide the setting and plot for her novels, as in *Le Sommeil délivré* (Sleep Unbound, 1952), *Le Sixième jour* (The Sixth Day, 1960), and *Nefertiti et le rêve d'Akhnaton* (Nefertiti and Akhnaton's Dream, 1974). In the latter novel she imagines both the life of Nefertiti as the Pharaoh's consort recounts it to her scribe and the effects of Akhnaton's mysticism on their love. In *L'Autre* (The Other, 1969), a desert parable that offsets a certain contemporary literary cynicism, an old man and his dog devote themselves to the saving of a young stranger who has been caught in the earthquake that has destroyed their village. All of Chedid's work bears witness to a belief in the spiritual forces that govern life and that can bring human beings to a recognition of their shared humanity. Many also speak to the disenfranchised condition of women in traditional cultures, in which they are often treated not much better than chattel.

Her theater pieces cannot be placed in any school or movement and are, indeed, quite distinct one from another. Nevertheless, each reflects a constant preoccupation with the paradoxical power and impotence of language. They range

This characteristic portrait of Andrée Chedid communicates both her candidness and the bemused pleasure she exudes in striving to fuse in her writing the complexities of war, violence, and women's fate with the simplicity of daily living.

from the rather classical, Shakespearian-inspired historical drama *Bérénice d'Egypte* (Berenice of Egypt, 1962), in which the younger sister of Cleopatra attempts unsuccessfully to maintain democracy in the face of the tyranny of her own father, Ptolemy; to the psychologically rich *Les Nombres* (The Numbers, 1965), which recreates the struggle of the biblical Debora against war-mongering and mass hysteria; to a morality play and political allegory in which puppets turn into living beings who do battle with the puppeteer (*Le Montreur* [The Showman, 1967]). As is true of her theater pieces in general, these three works make palpable an intense visual imagination. Chedid is adept at proposing arresting scenic frescoes. She organizes her pieces in tableaux rather than scenes. And her characters, highly stylized, speak a sparkling imagistic language.

The *Goddess Lar or Centuries of Women* (1977) is again unique among her works.[1] In this taughtly wrought and mock serious piece four symbolic characters represent the struggle to defeat the equation that makes *homemaker* the sole equivalent of *woman*. In eight movements structured to elicit the audience's participation the character Gynna (pronounced Djinna) gradually and with difficulty exposes the ruses of Mattaa, the Goddess Lar, goddess of the hearth and protector of the home. Mattaa would keep Gynna in chains. She would effect the kind of mythological configuration that keeps Mann, too, in a bind. His "bondage," however, ultimately functions by oppressing Gynna even more than himself. Her greater enslavement makes his life easier. Only the arrival of the adolescent and questioning child Chabb, at the end of the seventh tableau, suggests any possibility of real change in the stifling rapport established between Gynna and Mann.

A chorus of conforming women dance and sing. They are tempted, as is Gynna, by the comfort of the Mattaa figure. They are also, ultimately, cowed by her. Unlike Gynna, they will not revolt. They provide, instead, a portrait of the great female network, which reproduces ad infinitum women's oppression.

Five mimed outcomes to the conflict between Gynna and Mattaa—ranging from Gynna's defeat to her victory—are proposed in the eighth tableau. In all of these Chabb is the pivotal figure, his position representing what the future might be. It is up to the public to select the ending that it wishes to see come "true."

Like many plays by women writers in the 1970s, *The Goddess Lar* deals with themes of imprisonment and containment. Chedid would have these thematic concerns reinforced by lighting choices and staging. Gynna, for example, is never able to leave her "home." She is enclosed within a four-walled structure. Chedid also satirizes traditional notions about women by placing Mattaa behind a trompe l'oeil curtain, thus signaling the artifice surrounding the concepts of "femininity," "femaleness," and "womanhood," for which Mattaa stands.

When Mattaa emerges from within her shelter she resembles a child's version of a phantom, a mummified remnant of the West's Greco-Roman past. Teetering on her cothurni, Mattaa vacillates between being a real figure of horror for Gynna and a comic send-up of what horror is thought to be. Mattaa's powers, the staging would make clear, lie only in the eyes of the beholder.

A play of mixed moods and linguistic registers, *The Goddess Lar* combines moments of psychological interaction in a realistic vein with explosions of lyricism. And while Gynna is frequently inarticulate, she also finds new places from which to speak through dance and movement. She thus frees herself momentarily from Mattaa's control in gestures of physical release.

In its dual insistence on ritual and participation *The Goddesss Lar* combines consciousness-raising with exorcism. The play suggests that female identity should not lie exclusively in the realm of service to others. Rather, recalling other agitprop plays by women writers, Chedid's piece attempts to bring forth a new woman, one free to imagine a different future from the prescriptive and often restrictive one of "wife and mother." The final status of this "new woman" depends, however, on how audience members react to the potential endings of the play and, in the last result, on how they choose to live their own lives.

NOTE

1. This play was first performed in translation as a dramatic reading by the Manhattan Bridge Company in March 1985 at the Ubu Repertory Theater in New York.

Andrée Chedid

The Goddess Lar
or
Centuries of Women

"Lares: the name of the Roman gods who were thought to protect the home."
—*Le Petit Larousse*

"Household Lares: *foremothers and protectors of the souls of the home."*
—*Le Petit Robert*

Characters

MATTAA, THE GODDESS LAR, ageless and every age
GYNNA, A young woman, about 30 years old
MANN, Her husband
CHABB, Their son, 12 years old[1]
THE PUBLIC, When it wishes to participate[2]

Tableaux

Tableau 1. The Lair
Tableau 2. Some Space

---

1. In the hope of abolishing national boundaries, the names of the characters have been chosen from different languages. Mattaa and Mann have Germanic and Anglo-Saxon resonances. Chabb means adolescent in Arabic. Gynna (pronounced *Djinna*) is from the Greek *gynoecium,* the name for a place where women meet.
2. This sign indicates the passages in which the public may be encouraged to participate.

The titles of the different tableaux should be indicated onstage.

Setting

— Now, anywhere: a room.

— To the side and very visible an altar, painted in trompe-l'oeil. This camouflages the door behind which the Goddess Lar is sheltered. Her imposing
subterranean voice will be heard through this partition.

— The play can be adapted to any scenic space, from the most conventional to
the freest. It can take place on one or several levels, in front of or in the midst
of the public. But in every production the impression must be given that
Gynna moves in a restricted space from which she tries, at times, to escape. If
there is no set it would be sufficient, for example, to define the strict limits of
her territory by the lighting.

Situation

Sometimes ahead, sometimes behind, torn between her future and her past,
woman fights to break free of herself.

Manipulated by her depths, fashioned by centuries of women, of which
Mattaa, the Goddess Lar, is the all-powerful incarnation, Gynna—a creature in
transit and of our times—attempts to escape from the mold.

She searches the breach. A breach that would simultaneously disclose her true
face and the world around her, a mutation that would take its place among so
many others in this pivotal century.

At her side: Mann. He, too, shaken by the immense and fertile tumult of the
entire planet—not knowing if he should give or refuse his hand to this unknown
woman yet to be born, whose coming, despite everything, he perceives.

Suggestions for Performance

Guided at moments by a concern to offer more interpretive freedom to the actors, I've built into the action some free spaces. These intervals give the actors the chance to improvise and the public the opportunity to respond.

But this participation is optional.

On the evenings when the actors feel less inclined to invent, or those when the public would be unlikely to intervene, the play will take place without interruptions. This play of mixed moods juxtaposes myth and dream with day-to-day life; incantation with quotidian language. Music, dancing, and lighting should play major roles in its realization.

TABLEAU I: THE LAIR

GYNNA, *while often and nervously looking toward the door, which indicates the presence of* THE GODDESS LAR, *prepares dinner. A large pot is on the fire. She stirs mechanically with the soup ladle, tastes, makes a face, adds everything that falls into her hands: a faded flower, a piece of newspaper, some leeks, salt, an old comb, etc. Once or twice, approaching the altar in trompe-l'oeil, the woman displays her devotion: genuflections, sprinkling of holy water, rapid prayers. . . . But she cannot contain signs of impatience and fatigue. The clock strikes seven. The door opens slowly. It creaks. We hear, tyrannical, strident, the voice of:*

MATTAA: So . . . the soup isn't ready yet? I'm waiting for it, Gynna! I'm waiting. (MATTAA *does not appear. During all this scene she will continue to speak to* GYNNA *through the partition.*)

GYNNA: (*Exasperated*) Yes, yes, Mattaa, just a few more minutes . . . a few seconds! (*She goes into a panic, tastes, tastes again, adds some spices.*) It's nearly finished.

(*The clock again strikes seven.*)

I'm always late. No matter what I do, I can't seem to keep up with your schedule.

MATTAA: And yet, I am patient, so patient. I do what I can to help you. I even hold back the time.

(*The clock strikes seven yet another time.*)

It's seven o'clock, seven o'clock, and still seven o'clock.

(*The clock strikes seven more and more rapidly.*)

I'm waiting . . .

GYNNA: (*Softly*) You *can* wait! You're used to it. With your elbows cushioned by the pillows of the centuries, you have all the time in the world! You float,

unsinkable, over flat ground, without any obstacles, without bolts from the
blue. You're waiting, so what? Do you have to be thanked for that too?

MATTAA: (*Speaking as though a "spirit-of-the-dead"*) Patience . . . Patience imme-
morial! Where would we be without it! (*Livelier*) It's you, Gynna, who doesn't
know how to wait anymore! You're in a hurry. In a hurry to do what? Why
hurry? What do you do with the time you save?

GYNNA: (*To herself, with intensity*) In a hurry to live . . . (*Toward* MATTAA) I
recognize you, Mattaa, my Goddess Lar: you're trying to scare me. You want
to keep me at your mercy. But this time it's me asking *you* why? It's *me* who's
asking the questions! (*Screaming*) Why? It's your turn to answer! Why?

MATTAA: (*More intimately*) I watch over you, Gynna. I'm inside you, restraining
your whims.

You refuse to understand.

GYNNA: (*Walking toward the altar*) I've had enough of your protection. I have
your scales on my eyelids, your roots under my skin, your bowels in my guts.
You live at my expense. I've been listening to you for so long that I no longer
know who I am.

(*Crying out*) You tear me from myself.

(*A pause*) You rob me of the world, Mattaa!

MATTAA: How you go on! Your protests are useless, Gynna. You and I, we're
inseparable. Stuck with each other! For the moment you're in the spotlight,
right now on everyone's mind, and it's going to your head! But you're only a
bubble on the ocean of the ages.

The true protagonist is Me!

The most important role: It's *Me* who's playing it, in the wings, backstage, in
the lair! You can't do anything about it; you're only a woman. Brief. Transi-
tory. Me: I belong to centuries, litanies, entire generations of women. Do you
understand? That's what you are. And that's what I am!

GYNNA: (*Shrugging her shoulders and returning to her pots*) I've been listening to you
so long that I don't hear myself anymore.

MATTAA: (*Tyrannical*) My soup, Gynna! I must be fed!

(*She rings a small hand bell several times.*)

GYNNA: Stop playing the terrorist! You'll get your soup.

(*During the rest of the scene, as if magnetized by the alcove where* THE GODDESS LAR *is hiding,* GYNNA *approaches then withdraws. Sometimes she speaks in a monologue. Sometimes she
speaks through the door to* MATTAA, *who remains invisible, intermittently ringing her bell.*)

MATTAA: You're going to allow the hour to slip by again!

GYNNA: (*While busying herself, to the audience*) Ceremonies, rituals, bowing and
scraping, routines, schedules . . . she ties me down, she wraps me up in

chains! . . . But it's not working anymore. By repeating herself, entrenching herself, Mattaa is starting to stink of decay.

(*Toward the door*) You're growing numb. You're becoming anemic, Mattaa. You're paler than a piece of chalk! You're fastidious, a hoarder. You're petrifying yourself, walling yourself in. . . . You, who ought to be free, lavish, immeasurable. You, who, released from time, ought to be everywhere!

(*Louder*) The gods belong to everyone, everywhere. Let them either disappear or resign! They should leave us alone!

(*Heavy silence*) Aren't you listening to me anymore?

(*Slightly nervous*) Hey Mattaa, aren't you listening to me anymore? . . . I know you. Come off it. You're angry, you're scowling, but you're there. Always there, listening. You're on guard. You prevent me from withdrawing, advancing, going . . .

MATTAA: (*Interrupting*) Going! Going where?

GYNNA: (*Haltingly*) I don't know. . . . I'm looking for. . . . I'll find it. Going. . . . Going . . . further . . .

MATTAA: Where's that, further?

GYNNA: (*With a mixture of fervor and apprehension*) In front of me. . . . I'm looking. . . . I'm looking for myself . . .

MATTAA: (*Scathingly*) You're looking for yourself! But, first, what are you? The future is amorphous; only "yesterday" belongs to us. You're only a past, Gynna. You're all part of a past. There, where I am, that's where you are. (*Soberly*) Billions of years shored up in your veins. You belong behind, Gynna. It's in all of your sinews, far, far behind.

(*While* THE GODDESS LAR *continues to declaim—her voice becoming incantatory by moments—*GYNNA *mechanically finishes her work. Little by little she is subjugated. At times,* MATTAA's *words seem to be* GYNNA's *own. She seems to listen to them inside herself.* GYNNA *pours the soup into a tureen. Meticulously, she prepares a tray, decorates it with flowers, puts a starched napkin on it, a glass, silverware, etc.*)

MATTAA: (*Rhythmically*) What would you become? What would you be, you the living, if the gods and the centuries were to desert your shores? With your mushy brains and rubber legs, how would you manage to stand up? You need a well-stocked pantheon. As soon as a divinity disappears, you have to resuscitate it. Or else you'd create idols out of the next thing that fell into your hands. Can't you just see it? Living beings without frames of reference, without altars, without laws! All capriciousness and effervescence! Imagine women far off that path beaten by centuries of other women. Imagine them without the womb of the past to snuggle up in. Imagine them. On the alert.

Alone. Having to deal with anything that came along. . . . Come back. To your place. A woman among women. A stable Mother Earth. A refuge for those who carry the burden. That is how man dreams of having you, that is how he wants you.

(*Severely*) But there you are, protesting. There you are wanting control. There you are clamoring: *forward, outside, tomorrow, further.* There you are demanding your part of the adventure. There you are moving forward to question.

(*Prophetically*) Gynna, are you calculating the risks? Think about it, come on now, come back. Come back . . .

(GYNNA, *tamed, docile, carrying the dinner tray, hurries toward* MATTAA's *room. The steam that escapes from the soup tureen almost completely envelops her.*)

GYNNA: (*Subdued*) Here I am. I'm coming back, I'm coming, Mattaa. . . . I'm coming . . .

(*She pushes the swinging door halfway open and plunges into the lair. The door closes after her. Lights off.*)

TABLEAU 2: SOME SPACE

In a few moments GYNNA *reappears empty-handed. She closes the door after her, making sure it's firmly shut. Relieved, she takes off her apron, then her shoes, takes down her hair, unfastens her clothing, opens the windows {presence of wind and trees}, turns on the radio {news and music mixed}, then the television {a series of silent images}. It seems that the room is erupting, that the universe is invading it. The music grows louder.* GYNNA *begins to dance, a feverish dance. She stamps her feet to a strong rhythm, claps her hands, explodes on the dance floor. This lasts several minutes.*

At this point the spectators may also dance. GYNNA *will invite them to join her. Something happy, contagious, is communicated in this spontaneous movement. Even if the radio's news interjects a tragic note, the atmosphere is gay, animated. On those evenings when the public wishes to remain seated, the play will go on with* GYNNA *dancing by herself. She should, however, create a feeling of complicity with the public, of intimacy with the world around her. She must communicate both anguish and hope.*

MATTAA *opens her door violently. She throws the tray with everything on it from her room. The tray lands at* GYNNA's *feet. It looks like a tornado has struck. There is complete silence.* GYNNA *is stupified. If the spectators are dancing when this happens, they should go back to their seats.* THE GODDESS LAR *slams her door shut.*

MATTAA: (*Through the partition, thunderously*) Take it all back! I don't want it. I don't want to look at it anymore! You've lost your touch. You do everything at the last minute! Today, the 287th day of the year: you should have added four pelican eggs and three eagle feathers exactly twenty-three minutes after the soup started to simmer. And did you make the nine signs that destroy impurities over the cauldron? I'm sure you forgot. And you know it's crucial! Your heart is elsewhere. Your mind wanders everywhere. I waste my breath trying to instruct you.

GYNNA: (*Dumbfounded*) What's the matter with you, Mattaa? You must be sick! You know you don't ever taste anything. That it's all a sham.

(*Raising her voice*) Your tricks are old, you hear me. Your threats don't scare me anymore. You are a fiction, a myth. You are here because we want you to be here, but you have no mouth, Mattaa, no tongue, no body. You're all in trompe l'oeil! Just like this!

(*With both hands she attacks the door, which the altar camouflages. The lights go off except for a bright spot on* GYNNA's *fists as she pummels the partition.*)

TABLEAU 3: OUTCRY

A pallid light seeps through the hinges of the door. After a moment and with a calculated slowness the door creaks open toward the interior of MATTAA's *lair. When the door is completely open the same wan light fills the gaping hole. No one is in sight. Then the light is concentrated in a yellowish ball, a diffused spiral that moves out of the lair, hesitates several seconds on the threshhold, advances, as if to announce the invasion of* THE GODDESS LAR. *Suddenly,* MATTAA *emerges in person. Chalky, monumental, upright on invisible cothurni. She should look somewhat like a Roman matron. Her clothes are woven, stiff. Her face is petrified, made up with white paint, rather puffy. Her imposing measurements accentuate* GYNNA's *fragility.* THE GODDESS LAR *moves noiselessly, in measured steps. Standing still, she often poses her crossed hands on her stomach.*

MATTAA: You're abusing me. I won't let you do it. This is intolerable, Gynna!

GYNNA: Don't count on me anymore, Mattaa.

MATTAA: What are you saying? You can't get away from me.

GYNNA: Leave me to the present.

MATTAA: (*Curtly*) The present!

(*She breathes into her cupped palms.*) Here's what your present is . . . less than that! One minute you're here. The next you aren't. A breath. Then nothing!

GYNNA: In your hands perhaps. But not in mine. Watch! . . .

(*She cups her hands in front of her mouth and inhales with all her strength, then exhales for a long time.*)

Life. . . . My life. . . . A whole lifetime! You see how full it is?

MATTAA: Who are you fooling? The end is in sight, inexorably. What's a lifetime?

(*She snaps her fingers.*)

Not much. It's what preceded it that counts. What goes after.

(*Grandiloquently*) A speck on a continuously flowing river, that's what man's present is!

GYNNA: You speak from too far above and too far away.

MATTAA: The present is a fraud, a booby trap.

GYNNA: (*Louder*) I'm not listening to you anymore, Mattaa!

MATTAA: (*Breathing down* GYNNA's *neck*) What is it, this present? Pronounce it! Spell it! Living, what's that? Explain yourself. Since you know. Since you *think* you know, speak up.

GYNNA: (*Looking for the words*) Living . . . it's . . .

MATTAA: (*Sarcastically*) Come on, come on, you're overflowing with things to say, you're bursting with life. . . . Come on, speak up, I'm listening.

GYNNA: (*More and more upset*) Living, it's . . . living . . . how shall I put it, it's . . .

MATTAA: (*Parodying her*) Living, it's. . . . Living . . . how shall I put it, it's. . . . Living? Well, what is it? You see, you have no answer! You're all mixed up! Come on, let's go, speak up! Life is. . . . In your place, *I* wouldn't hesitate.

GYNNA: Life . . . it can't be translated. There is no key to it. . . . It shakes us. It ferments. It courses through us. It challenges the open sea: It . . .

MATTAA: (*Laughingly*) You're the one on the open sea! And you're getting lost. Life has order, a pattern. Come on, Gynna, articulate more clearly. I'll give you one more chance. What *is* life?

GYNNA: It can't be found among your pat phrases!

MATTAA: Then, where is it?

GYNNA: (*Catching fire*) It is *in* me. It rears up, speaks, speaks to me. . . . It's here, in my veins, in my flesh.

(*More rapidly*) It tempts me, quickens me, destroys my harmony then tunes me up again. Life uplifts me. It invents me . . .

MATTAA: You're mixing your metaphors.

GYNNA: Life has no other name than life.

MATTAA: (*Mockingly*) Your argument is formless, Gynna. You haphazardly follow all your inclinations.

(*Insistently*) A drop of a pin in the millennial ocean, a bit of dust on the circular course of the planets, a tiny fault in a monumental rock—that's all your life is. Already snuffed out, already destroyed, already stiff. While *we,* gods and forebearers, possess duration. Only the past is dense. It holds all of us: you, me, and even the future.

GYNNA: (*Plugging her ears*) I'm not listening to you anymore.

MATTAA: (*Badgering her*) You're at too many crossroads, Gynna. You don't even know which end is up! A double. A hybrid. Two-headed! Half of you wears my face. But, the other? . . . Who is the other?

GYNNA: (*Shaken*) Time. . . . Give me some time.

MATTAA: A muddled woman. Labyrinthine. Halfway there. Where is the other face hiding? When will you find it?

GYNNA: Leave me alone, you're hemming me in. I want other words, other visions, other dreams than yours. Go back to your sanctuary, Mattaa. Keep your "eternity" there.

MATTAA: (*A moment. Then pointing at* GYNNA's *face*) Don't fool yourself, Gynna. Your face is already the face of an ancestor. You're slipping into the well of time. An ancestor in the hollow of other ancestors. All women just as you are now. The past will swallow you up.

GYNNA: (*Screaming*) No! No! Not yet. . . . No!

(*Tearing herself away from the grip of* THE GODDESS LAR, GYNNA *rushes toward the public.*

She goes from one spectator to another, asking questions and gathering support from both men and women. Here, as before, she may either include the public in the action or perform alone. MATTAA *will remain upstage, withdrawn, rigid, monolithic. She is concentrating and mustering her strength.*)

GYNNA: (*To the public, feverishly*) Something in me, in you, is thirsty. Thirsty! Something in me, in us, is trying to be born. Mattaa must not hold us back. (*Going from one spectator to another*) There is something here. . . .

(*She stops, places her hands on her breast*) Something that is groping for words. . . . Oh! If you could just *listen!* Something is speaking. From me to you. . . . From you to you. . . . From one to another.

(*Silence, then addressing a couple*) Between this man and this woman . . . we dream of valleys with footbridges, of continuity and renewal. We want them: "together." We hope for: "a long time." But we hit our heads against the same walls; again and again we make the same grotesque moves. Somehow the same rust, the same venom creeps in.

(*She looks at herself.*) We're caught. But in which trap?

Sometimes we really see each other. Between a man and a woman every-thing is clear, crystalline. Then, suddenly, the shades are pulled and it's the darkest of nights. Somewhere the meeting has gone awry, and the landscape become hazy.

(*She crouches on her heels, speaking confidentially*) I'm speaking to you with all my force . . .

(*She hesitates, then . . . quickly*) Somewhere we went blind! Or maybe, we're only at the beginning. An appeal toward a multitude of other appeals. A cry that will no longer be stifled.

(*Still far away, upstage, as though seized by a sudden inspiration,* MATTAA *slowly emerges from her immobility. A broad smile stretches across her face. Then a silent laugh shakes her convulsively. After a moment, always silent, possessed and trembling, she tiptoes toward* GYNNA. MATTAA *stations herself behind the young woman, who does not yet suspect her presence. She raises and extends her arms, and her broad sleeves resemble the wings of a bat.* GYNNA *will become a prisoner in this shadow box.* THE GODDESS LAR *tries to alarm her, to cut her off from the public, to overwhelm her. She bends over her, whispers in her ear. In the beginning* GYNNA *resists these attempts to distract her.*)

GYNNA: (*Still to the public*) How do we pronounce *women?* How do we say *tomorrow?* Where is the freeedom that makes us grow?

(*Little by little,* MATTAA's *presence invades the stage.* GYNNA *is uneasy; her breath grows shorter and shorter.*)

I'm speaking with all my force for those who are still veiled, for those who are masked. . . . For those who are not heard. For all those aborted words, for those interrupted dreams. For those lives that never had, that will never have, life.

MATTAA: (*In* GYNNA's *ear*) Mann? Have you thought about Mann? . . . Have you thought about him in all this carrying on?

(*Again, this time to the public*) Has she thought about Mann? About what Mann wants?

GYNNA: (*To the public*) I'm not speaking against Mann. Not in his place. But with him.

MATTAA: Mann. With Mann! She says "with Mann"! *I* am with Mann. . . . Not her. Watch out Gynna, you are going to lose him!

GYNNA: (*Turning abruptly toward Mattaa*) Go away! I am with Mann, and Mann is with me.

MATTAA: (*Laughingly*) Mann. Mann carries woman along, but she mustn't weigh a thing.

GYNNA: You always speak of what was!

MATTAA: I'm speaking for eternity.

GYNNA: Today there is just Mann and Gynna.

MATTAA: Mann and Gynna. . . . You're imagining things! . . . Mann is looking for a female—second self, a womanly endorsement, a feminine echo.

GYNNA: (*To the public*) She doesn't really know; she doesn't know anything anymore. I know Mann.

MATTAA: She knows Mann!

GYNNA: (*To the public*) I know Mann! . . . Mann wants a companion, an equal.

MATTAA: Mann wants an Earth Mother, a housemaid, a baby doll . . . a charwoman—that's what Mann wants. You will lose him.

GYNNA: (*Less sure of herself*) A woman who is vital . . . a woman to complement him. . . . I know Mann . . .

MATTAA: (*In an oracular tone*) Where is this model that you're striving to become? Mann has his work to do. You're cluttering up the way!

(*As an incantation*) Mann needs a kitten, a mother, a lamb. Mann wants a reflection, a bodyguard, a shelter . . .

(*Like an echo*) You're going to lose him, lose him, lose him, lose him . . .

GYNNA: (*As if in the grips of a nightmare*) No . . . no . . . I don't want to . . . no, no, no . . .

(*Realizing that the young woman is weakening,* MATTAA, *like a spider, pounces on her prey, wrapping her in her veils.* GYNNA *doesn't resist any longer.* THE GODDESS LAR *appears to lift her from the ground. Walking backward, she clutches and pulls her far upstage. There* MATTAA *sits down and spreads her legs apart. Her skirts form a cradle.* GYNNA, *dominated, stretches out across* THE GODDESS LAR'*s lap . . .*)

TABLEAU 4: CENTURIES OF WOMEN

The following scene has a musical structure. Hand claps, whispers, inflexions, words, sighs, and hisses overlap. Sometimes, the "chorus of women" {recorded} controls the action. At other times MATTAA'*s voice is heard above all the others.* GYNNA *remains inert.*

MATTAA: There, there, let me take care of you. Come back to us, Gynna.

Chorus
Come back!
We steep
in the wisdom of the ages.
We toil
in the wisdom of blood.

MATTAA: Why oppose us with your fancies, your follies, your cries?

Chorus
Don't open the doors
The gale blows outside.

Everything begins
Everything ends
Between our legs.

MATTAA: There, there, Gynna, my child, my little sister. Let yourself be rocked.
Let yourself be taught.
(*Sotfly humming*) Sleep, sleep, woman sleeps. Forever, she will sleep and sleep.

Chorus

We'll help you.
Climb up on our shoulders.

MATTAA: Don't improvise
Follow our example
Let yourself be carried!
Let yourself be shaped!
(*She modulates her tone.*)
Sleep, sleep, woman sleeps
Forever, she will sleep and sleep.

Chorus and Mattaa

Your boundaries are cozy
Your boundaries are warm
Sleep, sleep, woman-in-a-trance
Men are on the watch
Men have great dreams.

Your home is right here
The planet is not your country.

Come back to yourself, Gynna
Come back to us!

Close your eyes
Clamp shut your lips
Plunge into the luscious breasts of women.
Lose yourself in our voluptuous flesh.

Sleep, sleep, woman sleeps
Forever she will sleep and sleep.
(*Silence*)

MATTAA: Yes, yes, don't ask questions. Don't move anymore. Yes, yes, do
as I say. Revived and dead, Gynna.

(*Taking up the chant again*)
Dead and revived!

Chorus
Dead and revived!
Woman, woman
Forever woman!
So that man resists
So that man exists
Come back, come back
to your past!

MATTAA: Back, Gynna, back! Back to the fabulous hank of hair of your ancestors. Mixed from the same matrix. Bound to the common stock.
(*Her voice tenderly scolding*) You thought yourself unique, Gynna, my little
sister, my child!

Chorus
All our wombs carried you
All our breasts fed you
You are there where we are
You will be nowhere else!

Chorus and Mattaa
Sleep, sleep, woman sleeps
Forever she will sleep and sleep.

Sleep, sleep, silky woman
Woman of the dunes
A conquered land.

MATTAA: Sleep, sleep, woman sleeps
Forever she will sleep and sleep.
(*The lights dim slowly.* GYNNA *appears to be engulfed in* MATTAA'*s body.*)
Chorus and Mattaa
Outside, men fit out their ships
For them, stars
For you, shelter.

Outside, men are on the look out
For them, dreams
For you, nests.

Female drone for the man-dreamer
Female sheep for the man-shepherd.

Inside, inside, women hustle about
While the hours pass
And time slips by.

Inside, seated, women rest
While life runs out
And vigor dies.

(Words come rushing out. Echoes, breathing, sounds. . . . The voices become more and more feverish. The director can orchestrate the words and vocal music as she or he chooses.)

Chorus

Sleep, sleep, sleepy-headed woman
Mother Daughter Tribe Home
Sssh! Silence! Simple-minded woman.
Graying woman
Golden woman
Go home, return to the hearth!

Long live the garden of delights
Long live the warrior's refuge!

Man gives himself to the universe
Woman withdraws into herself.

Man is a whirlwind
Woman a cocoon.

TABLEAU 5: HAND-TO-HAND COMBAT

Suddenly: jumping off the lap of THE GODDESS LAR, GYNNA *again runs toward the public. Facing the spectators, she stares at them and seeks their help as if drawing strength from their eyes. Around her the stage is dimly lit.* MATTAA, *seated again, is dumbfounded.*

MATTAA: Look at her! Just look at her! She's cutting the cord, she thinks she can stand without anyone's help. Without Mann, without me, without us . . .

(*Vociferously*) You have no strength, Gynna. You're going to collapse. And then, who will come to your aid?!

GYNNA: (*After a moment of silence, calmly turning*) Go away Mattaa!

MATTAA: What? What did you say?

GYNNA: Go away! I'm telling you to leave.

MATTAA: Leave? . . . Me? . . .

GYNNA: (*Calmly*) It's time that you left.

MATTAA: Leave? How? When?

GYNNA: (*Going toward* MATTAA) Now. Immediately.

MATTAA: What game are you playing now, Gynna? If I'm not here, think what Mann will say when he comes home.

GYNNA: I will tell him that you have left.

MATTAA: (*Menacingly, she grabs* GYNNA *by the shoulders.*) You have no right. It isn't me who's leaving; it's you who's throwing me out. But I don't have to follow your orders. I'll wait for Mann; I'll let him judge.

GYNNA: You're leaving, Mattaa. I'll explain everything to Mann . . . alone.

MATTAA: And what will you tell him?

(*Declamatory*) Woman, oh woman! You're unleashing a tempest! I foresee shipwreck for both of you.

GYNNA: Leave me alone.

MATTAA: But, Gynna, what are you becoming?

GYNNA: What I am.

MATTAA: What you are?! . . . But you are first of all *me!*

GYNNA: (*Bursting into laughter*) You! . . .

(*She pivots, her arms spread open.*) The moment I begin to move, you're unable to follow. . . . The moment I start to walk, to stride . . .

(*She pirouettes across the stage.*) The moment I take off, you fall behind!

MATTAA: I fall behind?

GYNNA: Prove the contrary. Do what I'm doing.

(*Hampered by her robes,* MATTAA *tries unsuccessfully to imitate* GYNNA. *In the distance the strong beat of a jazz piece.*)

GYNNA: Come on! Let's go! . . . Like this: one foot in front of the other.

Come on! Come on! It's me who's leading the dance now: bend from the waist; touch the floor. Stretch! Stand up! Improvise! More energy! Higher! Extend your arms! Move! Dance! Better than that!

(*She laughs. Her movements grow faster and faster. She holds her hands out to* MATTAA.)

All right. . . . Let's dance together, come!

(*Ossified in her clothes, grotesque,* THE GODDESS LAR *moves gracelessly. She loses her breath, stumbles.*)

GYNNA: Prove that you're *me!* Prove it!

(*Louder music.* MATTAA *makes one last and colossal effort, but she gets caught up in her skirts, slips, sags, collapses in a pile of robes.*)

MATTAA: (*On the floor, groaning*) You can't leave me!

GYNNA: I am leaving you. I'm casting you *out*, Mattaa! . . . I'm setting off for other shores. I'm inventing. . . . I'm free. I am a woman and more than a woman: a human being. A person, Mattaa! It's you who are in chains. Look at me!

MATTAA: Your footsteps are too short; I am a multitude of women. You'd never be able to catch up with me. There'd have to be hundreds, thousands like you.

GYNNA: (*Full-voiced and echoing*) But there are thousands like me Mattaa. Thousands. . . . I speak for those who haven't yet found their own voice. I walk for those who haven't yet found their way.

(*With difficulty,* GYNNA *helps* THE GODDESS LAR *to her feet. Then she pushes her toward the exit.* MATTAA *seems to be conquered.*)

GYNNA: You must leave now, Mattaa . . .

MATTAA: (*Letting herself be pushed*) If I step through this door, you might as well start mourning Mann.

GYNNA: (*Firmly*) Leave, Mattaa.

MATTAA: (*Regaining her confidence*) You're taking too many risks.

GYNNA: Even with all else lost, I'd bet on Mann.

MATTAA: It's a losing bet! He won't recognize you!

GYNNA: (*Angrily*) He *will* recognize me!

MATTAA: (*Prophetically*) Watch out, Gynna!

GYNNA: With Mann I'll take any risk.

(GYNNA *pushes* THE GODDESS LAR *firmly outside and bolts the door behind her.* MATTAA *bangs on the door and repeats her threats.* GYNNA *walks over to the former lair of* THE GODDESS *and tears down the backdrop, which represents the altar. Then, calmly, she crosses back to sit down and wait for* MANN. MATTAA's *poundings have stopped. The lights dim.*)

TABLEAU 6: THE HOMECOMING

MANN *enters, takes off his overcoat.* GYNNA *gets up, goes toward him. They kiss.*

MANN: What a day!

(*He collapses into an easy chair.*)

GYNNA: What happened today, Mann?

MANN: Let's not talk about it. Where is Chabb?

GYNNA: He's coming home later.

MANN: You ought to control that boy better!

GYNNA: I needed to be alone with you.

MANN: You seem . . . different. Is there something wrong?

(*He gets up, ill at ease.*)

It's colder than usual. Have you turned the heat up? . . . Would you close that window?

GYNNA: I had a strange day. I wanted to talk to you about it.

MANN: OK. If you want to . . . uh. . . . What did you do?

GYNNA: It's not so much what I did. I've been thinking . . . about you, about me, about us.

MANN: Oh . . . well. . . . Can't we talk about this later? There's no hurry. Let's eat first.

(*He puts his arms around her.*)

You know, I've got so much on my mind these days.

GYNNA: But we've *got* to talk . . .

MANN: What's wrong with you? Think about me for a minute; my life's a constant hassle . . . worries, responsibilities. It's a madhouse out there. You don't even realize it. I often envy your being here, where it's calm.

GYNNA: Here is sometimes nowhere.

MANN: (*He sits back down, asks rather tenderly*) OK. Let's hear it. What's bothering you? What's wrong? What do you need?

(*He looks around him, disoriented.*)

Something's been changed in this house, I've felt uncomfortable since I walked in . . .

(*A moment*)

Where's Mattaa? I don't hear her moving around. I don't even smell her perfume.

GYNNA: (*Sits down next to him, gently*) That's what I wanted to talk to you about.

MANN: (*Alarmed*) Nothing's happened to her, has it?

GYNNA: Nothing's happened to Mattaa.

MANN: That's good. That makes me feel better.

GYNNA: She's not here anymore, that's all.

MANN: Not here anymore? . . . What do you mean?

GYNNA: Mattaa has left.

MANN: Left?! You're kidding! So, you picked a quarrel again, OK, I know her—she's locked herself up; she's withdrawing. Let me take care of it. I'll fix things up.

GYNNA: You won't fix anything. I'm telling you that she has left.

MANN: Left? but how? Mattaa's never stepped out of the house.

GYNNA: This time she did. And not for a walk! Gone for good! Disappeared! Vanished! Checked out forever! Mattaa has left us, and I'm the one who kicked her out.

MANN: (*Shaken*) What did you say?

GYNNA: (*Calmly*) You heard me just fine: "I kicked her out!" If you don't believe me, go look for her. Have a look behind her door.

(MANN *walks toward* THE GODDESS LAR'*s door. He notices that the altar in trompe-l'oeil is now in shreds.*)

MANN: Who wrecked her door? Who did it?

(*He plunges into her lair.*) Mattaa! . . . Mattaa! . . . Where are you hiding? Answer me! . . . It's me, Mann!

(*He comes out.*) She's not there! We have to bring her back right away! Tell me where she was headed! Something could happen to her!

GYNNA: She's already too far away. She won't come back again, Mann. Never again.

MANN: So it *is* you. It's you who . . . ?

GYNNA: It's me.

MANN: Why? But *why?*

GYNNA: (*Coming nearer*) Listen. Listen to me, my darling . . .

MANN: Leave me alone.

GYNNA: (*Very tenderly*) Just imagine, my love, if there were only you and me. Imagine that tonight everything began again . . .

MANN: That's not what this is about.

GYNNA: That's all that this is about. Now everything is possible. If you want it too . . .

(*Gently*) Give me your hand, Mann.

MANN: Which way did Mattaa go? Which direction did she take? Why are you punishing her? Why do you want revenge?

GYNNA: Mattaa has grafted herself under my skin. I don't know who I am anymore. I want to know! Mattaa is like a screen between us. You see me through her. How *could* you have seen me? Look at me now Mann, look at me in my nudity.

MANN: I don't recognize you!

(*Panicky, he backs away.*) Without Mattaa, what will happen to me?

GYNNA: Do I frighten you that much?

MANN: I had faith in Mattaa! Look at what you've done! . . . You haven't stopped stalking me for weeks. I'm telling you, Gynna, you'll never take my place!

GYNNA: I don't want your place! To walk *with* you . . . that's what I want.

Come here, my love, discover me, let us discover each other. I'm looking for
my own direction, my own horizons. My way near yours. Help me find it.

MANN: You're speaking in enigmas, and more and more loudly!

GYNNA: I'm forcing my voice because you hear me so poorly. . . . And yet I'm
talking to you about us. Give me your hand, Mann. Life holds other promises
for us.

MANN: Don't touch me!

(*Suddenly, he runs to the window and flings it open. Shaken to his depths, he remains
suspended over the chasm outside.*)

MANN: Mattaa! . . . Mattaa!

(GYNNA, *backing away, tiptoes over to* THE GODDESS LAR's *door and sadly leans
against it.* MANN *turns back toward* GYNNA, *starts to reach out to her, then pulls himself
back. He seems indecisive, torn. The lights dim then go out. A few moments pass.*)

TABLEAU 7: CHRONICLES OF PAST AND PRESENT

*The rest of the scene will be dreamlike and accompanied by a lighting design that
reinforces its dreaminess.* MANN *will sometimes dialogue with* GYNNA, *sometimes with*
MATTAA. *The latter will occasionally be represented by an offstage voice, at other times
by the actor playing the role. The three characters must give the impression of being
many people. They should move about when they speak, peopling the playing area. The
voices will have three distinct modalities:* GYNNA's *sober,* MATTAA's *exalted,* MANN's
vacillating between confidence and fear.

MATTAA: Mann, I am here. Do you hear me?

    My history is yours.

    For centuries

    I have collected your exploits.

    I've only spoken out when it concerned your destiny.

MANN: Why are you leaving me, Mattaa?

    Haven't I always followed your advice?

    You forbade me girls' tears,

    You entrusted me with my father's weapons.

    You applauded my battles!

    And you, I kept you out of danger.

    Inside, where you were less cold;

    Inside, where you were less hot.

    I serve you. I protect you, Mattaa!

    On your altar, mistress of your domain,

    You inspire my adulation!

GYNNA: Suppose my darling
　　　　We were to dream of a different universe
　　　　Without divisions
　　　　Sharing all
　　　　With less blood,
　　　　With fewer wars,
　　　　With the tenderness of new grass,
　　　　With words like water.

MANN: If you reject Mattaa,
　　　　I will fall into the breach
　　　　Between the wreckage,
　　　　And both will have lost me!

MATTAA: Centuries have fashioned me
　　　　To your measure, Mann!

MANN: You, who decipher the great book of men,
　　　　You, who know its codes and its laws,
　　　　Take this novice woman back into the fold!

MATTAA: For you, I have intrigued and won
　　　　Bountiful suns,
　　　　Victory, prosperity!
　　　　Speak, and I'll listen to you . . .

MANN: I have come so far, Mattaa,
　　　　From the depths of ages past . . .
　　　　Life at first was an indescribable light,
　　　　Then were the terrors,
　　　　The nights of horror.
　　　　The cold froze my bones.
　　　　To survive
　　　　I sprang from the grottos,
　　　　I sharpened my vision,
　　　　I became a hunter.
　　　　While you settled the lair,
　　　　My territory expanded.
　　　　Stalking a desire that continually evaded me,
　　　　I lost sight of myself.

GYNNA: Hunter whom the hunt pursues
　　　　Hunting from beast to beast
　　　　Till the quarry was man,
　　　　Till the carnage was unbearable.

MATTAA: You run to the hills,
   I rock your descendants.
   You face the beast.
   I tame the homefire.

GYNNA: Hunter whom the hunt pursues
   With women in your snares,
   Women for your fanfare,
   Women for your homecoming.

MANN: My story is so long, Mattaa!
   Hunter, shepherd,
   One day, farmer.
   From nomad to settler:
   I stuck to the soil,
   I invented the future.
   You, you followed my footsteps,
   You you walked in my shadow.

GYNNA: Suppose, my love,
   That I leave your shadow.
   That I open other windows,
   On other gardens.

MANN: I took on myself the wars,
   On myself the torments.
   I tackled alone the seas.
   I tackled alone the wind.

GYNNA: Suppose that I see
   Other hopes, other spaces . . .
   And that here, together,
   You and I move forward.

MANN: Mattaa belongs to me
   Like the tree to the gardener,
   Like the moon to the air!

GYNNA: Suppose, my love,
   That I were neither slave nor goddess,
   Neither "all," nor "nothing" . . .
   Suppose that you chose to love a living woman.

MANN: The man-eaters are on the rise!
   Help, Mattaa!
   Soon, they will be everywhere.

GYNNA: (*With a sudden vehemence*)

Mann, you created Mattaa!
Your mirrors shut me in, Mann.
If you force me,
I will break them alone!
(*Approaching Mann*)
I too go back to the beginning of time, my love,
Look at me!
I am not only the muse,
The spirit, the hostage.
I am not only the mother
In an endless sweep of mothers,
I am not only your desire.
You are not my psychiatrist—keeper.
Approach me through all my avenues.
Board me from all my beachheads.
Discover my hidden language.
Under the taboos speak to my body.
Under the gags seek out my cry.

MATTAA: Yours is the cry, Mann!
     Yours the work.

MANN: Mattaa, "Yes" is your reason for being.
     Consentment your vital force.
     You are the open door
     Where I am always expected.

MATTAA: Your fingers give birth to beauty!
     Your forehead to knowledge!
     Where are Gynna's traces?
     What has she given to the world?

MANN: From the beginning of time,
     Gynna has tempted and terrified me.
     My hard body
     Has always feared to slip
     Into her sticky flesh.

MATTAA: A thousand meals cooked,
     A million sheets mended,
     Tons of dust displaced!
     I quickly lost
     My vigorous legs, my adolescent breasts!

But because of me the earth

Will never be empty for you, Mann.

MANN: You strengthen me,

You reassure me, Mattaa.

GYNNA: (*Walking upstage slowly, toward* MANN)

Suppose, my love,

That our adventure be printed on a double page,

That tomorrow be born of a shared dream.

Suppose, my love,

That my love is limitless.

Suppose that I love you enough

To be you

Without ceasing to be me.

Suppose that you love me enough

To be me

Without ceasing to be you.

(*With these last words* GYNNA *rejoins* MANN. *The lights and positions of the actors change immediately to those that preceded this dream sequence.* MANN *standing with his back to the audience and leaning out the window, turns and reaches out toward* GYNNA. *She goes to him and tenderly takes his hand.* CHABB *enters then looks at them a moment:*)

The weather's changing. They say it'll be a clear day tomorrow.

TABLEAU 8: WHERE NEXT?

—This part is subdivided into five mimed sequences; the characters do not speak; they gesture. Their gestures are clear. Each sequence will be short.

—To avoid confusion the name of each sequence should appear (in a projection, or on a sign) on the stage.

—It is possible to envisage some kind of exchange at the end of the piece in which the public chooses one of the proposed resolutions or suggests others.

RESOLUTION 1: TRIUMPH OF THE GODDESS LAR

CHABB *and* MANN, *both leaning out of the window, call* MATTAA *simultaneously. In a corner of the room* GYNNA, *before her mirror, tries desperately to transform herself into* THE GODDESS LAR. *Suddenly,* MATTAA *appears out of the midst of the audience. Triumphantly, she walks toward the stage. Ceremonial music. The two men turn around, walk toward her to welcome her, each one taking her by the hand. They stroll around the stage.* GYNNA *cries silently.* MATTAA *laughs with unbelievable strength. Lights on.*

RESOLUTION 2: EXCHANGE

MANN *is still leaning out of the window.* CHABB, *an adolescent, kneeling before the former altar of* THE GODDESS LAR, *repairs the torn flat with a rectangular strip of paper. He touches up the strip with bright colors, attempting to create his own god, his own myth. Standing behind her son,* GYNNA *watches him work. She is immobile, perplexed.* MANN *turns around but doesn't move. Little by little another and indistinct figure appears from* CHABB's *dabbling.* MANN *walks toward his son, seizes a paint brush, writes* MATTAA *in flaming letters. Brusquely,* CHABB *crosses out the inscription and marks above it* AATTAM (Mattaa *in reverse*). MANN *backs away slowly to his former place at the window. Lights off, except for a spot on the highly colored flat.*

RESOLUTION 3: FLIGHT

MANN *returns by the front door, dragging* MATTAA *by the hand. He installs her in the center of the room, upright on a step stool. He forces* GYNNA *to come and prostrate herself before* THE GODDESS, *to dust off her clothes, etc. She submits to this.* MANN *sits back down. Satisfied, he contemplates the two women.* CHABB *enters. Surprised, he looks around. Then, in a gesture of revolt, he walks toward his mother, takes her by the hand, snatches her from her work, and pulls her away. They leave together.* CHABB *slams the door. The music explodes.* MATTAA *and* MANN *remain standing face to face. Total darkness.*

RESOLUTION 4: CHAOS

CHABB, MANN, *and* GYNNA *are seated. Someone knocks. The front door opens: it's* THE GODDESS LAR. *All three, in one bound, rush to keep her from entering, but* MATTAA *possesses colossal strength. She yells out horrible and indistinguishable threats. From inside they resist. They violently struggle to keep the door closed, pushing against it their furniture, anything they can grab in the room. The excitement mounts. They finish by fighting among themselves. Darkness descends on the clamor and the groans of* THE GODDESS LAR.

RESOLUTION 5: REBIRTH

GYNNA *arrives by the front door bringing* MATTAA *with her. The latter is no longer frightening. Still at the window* MANN *turns around, surprised.* CHABB *leans against*

THE GODDESS'*s door and watches them. The young woman pulls* MATTAA *to the center of the room. There, calmly, she removes her disguises, her battered adornments, her masks. It seems as if she's helping her emerge from a cocoon.* MATTAA, *more and more docile, allows herself to be undressed.* MANN, *fascinated by this transformation, approaches, at first prudently. Then, joining the game, he helps* GYNNA *unburden* THE GODDESS LAR. *A certain complicity is established.* GYNNA *and* MANN *laugh and joke while continuing to strip off most of* MATTAA'*s layers.* CHABB *turns around, writes in capital letters on* MATTAA'*s former altar, "The weather is changing . . . tomorrow. . . ." Lights off before* CHABB *has finished the sentence. Several seconds pass. Lights up: the transformation is finished.* GYNNA *has taken the place of* THE GODDESS LAR, *who has disappeared. She wears some of the articles* MATTAA *wore (symbolized by a piece of cloth, a necklace, etc.).*

S. Corinna Bille

THE FIRST AND ONLY real home of S. Corinna Bille (1912–79) was the Valais canton of Switzerland, an extraordinary and majestic region that extends from the Great Matterhorn to Lake Geneva. She left only for the duration of a short and unhappy marriage to a Parisian actor, returning to the Valais to develop her writing skills. Eventually she married a Valais poet, Maurice Chappaz.

Bille had always known that she would write. And in her fertile writing career, which won her many awards, including a Goncourt Price in 1975 for short fiction, she produced some twenty volumes: novels, short stories, poetic and dramatic texts. Tales for children—she had three children of her own—very short stories, numerous articles, and prose poems derived from dreams also figure among her published works. Scholars are currently editing the numerous projects she left behind at her unexpected death, notably several plays and her projected autobiographical texts, "The True Tale of My Life."[1]

Her talent is unusual and unique, marked by a free-flowing imagination and unsettling eroticism. Her passion for life did not prevent her from complete immersion in, to the point of possession by, her creations. On many occasions these states yielded some of her best writing, as in, for example, the novellas in *Deux passions* (Two Passions, 1979) and the novel *Theoda* (1944), a "true" tale of the last capital execution in Valais. There is nothing controlled or artificial about her work. It reflects, rather, her pleasure in transposing her own observations and experience, the spectacle of her mind's eye.

She wrote her dramatic pieces out of similar inspiration: local anecdotes, legends, and personal history. This is particularly apparent in her one published volume of plays, *L'Inconnue du Haut-Rhône* (The Unknown Woman of the Upper Rhone, 1964), which contains six one-acts designed to be performed in groups of three. Certain of these, such as *Le Diable et la mariée* (The Devil and the Bride), are farcical in nature, reminiscent of medieval popular theater. More

The impetuous and mystical S. Corinna Bille is pictured here in middle age. Lady and peasant, Bille forever marveled at the dream travels humans take "on the other side of the mirror," behind closed eyes.

often tragedy, sensuality, and a surrealistic sense of violence establish an uneasy intensity.

Such intensity colors "The Scent of Sulphur" (1963), the unpublished stage version of a radio piece originally broadcast by the Radio-Télévision of Suisse Romande. In her creation of this piece Bille was very influenced by the memoirs of a noblewoman from Jura. The noblewoman recounted the last time a witch, whose cabin she had seen in her childhood, was burned at the stake in Switzerland.

From the beginning of *The Scent of Sulphur*, in what Bille sketches as a red-tinged expressionistic set, the audience is plunged into the exteriorization of character Judith's longing for sexual experience. In the throes of discovering her own sensuality and in the midst of the forest, which is her only home, Judith, witchlike, implores the devil to destroy her. The death she imagines takes the form of orgasmic release. This longing, this protracted state of desire, character-izes and underlies the tension of the entire piece. Bille, through Judith, claims a woman's right to desire.

Instead of culminating in the satisfaction of Judith's passion, however, her proc-lamation sets her up to be literally obliterated. The play takes on the contours of a perverse fairy tale: unlike Red Riding Hood, Judith will not be saved from the wolf by her father but, rather, mortally attacked by both lupus and pater familias. The "wolf" (here a young charcoal maker) and her father (a misanthropic woodcutter) refuse to accept the autonomy of Judith's desire, submitting her to their own. The young man woos her and then disappears. Her father's sexual frustration manifests itself as incestuous love. Deceived by the young man, Judith will also be molested by her father. She must commit patricide in order to stop him from raping her.

Both Judith and her father find echoes for their conduct in the Bible: Judith recalling the heroic executioner of the oppressor Holophernes, and her father patterning himself after incestuous fathers Noah and Lot. Judith's biblical model, however, was rewarded for her courage, whereas in Bille's play Judith's personal strength results in her own execution. Refusing to acquiesce to the law of her own father, to his sexual longing, she is forced to succumb to the laws of the city and church fathers. Where she was "whore" to her would-be lovers, she can only be "martyred virgin" to the clergy who attempt to save her. These are the only available roles for the young woman Judith is.

The play can thus be read as the tragedy of woman's desire, its impossible realization: destiny for the sensual woman is death. There is no opening for Judith and no other mirror in which she knows how to see herself, except the mirror of men's eyes and masculine desire. Her major metaphor for herself is unsurprisingly the hanged man. And at the end of the play she takes on all the trappings of a medieval allegory of vice.

This is a Boschian world, an eerie space of dancing forest spirits and will-o'-the-wisps. Bille stages the return of the repressed in the witch's sabbath and reinforces the confusion between awakened sexuality and death in the "Ballad of the Red Rose," both musical interludes that punctuate the play. The boundless temporal dimension creates a dream space with scenes seeming mere fragments of a totalizing hallucinatory state. Time, however, stops when Judith kills her father with a clock, one of the gifts he has brought back from town in order to seduce her. When he returns as a ghost to haunt her in her prison cell, his head, Magritte-like, has turned into the very clock that arrested him forever. This is when Judith's life came to a halt as well, for she will never escape from the logic of the "fathers'" domination.

NOTE

1. See Corinna Bille, *Le Vrai conte de ma vie: Itinéraire autobiographique établi et présenté par Christiane Makward* (The True Tale of My Life: An Autobiographical Itinerary Established and Presented by Christiane Makward) (Lausanne: Empreintes, 1992).

S. Corinna Bille

The Scent of Sulphur

Characters

JUDITH
THE FATHER
THE MAN
THE CHAPLAIN
THE JAILER
THE EXECUTIONER

With Also

VOCAL SOLOS (several women's, one man's)
A CHORUS OF MIXED VOICES
BIRDS' SONGS AND CRIES
THE DANCE OF THE WILL-O'-THE WISPS
THE SORCERERS' ROUND

PROLOGUE

Behind the stage curtains we hear a woman singing:

RED ROSE

Ruby red rose
Of midnight
Not stirring
Shining bright

Wordlessly
Wisdom unfurled
Just a speck
In this vast world's

Infinity
Ruby rose
And the night's
Heart you are.

Lullaby
Sleepy rose
Ruby red rose

You must die
Slip away
To your repose.[1]
(*The* CHORUS *takes up the song.*)
(*The curtain rises.*)

ACT I

SCENE I

In a woodcutter's cabin at the beginning of the nineteenth century. The roof beams are a strange and lugubrious red. The door to the outside is open. We see a small window, a table, a bench, several stools, etc. The cabin is engulfed by a very tall forest, all black and deep red like a tapestry. A superb young woman, both forceful and delicate, is standing stage center. She has long thin hair and is carelessly dressed in a worn-out and dark-colored smock. Furious, she wrenches a wooden chest from its hiding place, opens it, and searches within.

JUDITH: Nothing. . . . Nothing but rags and stink! Rotted leather sacks, a torn vest. . . . (*She examines the vest.*) A vest that doesn't even have a lining, the kind of flowered silk that gave away the Fauret highwaymen. (*Daydreaming*) They cut up their victims' bodies and threw the pieces into the Devil's Pit, not far from here. A hole so deep there's always snow left at the bottom, even

---

1. The original score is by J. Quinodoz (Vevey: Bertil Galland, 1978).

in summer. One time I dared climb down, sliding along the rocks. . . . I wonder if anything's left of the dead men. . . . (*Frightened*) But I could hardly climb back up; I lost my nails in the cracks and my hair in the undergrowth. Oh! that hole . . . what if the murdered men should grow back up as trees? What a strange forest! What a terrible one! Some of them had come a long distance; there were peddlers and princes. . . . (*Changing her tone*) Those cutthroat Fauret brothers—the tailor who mended the vest told my mother how they were tortured! . . . (*With furious energy*) Men who aren't cynics are hypocrites! My father should have been an outlaw! (*She rummages through the chest.*) A scrap of paper, a letter! (*She unfolds it.*) How lucky I know how to read! (*Slowly, then quicker*) "For exorcising Evil, which must not be." This is magic! Foolishness! (*She throws the paper on the ground, hesitates, finally picks it up again, and glances through it.*) "In the name of the Master Charcoal Maker who lives at the bottom of Hell. . . . " (*She shrugs her shoulders.*) The Devil, always the Devil, that's all they ever think of around here! "In the name of our sweet little Lord. . . ." So, for them the Devil is grander than God? (*She goes on.*) "In the name of our sweet little Lord who is in Heaven, I beseech you, Bad Luck. . . ." Bad Luck? That's *my* realm, *my* luck! (*She fans herself with the paper, stands up straight, stretches out her arms.*) I'm beautiful, and I know it; I'm fragrant like a flower! (*She is exalted. She closes her eyes.*) Like foxglove! (*She looks down, caresses her breasts.*) They're about to burst! They're so full, so hard! . . . And there's no one to love me. . . . (*She continues reading.*) "I beseech you, Bad Luck, by the roll of furious thunder, and the blaze of the sun, the moon, the stars, of lightning and will-o'-the-wisps. . . ." (*In a strangely calm voice*) All those things are beautiful, too—those are what I love! Yes! A storm is my friend, I'd like a storm to go on forever . . . when I hear one chuckling away, shaking the cabin like a pair of dice in a gambler's hand, ah! I feel like screaming with joy! My father's scared. He hides in his bed. (*Silence*) He yells: "Shut the window! Close the door!" But I open the window, I open the door, and I go out naked in the rain, in the lightning, like this! (*She tears open her smock, exposing her magnificent shoulders, her neck, the deep valley between her breasts.*) And I stare at the lightning and offer it my heart. It could very well pierce me through. Lightning is Heaven's sword, which strikes trees down with one blow and kills the shepherds. (*Silence*) But what my father is most afraid of— and that's what I yearn to see—is a ball of lightning, a ball of fire. (*She stares straight ahead, as if transfixed, seeing the fire, tracing it with her hands.*) A ball of lightning, coming and going and wandering about. They say it will chase you, it will mold you. . . . (*She bends backward.*) It can follow the outline of your body without touching you, but you must stand completely still. They also say it can undress you without hurting you. Mostly, they say it makes you die. (*Silence*) I want to die, killed by lightning. (*She shivers, covers herself back up, and resumes her reading.*) ". . . will-o'-the-wisps . . ." I saw one the other evening, it was dancing by itself in the clearing, just as alone as I. I said to myself: What if it really is the spirit of a murdered man . . . ? (*Laughter that sounds like a sob. She reads.*) "In the name of Great-Friday, all Fridays, in the name of the number three, the number seven, the number thirteen. In the name of beauty and the name of ugliness, of goodness and meanness, in the name of honesty; by the first, the last, the beginning, the end. . . ." (*She pauses and repeats*) The end. . . . "In the name of spring, of summer, of fall, of winter. In the name of water, of earth, of air, of fire. In the name of death and of ghosts, of witches, of sleeping people and hanged bodies and frozen men. . . ." (*Pause*) Oh! I saw a hanged man three years ago in the forest; he had shoes on . . . it was the shoes I saw first. . . . (*She grimaces, counts on her fingers.*) A will-o'-the-wisp, a hanged man: those are my only lovers. (*She goes on.*) ". . . frozen men, shadows, specters, ugly spirits. . . ." (*Bitterly*) Mine! . . . "The cradle, the grave, the shroud. . . . In the name of nightmares and enemies, of angels and cherubim and the plague. In the name of day, of night, of the West wind and the North wind. In the name of Christmas, Epiphany, Candlemas, and Lent, Mardi Gras and Easter. By the Holy Cross and holy water, canopies, banners, and incense; by caldrons, boxwood, and beech trees. By the blind worm, the Rhône perch, the toad, the bat, the spotted salamander, and the snake: Oh Lord, rid us of what must not be! Satan, do good in place of Evil!" (*Ironically*) And so the circle is closed. We start with the Devil, and we end with the Devil. There's no keeping him out of things here. I should leave, run away, to the city. I lived there as a child. (*Proudly*) I was raised there, (*Sadly*) raised. . . . My mother worked as a maid for a great and kind noblewoman, Mme de Berny. There too, it was the Devil and the Good Lord. One day Monsieur, his lordship, declared that women were definitely not meant to be part of the heavenly host. The ladies present protested: "Why not?" "Because it's written in the Apocalypse that Heaven was *silent* for half an hour." That man and his Heaven! . . . He was so fond of sermons he once said at the dinner table—Mother was attending, she told me the story—he said: "Eternal Bliss will be an endless sermon." His granddaughter answered back smartly: "I'd rather go to Hell!" He sent her up to her room to think about it. (*With a sigh*) A room of her own. . . . Rooms, private chambers, all the chambers they had in that manor! And all the chamberpots I had to empty! But at least I learned to speak properly. "It's in our kinds of families—the masters used to say—that the best French is spoken." I learned to read, to write, to count. And maybe I could have become . . . maybe, a tutor, who knows, if my mother hadn't fallen in love with the coachman. And one night . . . she threw herself into the lake. (*She remains motionless, staring straight ahead.*) And my father came to get me; he took me away. (*Daydreaming a moment*) But I would run away much farther than that! To Paris. (*Silence*) No, that's not true! I only feel at peace in the forest: I am the forest's daughter. (*She closes her eyes.*) I couldn't survive without the scent of moss and cold . . . without the giant arms of the fir trees around me. I need the woods too much, what they reveal and, perhaps even more, what they conceal: their roots and their mysteries, their larvae, their leaves that turn transparent or blend with the stones, and all the living and dead bodies, buried . . . (*Suddenly angry*) Still, I can't marry a fir tree, a will-o'-the-wisp or a buried body, can I? (*Decisive*) Yes, I'll run away. That's why I've been searching. I'm still searching in all the nooks and corners . . . a little money, some good clothes. (*In despair*) And I find nothing. (*She looks at the paper in her hand.*) Not even a love letter . . .

(*Muted playing of "Red Rose." The cabin is bathed in a lovely light. A young* MAN *stands in the doorway.* JUDITH *does not see him.*)

JUDITH: . . . nothing but exorcisms and incantations. . . . (*She sees the man and stops speaking, stunned.*)

SCENE 2

JUDITH: (*In a different voice*) Who are you?

THE MAN: No one.

JUDITH: Why do you joke?

THE MAN: I meant: no one important. I meant: a man, that's all.

JUDITH: But that's already a great deal! There are so many false men, bad men. Don't you think so? (*Silence*) You're not answering?

THE MAN: I'm a charcoal maker.

JUDITH: My father is a woodcutter. I keep house for him.

THE MAN: I settled not far from here.

JUDITH: (*Drained by emotion*) Not far from here.

(*The muted but steady sound of an ax in the distance.*)

THE MAN: Can you hear?

JUDITH: (*Soberly*) That's my father.

(*Cracking sound followed by a crash.*)

THE MAN: The tree is down.

JUDITH: (*Trembling*) I don't like this moment. I always see Death.

THE MAN: Are you afraid for your father?

JUDITH: (*Abruptly*) Oh no! I think of the tree.

THE MAN: (*Laughing*) A tree!

JUDITH: It's a living thing. (*Silence*) I hear them breathe, especially at night. . . . And when they've been cut . . . for a long time it seems to me their roots bleed in the ground. (THE MAN *shakes his head*.) It seems it's my arms and legs that are bleeding.

THE MAN: You're dreaming!

JUDITH: (*Hard*) That's what my father tells me. . . . And now, you must leave!

THE MAN: I want to look at you, just a while longer.

JUDITH: (*Moved*) No! . . . He's coming.

(THE MAN *stares at her, uncomprehending*.)

JUDITH: (*In a panic*) He's coming, he's going to meet you. It can't happen!

THE MAN: But who?

JUDITH: My father. You mustn't. He can't stand people looking at me; he doesn't want me to talk to men.

THE MAN: Why not?

JUDITH: I don't know. He's already beaten me for it . . .

THE MAN: Goodbye then. . . . I'll come back.

JUDITH: (*A surge of hope*) No! . . . Yes!

(THE MAN *disappears*.)

SCENE 3

The cabin grows darker while JUDITH *stands immobile. Pause. Then she lights an oil lamp. Her* FATHER, *a bearded giant, stands hunched in the door frame. Then he enters, his silhouette replaces that of the young* MAN.

JUDITH: (*Turning*) You're here!

THE FATHER: Didn't you see me? (*He shuts the door*.)

JUDITH: No.

THE FATHER: Has someone else been here?

JUDITH: (*Hesitating*) No . . .

THE FATHER: Someone came—I can feel it. The air smells of a young man. (*He stares at his daughter, who does not flinch*.) And I can see it on your face.

JUDITH: A charcoal maker came by.

THE FATHER: I saw him.

JUDITH: (*Eagerly*) Did you speak to him?

THE FATHER: I spoke to him. He will not come back.

JUDITH: He could have helped you!

THE FATHER: I don't need anybody. (*Scornful*) Not even you.

JUDITH: (*Hatefully*) One day you *will* need me! But I'll be gone!

THE FATHER: You won't leave, you can't leave!

JUDITH: (*Bitterly*) So, all I have left is to take a tree for my lover! Will *it* know how to make love to me? . . . is that what you want? (*Anguished silence*) Do you, man of the Bible, know what solitude means for me? (THE FATHER *tries to speak, but she cuts him off.*) A solitude filled with thoughts, with gestures that you label impure, that you call sin. (*Gently*) And that, perhaps, are only nature's laws. Surely, men are more cruel than God! (*Silence*) Oh! If only you knew what the solitude of a healthy woman is made of!

THE FATHER: Many a woman has lived in the forest, alone and pure, caring for a father or a husband.

JUDITH: I don't have a husband.

THE FATHER: You are still too young to worry about it.

JUDITH: Young? I'll be twenty next year. I can feel that I'm growing older; my life is flowing by . . . for nothing, like the blood from a wound, like the sap of a severed branch . . . for nothing.

THE FATHER: You ought to pray.

JUDITH: I can't pray anymore! One can only pray if God wills it.

THE FATHER: Judith, Judith, don't you believe in God?

JUDITH: (*Hard*) I believe in God, but He has forgotten me.

(THE FATHER *exits offstage into the other room.* JUDITH *extinguishes her lamp and very slowly exits after him.*)

(*It is darkest night. Dancing of farandoles and rounds about the cabin. Young dancers in red tights, representing* WILL-O'-THE-WISPS, *frolic to a strange and discordant music.*)

SCENE 4

The same cabin. Day is dawning; the sun shines. Birds are singing. JUDITH *enters from outdoors, her arms full of branches and flowers. She sits at the table and weaves a crown of ivy, which she places on her head. Two huge roses are visible in her bouquet.*

JUDITH: These are the last two roses of the forest, roses from my rose bush. I cut them myself. (*She gathers them up, one after the other, and weaves them through the material of her dress, each one over a breast. She closes her eyes.*) And now I shall try to see myself. Yes, I think I do. (*Silence*) Yes, I'm beautiful. (*She keeps her eyes closed a moment longer.*) One might think I were listening to the birds, but it's me I'm listening to. I'm listening to my blood sing in my body. I hear it flow in streams, in cascades, in torrents. . . . How tumultuous it is! How violent! It makes me afraid.

(*Wild and desirable, she rises, facing the audience. In the still-open doorway appears the young* MAN, *who stares at her, as if in ecstasy.* JUDITH, *at last, turns toward him.*)

JUDITH: Don't come in!

THE MAN: Why not?

JUDITH: You're in great danger.

THE MAN: (*Fervently*) We're all in danger of going mad.

JUDITH: (*A finger to her lips*) Be still! (*She points to the offstage room.*) He's in there.

THE MAN: Your father?

JUDITH: My father, my guardian, my . . .

THE MAN: Doesn't he love you?

JUDITH: It's much worse than that.

THE MAN: There's nothing worse on Earth than not being loved.

JUDITH: Hush! You don't know what it is to be loved too much. It's like walking alongside a mountain that can will an avalanche into being.

THE MAN: Are you afraid?

JUDITH: I've lived in fear since my mother died. In the morning I wake up with my fear between my teeth, and I chew on it all day long. And in the evening it's like a chestnut burr in my throat. (*She clutches her throat; her movements cause one of the roses to fall to the floor. The young* MAN *immediately bends to pick it up.*)

THE MAN: I will take your fear upon myself. (*He straightens up and hides the rose under his shirt, next to his heart.*) As I will take you, all of you. . . . (*Lower*) The day you want me to, the moment you say.

JUDITH: (*Frozen*) Go away! (*Tenderly*) Please leave! He could kill you. (*Gestures toward the room in which her* FATHER *is sleeping*) He's sleeping now, he's been drinking . . . a great deal, but he's going to wake up.

THE MAN: Judith! Come!

JUDITH: I . . . I'm coming. (*She runs out the door after him. The second rose falls near the table.*)

(*We hear a man singing "Red Rose," accompanied by a flute or a guitar. The music fades away in the distance.*)

SCENE 5

We hear again the BIRDS' SONGS: *joyful, courting, or teasing ones. Heavy footsteps shake the cabin; the birds stop singing, and* THE FATHER *emerges and speaks, but his tongue is thickened. He is breathing heavily, nostrils flared.*

THE FATHER: There's something strange here, a new smell, a . . . (*He cannot find the word he's looking for.*) Something that wasn't here before. Before what? (*He sits down and slams his fist into the table.*) A horsefly! (*He crushes it with the palm of his hand, dismembering it with his thumb. And, suddenly, he sees the rose on the floor.*) A rose! (*He steps on it, flattening it.*) I've drunk like Noah. And who else was a great drinker in the Bible? (*He tries to remember, scratches his beard.*) Oh! yes, Lot. (*He recites*) "And they made their father drink wine that night and the first born went in and lay with her father, and he perceived not when she lay down nor when she rose." Yes. (*He shakes his head, more and more engrossed.*) And then there was Samson and Holophernes, too . . . (*He chases the last name from his consciousness.*) But Lot, lucky Lot . . . he didn't know what he was doing. Lot, the one just man, the only beloved of God. (*He starts to fall asleep, shakes himself, yawns.*) I can't work today.

(*On the threshold of the cabin* JUDITH *suddenly appears. Her cheeks are inflamed. She wears a crown of flowers, and her hair is wild. When he sees her, her* FATHER *stands up.*)

THE FATHER: Where are you coming from?

JUDITH: From the forest.

THE FATHER: (*Brutally*) You have no business in the forest at night! I forbid you to go there! Wolves lie in wait for you, and brigands. . . . The Fauret brothers may have been tortured to death once, but they keep reappearing, with different names.

JUDITH: There's no one in the forest.

THE FATHER: Our shadows are there.

JUDITH: Do you want to keep me from breathing?

THE FATHER: Breathe out the window!

JUDITH: I'm shut up like a prisoner!

THE FATHER: (*Calmer*) Why do you complain? You lead the life of a princess here. You have only a little housework to do. You want for nothing. If you were a servant in the city, like your mother, you'd be pale and famished, and so exhausted at night that you'd fall asleep without even taking your clothes off.

JUDITH: And what would be the harm of that? I hardly have one frock left. This one is falling apart; I'll soon have to go around naked.

THE FATHER: (*He looks at her strangely.*) Today I'll go to the city. I'll bring you a new dress. I'll bring you other things too. (*Silence*) But promise me you'll not leave the house. Swear it!

JUDITH: I swear it.

THE FATHER: You have washing to do. You have to knead the bread. I'll give you all the wood I have for the oven. Eighteen loaves![2] Do you understand?

JUDITH: Yes, I understand.

THE FATHER: And when I come home this evening I don't want to smell the odor of sin!

---

2. This baking would represent a month or more of their food supply. Old-fashioned country bread will keep for at least half a year.

JUDITH: (*Proudly, taking his measure*) You'll smell the odor of baked bread.
(THE FATHER *exits.*)
(*The curtain closed, we hear* A WOMAN *singing.*)

> Under clustered glass grapes
> Sleeps my lover.
> The chapel is a greenhouse
> Of virgins and martyrs.
>
> I enter and wake him:
> Do you hear me, sweetheart?
> For twenty years I wait
> Though his face is but wax.
>
> Under clustered glass grapes
> Sleeps my lover.
> The vines alone embrace him
> With virgins and martyrs.
>
> Yet I cry and call out:
> Open are his long eyes,
> Lighting the altar
> With their dark green fire.
>
> Under clustered glass grapes
> Sleeps my lover.
> At war is his soul
> But his body died here.

(*The* CHORUS *repeats this song.*)
(*The curtain is raised.*)

ACT 2

SCENE I

The same cabin, the evening. Eighteen loaves of bread have been placed side by side on the table. Two piles of clean, if worn, garments have been folded and arranged on top of the chest. JUDITH *remains immobile for a moment, then speaks.*

JUDITH: (*With a round loaf in her arms*) I've washed, sewn, kneaded, cooked.

Nineteen loaves! Everything's ready for my father's homecoming. (*She examines the loaf she is holding.*) But he won't get this one! This is bread for my engagement night. I've cut a circle into the crust. (*Silence*) Young man, slim and fine looking, man with a fleece upon his chest, with hands big enough. . . . (*Excited*) to take me. (*She looks about her, listens.*) I think he could crush my bones, and I wouldn't cry out. Oh, to die, to die with him in the forest. . . . To lie on the ferns and have their imprint on my skin. (*She dances, her cheek touching the loaf of bread.*) And, if he looked at me every day, I'd no longer need to see the sky. I could live in a prison. I wouldn't need the sun or fir trees or anything. His eyes . . . (*She laughs, suddenly becoming serious.*) His young man's eyes. He will tell me about my own, what mine are like. I don't even know their color. . . . Though I've already seen myself in his glance, as if in a mirror. (*She sighs.*) No mirrors here anymore, perhaps Father will bring one back to me. (*She smiles.*)

(*The young* MAN, *holding a fir tree before him, has been slowly entering the cabin. He is half-hidden by its branches.* JUDITH *finally sees him and screams.*)

THE MAN: Don't scream, Judith! Don't be afraid of me ever! I've been watching you for a while, admiring you. You are . . . (*Pause*) Judith, I want only good things for you.

JUDITH: Then why do you hide behind a tree?

THE MAN: Your father . . . doesn't like the smell of other men.

JUDITH: But now he's far away, gone to the city to sell his wood and buy provisions, maybe even a present for me. He'll only return very late tonight.

(*The young* MAN *drops his leafy disguise and shows himself to* JUDITH. *They take a long look at each other. Then they fall into each other's arms and kiss, passionately.*)

JUDITH: We'll live together in the forest, we'll die there!

THE MAN: There will be no blade of grass, no leaf that will not leave its mark on your body!

(*Still enlaced, they flee into the forest.*)

(*Twilight, then night falls. Music and the* DANCE OF THE WILL-O'-THE-WISPS)

SCENE 2

We hear an owl hooting. JUDITH *enters the cabin, lights a hurricane lamp and several candles. She at first seems lost in despair but slowly comes to life. During the entire scene her few movements and gestures will bring to mind a* SORCERERS' ROUND. *She, herself, will be unconscious of this subtle transformation. She will be both the specters and the wild beasts of whom she speaks.*

JUDITH: He took me and rejected me. Taken and thrown away. And he just simply . . . left. (*Silence*) He lied to me . . . the young man; he doesn't live in the forest. (*Louder*) But why, why do *I* stay here? Sequestered in solitude, ripened through absence. Dead. . . . Perhaps I'm dead, and I don't know it. Does one really know if one's dead? (*She looks at her arms, her legs.*) Does one know what death is when one's dead? You can only know death if you're alive! (*Softly*) All those tiny corpses in the forest, those fragile white skeletons, those bits of sugar cubes I find at the feet of trees in the morning. . . . (*The owl hoots.*) Who will find me? Which ant will feast on me? Which rat? (*Gravely*) I should have ended up with my legs swinging in the air many seasons ago. I should have, a longtime past, become a bleached cage for the birds, a perch for their claws, my skull a watering pool. (*Silence*) I'm thirsty. He is far away now. I will never catch up. I couldn't make him wait for me . . . I'd waited too long for him. I thought I was his destiny . . . but I didn't mean any more to him than . . . a plane tree's leaf ready for the fire. He ended up telling me: he doesn't live near here. He was just passing by. No one ever stays in this forest. (*She makes fists of her hands. She is furious with herself.*) He had me so quickly—and he won't ever come back. (*Suddenly, she becomes threatening.*) Oh! I wish they were real, all those other ones, the ones who do come back . . . (*She walks like a sleepwalker.*) I summon them: the bewitched, the sorcerers, the hanged bodies, the frozen men, enemies, angels, cherubim, kings, club-footed monsters, and even (*Very low*) the Master Charcoal Maker . . . in whom I cannot believe. (*A pause, then she screams.*) But the forest is empty!

(*Long silence*)

Oh! How I want them to be here tonight. They would keep me company, all of them, the assassinated, the crippled, the madmen, the drunks, the scourges, the helpless, the homeless. Come to me! Come! (*Silence*) But the forest is empty! And yet were they to come . . . (*Softly*) You desperate ones, you living dead, and, yes, even you long-dead, you in the Devil's Pit and you who fell years ago into the waiting chasms and were buried forever . . .

(*Hoots of an owl*)

Yes! I will be your queen, and you will all come to me! (*Exalted*) You will be resuscitated; you will know pleasure once more! I *am* the queen. You *are* all present: the living and the dead and the red-haired beasts and the gray ones, the wild cat, the wild boar, the black cock! (*She raises her arms over her head and mimes the mating strut of the wood grouse, then stops; more softly*) And everything living, under rocks and mold, all that we step on without knowing it, all that's rotting, everything we cannot bear to look at: vermin and toads, snakes and spiders. (*She cries out.*) All of you . . . here now! (*She opens her arms.*) Get ready for the great round: the rooster with the woman, the man with the vixen, the rat with the child, and the horned stag with me. (*Seductively*) And you, Master Charcoal Maker . . . (*We hear footsteps. She goes to the door and opens it wide. No one is there.*) But the forest is empty! (*She laughs. In response we hear the moan of a cat.*) There's just a small lynx and me.

(*Brutally slamming the door, she returns to center stage. She takes her head in her hands and groans strangely, like a wild animal. Then she begins to turn in place, faster and faster. Exhausted, she slides onto the bench.*)

JUDITH: I don't need wine to be intoxicated. Not me.

(*She falls asleep. Music and* THE SORCERERS' ROUND: *with women bewitched, witches and whores, hanged men, frozen men, fallen angels, kings, princes, club-footed humans, murder victims, cripples, madmen, drunkards; beings with mange, struck by lightning, dead by their own hand; peddlers, mountebanks, outlaws; wild boars, stags, wild cats, foxes, grouse, owls, serpents, devils, etc.*)

SCENE 3

Head cradled in her arms on the table, JUDITH *sleeps. We hear again a heavy footstep.* THE FATHER *enters. He closes and bolts the door. While undoing an enormous bundle, he speaks to himself as though his daughter were not present.*

THE FATHER: (*Singing vulgarly*)
She's my daughter
Because I loved her mother.
She's my daughter
Because I'm
A man . . .
(*Changing his tone*) Stay away! Renounce! My head says: Yes. But the rest of me says: No. If they cut my head off, my body of its own accord would walk to her. (*He takes a few steps toward* JUDITH, *looks at her. He is startled and moves away.*) My desire for her mother was nothing in comparison. Twenty years ago . . . (*He remembers.*) Twenty years ago she was born; it's been ten years since her mother drowned herself, and for all ten I have lived alone—with Judith—but alone. And I thought the demons inside me were dead; I thought I could laugh at them, and I wasn't much troubled by the teasing whores when I went to town. I used to answer back: "You're a necessary plague but *I*, by God's grace, have no more use for you!" They'd grin and say: "We'll wait for you, wait till you turn fifty!" But I still don't look it, not yet: (*He straightens up.*) Today I spoke with those women; I went with them. (*He puts his head in his hands.*) It's as though I'd been unfaithful to her! (*He drops his hands to his sides.*) I liked to think of myself as a good man, a just man before

the Lord. I stood before God as straight as a fir tree, and I murmured: "One day, O Lord, I shall fall under Your ax." (*He looks about; the candles have almost all burned out.*) I encountered strange smells in the forest tonight, smells of flesh and marvels; life and death are fornicating; resin flows like wine or sperm; ferns clasp each other like hands; the blue thistle wounds and the purple gentian is sweet. . . . There's plenty to set astray a soul weaker than mine. (*Slowly, he approaches* JUDITH, *who has awakened. She pretends she is still sleeping.*) Daughter, you are Evil and you are Good, you are Woman and you are Forest. (*Silence*) People of the cities don't know all that can be seen out here. "Oh no, ladies and gentlemen, they don't hold Sabbaths in the forest anymore; there aren't any witches left, nowadays. They were all burned! The land was overflowing with them. They grew like wild blueberries!" (THE FATHER *undoes the rope tied around his bundle.*) What you can see in the forest these days is much more awesome. It's our desires that thrive in the forest; they multiply under the trees. No shade's darker than the shade of the forest! No sun's more blinding than the sun of the forest! And when you walk the ground isn't mute like the ground of the wheat fields; it moans under your feet; it stirs and resounds; it's a dark ground pervaded by millions of roots crossing and intertwining! Ah! I can feel the entire forest vibrating . . . and when one of my trees dies . . .

JUDITH: (*Who pretends to wake up*) Father! Is that you? (*He bends over her and touches her breasts.* JUDITH *stands up quickly and backs away.*)

THE FATHER: See what I've brought you. (*He pulls out of the sack a lustrous black clock, inlaid with copper and glass. He sets it proudly on the table. It is three o'clock.*)

JUDITH: (*Stupified*) It works!

THE FATHER: Yes, and it even . . . chimes. (*He shakes it, and we hear a small chime.*)

JUDITH: What time is it?

THE FATHER: I don't know . . . but I'll learn. You'll learn. And here's the key to wind it. It's made of gold.

JUDITH: (*More and more astonished*) But why? Why such a gift! It's worth a fortune! (*Suddenly angry*) And the dress you promised me! And the shoes?

THE FATHER: You're not happy with this?

JUDITH: No! I need clothes. (*Very angry*) This winter I'll go barefooted in the snow; I'll have to go completely naked. What do I care what time it is. I've gone this many years without knowing.

THE FATHER: (*Good-naturedly*) Well, then! You're going to be very happy. Wait just a minute. (*He reaches back into the sack and pulls out a long, splendid silk dress, embroidered with glittering jewels.*)

JUDITH: (*Who doesn't believe her eyes*) A dress of sunlight! A dress for a queen! (*She takes it and runs into the other room. She returns very quickly, almost unrecognizable, dressed in the new costume, her hair piled on top of her head.*)

THE FATHER: Who are you now?

(*They look at each other in silence.*)

JUDITH: Another Judith.

THE FATHER: You're the one I've been waiting for all my life.

JUDITH: (*Troubled*) Perhaps in appearance another Judith but, in reality, one more dangerous than ever.

THE FATHER: Come here.

(JUDITH *is very careful to stay away but bows graciously.*)

JUDITH: It's good to be beautiful; it's a consolation.

THE FATHER: And I still have more for you.

JUDITH: More?

THE FATHER: More dresses and shoes. But here's the best. (*He takes a pearl wedding band from his pocket.*)

JUDITH: (*Very seriously*) Now I understand, Father.

THE FATHER: If only you could understand . . . everything . . .

JUDITH: I'm not afraid because you've become a thief; I'm even glad of it.

THE FATHER: Some things a man does only once. One terrible act can be enough for a lifetime. Give me something to drink, Judith! I'm thirsty, and I feel tired. Pass me the wine.

JUDITH: (*Cruelly*) I've never known you like this. You always used to say that wine was the Devil's invention to tempt men and lead them into sin.

THE FATHER: (*Begging*) Bring me the cup, Judith; I want to drink from your hands. They're even more beautiful than your mother's. (*He sighs.*) She was a tame dove who gave birth to a wild one. (*He is confused.*) But what wildness . . . glistening . . . moist . . . shining . . . how beautiful you are! (*He gestures toward* JUDITH's *breasts.*) You've two roses under your dress. (*He stands up brutally.*) Show them to me!

(JUDITH *has moved away and is looking disgustedly at him, but he catches her by surprise, grabs her waist. She struggles, manages to escape. He runs after her, grabs her again.*)

JUDITH: Father!

THE FATHER: (*Suddenly calm*) It's not the wine. The wine didn't do anything. I'd need a river of wine to forget you're my daughter. Ah! Lot was luckier than me . . .

(JUDITH *has reached the door, but she can't open it. She tries to get to the window; her* FATHER, *however, realizing that she's getting away, throws himself on her. She fights*

him off, grabs the clock from the table, and throws it at his head. He falls to the
ground.)
(*Curtain closed; the chorus sings "Dies Irae."*)[3]

Dies irae, dies illa
Solvet saeclum in favilla:
Teste David cum Sibýlla.

Quantus tremor est futúrus,
Quando judex est ventúrus,
Cuncta stricte discussúrus
Tuba mirum spargens sonum
Per sepúlcra regiónum,
Coget omnes ante thronum
Mors stupébit et natúra,
Cum resúrget creatúra,
Judicánti responsúra.
[etc.]

(*The curtain rises.*)

ACT 3

SCENE I

A white-washed prison cell in the summit of a tower, suspended in a bare gray sky. A
raven's cawing penetrates the space. There is a door and a small barred window, a
straw pallet, and an earthen jug. The whiteness of the cell, its emptiness, are in
complete contrast to the deep red-purple hues of the cabin in the forest.

JUDITH, *in a formless, loosely woven dress, her hair clipped nearly to its roots,*
paces back and forth, talking to herself.

JUDITH: They came looking for me; they took me away; they undressed me; they

---

3. "Dies irae" is a medieval hymn attributed to Thomas of Celano:

Days of sorrows, dreadful day,
When the world shall pass away,
So David and the Sibyl say.

Ah, what terrors shall appall,
Systems ruining shall fall,
When the Judge his roll cloth call.

K. M. Jones, trans., *Latin Poetry in Verse Translation,* ed. L. R. Lind (Boston: Houghton Mifflin, 1957).

beat me; they tortured me. (*She keeps on walking a moment longer, does not speak. Then, haggard, she throws herself at the door, shakes it violently, goes to the window. Same gestures as at the end of act 2. She grasps the window bars then slowly slides to the ground.*) I *will* get out of here! I *will* return to the forest! (*Her voice grows weaker and weaker.*) I'm so tired, I don't know if I can go on. . . . But he will carry me away, kiss me, crush me . . . my lover.

(*We hear a huge rattling of keys in the lock. The door opens.* THE CHAPLAIN, *all in black and very dignified, enters. He has a book tucked under his arm.*)

THE CHAPLAIN: Stand up, Judith!

(JUDITH *stands up. Silence*)

THE CHAPLAIN: Do you repent of having killed your father?

JUDITH: No . . .

THE CHAPLAIN: Unhappy child!

JUDITH: In the Bible, Judith was treated like a heroine for having freed her city from the tyrant Holophernes, and the trumpets of glory have celebrated her name ever since. But I, Judith of the forest, I am condemned for having freed myself of a monstrous father!

THE CHAPLAIN: No crime is more heinous than parricide.

JUDITH: What if he were an unnatural father? If I told you . . .

THE CHAPLAIN: Never mind words—you need evidence and witnesses. Do you have them?

JUDITH: (*Defeated*) No. (*Silence*) And if I told you he desired me, pursued me?

THE CHAPLAIN: You could have run away.

JUDITH: I was his prisoner.

THE CHAPLAIN: You were only the prisoner of yourself, Judith.

JUDITH: I could not leave! (*She begins pacing again, like a caged animal, and will not stop until the end of the scene.*)

THE CHAPLAIN: We are all prisoners in this world. Only death can open the gates.

JUDITH: (*Screaming*) I don't want to die!

THE CHAPLAIN: Come, my child, let us pray. (*He opens his book, kneels, and whispers a prayer.* JUDITH *keeps pacing, staring ahead. Pause. He gets up, closes his book without looking at her.*) There's more rejoicing in Heaven for one repentant sinner than for ten just men.

JUDITH: (*Gently*) I'm not repentant.

THE CHAPLAIN: You lived a very secluded life in the forest?

JUDITH: (*Suddenly confident*) Yes, I lived alone with my father for ten years.

THE CHAPLAIN: But there were other families, weren't there? Woodcutters?

JUDITH: Sometimes one would pass by.

THE CHAPLAIN: Poor child!

JUDITH: (*Refusing his pity*) I was at home in the forest. I want to go back. I liked living there, I like living alone. . . . The trees were my real family. I'd listen to them sing all around me; they protected me with their branches. They rocked me to sleep and stroked me awake. (*Reflectively*) And their taste! I loved them so much I'd sometimes bite into their trunks, under the bark. There's tender juicy flesh underneath . . . white, so very white . . . (*She smiles.*)

THE CHAPLAIN: (*Aroused*) Didn't you have a lover?

JUDITH: (*Hostile*) No.

THE CHAPLAIN: Didn't you ever come to town?

JUDITH: No . . .

THE CHAPLAIN: (*Surprised*) But who raised you? You're educated; you speak properly.

JUDITH: Until the age of ten I was with my mother, in a noble family, in the service of Mme de Berny.

THE CHAPLAIN: Ah! Now I understand better. (*He thinks.*) You should have returned there. That was the place for you.

(JUDITH *remains silent and stops walking.* THE CHAPLAIN *lets himself out while gesturing toward her.*)

THE CHAPLAIN: May God bless you. I shall return. (*He leaves.* JUDITH *collapses on her pallet.*)

SCENE 2

The scene takes on the reddish-purple tints of the cabin. The lighting is odd, unreal. We hear the heavy footsteps of THE FATHER. *The door opens.* JUDITH, *sitting bolt upright, stares.* THE FATHER *enters. He no longer has a head—that is, in place of his head is the clock that he had brought home the night* JUDITH *killed him. Its face is now his. The hands read three o'clock.*

THE FATHER: You didn't expect me.

JUDITH: (*Composed*) On the contrary, I knew that you'd come.

THE FATHER: (*Humbly*) Judith, I've come . . .

JUDITH: You don't scare me with that mask!

THE FATHER: It's the face you gave me. I have no other.

JUDITH: Only your mother gave you your face!

THE FATHER: Judith, now I know that children create their parents . . . far more than fathers form their daughters.

JUDITH: (*Annoyed*) Have you gone crazy or become wise?

THE FATHER: What I'm about to say will astonish you, I know. I've come to ask your forgiveness.

JUDITH: Forgiveness! Of me who killed you. (*She laughs.*)

THE FATHER: How your laugh pleases me: it's the laugh of the desperate.

JUDITH: Men's justice is still your justice. You always scolded me for being ungrateful.

THE FATHER: (*Energetically*) And you were! Your only instincts were like a savage's. (*Silence*) But I, Judith, I . . . what did I do to you?

JUDITH: (*Begging*) Father, please take off that mask!

THE FATHER: But I haven't another head.

JUDITH: I can't bear it anymore! (*She covers her eyes.*) They called me the hand of Evil. (*Screaming*) Anything would have been better . . . a sword . . . but not this! Not this!

THE FATHER: Do you know what time it is now?

JUDITH: Time doesn't exist for me anymore.

THE FATHER: It's three o'clock. For you it will always be three o'clock, three o'clock in the morning. (*He backs toward the door.*) Farewell. I shall return.

(*He leaves; the door shuts. It is very dark in the cell. Pause. We hear a nightingale. A grayish light, then a rose light bathes the cell.* JUDITH *slowly awakens. She listens.*)

JUDITH: (*Her eyes still closed*) It's the lament of the nightingale. . . . How he calls out! How he desires. . . . In those repetitive whistles, sometimes as many as ten, there's all the hurt and all the balm of love. (*She opens her eyes.*) Of course, it's spring. It's the month of May. . . . In the early morning dew I can go look for new buds on the branches. . . . I'll cook them . . . for a long time . . . over a fire of sweet pine . . . in the copper kettle, with the sugar he's brought back. What good syrup it will make, this black sap of the fir trees. It will cure us. It will save me!

(*Suddenly, we hear the voice of the Young* MAN, *far away, then coming closer: "Judith! Judith!"*)

JUDITH: (*Running to the window*) It's you! I've been waiting for you.

THE MAN: But I can't come in.

JUDITH: Why?

THE MAN: I'm far away, so far from you.

JUDITH: Where are you?

THE MAN: Over here in the light.

JUDITH: I see it. It's the light of springtime. The air is springlike, and so is the wind. But where are you?

THE MAN: In the forest.

JUDITH: I still can't see you. There are too many trees between us, too many odors of wild clematis and bark. Oh! Come! Come! You're strong! You can destroy these walls and tear down the bars! Come!

THE MAN: No Judith. I can't come to where you are.

JUDITH: (*In despair*) I'll die if you don't help me! Young man! Young man! I don't even know your name.

(*A long silence. The rose-colored light fades away. It is once again icy daylight in the prison cell.*)

SCENE 3

JUDITH *is lying on her bed like a sleepwalker. We hear again the rattle of the key turning in the lock, and the door opens slowly. But we see no one.*

JUDITH: (*Mechanically*) Come in.

(THE CHAPLAIN *enters her cell. He is both sensitive and aloof, authoritarian and timid. He will remain an enigma to us until the end.*)

THE CHAPLAIN: It's been light for a long time now, Judith.

JUDITH: (*Gravely, she sits up, cross-legged on the edge of her pallet.*) It will be a bad day; I've had a bad night. I've been dreaming. . . . I saw and heard them.

THE CHAPLAIN: They return. They shall always return. We never master the absence of the people who once loved us.

JUDITH: (*Hard*) They didn't love me! No one has loved me!

THE CHAPLAIN: No one? And your father . . .

JUDITH: He loved my mother, and my mother . . . loved the coachman. No, it wasn't me whom he loved; he was seeing my mother in me. I was my mother! (*Scornfully*) He wasn't even sinning, you see!

THE CHAPLAIN: And you killed him!

JUDITH: (*Cynically*) If it had been me he wanted, maybe I wouldn't have killed him.

THE CHAPLAIN: Man never knows how to love enough. Only God knows that.

JUDITH: But this God you speak of, this loving God, why does he need us?

THE CHAPLAIN: It's a mystery. After death we'll know everything and be delighted with our knowledge. We should rejoice.

JUDITH: I won't rejoice about Heaven . . . (*Brusquely*) And what if God were the Devil?

THE CHAPLAIN: Good and Evil cannot coexist in Him.

JUDITH: (*Stubbornly*) And if they were *one*—One God, both good and evil—I would understand then!

THE CHAPLAIN: The human being's a mixture, of course. But God! . . . Don't you believe in Him?

JUDITH: I feel blows, blows over all my body, all the time, always. As long as I keep on being beaten, I shall not see God.

THE CHAPLAIN: You must separate God from Evil, Judith. God is the absence of Evil. (*Silence*) That is why so many people believe in the absence of God. But he's coming, Judith. He'll arrive without your expecting him, without your desiring his presence!

JUDITH: (*Angry*) Words! I want to *live!* Help me get out of here! (*She gets up.*)

(THE CHAPLAIN *doesn't answer.*)

JUDITH: You, too, you imprison me.

THE CHAPLAIN: You're only a prisoner of yourself.

JUDITH: (*Pacing again*) You've already said that. Words! Just words! I'm a prisoner of my life. It's not the same thing.

THE CHAPLAIN: Life works out according to who one is.

JUDITH: (*Crushed*) Oh! Your words are a mockery. . . . If I were you, I'd be ashamed.

(THE CHAPLAIN *doesn't answer.*)

JUDITH: I'll never know what you're really thinking because one never does know what the church believes.

(THE CHAPLAIN *smiles.*)

THE CHAPLAIN: (*Less aloof*) The young man you mentioned . . . your charcoal maker.

JUDITH: (*Between her teeth*) The Master Charcoal Maker.

THE CHAPLAIN: Was he the only man you've known?

JUDITH: (*Not moving*) Yes, but I don't know him anymore.

THE CHAPLAIN: (*Tenderly*) He ran away. He abandoned you, you understand.

JUDITH: (*Cutting him off*) So did God.

THE CHAPLAIN: God? The Lord has never been closer to you than He is today.

JUDITH: How do you know?

THE CHAPLAIN: In order to experience the terrible tenderness of God, you must feel abandoned by everyone, including yourself. (*Silence*) Believe me, Judith, God loves you more than any mortal man could hope to.

JUDITH: (*Listening, sarcastic, astonished*) If God is my witness, He will see that I'm ashamed for you!

THE CHAPLAIN: God humiliates no one! It is the law of the world that mortifies us. God forgives everything, understands everything. (*Silence*) Allow yourself to be comforted in His arms. He is your Father.

JUDITH: (*Horrified*) My father!

THE CHAPLAIN: Your true Father.

JUDITH: Sleep in his arms? I've always wanted to have my *own* bed. (*Enraged*) Really, do you know what you're saying? Sleep in his arms . . . (*Bone-chilling laughter*) God's not my lover.

THE CHAPLAIN: He's the one and only Lover.

JUDITH: (*Insolently*) I had a lover in the forest. A flesh-and-blood man! And young, too; the charcoal maker. . . . I can still feel the pressure of his body against mine; I can feel the wound of his kisses on my lips, the coolness of his breath. . . . I can believe in him!

THE CHAPLAIN: It's your youth speaking now. If only you could grow old!

JUDITH: That's a queer wish! What's the use of aging? You know as well as I that old men are the most dangerous.

THE CHAPLAIN: Old age would teach you that what you call earthly love is deceptive. It exists . . . yes, no one denies it, but it's infinitely small. (*Silence*) And yet it's the force that stands between God and man; it makes us heavy, so weighty, that we think we are richer than Heaven. But time wears away at us, and when the end is near we become light. (*Silence*) Judith, you can't tell from what *you* can see, but *I* tell you: the death that awaits you is God's gift.

JUDITH: (*Hoarsely*) I've been sentenced? You know it?

THE CHAPLAIN: I don't know anything yet. I've talked with several people. . . . The clock and the clothing were stolen from Mme de Berny. We don't know how your father got in. The countess testified in your favor. She liked your mother, and told us you were a good little girl.

JUDITH: (*Calmly*) I was a good little girl.

THE CHAPLAIN: I will do all I can for you. And I shall pray. . . . Farewell. (*He leaves without glancing backward.* JUDITH *lies down again.*)

(THE CHORUS *intones a Gregorian chant.*)

SCENE 4

THE JAILER *enters with a tin of soup and a hunk of black bread.*

JUDITH: I'd like a mirror.

(THE JAILER *appears not to hear her.*)

JUDITH: I said: a mirror!

THE JAILER: (*Suspicious*) That's not what the condemned ask for, usually.

JUDITH: (*Change of tone*) The condemned! (*She refuses to think about it.*) What do they ask for?

THE JAILER: Something really good to eat or to drink or smoke.

JUDITH: (*Furiously*) You don't want to *give* me a mirror?

THE JAILER: Of course, my precious, I'll get you one. But what do you want to do with it?

JUDITH: What do you think? Look at myself.

THE JAILER: That's all?

JUDITH: (*Suddenly understanding*) Are you afraid I'll use it as a weapon, a dagger? That I'll stab you in the heart or cut my veins . . . ?

THE JAILER: Women do that sometimes after looking at themselves.

JUDITH: (*Upset*) Have I become so repulsive?

THE JAILER: (*Admiringly*) Oh no! Everyone here calls you "Beautiful Judith."

JUDITH: (*Approaching him*) Please, let me go.

THE JAILER: I'm here to guard you, and I *will* guard you.

JUDITH: What if I were to give myself to you? I'd do anything you wanted . . .

THE JAILER: (*Lowering his eyes*) I don't like to make love.

JUDITH: Not you, too! (*Silence*) Do you really know what you're talking about?

THE JAILER: (*Bragging*) Of course, like everyone else.

JUDITH: And you really don't like it?

THE JAILER: Well . . . sometimes it's all right. But I get anxious afterward.

JUDITH: Fool!

(THE JAILER *leaves, ashamed; we hear the key in the lock.* JUDITH *goes to the window and carefully examines the bars, which she seizes in both hands and tries to pry loose. To her great surprise they come unfixed rather easily.*)

JUDITH: Hah! Who did this? Was it a prisoner before me? Or could it have been? . . .

(*She puts everything back in place, exulting, and sits on the pallet to think. Pause. The door opens, and* THE JAILER *arrives with a mirror, which he holds out to her.*)

JUDITH: (*Looking at herself*) "Beautiful Judith" (*Silence*) So, it's true, I *am* still beautiful, in spite of my shaven head. Beautiful and sad.

THE JAILER: Why don't you eat?

JUDITH: (*Who begins to eat her soup; between mouthfuls she speaks.*) I can hear voices. But they're still too far away. What are they saying?

THE JAILER: They say that you're a witch, that they saw you fly out of the window riding a broom. (*Clever*) Between us, I know it's stupid. I don't believe in such stuff myself. *I've* been to school. But maybe it'll work for you if you say you're a witch. Sometimes confessions have saved people. (*Silence*) Here, right here in this room, I've heard lots of them confess to copulating with the Devil . . . even up the ass! (*Silence*) The registers are full of such declarations. I've read them. It's always the same story . . . (*Silence*) makes it sound like paradise to get it up the behind. Ugh! In any case, the so-called Master Charcoal Maker, you know, doesn't even exist; he never existed. He was invented by idiots. Lucky for us we've entered the age of enlightenment.

JUDITH: (*Who has been listening as if dreaming*) The Devil is man himself.

THE JAILER: Maybe so, yes, you're probably right. But sometimes it's also woman. I don't say that in your case, but, believe me, I've known a few.

JUDITH: If you don't believe in the Devil, you can't believe in God.

THE JAILER: Don't tell anyone! . . . (*He whispers in her ear.*) No, I don't believe in God either.

JUDITH: Really, you don't?

THE JAILER: No . . . (*He sits at the other end of her pallet.*) Did you really work for Mme de Berny? Her rooms are much prettier than this one, aren't they?

JUDITH: (*Trying to remember*) Madam's bed. . . . There were two dressing tables on either side and a small chamber behind it. And I can still see the fabric of the drapes and the furniture. It was linen with big sprays of blue flowers, printed right there in the manor, because they had their own tools. (*She finishes her soup.*) I'm still hungry.

THE JAILER: Eat your bread.

JUDITH: It's too hard. They had formal dinners. . . . They served two of every-thing: two hors d'oeuvres, two soups, two plates of cured meats, two roasts, and vegetables, and cheeses and salads! For the main holidays they even served three or four of each course: I remember veal heads, a creamy white, with a parsley garnish and a lemon wedged right in their mouths, old wines in crystal glasses, meats on silver platters, desserts in fine China or English crockery . . .

THE JAILER: Did you have time to eat?

JUDITH: (*Absorbed in her description*) And sweets! Little cubes of cake glazed in red or yellow, and nests made of nougat with four candied almonds for eggs, olives made of pistachio nuts and ginger cookies . . .

THE JAILER: I'll bring you some!

JUDITH: For Christmas we'd hang painted-sugar candies on the tree.

THE JAILER: I'll bring you some! You wait! I'll bring you some. (*He takes a pack of cards from his pocket and spreads them on the bed.*) Do you want to play?

JUDITH: (*Taking the cards he hands her*) They came from Germany and were shaped like apples, pears, walnuts, oranges, roses. . . . You're cheating! (*She slaps his hand lightly.*) . . . and blue-bells, daisies, monkeys, lambs, children, angels . . . there were even entire family scenes . . .

THE JAILER: (*Excitedly*) Ace of spades! Jack of hearts! . . .

JUDITH: (*Dreaming on*) . . . and little quince-paste sausages, miniature marzipan hams . . .

THE JAILER: I win! (*He picks up the cards and runs out as though there were a fire within.*)

(JUDITH *looks at herself in the mirror then closes her eyes.*)

JUDITH: And now I'll look inside myself. I'm my own mirror. Yes, I see, I'm afraid of death. And yet, even at the time when I was at my fullest and freshest, I could feel myself decaying. Not the decay of sinfulness, the other one . . . the one they never talk about. The decay of fruit that hasn't been picked. (*She lets the mirror slip and break. She bends over it.*) Here I am, shattered, in pieces, my true image.

(*She picks up a piece and examines it to make sure its edge is sharp. Then she hides it under her pallet and lies down. Night falls slowly. In the faint light* JUDITH *is stretched out, immobile, her eyes open. Pause. She stands up, takes off her leather belt and the loose tunic she is wearing. [She will have a gray bodysuit on underneath.] With the bit of mirror she cuts up her dress and the blanket covering her bed; she makes ropes of the pieces. All this rapidly and with skill. She hikes herself up on the window ledge, removes the bars, attaches the rope, and slides off the edge. Pause. A muffled scream and silence. Deepest night.*)

(*The* CHORUS *sings a Gregorian chant.*)

SCENE 5

The prison cell. It is dawn, then the explosion of a very bright white day. A man's foot pushes the door open. THE JAILER *and* THE EXECUTIONER *enter carrying* JUDITH. *She has fainted. There is a cloth bandage around her head. They place her on her pallet and leave. Pause.* THE JAILER *returns, makes her drink something.*

THE JAILER: Good, you're coming around. It's only a small cut. Shall I tell you another story?

JUDITH: Yes, tell.

THE JAILER: I've seen things all right! I once saw a simple soldier, who was standing at attention in front of his general, start to walk like a wind-up toy. (THE JAILER *mimes the scene.*) He says, "I've come chou, chou, chou, chou all the way to you, mein commandante."

(JUDITH *laughs.* THE CHAPLAIN *enters. She stops laughing.* THE CHAPLAIN *kneels and prays.* THE JAILER *and* JUDITH *watch him, then* THE JAILER *exits.*)

JUDITH: (*Weak*) Tell me that you love me. I can't die if no one has ever loved me.

THE CHAPLAIN: I love you . . . in God, Judith.

JUDITH: I only ask for a little earthly love. She holds out her arms to him.

THE CHAPLAIN: (*In a different voice*) The earthly need to be loved is a shadowy one.

JUDITH: Oh! Why?

THE CHAPLAIN: All *natural* movements of the soul belong to the Earth, which is but a realm of shadows.

JUDITH: (*Revolted by this*) Because the soul sits in the body, of course! But I'm obliged to carry my own weight. I'm not a ghost! (*Gravely*) I understood that this morning. And I thought about what you said to me. I think, yes, I think that all beings are unloved and alone—and you, first of all—if God doesn't exist.

THE CHAPLAIN: Even if that were true, I would not regret having lived.

JUDITH: But you haven't lived your life. Loving God isn't living.

THE CHAPLAIN: (*Impenetrable*) Even if God didn't exist—and I know that He does—I would regret nothing. You must pray, Judith.

JUDITH: I don't hear him listening to me. (*Silence*) Why is Christianity so sad?

THE CHAPLAIN: It's a serious religion but a joyful one, too. I believe we must denounce earthly pleasures in order to realize ourselves fully in God. Only renunciation allows us to attain Perfect Joy. (*Silence*) It's men who have made Christ's face sad.

JUDITH: But why did he always curse the flesh, flesh, which is the sun of human life?

THE CHAPLAIN: It's men again, Judith, who have cursed the flesh. And that's because they've suffered from it. Even the greatest saints are somber in front of God, who is Light itself.

JUDITH: If men were less somber, women would be brighter. . . . Women know how to be happy on Earth. I was!

THE CHAPLAIN: (*Surprised*) You were?

JUDITH: Terribly. Without any reason. I used to be able to cry out with happiness, alone in the forest, until the day . . .

THE CHAPLAIN: . . . the day?

JUDITH: In a low voice . . . the day my solitude began to smother me.

THE CHAPLAIN: You will never be alone again, Judith.

JUDITH: (*Exasperated*) But I can't make love to God!

THE CHAPLAIN: (*Covering his face in horror*) Oh! Woman!

JUDITH: (*Furious, standing*) You will never be able to understand us! God isn't a woman. He made himself into a man. And didn't one of you say that a woman had no more soul than a goat? Well I, I, say to you: "Animals have greater souls than men."

THE CHAPLAIN: Don't blaspheme, Judith! Your death is near.

JUDITH: (*Shaken*) Near?

THE CHAPLAIN: Death is not far from any of us. We must prepare ourselves for it. (*Very softly*) You spoke to me of your joy in the forest—tell me more about it.

JUDITH: All right . . . but the forest was dark, too, sometimes dismal. The grayish lichen, which hangs from trees, looks like shrouds torn away from graves. Even when the sun plays with it you think of the dead.

THE CHAPLAIN: Have you never felt the presence of God?

JUDITH: (*Lost, full of forebodings*) Yes, one day I did . . . (*Choosing her words*) One morning at sunrise . . . a tall, very dark fir was hiding the sun, but the sun was shining through it all the same—very, very forceful and strong. It was so . . . I told myself, yes . . . that God was coming.

(THE CHAPLAIN *prays silently.*)

JUDITH: And what if everything you say is false? If the love you speak of is just a trick! (*She screams.*) God does not love us!

THE CHAPLAIN: He sent his only son to save us.

JUDITH: Yes, but this Son isn't really God. What if He were just a compromise between God and man?

THE CHAPLAIN: (*Severely*) You must not separate the Father from the Son.

JUDITH: (*Obstinately*) If Christ were God, why did He cry out on the Cross at the last minute: "My Lord, why do you abandon me?"

THE CHAPLAIN: Human nature was still part of His Divine Self. That's why He cried out. (*Very upset, changing his tone*) Prepare yourself, Judith, your hour has come.

JUDITH: (*Refusing to understand*) My hour?

THE CHAPLAIN: You will be burned at the stake.

JUDITH: No! Judith killed once to save a city! And she was glorified! Today Judith kills to save herself! Why is she sentenced to burn?

THE CHAPLAIN: For men it's numbers that matter; numbers will always prevail. How many people in a city? Hundreds, thousands. What's a single girl compared to a city? The crowd will reign over the earth, Judith. (*Silence*) For God alone you are unique. And He will receive you.

JUDITH: (*Terrified, not listening to him*) No! No!

THE CHAPLAIN: I'd like to help you, Judith. (*Lowers his voice*) I'm alone too, tremendously alone.

JUDITH: I don't want your help! You only love God! I don't want to die. They won't make me die; you're lying!

THE CHAPLAIN: You will be burned alive, Judith.

JUDITH: It's not true!

THE CHAPLAIN: The law . . .

JUDITH: Men's law . . .

THE CHAPLAIN: . . . isn't the same as God's law.

JUDITH: (*On her knees*) Save me!

THE CHAPLAIN: I can do nothing more. I was only able to make sure your robe be sprinkled with sulphur to shorten the suffering.

JUDITH: (*Muffled voice*) Burned. . . . My body won't even have its true death. They'll have robbed me of everything, even my death. Ah! I'd rather have my head cut off three times than die like that, reduced to ashes! (*Pause*) I won't be able to return to the nurturing soil like the animals I used to bury under the trees. (*Sobs*) So, I'm punished for once wishing to be killed by lightning! My lightning is this fire.

THE CHAPLAIN: You shall see God, Judith. He said to the living: "You will not contemplate my face, for none shall see my face without dying." And he added: "There is a place near to me; you will stand on the rock . . ."

JUDITH: No!

THE CHAPLAIN: "And when my light passes over you, I will place you in the hollow of the rock; I will cover you with my hand, until I have gone by."

JUDITH: No! No!

THE CHAPLAIN: But you, Judith, you'll see God's face.

JUDITH: (*Abruptly, fervently*) Yes!

(*We hear the murmurs and clamors of a crowd that is gathering before the prison. Men's voices "To the stake! To the stake!" Women's voices: "To the pyre! Fetch the parricide! The witch to the stake!"* MIXED VOICES: *"Death! Death!"*)

(*In anguish* JUDITH *and* THE CHAPLAIN *look at each other. The door opens, and* THE EXECUTIONER, *dressed in red, appears. He is carrying in his arms a long robe, which has been smeared with sulphur. It is as brilliant as a mountain primrose.*)

THE EXECUTIONER: It's time.

JUDITH: (*Strangely calm*) What time?

THE EXECUTIONER: Can't you hear the bells?

(*Three bells sound.* THE EXECUTIONER *dresses her in her sulphured robe.* JUDITH *looks at* THE CHAPLAIN. *He cannot sustain her gaze. Dressed like this, the bandage around her head like a small white crown,* JUDITH *looks more and more like Joan of Arc.*)

JUDITH: My wedding dress! My wedding dress to marry the fire.

THE CHAPLAIN: To marry death, Judith, and wed your Lord.

(JUDITH *straightens up and slowly exits to her death.*)

(*The* CHORUS *sings a Gregorian chant of celebration.*)

(*Curtain closes.*)

Chantal Chawaf

CHANTAL CHAWAF (B. 1943) ENCHANTED readers with her first poetic novels: *Retable, La Rêverie* (Mother Love, Mother Earth, 1974), *Cercoeur* (Heartcrunch, 1975), and *Blé de Semences* (Seed Wheat, 1976). Her enthralling metaphors, her insistence on alliteration and constructions built on repetitive rhythmic patterns, on unstoppable "vegetal" growth, on an accumulation of perceptions and the materialization of the senses, gives to her works—some seventeen in all—a particular delicacy, a lightness that charms. For Chawaf words are liberating, living matter.

Women readers especially have been invigorated to find expressed in her works so freshly and with such beauty the way they experience their sexual bodies, their "femaleness." Readers are not insensitive either to a kind of sadistic revolt, a skewing of expected emotional responses, that hovers about Chawaf's texts. Her feminist meditation on fairies, *Fées de toujours* (Fairies Forever, 1988), which was re-created for the stage in Brussels by Monique Dorsel, is an especially playful creation of new syntax as well as of new approaches to old stories of princesses and wood spirits. In this text Chawaf identifies words as the true fairies. Of late, as in her novel *Rédemption* (1989), the same syntactical playfulness contrasts markedly with themes of maniacal passion, contributing a grotesque coloration to the characters' blending of metaphysical and sexual abandon.

Chawaf's works cannot leave her readers indifferent. They are as far removed as possible from anything even remotely considered a traditional "woman's novel." Rather, they are exemplary of what has come to be known in the United States as "écriture féminine."

Chawaf wrote her only dramatic work, *Warmth: A Bloodsong*, in 1976,[1] having been inspired both by the vituosity of Parisian actress Garance and her own overpowering love for her infant daughter. As in all her early texts, in *Warmth* she seeks to create a space-time out of time, a union with the "mother." This has

Chantal Chawaf and daughter Jinane share an exceptional intimacy that has inspired much of Chawaf's writing, particularly in *Warmth*, *Fairies Forever* (*Fées de toujours*), and *Towards Light* (*Vers la lumière*).

been a primary literary search for her, perhaps in response to the uncanny and cruel circumstances of her own birth, in which she was pulled from her mother's body just after her mother had been killed on the way to the hospital in a World War II bombing.

In *Warmth,* as elsewhere, Chawaf's aim is to sing the sensuality, the orgasmic joy, of the female body engaged in female functions. Chawaf attempts to realize the potential of words to free the unconscious, to regenerate woman's sensuality, to disintellectualize her body, and to give voice to experiences rarely depicted. Her work cannot and should not be read for its themes or story but, rather, for her phonic games, her syntactical and semantic inventions, and for the images she creates. Readers should, indeed, as in approaching Hélène Cixous's *Name of Oedipus: Song of the Forbidden Body,* read or sing the text to themselves, keeping the vital rhythms and the music of the unconscious in mind.

In *Warmth,* a play of birthing and pregnancy, Chawaf abolishes hardness, solidity, geometry, linearity—all those images commonly associated with masculinity or maleness. Instead, images of liquidity—of flowing blood, of spurting milk, of creamy butter fat—abound. When she imagines impregnation, for example, Chawaf sees it in terms of nourishment rather than conquest. She fills her play with an incessant cataloging of organs, sinews, waters, fibers— establishing subjectivity through this ebb and flow of life. As is true of Monique Wittig's techniques in articulating her novel *The Lesbian Body,* Chawaf's stylistic inventions forbid the body's objectification.

In *Warmth* Chawaf gives voice to the experience of prebirth, birth, and afterbirth as lived and felt. She does so through three "characters" whom she terms "The Mother," "The Daughter," and "The Heart"—the last of these a choral character, as suggested in the homophonic analogy *coeur* (heart, or core) and *choeur* (chorus). [2] Her work might be considered complementary to the visualizations in American artist Judy Chicago's *Birth Project,* for Chawaf transforms the functioning of the reproductive organs into poetic matter. The Mother, for example, follows the Daughter's passage through the birth canal by seeing her own body as if outside of itself and in the process of erupting into a wholly new universe.

While Chawaf does indeed designate and ascribe lines to her characters, the appellations in fact only signal the places where the body's voice has momentarily settled. Mother, Daughter, and Heart do not have distinct characterizations. Frequently, they do not even directly pick up one another's lines. They are, rather, a voice shattered and circulating, each intervention a rhythmic response to the one before. The voices, therefore, interweave and mingle, refusing any kind of chronological ordering in their hymn to mother-daughter love and bonding.

Chawaf describes the desired space for the performance of her prose poetry as uterine: warm and tender, "crossed," as she says in her stage directions, "by the rhythmic poundings of life." She would have the audience incorporated in this space as well. She imagines both an ahistorical and atemporal space, an undifferentiated magma that is all-encompassing and secure. She sees both the space of the production and the space that mother and daughter inhabit as a nurturing association of body and nature, a feminine paradise protected from civilization's incursions: "a refuge in warmth, in the beginnings of the body"—as a line in the play evokes it.

Warmth has no consciousness-raising intent. There is no built-up critical commentary, nor is the staging meant to distance the spectators so that they think about the images being presented. The production expects, instead, to involve the audience in its rhythmic structures, to seduce it both through the vibrating light pattern suggested in the stage directions and by the vocal quality of the actors. The spectators should be engulfed in the tide of words, both hauntingly melodic and deliberately troubling.

Chawaf, however, does wish to image a new woman, a speaking woman—one who will create herself anew out of her body's energies. Chawaf's project, to abolish all distinctions between spirit and matter and to figure unmediated life onstage, rejoins that of Antonin Artaud, the twentieth-century theoretician, who also sought a ritualistic and therapeutic theater. Whereas Artaud, through participation and purgation, would reconcile human beings to the most dreaded and repressed elements in the psyche, Chawaf would sing that part of the repressed female psyche whose liberation, she believes, means empowerment.

Chawaf thus breaks down all boundaries: inside-outside, female-male, mother-child, audience-performers. Chawaf's *Warmth* is a radical attempt to abolish categories and to establish mother and daughter as the originary couple. The play can then be read as an exalted celebration of woman's biological and psychological strength and as a paean of hope for a new world from which aggressive masculinity has been banished. The last lines of the play bear witness to this vision: "With our hands we can turn the world into a caress."

NOTES

1. This play was created in Paris at the Théâtre du Lucenaire by the actress Garance and her troupe L'Obsidienne in January 1977.

2. The Heart: a euphonic analogue of the chorus in Greek tragedy. The French words for *heart* (*coeur*) and *chorus* (*choeur*) are homonyms.

Chantal Chawaf

Warmth: A Bloodsong

Translated by the Editors and Cynthia Running-Johnson

To Garance, who exudes theater
and who, one spring afternoon,
asked me to write a script
for her troupe L'Obsidienne;
and to Jinane, my daughter;
and to those forces of tenderness
that make life possible.

Characters

THE MOTHER
THE DAUGHTER
THE HEART, or pulse, of the play

The Heart is a multiple character that intimately connects the Mother and Daughter to each other and to human life in general. It is a rhythmic synthesis of man and woman, a locus where the body speaks to others and to itself. The Heart should therefore be played by several actors, male and female, who appear successively onstage, creating a kaleidescopic, pulsating movement that both surrounds the Mother and Daughter and emanates from them. And these actors and actresses, while dressed differently and according to their sex, should also display a common sign, a sign that designates them as the symbolic origin of the body's voice. The sign might be a mask or a jeweled emblem.

(The "body" will also speak through the words of THE MOTHER and DAUGHTER.)

Playing Area

The playing area should be covered by a protective vegetal layer that nourishes the body and shelters it from oppression. This performance space should be both internal and external, as intimately tender and warm as possible: ventral, uterine, and throbbing. And also epidermal, tactile, and palpable; pulsating with the inextricably linked vibrations of heart and body. Modulations in the lighting, a dance of electric intensity, should reinforce this continuous pulse beat.

THE DAUGHTER: Weaver of dewdrops, of buttercups and hyacinths, of wild violets and strawberries, weaver of the toad belly's black and yellow stripes, of the forest's cool penumbra lit by flower-covered reflections, weaver, you pass, a fountain between briars and mulberries; you foam into mist and steam, and your flowing waters fall in cascades, and your rivulets dissolve the moss and sandy ground and scar them—a spring where light changes, where movement wrinkles into waves and traces its most fleeting forms, where the trees' reflections sparkle green, where the day divided by spiderwebs, air threads, stems, and showers is born and dies—where a hand, wet, surging out of the emerald water, is pearled with droplets, refined by rainbow light until it is only a pellicle of paleness, only wild rose petals and the woody wrinklings of leaves around flower buds in the dampness of daylight—while your waters play beneath the dragonflies.

THE MOTHER: At the communal fount soapy bubbles caress and surround our fresh-scrubbed linens.

THE HEART: Her eyes are nearly dead; her gaze is fixed: two pale and sickly eyes touched by unfamiliar breath grow dim and hazy as if the doctor were blowing on window glass in winter.

THE MOTHER: Her eyes—a faded, glassy, water blue—mist and blind her. Too cold: her extremities were freezing to the touch. We enveloped her in warmth.

THE HEART: She uses her hands to find her way.

THE MOTHER: Little by little her eyes begin to clear.

THE DAUGHTER: It is dark. The corridors of the labyrinth are narrowing.

THE HEART: While the vessels, the lifeblood, the fires are red.

THE MOTHER: Unable to see—the waters were black and stagnant.

THE DAUGHTER: I was lost and alone. I refused to learn. I refused to obey. I refused. I cried. I was so cold. And I missed you. I was always cold, the cold of constant hunger. And the darkness at sunset frightened me.

THE HEART: It is hard to see. So very hard. We must strain our eyes.

THE MOTHER: Come. . . . Come . . .

THE HEART: I welcome you. You are flesh and blood now, blood that millenniums have mixed and nourished.

THE MOTHER: You are here with me. Your gaze moves the stars; it plunges to the depths of the universe. You are life with me, life before me, behind me, within me, life below me, above me, at my right, at my left, the width of life, the length of life, the heighth of life, life in the heart, in the mouth, in the eye, in the ear of my love for love . . .

THE DAUGHTER: You charm me . . .

THE HEART: Particles of light collide at meteoric speeds.

THE DAUGHTER: I hear your voice.

THE MOTHER: And the sun rings my right hand, and the moon rings my left, as day and night give rhythm to the Earth.

THE DAUGHTER: At dawn day comes out of night, and I can see you shining.

THE MOTHER: Shining . . .

THE HEART: The heart pumps blood through the arteries, red like the hearth's hot coals.

THE DAUGHTER: The rays of light from the moon to the sun grow stronger.

THE MOTHER: My fingers in your tresses, in your braids, undo them, searching for you, decorating themselves with rings of your hair finer than spun silken threads, and my hand under your hair explores the bony hollow where your brain is enclosed, your brain whose nerves I feel ending in the blinking of your eyes under their long, curved lashes, and you look at me tenderly, sweetly, and my hand strokes you, caresses you.

THE DAUGHTER: Slowly, I feel my way forward . . .

THE MOTHER: I can sense you.

THE HEART: We are sensitive organisms. We know when life is sick, and we cry out; no law has the power to desensitize us. Life propagates itself in us through our cranial nerves, which branch out to guide us.

THE MOTHER: We open our hands.

THE DAUGHTER: I cross the nuclear flames.

THE HEART: Meteoric dust falls from the sky to the Earth. The vegetal radiance of the grass illumines us.

THE DAUGHTER: I inhale you through all of my pores. If I do not, night darkens my senses.

THE MOTHER: Flower-laden branches reflected in the fountain offer themselves to life's sweetness, to the hand that gathers them.

THE DAUGHTER: I was in great danger.

THE HEART: Wearers of goat horns, our mothers, far from the fallow land, lived behind briars and shrubs in the darkness of the grotto's entrails.

THE DAUGHTER: The moisture of the twilight mist wet me; it seemed as though my vision were dimming. And roots and lumps of soil came with the ferns, with the heather that I uprooted while crouching in your wooded womb. I did not know what I was seeking.

THE HEART: It was I calling out to you.

THE MOTHER: The first old woman sowed the ground around her hut with hex signs to ward off suffering. The second, in the steam arising from the Earth's opening, placed her sacrifice beneath the stars in her search for light.

THE DAUGHTER: I could not speak.

THE HEART: The light reflected by our skin bathed our union. We found each other in the energy emanating from our faces and hands.

THE DAUGHTER: You keep life flowing through me.

THE MOTHER: Fibers and nerves give our gestures a calming softness. We have hearts, blood vessels, lungs, intestines, organs, dilations, contractions. We are alive. We function. Blood rushes through us.

THE DAUGHTER: I could not bear the loneliness.

THE HEART: Forces confront one another, bumping, circulating, banging against blocked passageways, accelerating movements, flashes, and poundings. Life erupts through the tips of my fingers, opening my hands to caress you.

THE MOTHER: The liquids within me make movement easy. And my arms, made to hold, to clasp, search for warmth. . . . With my arms, with my hands, I reach toward you. I need to touch you, to caress you. And in my hands your flesh again becomes matter, pliable like the burgundy-red placenta once attached to my womb. And in my hands your skin materializes, your sensitized skin. And your blood's spinning cells produce a light that invades me when I touch you.

THE DAUGHTER: I cry out because I am afraid.

THE MOTHER: We are linked by the softness of warm flesh, by your breath, which I approach till I can hold it in my hands, till we merge, till I hear only the music of your breathing, your nostrils and half-opened lips. . .

THE DAUGHTER: I am not afraid now.

THE MOTHER: I stroke you.

THE HEART: We touch and discover each other. The simple mortar made of dirt and straw, the layer of Earth that was molded and pressed as it dried, the clay pot used for coffee, connect me to your muddy, earthy flesh. I have known no nourishment to equal this.

THE MOTHER: It is as though I could touch even your breath when it brushes me.

THE DAUGHTER: We are connected by animal passions.

THE MOTHER: When you walk, when I see your blood flow through the transparency of your skin, when your legs, your hips, your heels, energize your movements, when your skin radiates clarity, when I watch you, weigh you, contemplate you as if to gather life . . . then the sun is like foaming milk, there for the sipping.

THE HEART: Our blood flashes darkness and light.

THE DAUGHTER: Touch me. Touch me everywhere.

THE MOTHER: So good to touch you . . . to put my fingers on your violet pulse, on your spinal marrow, to feel connected to your heart, your glands, your uterus, your bladder, your lungs, your fluids, your ligaments, connected to life through your nerves, through my hands on your back. So good to touch you because you are alive, because life circulates under my fingers, under my hands, because your flesh is living; because, even dead, flesh stays alive in living flesh and living emotions, because death does not interrupt love, because life transmits life, because all the ages of the Earth circulate in our body, because watching life enlivens, because, even outside the body, the heart continues to beat . . .

THE HEART: We revitalize each other.

THE MOTHER: A shiver dances across your skin.

THE DAUGHTER: Perhaps between us there is not merely love but, rather, life. It possesses us.

THE HEART: Your skin glows.

THE MOTHER: Your hair shines. It is alive.

THE DAUGHTER: I speak.

THE MOTHER: You are vital; your presence fills me to overflowing. In handfuls I sow my feelings. And feelings give life to my words.

THE DAUGHTER: I see.

THE MOTHER: I brought you into this world.

THE DAUGHTER: I walk. . . . Or did I perhaps welcome *you* to this world?

THE MOTHER: It no longer matters.

THE DAUGHTER: When I hold your hand in mine, it is as though I were holding your heart. . . . They will not destroy us. They will not separate us.

THE MOTHER: They will not find us.

THE DAUGHTER: Your arms are long and white—long, long like life, which never ends, and white like the milk moving through me after I have drunk and eaten and, satisfied, grown drowsy.

THE HEART: One hundred and fifty square meters of bloody vessels water our lungs.

THE MOTHER: Are you my mother . . . or my daughter?

THE DAUGHTER: We can no longer say.

THE MOTHER: Our ancestor was the night.

THE DAUGHTER: Wooded Europe of dark forests, flush with lofty beeches and oaks.

THE HEART: Our fluids glisten.

THE MOTHER: They flow.

THE DAUGHTER: We are women, bodies with folds and rolls of flesh. There is something full and heavy about us . . . full like a cow's udder. We are fields of veins and arteries and nerves and blood.

THE HEART: Human.

THE MOTHER: From the trees I take my sugar and from pollen the dye for my hair and from hawthorns the jam to spread on pieces of bread in the basket sitting on the table and from the maple its oil.

THE HEART: I eat.

THE DAUGHTER: Your voice is silky.

THE HEART: They say that we devour each other, that we are cannibals, that we succumb to the pressure of our instincts—of blood infused with solar gases, that man is mortal, that we are the sisters of roots and underground waters and killing fevers.

THE DAUGHTER: But our shelter isolates us like a layer of flesh, like impenetrable skin, like the womb where we were formed.

THE MOTHER: Your eyes are clearing.

THE HEART: She rubs her downy legs, covered with hair that is long and silky like northern velvet.

THE DAUGHTER: The roundness of your shoulder guides my caress toward your dimples, toward your elbow, toward your wrist, down to your fingers, which grip me, capture me in their robust pinkness.

THE MOTHER: You shiver; you tremble; you answer me with your fibers, your cells, your ligaments, your curves.

THE DAUGHTER: In our embrace even the blue hue of your complexion speaks.

THE MOTHER: Without you I barely existed.

THE DAUGHTER: How your face lights up!

THE MOTHER: You are so close to me.

THE HEART: They battled the trees; they burned the trees; they kept the sap from rising; trunks were reduced to dust. They stopped, surrounded, and strangled the forest; they tilled the ground with pickaxes; they *killed* the trees. There were wars and hate. And now—pain and exhaustion. But, still, air nourishes the leaves.

THE DAUGHTER: Then day and night were one.

THE HEART: I could hear you, but I could not see you.

THE DAUGHTER: Death reduced life to gasps.

THE HEART: Men kill other men.

THE MOTHER: Stay like this, leaning against me. Let me soak in your heat, warm myself . . .

THE DAUGHTER: I draw love from love.

THE MOTHER: . . . comfort myself.

THE HEART: Their soldiers, armed with axes, tried to split through our soft, compact flesh, and their great hunters, their great falconers tracked and ambushed the fleeing beasts. Long tresses, spread out on the ground, looked like branches of a felled forest, while their weapons continue to disembowel and dismember.

THE DAUGHTER: But you and I are the origin, the source; we have found a refuge in warmth, in the beginnings of the body, and there was nothing before us. There *is* nothing except us—and we are at the start of life that is forming. We feel only love passing from body to body, and we are intact, and our velvet flesh muffles the noise of our organs until they are almost silent, and I absorb the moisture, the knowledge of your skin, by embracing you, by pushing my whole self against the blue-green curve of your pupil. I cherish you. My life renews itself at the hot springs of your strength.

THE MOTHER: And I support you with my strongest ligaments.

THE DAUGHTER: You nourish me at your breast. You pour into my mouth in waves that spill onto me, and I am filled to overflowing.

THE MOTHER: Being this close to you, having my skin against yours, frees me. Life is stable near your mouth, your hands. I am fed by my own milk.

THE DAUGHTER: Your milk comes in great swells.

THE HEART: We are . . . together. The newborn presses her lips to the nipple.

THE DAUGHTER: Life is young.

THE MOTHER: Flesh takes root in flesh, in roots and in nodes and in lumps of Earth, and . . . in the future.

THE HEART: Mounds of flesh press down upon us.

THE MOTHER: And we prepare to eat.

THE DAUGHTER: Your voice flows freely on, like waves of butter and cream.

THE MOTHER: And your trembling beckons my caress.

THE HEART: And the air in our lungs creates light and fiery heat.

THE MOTHER: The foaming cascade runs on. I squeeze out my milk through the tips of my breasts.

THE HEART: Roots intermingle, flesh consolidates, large mouthfuls of milk harden the breasts.

THE DAUGHTER: And our meal continues here in the midst of the forest, among the pines and oaks, in this resinous and leafy solitude, to the east of oceanic Europe, in this central western shelter, where ancient beech trees live on, where history began, where we are far from cities and towns; and barefoot I lean against the tree, I drape my milk-drenched robes over my arm, I touch the curve of the earthen mound with its smell of wild boar dung, and, gently, pressing your fingers against your chapped breast, you hold your nipple to my mouth.

THE MOTHER: Flowing waters carry soil down the hillsides.

THE HEART: As though it were raining milk.

THE MOTHER: We have averted ruin. Life does not dry up. Liquid energy spurts forth from the sun's surface.

THE HEART: And water recharges itself with helium.

THE DAUGHTER: The sun's straw torch burns in the blue sky, preparing the Earth for cultivation.

THE HEART: A child is born.

THE MOTHER: Tendrils of hair cast shadows on your face.

THE DAUGHTER: Woman disguises herself as the sun's radiance. Muscles glow red through her skin.

THE HEART: Thick, elastic fibers strengthen her breasts.

THE MOTHER: My stomach is a pouch.

THE DAUGHTER: Saliva gathers at the corners of your lips.

THE HEART: Sustenance pours into our body.

THE DAUGHTER: I like to burrow into your breasts, into the fatty part of your milk, inundating you with cream, molding you with my hands and mouth, and I want your fat to flow thick and your flesh to be nibbled, suckled, gnawed, sucked, nursed, and I want the substances of my feeding to flush my complexion. Mouths rub against mouths like branches against branches to light the fire that illuminates and warms.

THE MOTHER: Your tongue fashions the mixture that satiates you.

THE DAUGHTER: Your upper lip is edged with down.

THE HEART: Man, drawn up by my vagina, secretes the sticky substance that nourishes me. He impregnates me, oily, slippery, slow, and he leans heavily and moves without haste, and I take time to savor him. He filters through my kidneys, passes into my urine, gives himself mouthful by mouthful to me. My fingers, my hands, encourage the nurturing juices, the fine buttery fat. And man's substance flows from his full testicles, and his mass spreads itself upon me in the rivers, hormones, plains, fields, and forests of life's rich countryside.

THE MOTHER: Leaves absorb water, acid, and oxygen from the air.

THE DAUGHTER: Once upon a time, jaws hanging open and on four legs, women ate raw flesh and placentas. Eyes crazed, they tore themselves to pieces in front of the hearth and, delirious, held up their bloody members. They strung potato beads around their necks and poultry feathers around their waists.

THE MOTHER: The juice trickles out, drop by drop, as chewing transforms the solids into liquid balls. We smear ourselves with sticky clay slip, with sludge, with cow dung, with slime. We mark our aprons with ochre and excrement. On towels we spread out the stems of young onions. And in the cook-house we take the hardened, gelatinous proteins from their molds and begin to beat the fat into the meaty paste. We tear the cooked, juicy flesh with our shining teeth. We eat it and, then, wipe off our mouths.

THE DAUGHTER: Women's breasts are soft-curved masses.

THE HEART: Whose skin is marbled with veins.

THE DAUGHTER: And dawn clouds in the sky are like a violet's chalky petal.

THE MOTHER: The milk you bring up has soured in your stomach.

THE HEART: It must be daybreak.

THE MOTHER: Your flesh moves in nervous ripples from the trembling of your open nostrils and half-closed eyes to the delicate skin of your head, wet with warmth, resting in the hollow of my shoulder, and I rock you. I feel you sensitive and vulnerable in my arms, and the tenderness, the smoothness, of your cheek touching my skin. You are folded against me. You digest warmly, and your earlobe is warm, and you inhale through wide nostrils, and I contemplate you to the sound of your breathing while the liquids of life wet you. And in your blood-red world you move on. And, if a lock of hair, displaced by your movements or by the wind, falls into your eyes, I push it gently back from your forehead.

THE DAUGHTER: You sit and your knees, your calves, your bare toes bespeak simplicity.

THE HEART: Our ancestors bled.

THE MOTHER: You tremble.

THE HEART: Oxygen revivifies the blood's redness.

THE DAUGHTER: I am calmed by the fat, bones, muscles, and cartilage of your lap.

THE HEART: I hear the blood flow through my vessels.

THE MOTHER: Our link is this penetrating softness. . . . Such fair softness when your face turns toward me. Oh, let the haze 'round your head evaporate and your hair tease me. And let me absorb your passionate energy.

THE DAUGHTER: Our hands can touch the infinity of the universe. Let our hands skim, caress, and cradle the body's contours.

THE HEART: Let them grip, and let our fingers grasp the flesh.

THE MOTHER: Our skin is too tightly knit together to allow destruction in. Oh! hold me close, so very close . . .

THE HEART: Our skin is stretched and taut.

THE DAUGHTER: Let me be sheltered . . . within the reaches of your breath . . . within the hollow of your interlaced fingers . . . within your animal warmth— as in a stable or under a brooding hen's breast.

THE HEART: Hold fast!

THE DAUGHTER: I can hear you swallow.

THE MOTHER: You are even softer than your flesh.

THE DAUGHTER: Your lips are silken.

THE MOTHER: You grow tiny in my arms.

THE HEART: Outside the wind whips the trees, while inside the oil from the beechnut thickens like molasses or honey, and the muscles lodge deep in the body and the torso shelters its organs.

THE DAUGHTER: We are as tightly woven as the fibers that cover the skull. We form one membrane under the skin, under the hair, a connection neither bone nor flesh but as strong as the flexible matter in the nose, the eyes, the ears, the hands, the feet. It pulls us together inside a single covering that gives us form, makes us round, makes us soft, gives us this texture of tenderness. I so love to caress you . . .

THE HEART: Their bodies are one.

THE DAUGHTER: My mouth is wet from loving you.

THE MOTHER: My muscles grow heavy, conquered by this mass of life, by the goodness of your flesh, by the warmth of your breath on my skin as I caress you.

THE HEART: We sate ourselves with ourselves.

THE MOTHER: Her chest swells.

THE DAUGHTER: Wrap me in your nourishing fattening flesh.

THE HEART: In the grassy prairies of your hair.

THE MOTHER: Air penetrates my expanding tissues. Vermillion and scarlet matter harbors densely floating particles, while soldered masses detach themselves from my walls. Life carried along in the flood descends and begins to emerge, and our bodies reinforce each other's movements. My blood boils, my flesh explodes; forcing a passage, growing salty with milk; my blood cells, my plasma are electric, my belly, my breasts, are stretched, engorged, overfilled. They unfold themselves, their expansion mirrored in the release of red energy, swelling, bloating, bursting forth; and the other red matter, the blood clots, melt; and the umbilical cord presents its seven knots, and life empties into the day . . .

THE HEART: . . . and breaks the membrane with a cry.

THE DAUGHTER: You shine gloriously from the inside outward.

THE MOTHER: A pouch of warm water fell from my belly and inundated my thighs.

THE DAUGHTER: Blood surged through the placenta.

THE HEART: Perspiration calms the body's heat.

THE HEART: And still with my blood you were carried from the depths of matter's divisions to the birthing bed, where my muscles rest from the strain of pushing so hard . . .

THE HEART: Now you are one. You are out of danger.

THE MOTHER: I apply a dressing to your navel.

THE DAUGHTER: I lean against your throbbing heart. Still overwhelmed by the effort of birth, it beats and palpitates. You breathe more quickly . . .

THE HEART: The space between the sky and the Earth becomes transparent.

THE MOTHER: I cleanse you.

THE HEART: The effort brings such pleasure.

THE DAUGHTER: We lie here on the ground.

THE MOTHER: The walls of my muscles and skin have elastic contours.

THE DAUGHTER: Sap rises in the trees. The Earth is the source of all flesh.

THE MOTHER: Beech leaves cushion our nights.

THE HEART: The short pale hairs of your breast shine like a clay jug in the sun.

THE MOTHER: I wiped you off.

THE DAUGHTER: It is daytime. The sun lights a golden fringe of sky between my lashes.

THE HEART: It is day.

THE MOTHER: In spring the soil clothes itself in greens.

THE HEART: Let life spring from our palms.

THE DAUGHTER: And strong smells ooze from us.

THE MOTHER: Wounds scar over.

THE HEART: We notice the skin's appearance—its feel, its thickness, its texture.

THE DAUGHTER: I touch you . . .

THE HEART: We inhale the skin's odor.

THE DAUGHTER: We watch the fingers stretch out, the hands spread their cover . . .

THE HEART: Hands that can be cupped to scoop up nourishment . . .

THE DAUGHTER: Hands that can mix dough into a mealy paste . . .

THE MOTHER: To thicken soup . . .

THE DAUGHTER: To feed us . . .

THE MOTHER: I am content to be nourished by your hair, by your lashes, long and fine like the legs of field spiders among the wheat; I am content to see your butter hair with its golden-threaded reflections; I am content to chew you and roll you around in my mouth; content with the feel of bread after it has been worked by my tongue, like soil after a plowing.

THE DAUGHTER: Women's breasts are pierced at the end to let the cream flow out and wet the teeth, water the tongue.

THE HEART: Women's breasts are rounded huts; women's breasts are fatted sows.

THE DAUGHTER: Women's breasts are full like a pregnant womb. They fill the eager mouth like a soft-cooked egg.

THE HEART: You astonish me.

THE MOTHER: Your pulse beats like skin, fur, plumage, animals between my fingers, like everything that has blood, and I come so close to your flesh that I can touch the blood at work, propelled from your heart, circulating in your veins, in your arteries, in your capillaries, in your lungs. I can touch the blood that irrigates your organs underneath the covering of skin and mucus. I am so close that I can feel its pressure through the texture of your skin.

THE DAUGHTER: I breathe.

THE MOTHER: I swell.

THE HEART: My open hand blankets your skin with warmth.

THE MOTHER: Folds of skin enwrap you.

THE DAUGHTER: You feed me as though the pulse of my umbilical cord had not stopped. The pounding of the blood in your arteries injects your love into the cascading of my blood, into the cells of my nerve endings, into the pulp of my fingers. They push forward, searching for life.

THE HEART: The flow is torrential!

THE MOTHER: My hand explores your skin, your body.

THE DAUGHTER: I touch the large vein. Its bluish robes shine through your skin.

THE HEART: Oxygen makes the blood red; the skin sends out sparks of light.

THE DAUGHTER: Currents of internal light soften you. Daylight is diffused in your fatty denseness. I touch its velvet texture. I feel its warmth. I can almost see it.

THE HEART: We are close, so close . . .

THE MOTHER: The skin of our hands is porous.

THE DAUGHTER: We must preserve this closeness.

THE HEART: Live!

THE MOTHER: I will look after you, make life surge within you.

THE DAUGHTER: Time will develop both bodies and trees.

THE HEART: From cheese and milk calcium will build our teeth.

THE MOTHER: Eat!

THE DAUGHTER: Our organs will not stop producing heat, the currents of tenderness that warm us . . .

THE MOTHER: My fingers sink into your flesh. I hold you. Do not be afraid. I hold you close. And when you push against my hand the folds of skin flatten. They lie down like the valves of the intestines when food passes through. Your warm, ruddy softness nourishes the hands that close around you, prolonging softness, prolonging warmth, slowing the passage of your skin into mine.

THE HEART: I breathe in and out.

THE MOTHER: I gather you into my arms. I pull you to my heart. Your skin lights mine. Your moisture makes me sticky, slippery, drenched, wet. It is good. Lymph bathes our cells. I feel you inside me.

THE HEART: I cover you with my hands.

THE DAUGHTER: You bruise my skin.

THE MOTHER: You stick to my fingers.

THE DAUGHTER: You are so near I can caress you with my tongue.

THE HEART: You have passed through me; you have traversed my boundaries.

THE DAUGHTER: I put one hand above you and one below you.

THE MOTHER: Outside in the forest garden pints of sweat ooze from the lettuce leaves. Seeds sprout.

THE HEART: We are one with the blood that circulates in us. Our fine skin grows even finer in our caresses, in our hands, until it is transformed from softness to life, like love linking one body to another, like capillaries joining the arteries to the veins . . .

THE DAUGHTER: Like small pieces of dough sticking to the hands . . .

THE MOTHER: Like the tongue reaching out to taste . . .

THE HEART: And your mouth shoots air into my breath . . .

THE MOTHER: And your mouth full of food presses its lips to my breast. I become stronger.

THE HEART: Golden and bloody film, cloth of the tactile organ, woven by the softness of words, woven by the softness of gestures, your skin filters the rays of light.

THE MOTHER: I hear something; I hear noises, someone moving.

THE DAUGHTER: Let me see what it is.

THE MOTHER: No, stay, I will go. But put the cheese on the drying racks.

THE DAUGHTER: Who is it?

THE MOTHER: A man and a woman. They are wounded and return from battle.

THE HEART: We should wipe dry their foreheads, their temples . . .

THE DAUGHTER: Calm them . . .

THE MOTHER: So that they may know warmth, show them into the fullness and softness of our cushions of flesh, that they may merge with the folds, the wrinkles, the smiles of our skin, our breasts, into the words that we whisper so softly . . .

THE DAUGHTER: Into our openings, our arms, our hands, our kisses, there where our life, through layers of muscle and fat, through lips, skin, and passion, makes us whole and animates us.

THE MOTHER: We do not want to suffer anymore. We will not surrender to despair.

THE HEART: Something soft is coming into the world . . .

THE MOTHER: With our hands we can turn the world into a caress.

THE DAUGHTER: The day infuses the atmosphere with a grass-green light, a grape leaf light, a bean-red light, a mulberry light, and from the forest comes a glow of yellow-gold.

THE HEART: We breathe, and our strength grows . . .

Hélène Cixous

DESPITE HER MYRIAD INTELLECTUAL and creative endeavors, Hélène Cixous (b. 1937) has built a remarkably coherent career. Inspiring teacher and lecturer at the University of Paris and abroad, the most prominent figure of the Parisian feminist publishing house Des Femmes, essayist of vision and conviction, notably of "The Laugh of the Medusa" (1975), inspired reader of great international female talents such as Brazilian writer Clarice Lispector, author of some thirty prose texts that experiment, among other things, with linguistic games and autobiography (*Vivre l'orange* [To Live the Orange, 1979]) or newly sexed pronouns (*Illa,* 1980; and *La,* 1976), Cixous has ceaselessly required her readers and students to think about the connections between language production and the place of women in society. Through her insistence on the liberating potential of writing she has also encouraged many women to take pen in hand themselves.

She has produced a vivid body of theatrical works, which range from avant-garde protestations of Freudian concepts (*Portrait de Dora* [Portrait of Dora, 1976]) to historical epics that link a broad-based philosophy of "mothering" to the functioning of theater (*L'Histoire terrible mais inachevée de Norodom Sihanouk, Roi du Cambodge* [The Terrible but Unfinished Story of Norodom Sihanouk, King of Cambodia, 1985]; and *L'Indiade ou l'Inde de leurs rêves* [The Indiad or India of Their Dreams, 1987]). In one of her most recent plays, *On ne part pas, on ne revient pas* (You Don't Go Away, You Don't Come Back, 1991) she stages the anguish of living and growing into a couple and paradoxically into oneself. Her own textual inventiveness, heeding in part Jacques Lacan's psychoanalytical reformulations and Jacques Derrida's attention to language as the site of cultural disruption and negotiation, affirms a libidinal economy of expansiveness. Cixous's work makes tangible the empowerment contained in the postmodern notion of the "slipperyness of meaning."

Of her ten plays published to date, *The Name of Oedipus: Song of the Forbidden*

Hélène Cixous stares intently at a rehearsal of her play *Portrait of Dora* (1976), while director Simone Benmussa (to her immediate right) confers with an assistant. (Photo by Roger Viollet.)

Body, originally written and performed as the lyrics for a muscial score by André Bouchourechliev in 1978, can be placed among her dramatic productions meant to posit theater as the space for questioning sexuality.[1] Director Claude Régy's staging, in fact, concentrated on building a stark and extremely intense web of recitation and modernistic vocalizations to convey the convoluted interaction of conscious and unconscious discourses. In *The Name of Oedipus,* as in *Portrait of Dora,* Cixous adopts a theatrical form to challenge what is considered to be the "normal" relationship of the body to unconscious desire and patriarchal cultural heritage.

Her most recent history plays, in contrast, imagine theater as a place of innocence, a free-flowing transformational space in which cultural and political differences can be probed. In both *Oedipus* and the later plays, however, utopias are suggested and egos transcended. Linguistic alchemy and mystical love promise to abolish the dangers of difference.

In *The Name of Oedipus: Song of the Forbidden Body* Cixous comes to grips with the incest taboo insofar as it reinforces a psychosocial order that rigidly incarcerates "men" and "women." Confined by the well-known plot, Cixous begins, nevertheless, by fragmenting the characters: all the principal roles are doubled; no one character has total authority. Cixous also challenges Freud's interpretation of Sophocles' hero by creating a split Oedipus who is ultimately incapable of surrendering to the city's demands. Moreover, her lucid and accepting "Jocastas" refute, from the beginning, the distance that the laws of the city and "the father" have created. Jocasta's struggle is not to give in but, rather, to move out of a system based on binary opposites.

The play's title, and especially the subtitle, suggests the playwright's intention. Because of its homophonic quality, "le nom d'Oedipe" can mean either the "name" (*nom*) or the "no" (*non*) of Oedipus. Cixous contends that Oedipus' name determines and delimits his possibilities. Oedipus is "Oedipus"—he who (unintentionally) kills his father and sleeps with his mother, a man who cannot freely claim his acts once he completely understands them. His "no" is his refusal to cast off his name, his role, an inability to reject the myth that defines him as incestuous and homicidal. Cixous's Oedipus says no to the passion he has known for Jocasta, no to life conceived as the liberty to create oneself without subscribing to expressed norms. The myth of "Oedipus" imprisons Oedipus. The more he knows, the more Oedipus falls apart, disintegrating into the myth of himself.

Jocasta, on the contrary, embodies the dream of primary love: she knows the secret but chooses not to know. She does not see herself as bound by political responsibility and the internal laws of conformity. She sings her forbidden body, delivering in song and dialogue her passion and her desire. Through Cixous's

Jocasta what society has proscribed finds a voice. Jocasta is "the mother who exults in orgasm," a totally different mother from the sexless and nonorgasmic Madonna who embodies the essential maternal myth. Chanting and intoning, she subverts a syntactically ordered, male-centered and -generated language in pulsating verses in praise of her love. Like Molly Bloom, Jocasta says yes.

Jocasta dominates the stage in seven of the play's twelve movements, sharing the focus with Oedipus in only four. Her character has appropriated the energy and "oedipal drive" for self-assertion supposedly limited to men. She challenges the fundamental taboo against incest, an interdiction presumably based on society's need to exchange women in order to maintain its structure.

In her *Oedipus* Cixous upsets any definite spatiotemporal frame through switching verb tenses and juxtaposing confrontational scenes with memory sequences. Because of this associative scenic logic, because of this absence of temporal and emotional progression, the play's revelation scene, in which Oedipus learns of his patricide and incest, is experienced as anticlimactic. Indeed, Tiresias, rather than prefiguring Oedipus' end and representing the cosmic order as in Sophocles' tragedy, is just another member of the Chorus.

Through language Jocasta, on the other hand, recreates the world as she wishes to see it. Furthermore, she attempts to convince Oedipus to redefine himself. But Oedipus has slipped away, out of reach, into silence. Muteness, rather than blindness, handicaps him. This speechless withdrawal supplies the controlling metaphor for Oedipus' plight. It supercedes the image of blindness that structures the original Sophoclean drama. Thus, Cixous' Oedipus, rather than suffering through a voyage of self-discovery, agonizes in his reluctance to acquire a new language. This is what, in effect, constitutes the "plot," a dramatic warning against the tyranny of single signifiers.

In a poetic apotheosis made possible by rejecting linguistic laws of gender and number and accepting the alchemy of the verb, a new being emerges at the play's close. Once Jocasta has expired Oedipus finally speaks, incorporating the mother-lover in his last monologue by matching a singular French verb to a plural pronoun: "Nous continue" (We continue/s). "His" enthralling love song creates an ongoing present, a space beyond words and time, a dimension usually outside the limits of narration, in which "woman" is not the object of desire, in which characters are awash in one another.

No longer uniquely male, the Oedipus character is now dual-sexed, doubled, bisexual. The mother, and not the symbolic father posited by Jacques Lacan in his rereading of Freud, has been essential to his acquisition of language. This Oedipus is a character-in-progress, an unfinished and open-ended mythic figure, a utopian projection of an emerging human undefined by the old "symbolic order."

NOTES

Part of this introduction appeared in Judith G. Miller, "From Cocteau to Cixous: S/M/ Othering Oedipus," *Themes in Drama*, 1985, 203–11.

1. This piece was originally performed as an opera at the 1978 Avignon Theater Festival with the following staff and cast: Music: André Boucourechliev; text: Hélène Cixous; choral direction: Stéphane Caillat; instrumental ensemble, music management: Yves Prin; staging: Claude Régy; set: Jean-Paul Chambas; costumes: Patrice Cauchetier; Jocasta 1: Sigune von Osten (soprano part); Jocasta 2: Catherine Sellers (spoken part); Oedipus 1: Claude Meloni (baritone part); Oedipus 2: Michaël Lonsdale (spoken part); Tiresias 1: Daniel Berlioux (singing part); Tiresias 2: Axel Bogosslavsky (spoken part). In this translation we have not signaled the difference between the speaking and singing roles. A director, however, might choose to give each part to two, or to several, different actors playing Jocasta, Oedipus, Tiresias, and the Chorus. Actors could be cast according to the pitch and resonance of their voices. The result would be a type of "tone poem" rather than an opera. It would be possible to use the variations in typography of this translation, which follow the original text's, as a guide to this kind of casting option.

Hélène Cixous

The Name of Oedipus: Song of the Forbidden Body

Characters

JOCASTA   OEDIPUS   TIRESIAS   THE CHORUS

PROLOGUE *(All, incantatory)*

Afraid	Afraid	No!	Without
Afraid	The lover	I do not want	
I am afraid	Will die		Sense
Mother	Not to return	To die!	
Child	Afraid	No!	Senselessly
See each other	Not knowing	I do not want	
Die	Where	Not to	Bloodlessly
The Mother cries	The body		
The child	Is	Die	Bloody
Hears	For	Without	
Her	Burial		Sense
Mother!	Afraid		
Mother!	His dying		Incense
Do you not	Alone		
See	Fallen		The child's
I am dying	About to die		
Mother!			Senses
She dies	Mourn		Slipping
Afraid	The lover		
To see his death	Dead		Away
	In the street		
To die first!			With

253

Afraid   Stay
To see her   No one
Dead   Alone
Dead   Lone   Holding
                    Lone
                    Lone   Embracing
                    Lone
                                        Him.

                                        Murmurs
                                        Mothers plead with death
                                        The child first
                                        Once dead would not see
                                        The dying
                                        Mother
                                        Mama
                                        Do you not
                                        See
                                        My death
                                        Coming?
                                        Mother
                                        Speak
                                        To me
                                        Speak to me
                                        One more
                                        Time.

JOCASTA: You
           My life
           Stay, today
           My love
           Stay for me
           Entirely.
           Do not move away
           From me
           One second.
           Do not go outside
           Do not answer anyone

Do not hear anything
But my voice.
This once
Because *I* want it.
Do not be the king
Stay for me
Be mine
Forget the world
Forget the town
Forget the time.
Do not be someone
Today.
O my love
Be my love
Be my blood
Be my bones, be in my bones
My marrow fired up.
Forget men,
Women, the dying.
They do not call
They do not cry
They do not die
They do not blame you
For not going out
To save them.
They do not crawl
In the streets
In their own feces
Begging death
To come and rescue them.
There is no one in Thebes
No need to go out.
There is no town out there
No Thebes, no streets
Not one cat, not one ghost
Of even a child.

JOCASTA: *No, Oedipus! Do not be Oedipus,*
Today, you are not the one
They are calling.

Do not be the one they beg,
Disown the dying,
The envious, disown the name
They cast on you.
Come to me, come closer,
Closer still
And do not be him.
Become yourself just with me
For me as I am you for yourself
And I shall tell you our true names.

OEDIPUS: *No, even love cannot*
          Blind me.
          How could I enjoy the flesh
          Of love
          And ignore death
          Feasting outside?
          Woe! To loose my senses, to forget,
          To allow the weeping? . . . No
          Even if my mother . . .

JOCASTA: *Ah, do not say: mother, do not say: death.*
          Forget death forget
          Oedipus. Give me
          Not even a day, but an hour
          And then . . .

OEDIPUS: *Then?*

JOCASTA: *One hour only, but no limits*
          And no names.
          If only you knew who you are! Stay and I
          Shall tell who you will be.
          O my lover son, my lover
          My husband son, my lover
          My mother my life, you.
          And then . . .
          Be. Be the one you want
          The one you need.

JOCASTA: Stay
          Not even for an hour.
          Only for a time . . .
          Time without length, barely a minute
          Without depth, without time.

But a moment. . . . Profound enough,
Present, ancient enough.
So our entire story may be relived in it
All at once.
For the last time.
Pray, give me this instant!
This nothing.
More than all things to me.
Give me the gaze
That unveils everything.
That would tell me our life
In one flash.
Then I will not hold you back.
Give it to me, thrust it at me.
Turn that face toward me

JOCASTA: *Which makes me breath*
Which means: I know you, I keep you.
You are in me, even if one of us were dead.
Not the one that the void disfigures.
Do not look at me without smiling,
Without telling me with your eyes: "I am not leaving; yes
I am staying: when I am gone, you are me. You are us both."

JOCASTA: Do not look at me absent. Look at me present.
In you as we were yesterday.
Where are you? You, who are here without yourself?
Where are you? You, who are not here?
You are here, and you are not . . .
How did you leave? Without yourself?
Without me?
Answer me! Beckon to me!
Do not leave me by myself
In front of you!
Such silence! Suddenly this boundless
Heavy silence, your silence
Unfolded over my head . . .
I have already heard this silence
Fall.

CHORUS: *Suddenly his face is empty.*
She would like to reach it,
To touch it, to caress it

With a word, to touch his chin
To lay
A word, on his eyelid, his eye
To wound him slightly.
But a barrier,
A glass barrier forms
And darkness flows
Between their bodies
And his body is gone.

JOCASTA: The heaven above splits open.
A dark heaven descends from the other. Its dark drapes rush forth.
I have already seen the heavens bleed.
The world has been shattered. A dark heaven poured out;
It was the Primeval Terror.
Nothing could stop it.
Darkness flowed, flooded forth.
It was the doomed night. Dark tears drenched me
As if the gods
Who do not exist
Were crying, crying over me,
Over my face, all over my neck,
My shoulders, my breasts, crying his tears.
I bathed in terror,
Paralyzed. I cannot even
Close my eyes
To stop watching the night
That continues to fall, continues,
Continues.
This silence . . . opens. I am hurled
Into fright. And times closes upon me.

JOCASTA: **There is a silence in my story**
That I cannot forget. My father's final silence.
Night was falling. I was walking across the garden of
  childhood.
A fear made me stop. I could see my father wavering in the
Distance.
He was out there. I sensed him.

I knew there would be no worse sight ever. A silence was
Spreading.
He was growing stiff.

JOCASTA: I could hear him panting, his body bent
Forward
Waiting without a motion. He was a young and grave man,
    watching
His own death.
I was standing at the corner of childhood, in front of a tree,
Amid silence.
Out toward a sky descending lower and lower. His agony gave me
Roots.
I did not see his new face. I cannot tell of it.
What was that sudden face?

CHORUS/
TIRESIAS: Seek no more! Imagine!
A scene without a witness.

JOCASTA: I cannot forget.
Yet I can hardly tell of it. I was unable to move.
I watched him in the distance. He was drifting further away.
I wanted to pray, to beg. My voice was gone.
He was bent over. Intent. The air grew cold.
A barrier stood between us. Engrossed in his dying
I was his child, he my mother
And I watched him leave.

JOCASTA: SUDDENLY THIS THOUGHT: "I KNEW IT."
WHAT WAS TAKING PLACE HAD TO BE
I WAS SURE OF IT, I WAS EXPECTING IT.

JOCASTA: His face suddenly turned
Against me, eyes full of anger.
The air became darker. His look was sending me away.
He gave me glances of hostility:
"What are you doing here!
Go away! Off, off with you!"
The barrier stopped his voice. I did not hear:
"Off with you!" I did not hear the pain, the shame,
The softness in his rage.
"Off with you! Do you not see I am dying?"
I could see it. I was about to see it. I would never see it.

TIRESIAS: . . . You should not have watched.

JOCASTA: . . . I did not hear. I guessed.
I obeyed. With closed eyes.
I could see him no more. I did not see him die.
I had just seen him for the last time.
I didn't see him dead. The last time he was alive.
Sending me away with his look. I stepped back; I left.
The last time
His look was pushing me away.
I left. I did not come closer.
The end must have come. I know it must have.
I can still feel myself moving back, step by step,
Until the last moment
Without a cry, without calling his name out,
Without hope. I kept silent. I saw him no more.
I left; I was outside; I had just lost his life.

The sky opens. Night falls upon me. I see the worst.
What a daughter cannot see without losing her blindness.
Since then, no childhood left, no peace.
Why could I not call out his name
To hold him? Speak the words that stop death?

JOCASTA: THAT THOUGHT: I KNEW YOU WOULD DIE:

CHORUS: . . . WHERE DID THAT THOUGHT COME FROM?

JOCASTA   . . . MY DESTINY WAS TO LOSE YOU ALIVE: TO NOT SEE YOUR
DEATH: TO BE UNABLE TO CALL YOU BACK TO ME.

JOCASTA: And ever since I have felt suspended
Between his life and his death.
A death that will never be real to me.

JOCASTA: BETWEEN THE MOMENT BEFORE DEATH
AND THE MOMENT OF DEATH.

JOCASTA: I did not touch him: I did not lay my head upon his chest:
He did not take me in his arms; I did not kiss his mouth.
No one told me his final name.

Lost without being lost.
Withdrawn. Become. Begone.

Never seen but alive. Disappearing.

Time broke down. Silence spread.
I felt the past sink. Suddenly.

I am falling and no longer present. Solitude closes in upon
    me.
I no longer know where my life is.
My life is here. But I do not know where here is.

TIRESIAS: AND EVER SINCE THEN NOT KNOWING IF THE OTHER
    IS STILL ALIVE OR ALREADY DYING:

JOCASTA: Terror has returned.
    It began with a new fear.
    I heard the city crying. The word *afraid*
    Resounding. Afraid, afraid, afraid, mingled with names, with
        calls
    Of tenderness and worship, and I could hear his bold
    And gentle voice, the tireless answer of his passion. The word
    Afraid, afraid
    Rising, expiring, vanishing among the names that
    Urged him to come, that elected him.
    Their voices unchaste, naive wanting him
    For a god. As if Afraid had become this man's first name.
    Fear pervaded me. It was an unknown fear.

CHORUS: *When she heard how the city*
    Had called him out
    In a low voice, had spoken his name
    In a trembling voice
    Of love, of shyness,
    She suffered.

JOCASTA: A sharp, beastly fear. I felt wounded.
    What pain! Oh city!
    My journey through a long stifling night had just ended.
    This city . . . resembles that night.

    I did not tell him my fear.
    Fear of any moment when he is elsewhere,
    Seen by others, followed, entreated, desired.
    My fear, my resentment. His need.

A good king, a good father. How could I not resent him?
"Is my love not enough for you?" He would entreat me:
"Promise you will never have any king but me."
"I swear it. Never a king but you." I swore.
What about me? You never swore to me.

CHORUS: *He is a man. As with all men*
            His desire is
            Always the same:
            To stand great and pure in his children's eyes after his death.
            To be, in the children's eyes, the only king for you.
            It's not enough.

JOCASTA: They follow him, they conjure him up, they trust him,
            They detain him, they wish him well, they love him.
            Elsewhere,
            I can hear the city, her woman's voice calling to him
            A thousand times stronger than mine.

CHORUS: *That is normal. He is a man.*
            He is a child. Never adored enough.
            No love could ever love him
            As much as he would wish.

JOCASTA: No.
            Not a child. He is the father he never had.
            The father without fault, without threat, the boundless father
            He would have liked to have. Powerful and gentle like a mother.
            And that city is his daughter, the one he loves, his lover.
            She resembles him, I can feel it.
            She has a body, I sense it, I imagine her face.

CHORUS: *What does she give him?*
            What did you not give?

JOCASTA: All that he does not want from me.
            Her needs, her distress, her fragility.
            Her voice—so weak. Who could resist it?
            She draws him. He is drawn.
            I understand it. Such a voice. The softness
            Of a sad humid breeze. Irresistible.
            Weak *and* strong.

JOCASTA: *The strength of weakness.*
            The moment he hears her whisper. "Come," he comes,
            He dashes forth. And he forsakes me.

Such a feeble voice. It is natural.
The moment I hear the city call him,
An awesome pain strikes me. Grabs me by the throat.

JOCASTA: I am *not* forsaken. I am sure of it.
The voice pulls him. It exiles me.
Distance
Pushes me away.

CHORUS: *Sends her away. Faraway.*
Distance sneaks between their bodies.
Distance grows.

JOCASTA: The word *distance* sickens me.
I have no word to counter it. I am so faraway.
Distance swells, it takes over, the world diminishes.

When he left . . . a sentence formed on my lips.
I thought:
"He just left." It was a simple sentence
Heartrending.
A phrase of cruel innocence.
It was like those sentences I used
To begin our story.
Transported with joy, with ecstasy
I would say: "He is here!"
And I said: "You came back!"
And I kept telling myself:
"He has just arrived!"
And then I told myself:
"He just left."
It was the same sentence: I started
With terror.

CHORUS: *When? Where? Did he just . . . leave?*
Do you mean years ago or yesterday?

JOCASTA: Yesterday: years ago.

JOCASTA: *The pain was abominable. Life destroying.*
Fangs sunk into my heart
Sucking my blood. Poisoning me.

JOCASTA: I thought:
"He should not have come."
The cause is his coming.

He could have stayed away.
I would have waited for him. I would still be waiting.
That thought repulsed me.

If he comes back. . . . When he comes back
I will tell him, I will not hide it from him.

It was hard not to scream.
I could not understand.
Such pain! With no reason.

CHORUS: *Was it seeing him leave that hurt you so?*

JOCASTA: Hearing him answer
The other's call.
He said: "I am coming. Here I am."
In such a strong and firm voice.
As though she were his daughter.
And he, her divine mother and father.

CHORUS: *Because the city called on him*
It was natural
Not to waste a minute, not to look back
Or even glance at you. It did not mean:
"You do not exist for me."

JOCASTA: Natural to reassure her
With a tender, godlike voice?
At once answering her call. Without taking time to tell me
"I am coming back. I will be back?"

CHORUS: *He did not say: "I will be back."*
But he did not say: "I will not."

JOCASTA: When he comes in,
I will make fun of fear, the moment
I hear his step, even before
He comes in. At a sign of him,
A word, the most remote echo
Of his voice, of his presence
Fear will be gone, forever.
The moment he comes in.
My fear did not come from me.
I believed him. Did he not
Swear to me? I would never dare

Forfeit my trust. Trust
Did not fail me. It was faith
That bowed.

CHORUS: *Do you think he might have . . .*
Did he not swear . . .
No trust? Since when?
Why?
Before leaving,
Would he not have told you . . . ?

JOCASTA: *Nothing.*
Just before going out, he was standing by the door, his back to me,
He spoke a few words.
I think they were:
"How brief life will have been."
But I could not swear to it.

TIRESIAS: The oracle spoke to Tiresias. It said: "Rise up, go to Thebes, the great ailing city, and prophesy against Oedipus for the stench has risen even to me." Tiresias stood up, wanting to flee. Messengers stopped him.

JOCASTA: I tell you: listen to me.
Do not listen to him.
You must know not to know.
To withdraw.

CHORUS: *—Listen to her!*
—Do not listen to him!
—He will never change.
—Still the same thirst?
—And she—so weary, exhausted.

OEDIPUS: I must go
To what I fear most.
What I dread
Beckons me.
As if the Singing Beast
Were coming back.
Or else her living shadow
To defy me, to point
The danger out to me.

CHORUS: *—Is he deaf?*
            —He has ears only for Horror . . .
            —He only listens to the voice
              That speaks of terror.

JOCASTA: Do not listen to it!
            Listen to me!
            Do not get trapped
            By blackmail!
            Come, come away!

CHORUS: *—Do not listen*
            —Listen
            —You must know
            —Not to know

OEDIPUS: To love each other is not enough.
            The end of the story
            Must be lived for love to be
            True.
            Come, let us go further,
            To the end, both together.
            I say: come, I want
            To live through this mystery with you.
            Do you know me?

JOCASTA: I know you.
            You always want to get closer
            To the source. I am responsible.
            I was unable
            To give you the love that brings peace.
            Unable to wean you.

CHORUS: *—He could only be happy*
            If he were the maker of light.
            —There is no source.
            —There is never real light,
            Not enough light for him.

OEDIPUS: I am not
            A man of doubts and disguises.
            To lack light
            Is to lack air.

JOCASTA: Why believe
            The oracle's poisoned tongue?

Escape from what is concealed.
Do not look for it.
Do not go out. Stay here.

OEDIPUS: My life for the answer!

CHORUS: *To fulfill and not fulfill*
What the oracle did not predict.
A consuming desire for death.
For dying.

OEDIPUS: What do you know?

TIRESIAS: Nothing
That can be spoken.
What I know cannot be told.

OEDIPUS: What stops you from speaking?

TIRESIAS: Words. The truth.

OEDIPUS: You are blind but not mute.
Your silence destroys me.
Tell me the name of the man
On whose account the city is tortured.
Speak, speak!

TIRESIAS: What cannot be spoken, you might hear
Another way. But you are only
An ordinary man. You do not see truth
As long as words have not pointed to it. Encased it.
It is not forbidden to know.
Look for yourself.

CHORUS: *—They struggle*
In the dark.
Because of the secret.
—One slows down, the other
Hastens the end.
—One preserves for the other
One last day of blindness.
—A struggle of words with the secret.

OEDIPUS: You let us hover between Life and Death!
Mothers will call down curses on you.

CHORUS: *—Soon*
No Mercy!

TIRESIAS: You are
Strong but

Weak.
I saw you confront the Sphinx.
You see nothing, you guess nothing.
You speculate, calculate.
No birds nor gods
Reveal anything to you,
Nor the oracle of your blood.

CHORUS: *—One suspended*
Between the said and the unsaid.

OEDIPUS: He is mad. You are horrifying!

TIRESIAS: Listen: I have nothing to teach you. Listen:
The worst will be known. You already know
without knowing. You cannot avoid it.
You already know what you will learn.

CHORUS: *—What man?*
What mortal can understand
What the gods want?
Their desires are not ours.

TIRESIAS: Slave of words. I shall speak . . .

OEDIPUS: Your words interest me no longer.

TIRESIAS: I shall speak. Your terror will erupt.

OEDIPUS: Too late. I have no trust left in you.

TIRESIAS: Stop seeking to avoid the truth.
You are the one you fear.
The one you cannot find.
Did you hear me?

OEDIPUS: No.

TIRESIAS: Ah! but you did hear me. You know
Who you are. Yourself,
The murderer.

OEDIPUS: You do not scare me.
Your words do not reach me.

TIRESIAS: You are not deaf.
You are the one,
Yourself, the calamity, the poison,
The cure, the source of torture, of salvation.
You have heard me.

OEDIPUS: There is a force in his voice
That no man could break.

It enchains me. I want to resist,
But it is stronger than I am.

CHORUS: *He will not escape.*
—There is a voice
In the blind man's voice
That reminds me of . . .
—What voice?
A sad voice, ancient
And inexorable.
—More ancient than memory.

OEDIPUS: There is a voice saying:
"You want" against my own will.
If it so desires
I shall want what I should never want.

CHORUS: *A voice that encloses the world.*
Like a wall.
—More ancient than the city.
More distant than the past.
—Which does not know all that it does not know.
—An ancient voice, more ancient than all the past.

TIRESIAS: You would have heard it tomorrow.

OEDIPUS: You said I am the one?

TIRESIAS: You are the one you hate.

OEDIPUS: I beg you
Say no more.

TIRESIAS: There is no more to tell.
You have lost your blindness.
Oedipus has lost the night.

JOCASTA: Thought returns, once cast away, returns
To tell him. No! To call him
With my voice, not with words that bite,
That lacerate the throat.
To make him hear the secret
Only with the song, the murmur of the blood,
Senseless wish, to tell him with my eyes, without words:
"Before leaving promise you will
Look into my face . . . my life . . . entirely

So you can see then who I am,
So you may understand all
The strength with which I love you. I will have loved you."
Such a thought, not to be thought.
Let chance decide.
Chance, chases away . . . if only
To tell him so softly, so quietly,
So secretly, without moving my lips,
Without telling him, to breathe the strangeness,
The image into him while he does not heed me.
Slowly, tenderly, to draw him by force of love,
To bring him closer and closer and tell him his name.
No, I shall not tell him.
Chance . . . but he may never know.
If only I could be sure he is about to know!

CHORUS: IT IS BEST—AS HE WILL KNOW—THAT YOU
            SHOULD HAVE BROUGHT HIM SO CLOSE.
            HE ALREADY KNEW; HE WOULD HAVE ALWAYS KNOWN—OR
                ELSE—HE
            WOULD SURELY KNOW ONE DAY.

JOCASTA: I had already told you in a dream,
            In daydreaming,
            And now, my lover son,
            Who is waking?
            Now, who will you be?

CHORUS: BRING HIM THERE ON THE VERGE
            EXTREMELY CLOSE, JUST WHERE HE DOES NOT QUITE KNOW
                HE KNOWS
            WHAT HE ALREADY KNOWS, BUT ELSEWHERE, AND WHAT HE
                WILL CEASE
            TO FORGET.

OEDIPUS: What if I told her?
            The terrifying
            Tide of words.
            My throat is gorged with blood.
            I am choking.
            If I told her! And then!

If I did, without meaning to
Tell her, at last, to have told her
At last! But I can no longer
Breathe.
I am choking.
Horrid agony.
No use to tell,
Horror. Words elude me.
Silence eludes me.
I feel my soul
Eludes me. Outside myself.
My head! My head!

OEDIPUS: *I no longer know if*
What is true
Is not false.

CHORUS: *She says: "Speak to me*
Tell me, my dear, my love."
She says: "I am here.
I am always here."

OEDIPUS: To tell her: a disaster
Sends me away into exile.

CHORUS/
JOCASTA: *—It is dark, she is patient.*
You can say it.
—I am not afraid. I am here,
It is I, my love,
Me, alone, with you.

OEDIPUS: To tell her all myself;
No longer knowing who is me.
Self without self.
But it is I who never stops
Suffering, I who stops
Being myself.

OEDIPUS: If I could only tell her:
Call me! Make me come back
To myself! Tell me the name
That brings me back!

CHORUS/
JOCASTA: *—She calls you.*

—I call you: My love!
I listen to you. I keep you.
You are here, love,
Before me.

OEDIPUS: What I will not tell anyone
            Not even my mother.
            What I cannot tell
            Myself
            I shall tell you.
            Will you hear me?

CHORUS/
JOCASTA: *—She calls you.*
            —I call you: My love!
            I listen to you. I keep you.
            You are here, love,
            Before me.

JOCASTA: I will understand you.
            Even if you should speak a foreign tongue to me,
            I shall understand you.

CHORUS: *Man . . .*
            Sees himself hunted down
            Turned a stranger
            Even to himself . . .
            On the verge
            Of tears.
            But no tears come.

OEDIPUS: If I should tell you: "I killed my mother.
            I killed her—with my own hands?"

CHORUS: *Man's need:*
            To be the son of the wife;
            Lover, to be the redeemed
            Child; to be the apple
            Of her eye.

JOCASTA: I will accept what you have done.
            You can tell me.

CHORUS: *She would understand*
            Ahead of time
            What he had done.

OEDIPUS: I will tell you.

All will be told. And then?
Fear. And plunging even further,
Deeper. Too far already.
Do not look at me.
I will tell you everything. Close your eyes.

JOCASTA: *Eyes closed*
            As if you were asleep
            My night body around you.

JOCASTA: My night body around you
            As if you were asleep.

OEDIPUS: I see myself.
            I am standing.
            At the crossroad
            A black road cuts
            A white road.
            The sun has turned black.
            Two snakes rise before me.
            I cannot proceed.
            The snakes stand in my way.
            I cannot step back.
            Lightning strikes a rock.
            I feel my heart stop,
            My eyes revulse.
            I see myself in front of the smitten rock.
            Blood flows from the wound.
            The white road has vanished.
            I hear the Earth moan.
            Suddenly a man at my side.
            I did not see him come,
            Right against me,
            I cannot turn around,
            Leaps on me.
            I did not see his face.
            I felt his arms enclose me,
            Crush me on his chest.
            A man struggled with me.
            Hand to hand in the dark,
            He embraces me, I encircle him,
            Speechlessly, there will be no end,

Wondering who is about to die,
So tightly entwined,
His heart beating in my chest,
Only death can part us.

OEDIPUS: *At least tell me who you are!*
What is your name?
Who wants to die?
I want to see you face to face!

OEDIPUS: At that moment he hit me
With all his might in the face,
My temples were ripped,
A rage uplifted me,
I was blind with blood.
I was about to throw him down
When I felt my body fall over him
Like death.
Like a mountain.
Tell me! you do not want to tell me?
At once I cut his throat
With my own hands.
With these very hands. I killed.
I did not know the man.
An entire night I yearned
To feel death.
Can you love me?

JOCASTA: I love you.
I love your hands. I owe them life.
Let me kiss them.

OEDIPUS: No!
I can still feel
The warmth of his blood
In my palms.
Had he told me his name . . .

JOCASTA: He has no name.
Let the dead die.

CHORUS: —*Man*— . . . *needs to forget*
The dead, and their names.
—*Which name?*
—*If he had known?*

—What about her?
—Only she knows
All that she knows.

OEDIPUS: I would have known whom to forget,
Whom to bury.
I would have buried him.
He could be erased from my memory.
What if I knew?
What if I were to tell you?
If he had been? . . . Your husband?

JOCASTA: Do not say "Your husband!"
The dead have finished dying.
I am the wife of a living man.

OEDIPUS: You are not answering me.

JOCASTA: Why
Torture ourselves endlessly?
Again I say to you: I love you
Absolutely, every day,
In all the motions of your life. Ever since your first breath,
Before that and without end.

OEDIPUS: You would forgive me the worst?

JOCASTA: *Between you and me there is no worst*
No god, no law, no time
No thought
Only us, Naked.
No measure nor limit
Between us, no wall
No memory, no look
No veil. No skin.

JOCASTA: That man, if he had been my father . . .
You might have killed him; if you had killed him
I would love you.
You could tell me.
Would you tell me?

CHORUS: *Is there something you did not tell?*

OEDIPUS: What must not be told.
Only whispered, with eyes closed, my head on your breast
So nobody can hear.
Burying my face between your breasts,

Burying words in my voice,

My voice in my mouth,

Burying my mouth on your breast.

JOCASTA: How well I know you.

CHORUS: *Forever the need to disappear*

Into the body of the other.

To be the son of woman!

Is it something you have done?

OEDIPUS: Nothing

I could have avoided.

As though crimes

Got themselves performed

By me, in spite of me.

To inflict death

Yet to have done nothing.

To kill. As if I were forbidden not to.

Even to kill my mother . . .

Perhaps even now

To unleash her murder.

CHORUS: *To be condemned*

Having done nothing.

Guilty beforehand

Whatever he does.

Infinitely.

JOCASTA: Whatever you have done, let me know it.

You can do nothing,

Have done nothing

That can be held against you.

Look at yourself in my eyes.

I see you as you are: untouched. Without fault.

Just as I wish you would see yourself!

OEDIPUS: If only you knew where I am,

In what state, how disjointed,

You would tremble at your words. If you knew

What I have just discovered,

You would see me as I am.

The quarry of a fatal wrong.

I can talk of myself no more,

Barely can I think of myself. No longer do I know who says: "I"

With my voice.
Where I was there is but pain.
I feel someone in agony
Where I took pleasure.
Do not cry.

JOCASTA: *(Her tears flow noiselessly.)*
I do not cry. I am coming closer. Do not move away.
Do not get lost without me; do not close yourself in.
Let me enter your suffering with you.

OEDIPUS: This suffering will draw us apart.
The dead man's name . . .
A man disclosed it to me this morning.
The dead man really was yours.
Can you love me?

JOCASTA: I have never had
Any lover but you,
Never.

OEDIPUS: It was Laius. I killed him.
Your innocent lover is a murderer. I shed his blood.
One of a kind. Matchless blood. I can never redeem it.

JOCASTA: You were innocent.

OEDIPUS: I was so yesterday.
How young I was then!
I was strong. I lived in broad daylight,
Walked straight, growing closer to you,
To myself, without looking back. The path going upward,
The light getting brighter, my love for you more and more
Peaceful, despite the fear,
Despite the city, the plague.
I felt content.
I was home. I loved myself
As though nothing could happen.
I did not sense the crime stalk me,
Catch up with me, suddenly
Pounce on me.
The sky turned black. Blood rained on my head.
I let death into your life.

JOCASTA: No. There is no other death in my life
But one that would take you away from me.

This blood does not blind me.

I see you as you are

My love, my innocent one. This blood

Does not stand between us.

OEDIPUS: I can feel this dead man killing us.

I shall have to go away.

Do not call me: my love.

I am the one who stands between you and love.

CHORUS: —*She does not want to know.*

Cannot, fails to

Think their death.

—*Both dead, already. She is dead.*

—*Separate.*

—*No point in beseeching . . .*

JOCASTA: You can kill me

With a word; you can separate us, snatch life,

Snatch death from us

With but one word, you can

Preserve us, you

Decide

Alone, as if you were a god

And I had ceased to be.

You. And if you wanted,

Yes, if only you did, one word would suffice

And we would be saved

And alive still.

CHORUS/

TIRESIAS: —*You are only a man.*

—*A man*

Like the others.

He believes the worst.

He fears the worst.

As long as he is kept in terror.

OEDIPUS: How could I be free of fear?

JOCASTA: Man is allowed not to fear.

OEDIPUS: I fear I no longer understand myself.

JOCASTA: It is not forbidden to live

Without consulting the gods.

OEDIPUS: I fear I no longer can love myself.

JOCASTA: Soon I will not know how
To love you.
To give you
This love.

JOCASTA: *(To herself)*
I harbor the secret.
And no one is more intact
No one more violated.
I sense
A silence forming
Between myself
And the one I was.

CHORUS: *Nobody knows*
What she knows.
—Did the seer speak to her?
—No
—Maybe
—No
—Crazed? . . .
Separate
From herself.

OEDIPUS: All is darkness now!
I have such craving for light!

JOCASTA: I would have
To watch him go
As if he were already gone
As if he knew he were going.

CHORUS: *—No longer knowing who you are*
For the one you love.
—For the first time
This time
His glance deserts her.

CHORUS: For eternity
He would be unable to stop
Moving further
Infinitely
Into the dark. Without telling her.

CHORUS: *Jocasta, now a stranger draws him.*
A source he cannot resist; he wants to give in,

To be pulled back,
Bound again.

JOCASTA: Already I feel you elsewhere,
No longer do I know where I am
For you.

CHORUS: *No more love, so abruptly?*
—Perhaps no more love . . .
Not that simple:
He still loves
Love.

OEDIPUS: Do not follow me. Let me
Bury this horror by myself.

JOCASTA: Then you will never know
How much I would have loved you.

OEDIPUS: I feel a great need for desert space.

CHORUS: *Detain him not, stop him not, follow him not.*
Soon no reason left
To be called
Wife.

JOCASTA: Far, you are so far.
I shall lose you to your darkness
Soon, and you
Will not know me anymore.

OEDIPUS: Let me cross this desert alone.
May I leave this world
And find myself elsewhere!

JOCASTA: I should not have seen him go away
With his eyes closed
I should not have seen myself losing him.
I should not love him at all
So that love would withdraw itself.

OEDIPUS: Oh! Let me know what I fear to know
And not lose my mind!
But I do not know if it is what I truly want.
Horrible dreams woke me up.
They screamed: "Nevermore shall Oedipus know."
They transported me.

They dragged me out of the room
Through the walls, my body torn apart.
I cried in my dream: "I am not sleeping!
No need to wake me! I beg you do not wake me up!"
Their fingers plucked my eyelids off.
They shouted: "Are you sleeping? Do you not see what you
    are doing?
Never shall Oedipus forget!"
I writhed in agony. I could see! I could see!
I was in a strange city.
I knew you were waiting for me in vain.
I was not coming. Not sending you word.
You knew nothing. I was giving you no warning.
The news was brought to me, standing in my room.
A voice was proclaiming: "He is the lover
Of his mother." I did not hear it.
The news was not reaching me, it came in, it screamed:
"He is the son of his wife," but I was not listening.
I had become another; the news stunned me.
I did not know who I was. The one I had been
Was not me. No one could understand.
And yet, it was I crying. Tears
Were running down my cheeks, down my chest.
I had already heard that voice.
I could have ignored it. Not believed what it was saying.
How could I ignore it? It was my mother's voice,
A very ancient voice, and infinite sorrow,
A voice low and tender that insisted:
"Forgive me for telling you the truth,
Pretend that you do not hear. If I say:
Oedipus is his mother's lover, do not listen to me.
Do not believe me."
I wanted to lose my mind. I wanted to dream
I was killing my mother with my own hands,
Strangling her, burying her voice in silence,
Covering it up with my screams.
I screamed: "Do not wake me up. I am dead."
I was screaming: "I always knew."
In my dream, I thought:

"Act as if you knew."
That is why I screamed: "I know! I know! I always knew!"
But I did not know anything. Yet I had this maddening
Fear to know
As though fear knew more than I did.
As if truth preceded me, called out to me;
"Come," commanded me: "Follow me to the end,
Your eyes closed, and I shall tell you who you are."
In the dark, I followed her,
Step after step; how could I disobey her?
I would have liked to wake up. Before appearing in front
    of you.
Not to see you, not to hear your voice
Calling me by the dreaded name. Never to have seen you,
Touched you.
Fleeing from dream to dream, I wanted to go further,
To run out of the world, to rush into oblivion.
The world was closed, walls stopped me,
Memory haunted me, taunted me,
Pressed me harder and harder and drove
Seven blades into my back.
How would I ever reach the brink of oblivion?
I was dashing through my shadows, between dreams
    and truth.
It was an endless race. Through dead bodies. The bodies of my
Dead.
I wanted to arrive in front of you.
What bliss to set my eyes on you, what ecstasy to be saved,
At last to rest my face upon your breast,
To ease my soul into your flesh.
I was unable to want it.
I was afraid to recognize you, to find you again
Only to lose you.
I was afraid to hate my mother, my beloved.
I was afraid to see your other face.
Not to recognize you. To dread you. To grow
Unable to love you. To love you. To grow unable to say:
"I love you."

JOCASTA: Even if it were not a dream,
             If you should appear as misfortune in front of me,
             I would be so immensely happy to see you.
             Even if you told me: "I am your son"
             And I believed you, even if it were true,
             If I had always lived in fear of it,
             If you should come, I would love you as I love you
             With my flesh and soul
             Without names.
             Nothing, no secret, no revelation would prevent me
             From getting close to you, closer
             And closer still.

OEDIPUS: Do not say that! Do not!
             If fate had decided that you were my . . . ?
             No. Not to be said. There are thoughts
             That put words to death. Not even to be thought,
             Not begun to be imagined,
             Without falling into abysmal Silence.
             If fate had allowed my mother to be . . .
             Words . . . I hardly breathe.
             My voice would flee. It could not bear it.
             Even in dreams it was forbidden.
             If it were not a dream,
             If I am in fact he I cannot be,
             I would never speak again.

JOCASTA: Look at me!
             Have I not begged enough?
             My silence has not said enough?
             My love, do you not understand?
             Have I not shown you? Did I not open my door?
             Did I not unveil my body for you?
             Did you not enter my flesh like your home?
             I did not name. I did not hide. I gave.
             I did not lie. I did not escape. I did not turn away.
             I stood before you. I turned my face toward you.
             I did not close my eyes.
             Do you see me? Did you see me?
             Come look at yourself in me. Did I not harbor your reflection?

Do you see yourself? Yes? Perhaps?
You, who enters and leaves my eyes
Did I not allow you to guess
The secret?
Did you never perceive in me
Your resemblance?

OEDIPUS: That fear!
That resemblance!
That awe . . . never ceased growing.
My fate was in your eyes.
I read my life in them yesterday.
And now I can look at you no longer
Without seeing my death.

JOCASTA: But *I* look at you
And do not see my death. Look at me
Loving you just as you are.

OEDIPUS: No! Stop looking at me!
Stop seeing a me who no longer exists!

(This is a lengthy sequence: crowds, confusion. OEDIPUS *with his back to the sun.* OEDIPUS *and* JOCASTA *are turned away from each other and sit on a diagonal axis.* OEDIPUS *never looks at* JOCASTA*—as if he cannot turn his head in her direction. A "natural" impossibility. She seems to be the one, at times, to venture a glance at him, but it rarely reaches him. Her eyes do not rest on his face. Only once, perhaps. And perhaps he smiles, but not a true smile. Perhaps he does notice her dazzled, uncertain look. But for hours, aware of each other's presence, their eyes do not meet. Except once, perhaps, for a second. . . .)*

JOCASTA: *(Speaking to herself slowly, afraid of her fear)*
I am afraid. Afraid.

CHORUS: What is this? . . . What has happened? . . . Nothing? You look . . .
frightening. There is no . . . ?
Did it happen . . . ?
—Yes? . . . It happened? . . .
—I do not know. There is such silence. A silence of . . . I cannot
describe the . . .
—The Air is not moving. This silence. . . . They . . . Stopped
speaking. This silence . . .

JOCASTA: Choking me.

CHORUS: Nothing is known? No one here. And the torpor. . . . Impossible to
            say. To know when. The air . . . inert, sick. Life is not coming
            through. To destroy the silence.
            It cannot come through. It does not dare. A shame to see.
            Is it about him? Not really. He is not the one who. . . . It is because
            of . . .

JOCASTA: I am . . . afraid.

CHORUS: It is because of her. I think I understand. He must . . . agonize.
            Pain. Suffer to see her suffer. Yes. To see her so close. And she too.
            Seeing him. Not seeing him seeing her suffer. In pain with so much
            suffering. So close to death.
            She too. So close to dying.
            A final death.

JOCASTA: I am in darkness.

CHORUS: In this silence. Struggling against nothing, with nothing. Is it
            impossible to accuse someone?

JOCASTA: In the darkest night. I do not think. . . . Yet I think I could . . .
            understand. No. I do not understand. I dare not hold my hand out,
            nor a word. In this dark. Afraid to touch. Why? Does not want to be
            touched, I feel it. By anybody. By me.

CHORUS: Is there a reason? Suddenly? There must be. Suddenly. A reason.
            Without reason.

JOCASTA: It is the city. Suddenly. That is the reason. I imagine.

CHORUS: He must think. His fault. A fault being paid for.

JOCASTA: No, no. No fault. No. No reason. There is death. I feel it. It is anger
            against him: death. Wants to fight. But all his strength is faraway. I
            feel it: happening away from here, very far, not thinking, just the
            struggle, within the body. In the dark. In the heart of the dark. I do
            not know where. When. Suddenly it is dark. I have become nothing
            for him. Death . . . how can it be lived?

CHORUS: Are there signs? No, there are not signs. Precisely. He does not
            make a sign. Paralyzed. Suddenly. It is life failing to come through.
            Failed yesterday.
            The cessation of life.
            And her, in the dark, the bed chamber, the air dark, too. Light
            cannot come in. Motionless. Wandering. He says nothing?

JOCASTA: His silence . . . speaks. So long, so pregnant. This silence means.
            But I do not understand. I think I understand, but I am not sure.
            What I understand—I do not understand. He does not believe me. I

am the one who cannot hear. This silence. As if he were saying . . .
Ah! I am wrong, it is not true. It is nothing. Only silence. Human
silence.

CHORUS: To endure. Must not think. Must not interpret. Must not. . . .
Rush onto. . . . Must not suffer . . . but . . . pain . . .

JOCASTA: Impossible to live if the only one I can talk to is not alive. Withdrawing suddenly, without a word. Not arriving. Not coming. If he had
told me. But he did not say a word. My love, I am so afraid, I would
not want to. . . . Move apart without meaning to, to be faraway
from you in the dark.

JOCASTA: *Cannot live*
Nor speak. Nor keep quiet
Without betraying
Your will. Nor think.
Who controls you?
You, no longer allowed
To speak. Nor think.
What you think is forbidden.
Do not think. Stop.
Do not ask me if . . .

JOCASTA: Your silence . . .
As if he were telling me:
I am alone. There is no one.
But I am the one who is no one.
He speaks to no one, and it is I.
As if he were my absence
Not even absent.
Not him, not his death. It is I,
His wife, erased.
Instead of me, as if I
Were not here, had never been
But a ghost.

CHORUS: *Not to suffer*
Too much; to suffer less, better, without becoming
Mad. Without betraying.

JOCASTA: I wish not to be misled.
Not to mislead him. To live, if he wanted.
If he wants to die. Horror
Not to know his true desire.

CHORUS: *Does he also not know it?*
His difficult silence
Forbids translation.

JOCASTA: Had he only said:
"Everything is trembling.
I need your help . . ."
But he did not ask me. Did not say
A word, not even
"Do not ask me anything."
Everything is trembling, and I am helpless to interpret.

CHORUS: *Ask him nothing.*
Give him . . . Nothing.
Trust him infinitely.

OEDIPUS: *A word—*
With which voice?

JOCASTA: He did not tell me:
Trust me.
He did not tell me:
Wait for me.
He did not tell me:
Later. Someday.
Before death.

CHORUS: He is not dead.
You must wait. Suspend your existence
Over your strength.
The last time he spoke to you?

JOCASTA: He said:
"Several times, without success,
I tried to tell you,
It is all too difficult . . ."
He was talking to me, his lips moved. Tell me, tell me,
Carry me with you.
The words stopped.
Several times, without success
Calling him, holding him. In front of him
As if not there. Suddenly. Vanished.

CHORUS: All kinds of thoughts,
None false, none true.
How to

Chase them away: evil thoughts,
Thoughts of evil.
Close your eyes;
Keep faith.

JOCASTA: The air had become unbreathable.
O my beloved, my distraught lover, I am in pain.
I cannot breathe if my life's breath
Will not breathe for me.
O my madness, my lover, my mother.

CHORUS: A slow gentle breeze is blowing
Like the sigh of a lover, of a tormented mother,
A tender humid breeze.
The winds of fear. A soft shy breeze . . .

JOCASTA: The breath of bereavement takes form.
I shall again live in fear
Of chance. O my beloved, your face has turned somber.
Your face frightens me. No longer the same,
The old anxiety has been roused.
I am afraid to open the window
And see the black sail faraway
Unfurled and rising,
Snatching from me my sight, my life.
I am afraid to open my eyes
To see your face altered, already veiled.

CHORUS: Stop beseeching misfortune!
Death cannot reach you here
As long as you do not summon it.
Do you believe me?

JOCASTA: It is not hope that is wanting.
It is *I* failing to reach him.

TIRESIAS: There is no black sail
Only the sky turning darker.

JOCASTA: No, it is he already so far away
That he is no longer himself.

CHORUS/

OEDIPUS: **Emptiness, Silence. Silence has taken hold.**
If you move too far away. Silence calls him. He cannot resist it.

Drowns in it.

Where now? Submerged.

The essence of emptiness: you cannot emerge from it. Emptiness grows deeper.

No one to ford it, to retrieve you from the void.

God will not help. The essence of empty space: God does not hear.

Does not speak.

Silence is a dead man's tongue.

Death does not come. Silence sucks you up, without desire.

What does it want? Nothing. There is nothing to want.

There is no one to want?

I lack myself. Separated from my name. Less and less here.

Further and further from myself. From the door.

There is a glass barrier. O to open it! So far. Three infinite steps away.

Poisonous silence. I shall speak tomorrow, tomorrow, tomorrow.

Numb. Words not empty, rather—full. Each word becomes boundless, dangerous, monumental.

—After such a long silence what word will serve to break through.

To free. To name oneself.

No more silence, no hollow, no blank, no void; no slaughter of stifled phrases, murdered words, charnel houses of dead bodies. No massacre of all that wanted or did not want to be said. Every minute, thousands of victims. Of thoughts, condemned and executed. (Assassin: Assassinated: Self-assassinated) Why? Distrust. Everything lies. Everything speaks untruths. There is no truth. Truth lies. Everything said is too long, too true, too cruel. But mute truth—perhaps not true? Then truth—not known? Nontruth? Nontrue?

JOCASTA: I am . . . in pain.

As if he were telling me:

Do not love!

Stop loving!

CHORUS/

OEDIPUS: *Several times*

Without success

I tried to
Tell you: Do not fear.
But I failed
To say it. Everything became
Too difficult.
Not absentminded, not forgetful
I wanted to tell you.

CHORUS/
JOCASTA: He did not tell you:
           Wait for me.
           You did not tell me:
           Do not love me.
           You did not say: do not wait for me.
           But you did not say:
           Love me. I want you to love me.
           You did not say:
           Love me. I want you to love me.
           Leave; go away.
           But you did not say:
           Stay, I want you to be here.

JOCASTA: *You did not tell me:*
           "Please erase me
           From your memory."
           But you did not tell me:
           "No, I shall never erase you."
           You did not tell me:
           No, but you did not tell me:
           Yes, I tell you yes,
           I tell you yes.

JOCASTA: Nothing. He could tell me nothing.
           There is nothing to tell me.
           Not knowing where I am
           Is not death,
           But silence
           Unshared. He cannot speak to me.
           Words have exiled themselves
           Overnight. No meaning left.
           Not a word. Suddenly I understand.
           It is hard. I understand him. Even his

Hardness within me. I love, within me,
His sudden hardness.
And I understand.

CHORUS: *And now there is no love left?*
Or less love?

JOCASTA: Nothing more to give.
I gave beyond myself more than once.
I could see my strengths exhausted.
With no resource left always finding a little more love.
In the end, with everything gone, I was still drawing
From my heart more than I thought I had.
How fine it was! To struggle on and on to doubt, to win.
To give him all I had.
All I could ever have, more than all.
Now to give him
Nothing. Forever nothing. Not even thinking.

CHORUS: *Like a crazed woman*
Holding him back with words
Clinging on. You are mad!
Already this silence. . . . He has long stopped speaking to you!

JOCASTA: Will I hear you say "you" again,
My love?

OEDIPUS: I do not know, I do not know.

JOCASTA: With one word you can
Give me death
Or Life.
The strength to die
For you.

OEDIPUS: Why
Push me too far?

CHORUS: *Wanting*
Almost nothing,
Ah, not absolutely "nothing"
But little, so little
Not even a motion of the hand.
Not a sign.
Not a smile.
Not touching, no,
But only to speak to him.

No.
He must leave.
Be himself no more.
Though he does not know how to stop being.
She . . .
Cannot . . .
Does not understand that she must die.
And all this—yesterday.

JOCASTA: Tomorrow if you wish
Do not speak to me,
Do not touch me . . .
Now simply tell me
That you will keep me in you
Once I am gone. There will be no you without me.
Today, for the last time.

CHORUS: *—Do not insist.*
—He will soon start
Calling her "my enemy."
—In a minute, no mercy.
At the end of a minute
Gone.

JOCASTA: Tell me I shall stay in you
Even in thought
A mere image.
Even erased.

CHORUS: *—Stop calling him "my love."*
—He will soon detest her.
—You will regret his silence!
—Put your hand on your mouth.

—Do you not see you are hurting him?
—Every love name pushes him further,
Overcomes him with horror.
—Her mad hopeless need
To hear him
Give
Her
One of love's names . . .
Mad madness!

Do you not see
You are destroying yourself?

OEDIPUS: It is so late. I must
Leave you.

JOCASTA: I beg you do not go
Without looking a last look at me.
Do not close the door
Against me.

OEDIPUS: You will be the one to close it.
Let me leave now.
Do not follow me with your eyes.

JOCASTA: Say but one name
And I shall close the door.
A name to carry me through the abyss.
To call myself as you would have
If you should cease to . . .

OEDIPUS: No name can name you anymore.
Must I scream this at you?

CHORUS: *Madness, wanting to die*
With his name!

JOCASTA: I will be quiet.
Just tell me *your* name.
It will be the last name I ask
And I shall close my eyes.

CHORUS: *A name, a word,*
A mere breath.

OEDIPUS: No,
That name . . .

CHORUS: *Tell her. So she can stop*
Being unable to let herself
Die.

JOCASTA: Ah! Let me
Grow quiet
With your name
marking your exit.

OEDIPUS: *(Says his name, almost inaudibly)* Oedipus

JOCASTA: *(Screaming)* Oedipus!

OEDIPUS: Oedipus . . . no longer means anything.

JOCASTA: *(Eyes closed)*

How cold your name is.
How pale your voice!
How changed your name!
Even yesterday as I called out, the air spread you all around.
It was an enchanted space
And all words grew and multiplied.

CHORUS: *What madness drives her still*
To shatter the silence?

OEDIPUS: The name of Oedipus no longer names
Anyone.

JOCASTA: *(With formidable violence, calls in all directions, for all times)*
Oedipus!
I love you Oedipus!
Oedipus! Oedipus!

JOCASTA: My voice can no longer find him.
My voice has grown blind.

CHORUS: *She might as well speak to the silence!*
Forget
Now, if you can, do not stay
In this present. Come let us turn to the past,
Where love and death are divisible.

CHORUS: And then
What did he say to you?

JOCASTA: Speechless.
Three weeks without a word.

JOCASTA: *Except for the phrase.*
"How brief life will have been."
But he did not mean it for me.
He was talking to himself:
"Is this life?"
He was still in his room and yet
I could see him. I looked at him, devoured him
With my eyes from head to foot.
But he had already left. Is that the way life
Deserts us? The way we die?
There would be no end
To his absence.

JOCASTA: As if I too were no longer there.

CHORUS: He could remember only terrors.
Pursue them. Desire them.

JOCASTA: Without wanting to, he sentenced love,
Executed it, put us to death,
Without seeing himself kill.
We are dead, dead,
And there is only I to mourn us.

CHORUS: He had to call forth the horrors. To get close to them with open eyes.
To stand in front of them in disarray, as if he were confronting love
itself. In total surrender to disaster.

JOCASTA: And so . . . I am dying for us. Without him!
That is what gives suffering this air of madness.
How can disaster be avoided,
If it had already happened? Yesterday
I will be dead.

CHORUS: His eyes are only for the shadows.

JOCASTA: The worst is to live, day after day, always
Expecting the worst.

CHORUS: He would have wanted to
Retrace the steps within himself.
To the roots of disaster.
That was impossible.

JOCASTA: His entire life spent amid threats, deaths, and murders of his kin.
Among those he loved—while causing their ruin . . .

CHORUS: He was meant to keep away from his parents.
Never to see his father, his mother.

JOCASTA: So he would not kill them with his own hands. So they would die a
natural death. So he would not kill them and deprive them of
himself—who was their life.

CHORUS: Not dead, but lifeless.
How can one know
Enough to keep life alive?

JOCASTA: I wanted to deliver him from names.
All the names that pass for gods.
That impose themselves by fraud,
That we adore and obey as "pure beings":
Father, mother, truth, life, death, fault, debt, wife, truth,
Husband, king, birth, what man can say which he is?
It is words that rule.
I wanted to free him.

CHORUS: And yet the father has died!
            Which father?
            What death?

JOCASTA: As if there were only one death.
            As if I had ever ceased dying!
            As if I had not already lived this dying:
            Have I not already lost this life?

CHORUS: Already more than one death
            Through exile. Through absence. Through forgetfulness.
            What woman has not suffered these deaths?

CHORUS: *I have already seen her without life.*
            Dead.
            In his absence.
            Exile undoes her,
            Weakens, fades, exhausts,
            Detaches,
            Uproots.

JOCASTA: But not forgotten. Become
            A stranger.
            Not rejected, no. Gradually
            Separated from him without violence,
            As if he had to change bodies,
            To change memories.
            Gradually set aside,
            Not even erased,
            As if he had never known me
            Nor shared my life.

            O my beloved, to whom
            Shall I whisper your names:
            My mother, my love, my mad one.
            Silence has become
            Unbreathable.
            Love chokes me; I am overflowing
            With names of stifled love.

CHORUS/
TIRESIAS: *Do not say love,*
            Do not say mine, our,

My love, our room,
Our luck, my light of life.
Do not say the ill-fated words.
Do not say child, father, kin.
Let not the merciless,
Familiar words be heard.
What is done must not be said.
No longer say the delightful
Ancient words; spit them out.
What was done must be erased.
Buried
In silent sand.

TIRESIAS: I see her
In the far bedchamber
While he has been away.
If she is still alive, it is from waiting for him.
She is lying on her bed
Nearly dead with desire.
I see her mighty struggle not to slip
Into death.
Her eyes riveted to
The closed door.

CHORUS: *—Mighty struggle to save her life.*
—How much more time?
—The time to remember again.
—To love him both lost and found.
—Will he come if she calls him?
—Do not call him!
—You know he will not come.
—Not calling to avoid his not coming back.

JOCASTA: Awaiting him: the one who will not return.
Whether from madness or wisdom.
But yesterday you were so prompt in coming!
Without speaking, awaiting him still
Just one more time
As though he were about to arrive.

CHORUS: *—It is time to break with the lost*

Present, time to save the life of what no longer is.
—What force still carries her through
The impossible?
—Let her hear the desire
He no longer has?

TIRESIAS: She recalls the day
When they exchanged their names.
It was in the first bedchamber.
Lying on the far bed
She remembers.

CHORUS: *She would like*
To face the city again with him at her side.
—To never have seen him arrive.
—To see him appear in the distance for
The first time
—To approach the gates.
—To have never seen him walk by.
—To have been so unlucky as to have never met him.

JOCASTA: A silence was settling.
I watched the man
Come closer.
There was a lull in our despair.
I watched the Stranger's step,
Light, swift, measured
Across the square.
I did not move; his coming commanded space.
I saw his hair shine.
The noise subsided, the world had disappeared,
I myself no longer there.
Facing him, I followed him,
Accompanied him. I have never seen him.
But, as he grew nearer,
His look surrounded me.
Step by step, his hair shining,
My eyes caught in his locks,
I knew, I guessed,
I was sure, one more step.
His eyes on my hand, my arms,
My neck, all over, on my face, my brow,

On my lips, all over. I closed my eyes.
I began guessing.
No longer able to die.
No longer rich enough in lives
To watch him arrive
From the dead.
With this first sight
Already such pain!

TIRESIAS: *I see him coming. He is the hero*
Of chance.
Someone who comes to her from
A realm between death and love.

JOCASTA: From the start
Already sensing a new fear, a new grief,
Life failing me!
Unable to love him enough.
To touch him, to inhale—
His smells, his skin fragrant with jasmine,
With honey and young grass. Never able
To caress enough this man's immoderate beauty . . .
Feeling my sight falter,
Inventing the look that would reach him, seize him,
Enfold him just once.
Despairing from the start and blissful with
Knowing the agony of love.

TIRESIAS: *And from that moment forever unable*
To let herself die.

Seeking the pain that makes life worth living.
—Wanting and not wanting.
Looking at him, and looking and looking.
Wanting to see him without the space of looking.
—Having already seen him always and never having seen him before.
As she drew closer and closer.

TIRESIAS: I see a man. Approaching from the dead.
His gait is determined.
No one questions him.
He will not be stopped. I can tell.
Moving ahead and stepping forward his body

Does not walk. It makes each space swirl as does the night
Which slips in between low tones without flinching.
I know no one who can
Intimidate him.
No one. He walks past the winged virgin
Without stopping. As if she did not exist.
He does not hear her, heed her, give her a chance
To harm him. Does not let her speak out.
The instant her voice rose,
He took her breath away with a single word.
The word that makes beasts die.
I see him in the city. He has entered.
Here he is. He was bound to arrive. He stands
Before the palace. The silence has begun.

CHORUS: . . . *Who was he?*

TIRESIAS: A man who inspired fear.
A man who had not known fear.

JOCASTA: His joyless childhood, his strange serenity . . .
He was an ageless man, a frightening young man
With divine rigor.
I thought: "This man is not just a man."
He was a man of a different sort.

OEDIPUS: I was a man without a childhood.

TIRESIAS: His poise. . . . His way of approaching,
Neither too fast nor too slow,
Without looking back, impervious to distractions . . .

JOCASTA: Walking without walking, brushing the ground
With winged steps. Without resting, parting the air . . .

TIRESIAS: A flight without wings, the ground giving way,
Carrying him on the strength of his desire.
Arriving without delay, without a second wasted,
Without rushing, in front of her.

OEDIPUS: **I have arrived. I stood before your night**
Yesterday as I stand now. A night
That has opened to embrace me
As has the city.
I have walked briskly, tirelessly
For ten thousand years.
Now, as then: all is clear.

Then I called you my night.
And now my life, my virgin love,
My bride.

JOCASTA: You!
My life, my night, my
Virgin love.
I remember your remembering me. From the first smile.
I stood before the gates. The town had disappeared.
I see my life in front of me. You and my life are one.

OEDIPUS: The moment I saw you all laws and limits were abolished.
The doors of the universe swung open.
The Earth became the sea. I was born.
You were there, you would be there, the future had arrived.

JOCASTA: Oh to wrestle free of time!
Before him: no one; after him: no one. He, alone—the first, the last.

TIRESIAS: The last man, in person.

OEDIPUS: Soon you will be everything. You are mine.
I smile at you
And no longer want to die.
I want to be all there is. Never again to sleep. Except in
  your night.

TIRESIAS: I see her as if at that very moment.

JOCASTA: If the gates were to open
He would not walk in. But spring forth . . .

OEDIPUS: Come, I want to show you where I came from
There is where we were born.

JOCASTA: Where will you take me?

TIRESIAS: *. . . And he said words*
Keep her here . . . Hold her back from death.

OEDIPUS: Very high between the sky and the night
Into the crystal chamber that lies
Between my skin and my heart.

TIRESIAS: She remembers.

JOCASTA: I was about to get up yesterday
To go to the gates
From where he led me away.

TIRESIAS: *. . . Words that keep her love alive.*

OEDIPUS: One day, when we are old
I shall take you away to where

I shall never have seen you. I will see you
Run to me with your very first steps.
I shall take you in my arms.

JOCASTA: Take me, hold me, find me!

OEDIPUS: And I shall make love to you as if there had never been love
before.

JOCASTA: These are the words that detain me.

OEDIPUS: In twenty years, in thirty years,
I see you, your young face,
Your heart in my heart.
I come before you and I see you
When you are fifteen.

CHORUS: —*What madness?*
What delusion?
—*A life that does not pass* . . .
—*Existence always in the present* . . .

TIRESIAS: I see her
Plunge into her memory
To give the past the semblance of a present.

JOCASTA: Every night with you here
In this night.
And even though I expect nothing, I have everything.

CHORUS: —*What sort of light illumines her?*
—*A face that does not fade.*
A face never enough beheld.

TIRESIAS: She is a continuous night
Without beginning or end.
Where what has been is,
Never to disappear.

CHORUS: —*That love was love itself.*
—*That love was life itself.*
—*How could she think this love dead*
Without that thought tearing open her heart?
—*She cannot think it.*

TIRESIAS: That love is not dead,
Only astray, lost between present and past.

CHORUS: —*There are words which enclose her*
Between living and dying.
—*She cannot know where she is.*

JOCASTA: Am I dead? Yes. For him
           I am no longer here. I am dead.
           If only I could die also to myself.
           To no longer see myself dead and see him stand
           Before my body as he would
           Before my death.
           But I dare not die.
           If he ever . . .
           Came back . . .
           It does not depend on me.

CHORUS: —*She cannot go forward*
           Or retreat. She cannot forget his words.
           —*She would like to*
           See the past as present.
           —*Could she?*
           —*He could give her a present.*
           It is not impossible.
           —*That he keep her alive in the past.*
           —*If he wanted.*
           But wanting no longer concerns him.

OEDIPUS: I want to be
           Your night and become you,
           Who are my night.

JOCASTA: Are you—here?

OEDIPUS: Yes. I am.

JOCASTA: Is it—you?

OEDIPUS: Yes. It is I, myself, and you, you and I.

JOCASTA: Were you looking for me? Was it I
           Whom you were seeking?

OEDIPUS: You, the one I found.

JOCASTA: How frightened I am, you frighten me!
           Having seen you not looking for me
           But finding me. Having found you,
           The first man, the one I did not want.
           Having wanted you from the first sight . . .

OEDIPUS: I was not looking for you. I was compelled to come.
           I was not walking, I was drawn.
           I could not have failed to come.

TIRESIAS: She gets up. Tense, her body is tense.

Her skin is tight, her eyelids low. Opens the door,
Leaves the first bedchamber.
I see her waver seeing him come. Stunned,
Falling on him like night
Upon day. Silently.

OEDIPUS: You opened the gates.
You opened my breast.
I have your night on my face and in my flesh.
I entered. What happened
Is what had to happen.

JOCASTA: What if I had not been widowed?

OEDIPUS: I would have met you elsewhere,
In another life. And I would have loved you.

JOCASTA: This all happened! All that could happen
Happened to me.

TIRESIAS: Nothing better. Nothing wrong.
Except the worst.

JOCASTA: There is nothing to ask for then,
Except that every day be as the first day.
And that every night be like that night of nights.
The same and never the same.

OEDIPUS: How can you be the night?
I was not dreaming. And yet you were there.
You were my dreams. I was in you.
And yet you were in my dreams.
And you awoke me in your night.

JOCASTA: Still, those first moments . . .
I do not want to remember. I want to relive. The very first moments, relive them here, in a time that no longer goes by, that is no
longer the same. In a place that is not a place of memory and yet is a
memory, but new. I would not want to die without having heard his
voice yesterday promising me everything for the first time.

JOCASTA: *Forget me my love,*
Forget me. Close your eyes and call me.
Look at me, you have never seen me.
Go, and come to me again.
Ah you never came,
You have not arrived.
You are arriving, you are about to come,

To fall on me out of nowhere and for the first
Time. I want to live! I am alive!

TIRESIAS: I hear. I hear them look for each other. I hear the names they gave
each other.

That was in the first bedchamber.

OEDIPUS: Promise me never a lover but me.

Me alone: your strength, your child, me:

Your father if you will, myself:

Your spouse, mother, your lover.

Promise me never another king.

JOCASTA: You: my life, my day, my light, I promise you.

No, I will not promise you! I want you to ask me

Again and again. And every time tell me who you are for me.

OEDIPUS: If you wish I shall be your impulse, you my grace, I your
new strength, your dance. If you wish, I shall be your
mother, and then I shall be your child.

You—my child first, if you wish . . .

TIRESIAS: I hear their voices find each other, their breaths caressing each other,
fleeing, heeding each other.

JOCASTA: Tell me the time, tell me where,

Tell me when, tell me "us" in time, give me our time.

OEDIPUS: I see the future. I call it to me. The future is you.

The future is happening to us. It is the present.

There is no time.

JOCASTA: And now?

OEDIPUS: Now is the same as ever.

We are beginning. We are beginning.

JOCASTA: You will tell me everything?

OEDIPUS: I shall tell you everything. And everything will have no end.

JOCASTA: Everything that you think? That you know.

That you do not know. You will say everything?

OEDIPUS: I think so. I know it. Though I also do not know

It will be everything.

JOCASTA: Tell me where you are just now, at this moment in our story.

OEDIPUS: I am everywhere your voice calls me. Wherever I am,

I see us.

I close my eyes, I see you before having met you,

From the beginning. I do not sleep. Even in dreams, I sleep
Without sleeping to dive into time into your body,
To swim in your flesh that is the sea[1]
Your waves rock me. Say "the sea."

JOCASTA: I say: the sea, the sea, the sea.

OEDIPUS: As soon as you pronounce the word, I am on top of you,
against you, in you, I am awash in you, the whole of me.
But it is in me that you, the entire sea, is rocked.

CHORUS: *Look to your body for the words*
That set fire to the soul.

JOCASTA: Uncurl my waves,
One after the other, the whole
Of me in you. I, the sea,
My naked billows, my
Tongue, my fingers, my breezes, my hands on you.

CHORUS: SO VERY CLOSE!

BETWEEN THEM

NOTHING CAN SLIP IN.

—DEATH?

—NOT BETWEEN THEM. IMPOSSIBLE.

BUT PERHAPS IN HER?

—NO.

—IN HIM?

—POSSIBLY.

DEATH COULD NOT SEPARATE THEM,

NOT HAPPEN TO THEM,

IT MIGHT COME

AFTERWARD, AFTER THEIR LIFE,

ONE DAY AFTER THEIR DEATH.

JOCASTA: Are you here?

OEDIPUS: Yes. I am here.

JOCASTA: Here forever?

OEDIPUS: As long as I live
I am here.

JOCASTA: Here? Where? Tell me your name.

---

1. The French word for *sea, la mer,* is a homonyn for the word for *mother, la mère.* Here the double
meaning of the sound (*mɛr*) reflects the characters' fusion as incestuous lovers.

Say "I" again.

Tell me: "I am here."

Come here again and again. Swear to me.

Swear to me for every single day.

OEDIPUS: Every day I shall swear it. I swear it to you, today.

I am here. Yes. I am here. I am in Thebes for you.

JOCASTA: No, not in Thebes! Closer, closer. Do not be here. Be the city.

Be the air. Be the sky. Surround me.

OEDIPUS: I am the air. I fill the room. It is I you breathe.

JOCASTA: So far away! The room has disappeared! Everything
contains me!

Who are you in this bed? Who are you in my arms? You
are never enough me? I cannot go on! I am torn apart with
love. I do not know you! I do not envelop you! I fail to touch
you! I fail to approach you! I touch you; my hand burns on
your shoulder. Tell me that I touched you!

OEDIPUS: Yes. You *are* touching me. You have reached me.

It is I, yes, it is my body made flesh by your flesh.

Do you hear me?

JOCASTA: Ah! I have become a stranger to myself. Tormented by such
joy!

If you should feel the presence of such love within you, you
would be frightened.

OEDIPUS: Frighten me, then, share your joy!

JOCASTA: How can I stop this suffering? Stop feeling the grief of not
being you, of not being inside you.

When my lips touch yours?

OEDIPUS: We must find a way. I want to go where your heart beats. I
will enter your chambers and take your heart in my hands
and caress it.

JOCASTA: I will be your blood. For it is only there,

In the flesh, in the folds of the chambers

That pain can cease. That love can rest.

OEDIPUS: I will go where I am no longer myself. I no longer want to have
a name.

No other name than you, for you.

JOCASTA: No longer to know, no longer to think. But to live, to be life,
to be the fire and the light.

OEDIPUS: There is no word for this. Only gestures . . .

JOCASTA: This gesture: You are standing, I am in your arms, you turn
           slowly, and we see the entire Earth together. Say "we."

OEDIPUS: "We" is one. "We" continues.

JOCASTA: This moment was born of yesterdays before time.

OEDIPUS: Where is the shoulder that reaches further than the edge of the
           world? Now I am walking on the grass of your shoulder. I
           am going further than the Earth.

JOCASTA: Life opens up, it is within me, it is before me, it expands.
           And it is us. A breeze ruffles my hair. It is the breath of life.

OEDIPUS: Why? Why? Why are you woman? How are you woman? You
           must give me the whole of her, everything.

JOCASTA: Take Jocasta, tear her off, undo her, tear her off from me!

JOCASTA: *I remember being your*
           Life.
           And now, who?
           I remember loving
           Love, you, life in person. And now—
           Still loving you, but I do not know who you are. No
           Other lover but you, but who is
           "You," now?
           I see the one who was my life,
           Looking without seeing me, as if he were
           My death.

CHORUS: *Now who is loved in the place of the beloved?*

JOCASTA: Tear me apart, empty me out, shred me, weave a new space
           with the fibers of my body!

OEDIPUS: How many hours, how many years were my lips on your belly
           to have
           embraced you once?

JOCASTA: I expand to love you further and further still.
           Larger, wider, more vast.
           At night I think I cannot love you more. I have reached the
           limits of myself.
           But this morning infinity explodes, and I love you still further.

CHORUS: *—Who could believe that there was an end to infinity?*

OEDIPUS: I will not sleep anymore. I do not want to wake up
           Next to your body.

I want to live the night that is your flesh,
Turn the sky and Earth upside down.
This sky is not motionless; it is the sea.
I want to climb back up each vein, to follow your blood
Across all times, up until
The first drop.

JOCASTA: *I see my life before me*
But my life no longer sees me
And I feel myself dying outside myself.

JOCASTA: Yesterday, we are beginning; I entered us without delay, carried to the center of us—where my blood is your blood.

CHORUS: *Because it was written,*
Expected, promised,
Incredible, so very
Incredible.

Not desired, not hoped for—
A killing blow.

OEDIPUS: Before your voice called me
Who was "me"?
Where was I when I had not seen you?

JOCASTA: Yesterday, you were coming.

JOCASTA: YESTERDAY, SILENCE IS NOT SILENCE. YESTERDAY IN THE ROOM IN YOUR ARMS WHERE WE HAD WITHDRAWN THIS SILENCE WAS SINGING. DO YOU HEAR IT? IT WAS A PEACE SONG. WE HAD GIVEN IT BIRTH. IT LIVES OUTSIDE US FROM NOW ON. IT CONTINUES.

JOCASTA: *That was yesterday. I do not even remember it. Absence has become absence. This silence does not sing. This silence clutches my throat.*

OEDIPUS: *I hear everything, but I cannot turn my eyes.*
I hear everything with my dead eyes.

JOCASTA: Yesterday, you must go to Thebes. I know it.
Go. You must go. But love holds you back.
Love prevents you from leaving. You say: I am leaving.

OEDIPUS: I am about to leave. Right now. In a moment. Minute.

JOCASTA: Words drift like feathers
On our lips, I laugh. You stay.

OEDIPUS: Love is stronger
Than I. I say: I am leaving.

Love decided that I stay.

It wants me to carry you away.

Quickly we live several lives in one minute.

JOCASTA: That was yesterday.

Today: the desert.

The dance is dead.

My arms too heavy, my hands—too weak.

My blood—dried up. A metal hand rips

My heart out. I was us. Now I am no one. I am this desert.

Tonight, no longer alive, I see myself dead. I see my body lying.

I am alone as never before, my body laid in a coffin, not wept over,
  not hidden, not remembered. I want to die.

No one is free to die in such loneliness.

Tell me the word that gives death or life.

Tell me,

Say it. Give me a sign.

How to die, how not to die.

How to end it? When? Where? Why?

I do not know what you want.

JOCASTA: *The worst is to have seen him leave*
Without knowing if he would ever again
Return the same.

JOCASTA: I want, but I dare not. I cannot manage to end my life.

Your silence kills me. Your silence forbids me to die.

JOCASTA: *Without ever knowing what it is you wanted me*
To be—for you—,
Without ever having understood
What I might have been.

JOCASTA: Yesterday, I told him:

"If I should die, a breath from you would give me back my life. If I
stopped hearing, if I were lying in the dark, if I expired, if you lean
over me, call me by your name.

I will hear it. Tell me your name,

Oedipus! I shall cease dying."

It was the truth, I remember it was true.

I believed everything. Everything was true.

I believe even now.

OEDIPUS: *Every word hurts me; every question wounds me,*
I am not deaf.
I hear too much.

JOCASTA: I feel the past rejecting me
If he does not remember even if he does come back, *I* cannot come
back, not yesterday, today, or tomorrow. Nor forget. Nor stay.

CHORUS: *Because he does not turn around.*
Because he does not glance
At her.
He does not utter her name.
Not a word for a month.
Thirty days, thirty nights,
Thirty years without life.
He is not here. I saw him this morning.
And his face was hard.
He was gone, he was dead.
He was lost.
His body turned into a desert,
His heart rotted.

JOCASTA: Yesterday, I live, I believe, I hear your voice.
I enter, I leave, I have a body, I have a face.
My eyes dive into your eyes.
My blood surges; my blood exults.
Your voice fondles my heart.
Joy lifts me up, transports me
Over foreign lands, around the world.
I arrive at a wall.
A laugh of fire springs from my mouth.
The wall opens wide. I go through between times.
I move on, I roam through bottomless space.
The abyss is there, I do not fall in.
I accept everything, I dance,
I run on the air, pleasure carries me along.
I believed, I believed . . .

CHORUS: *This morning. I think he still wants to love.*
Love held firm.
Then love broke down. Suddenly
No strength left.
He wants to leave.

He cannot find the door.
No door left. No window.
No opening. His teeth—clenched. His voice—strangled.

JOCASTA: I was absolutely sure. This morning a burning wind wakes me, my
bed goes up in flames.
Time! Time has caught fire.
Leaping toward you my blood is ablaze.
I dash—
The ground gives way; love does not protect us.
The air does not support me. I collapse.
Infinity deserts and absence
Engulfs me.

CHORUS: *It was the season of*
Exaltation, the universe inflamed.
I, too, was burning.
I drew closer to him.
I was rushing
With discretion.
I was hoping for a long
Ardent day that would never end.
We were not alone.
The universe surrounded us.
We could not talk.
I was alone
Not far from him.

JOCASTA: I saw him, I wanted
To rush to him.
Something in
His eyes stopped me.
There was no longer a place for me
Beside him.

JOCASTA: The sun . . . I am in the shadows observing closely.
In pain, watching him so far away.
Absence in person held me back. His shirt was open. I could not
caress you.
My hands empty, my hands turned black, my palms dried up, my
hands burned.
I saw your neck. I saw your shoulders. I did not touch.
I felt my life oozing away. I was lying

In the shadow, on the bed. I feel my life
Going by, observed from a great distance, painfully,
Down to the last thought.

CHORUS: *He was out with the crowd,*
With strangers,
Fused with her, the entire
City.
I heard the words
Escape from his throat.
He was talking, responding,
Standing tall.
She was courting him.
I heard his voice
Laugh.

JOCASTA: Alone.
I descend time
Step by step.
Grief. Misfortune.
There is no place for me
Up here.
Hour after hour
Down to the lowest step of time
Alone.
Descending silently,
Gradually,
Entering, sinking,
In phrases unspoken
In lost words
Of thought.
Deep in the silence within.
Down to the last word.

(*Jocasta is standing, turned toward the door: three steps away the bed is untidy. Alone with* TIRESIAS. TIRESIAS *at that time is {why?} a tall, trim, and handsome young man who seems to be drawn to her. Not taking his eyes off her face, as if he were beginning to see her. As if he would soon be able to touch her, to watch her. She never stops looking over his shoulder, toward the door.*)

JOCASTA: If only you knew

How I suffer.
How difficult it is.
Will you tell him?

TIRESIAS: *Yes.*

JOCASTA: *You will tell him: all is well.*
How I have loved him! If he should
Ask you a question?

TIRESIAS: Yes.

JOCASTA: When he comes back,
If he were to come back, that I wanted to see—just
For a moment before the end.
A second after the final moment
There would still be time. Would you tell him?

TIRESIAS: Yes.

JOCASTA: *How I never hated him,*
Should he ask it.
If he felt uneasy; if he should come to think
I might hold it against him,
Would you tell him?

TIRESIAS: *I would tell him. Yes.*
If he asks me
I will tell him how you love him.

JOCASTA: No. I must no longer want
Nor think. Nor tell.
I do not want to desire
Any other favor than death.

And so you will never know
How I love, my love.

(*Now lying on the bed,* JOCASTA'S *gaze drifts away. She is dying,* TIRESIAS *looking on.*)

JOCASTA: How difficult to die.
To be done with it.
I am dead, I know it.
It is so hard.
I would never have thought that
Tearing my soul and flesh apart
Would be so very painful.

TIRESIAS: *Perhaps*

Not
Dead enough.

JOCASTA: You did not even deal the last blow!

TIRESIAS: *She was dying.*
She was meeting her death
With undue eagerness.

JOCASTA: You did not kill me!

I must die by my own resources.
Force myself to my death.

How slow it is, how feable and shy, how slow this death.
How enticing its ways!
It almost amuses me!
It would seem death is afraid!
Perhaps I am too devastated?
Still distraught by too much love?
Or is it that I no longer have enough
Strength to die?
Though I need death so much,
Though I need death's body to rest in.
Does death feel it? It seems it is afraid.
Perhaps my desire is not dead enough?
Yet for weeks . . .
Outside my body . . .
My breasts are dead. My hands,
My stomach, my womb—dry,
My arms, for weeks—metallic arms.
My skin has forgotten everything.
It can no longer remember.

TIRESIAS: *Too much strength perhaps,*
Yes, too much desire for death.
Too great in need of its mercy.
Unloving, unmotherly,
Death does not want to be loved.
To step in where love was.
It can be there only
For no one, for nothing.

CHORUS: Seeing her die halfheartedly
            So woefully
            I cannot stand it.
            What force detains her here?
            In spite of her relentless will?

TIRESIAS: *All the power of love*
            All its powerlessness.
            She has no life left
            But love refuses to die.

CHORUS: If I could only believe there is
            Some good in love's pain . . .
            But there is none.

TIRESIAS: *Even dead, love*
            Invades her, its poison
            Embalms her and keeps her in pain.

CHORUS: When, then? How?
            Can she find peace?

TIRESIAS: *In sleep. If she could dream of*
            Him. Rejoin him in dream. Let him come!
            He who is her death.
            Let him take her in his arms.
            He who does not come.

CHORUS: Will he come?

JOCASTA: He will not come.
            You will not come?

CHORUS/
JOCASTA/
TIRESIAS: I am not going. Let him come!
            I did not want. She wanted. Him to come!
            Not to die without him. Because he is death.
            Prevents herself from dying. Waits for him. To die.
            Life runs out.
            But does not wait for him.

TIRESIAS: *Let him come.*
            Do not wait for him
            Because he cannot come.
            He will not come.
            He cannot arrive

Because he is death
Which does not happen.

CHORUS/

JOCASTA/

TIRESIAS: Love, nothing but love . . .

How can she love he who is death?

He gives you nothing. He takes everything from you.

He took everything from me. Gave all and took it all back!

He gives me agony—and still—love.

She begs him to come. Not to come.

TIRESIAS: *If he comes?*

She would die of it

She will die of it.

Let him come!

Do everything.

Tell him to do everything

Not to arrive.

She will die of it.

CHORUS/

JOCASTA/

TIRESIAS: **She will be unable to stay alive.**

And if he comes

I will die of it.

Death was interminable.

It would not stop ending.

Do not let him come!

Keep him from coming!

(JOCASTA *turns to the wall.* TIRESIAS *caresses her entire body with his sightless eyes, eyes that see differently.*)

JOCASTA: Sing me a song, will you?

A childhood song

From when I was small. My mother's low voice . . .

I would turn to the wall. . . . The wall became the sea.

Waves lifted my bed. I felt content.

CHORUS: Sing the song

To her.

TIRESIAS: Sleep. I shall sing.

(He sings an enigmatic song in a foreign language: "Erlkönig" or "Die Gedanken sind frei.")[2]

JOCASTA: She would sing
         A foreign song.

         While he
         Never ever
         Wanted to sing for me.
         Not a single time.
         And yet his voice was
         Deep and beautiful.

TIRESIAS: *Be patient. Let sleep come.*
         Watch no more. Hope not.
         Doubt not.
         Let an other silence come to you.
         One that is just beginning.

JOCASTA: I feel sleep
         Win me. Penetrate me.
         An immense tenderness
         Embrace me,
         Rock me. How strange . . .
         A being—not man,
         Not woman.
         Yet I feel its arms
         Carrying me, its lips on my skin,
         My mouth on a vast breast.
         Ah! it is you! it is you!
         It is she, is it not? Yes
         I did not guess wrong, it is he.
         This sleep, how delightful.
         I feel a dream wanting me,
         I guess I know nothing.
         But I am sure. It is you, here
         Looking for me. You came to dream me

---

2. The "Erlkönig" and "Die Gedanken sind frie" are German-language folksongs, stylistically connected to the Romantic movement, therefore at once mysterious and anguished.

To preserve me though gone. It is you,
I do not know your name,
I have never known it,
I will never know it, the one
That will not wake me up . . .
I am content, at last.

TIRESIAS: *Forget yourself. Forget everything.*
Forget the world. Sleep.
Let a dream
Dream you,
Lead you away, unname you.

CHORUS: At last
Now you can come. Oedipus.
Too late.

CHORUS: *I am at peace*
Now she is dead!
And now he can come.
You may return, beloved.
This is the hour, your hour.

She said: he will not come.
No need to call him.
Not this last night. Not in the dark.
Not in this life.
But he will come, I am sure of it.
Too late.

(OEDIPUS *appears when the door opens. The instant he opened the door the ancient voice* *stopped.* JOCASTA's *heart stopped. And then silence. . . . He heard the words of silence. It* *was a silence never heard before.*)

CHORUS: *I am at peace*
Now she is . . . Dead . . .
Now she is
Dead.

OEDIPUS: My love! My strength! I am here,
My beloved, my child.
He has come back for you!

Oedipus is here, as I told you.
Take my voice! Take my breath!
Come! I am calling you, Oedipus.
I could not return any faster
From among the words.
From among the dead.
Come now. I know it is
Almost too late. But not too late.
You once told me: "I would stop
Dying."

TIRESIAS: *It was still true*
Yesterday. A moment ago
When you opened
The door.

OEDIPUS: "Oedipus! Oedipus!"
Come now,
To where I am,
Telling you the name
Of the one who loves you!

CHORUS: *It is no use crying out.*
You must seek the moment between light and dark.

(OEDIPUS *calls out his name, calls until his voice breaks.*)

OEDIPUS: Tell me again the words that hurt.
Tell me the worst. Tell me the truth ten times over.
Call to me; tell me the true name of Oedipus.
Torture my ears with words that pierce.
Tell me! Tell again! I want to hear with my blood.
Tear into my eardrums, I am deaf.
I cannot even hear my voice.
Wound me; make me hear the truth.
Are you speaking to me? Your mouth opens.
But I do not hear a sound. Before they reach me
Your words lose their blood, their substance.
I hear nothing. I heard nothing.

CHORUS: *Oedipus, Oedipus, do you not see*
She is dead?
Do you not see?
Are you blind?
Do you not see?

Do you not see?
The instant you opened the door . . .
Dead.

OEDIPUS: My love, what are you doing to me?
Even in dreams you should not die
Without me. No, not dead . . .
Just without voice. Speechless, my love.
Will you speak to me again? Tell me?
Will you never again speak to me?
We have as yet said nothing!
Listen! Ancient names are buried.
Everything has yet to begin. Whenever you wish.
Nothing has been named.
Speak to me. Do not leave me without a name.
Who am I, if you do not tell me to be here?
Who is speaking? I think I am shouting. I cannot hear myself.
This air will bury us alive.

When I arrived at the door
My pulse went wild. I was—Oedipus.
But now who is wailing?
A man about to become no one.
My love, that man looks at you.
Your face hurts him. It is so calm.

Too young. So serious. Your stare—
So grave, so vague, so remote.
You must talk to him.
Or you might kill him. He will forget his name.

CHORUS: *—He beholds her. Loses his mind.*
—He was a man.
—Without a name?
—Without a regret.

OEDIPUS: *My suffering cannot stop*
Because our deaths are now separate.
We had decided to die together.
Why did you not wait for me?

CHORUS: *How could you forget?*
—Without her . . .

No life, no death,
No rest.

OEDIPUS: My love, do you not hear him?
I ache for him.
So wretched . . . so utterly alone.
He does not even hear himself scream.
His pain hurts me.
And now
To whom can he say: "I am alone?"
Who will listen to a man
Who is loneliness itself?

OEDIPUS: *You had promised me not violent death*
But death without loss of each other.
In the sweetness
Of dying together we would become one. We were to
Intertwine our bodies.
Did I not swear it to you?

OEDIPUS: Do you not hear him?
Do you not hear him?
If you do not answer him
Who will rupture the loneliness
That buries him alive?
He must break out
But there is no exit. He must break
Through the walls.
Crack, gouge,
Carve a door
Through the horror
Of this loneliness.
Must get out!
Who will offer a hand?

But
Loneliness is within and without,
Is everything, is horror itself,
Throughout his flesh.

OEDIPUS: *What mistake my love?*
What mishap brought us to this?
I promised you such ecstasy.

In the crystal chamber
Between day and night
Enclosed in your arms,
My mouth on your mouth.
Such a wedding night in my arms . . .
Take me. Hold me.
Hold on with all your strength.
I breathe your breath.
You breathe mine.
I sweep you away. Such strength . . .
Such ecstasy. . . . To whom did you promise your life?
You were looking at me. You were swearing to me.
Your eyes were burning.
Was your radiance then
For someone else?
And now who are you
Looking at me from such a distance?
Do you not remember me? And the other?
You are another where you are now.
I do not know who.

I had seen death in a dream.
It was a sea.
We were climbing toward death.
But it had receded
By degrees. There were marble steps.
I discovered
The coldness of bare marble.
I was afraid death might come back
And catch us unaware. You held my hand,
Reassuring. Death would not return against our will.
And if it came back?
You would manage death with gentleness.

OEDIPUS: I want
          To cry and cry.
          I fear hate, my love,
          And I fear that Oedipus will hate you.
OEDIPUS: *How strong your hand, my beloved,*
          So gentle and delicate.

My life is in your hands.
Between your fingers.
If you wished you could destroy me with one stroke
Of your fingertips.
Or you could save me.
Or lead me to the top of the stairs
To the crystal chamber.
Do you not see that death has retired?
It will not return to catch you unaware,
To take your hand.
You will not ascend the last step.
You will not even begin the journey.

OEDIPUS: I must close my eyes, fight back the tears.
She must not see
Leaning over her
A hostile face.

OEDIPUS: *No, death has not gone! It stays.*
Its presence grows stronger, I feel it. It has stretched out over me to sleep, and
my body has turned to sand for you.
How could my body cease feeling death
With yours lying upon me?

OEDIPUS: One day in eight days
In eight years
I do not know when
I shall cry
Over you, over him,
Over your body.

OEDIPUS: *I still feel her. Yet I do not feel her*
Slipping between my legs,
Her breasts resting on my stomach.
On my skin I feel
Yet I no longer feel
Her fingers running, her breasts,
Sweet birds, alighting.
Her tongue calling forth a torrent
Of sperm.
From my head to my knees
To my ankles and now I am
Filled and on it goes.

My arms spread out,
My head bent back, desire was
Indomitable.
I fly and it traps me. I moaned
And surrendered, my eyes
Turned round in their orbits
Seeing no more
Than the sun.

OEDIPUS: No! Her eyes are not closed.
But . . . mine . . .

OEDIPUS: *And I sense love*
Out of love
Allowing love
To die.
I sense her flight.
I am consumed
For letting her flee. For letting her go
Without being able to desire
To hold onto her. And I feel
The sand disperse, and
The cold creeps into me.

OEDIPUS: *Now my bride is laid upon me,*
Laid to rest, and I do not need to
Vie with the air to envelop you.

OEDIPUS: Eyes closed I see us.
Before the world was empty.
Now we rise in each other
Filling the world.
Before the world was dry.
Now we join each other
Bathing the world.
Before the world was pale.
Now we warm the world
Between each other.
Nurturing, cleansing, illuminating,
Giving each other peace.

What is my trembling, then,
And what my joy to have found you again!

Found you in loneliness, my love.
My wife—born of me!
And my loneliness . . .
Vanished.

OEDIPUS: *Without fire, without movement,*
Without possessing you,
Nor you possessing me,
I feel you rejoin me
Elsewhere, at last.
No longer looking for you
We found each other,
For you were the one to go beyond the barriers
In a single breath.
And you shine upon my flesh
As the night's sun
Upon the day's.
Our lips are frigid
But our tongues are burning.
It is you, my night, surging
Over me
As surely as I am the silent sea
Whose flesh has just opened
So that you may fill it.
And we are entering each other
My mother,
My child.
My flesh is restful here.
I shall cease to suffer.
I have forgotten everything.
I no longer know who is dying.

Selected Plays by Contemporary French and Francophone Women Playwrights

Compiled and Annotated by Cynthia Running-Johnson

Note

The plays in this annotated bibliography, chosen from some one hundred pieces, were selected with a threefold purpose: that they be worthy of reading and production, that the group include works from French-speaking countries other than France, and that, as often as possible, good English translations of the texts be available. In these ways the bibliography corresponds to the spirit of the volume as a whole. Bibliographical annotations have thus been written with a view to the production as well as to the reading of the plays: they include character distribution and an indication of staging possibilities.

The annotations embrace both established dramatic and literary authors and newer voices. Certain among the better-known figures, such as Marguerite Duras, Nathalie Sarraute, Marguerite Yourcenar, and Simone de Beauvoir from France and Antillean authors Simone Schwarz-Bart and Maryse Condé, are noted for their writing in prose as well as (or even more than) in theater. Others of the writers have made their mark mainly in drama—in theatrical production as much as in the creation of scripts. Among them are Jovette Marchessault and Pol Pelletier from Quebec and Simone Benmussa, Loleh Bellon, Françoise Chatôt, Anne Delbée, and Brigitte Jaques from France. The newer and/or less often produced playwrights from the French-speaking world include Abla Farhoud from Quebec, Diur N'Tumb of Zaire, Michèle Césaire from Martinique, Michèle Rakotoson from Madagascar, Werewere Liking, a Cameroonian working out of the Ivory Coast, and the Algerian author Fatima Gallaire-Bourega.

In the case of younger Francophone writers the publication of scripts and of their English translation tends to be rather limited. Two remarkably energetic organizations, however, specialize in the location and distribution in French and

English of French-language drama: Ubu Repertory Theater in New York, 149 Mercer St., New York, NY 10012. Tel. (212)925-0999; and, for Québécois theater, the CEAD (Le Centre d'Essai des Auteurs Dramatiques) in Montreal, 426 Sherbrooke est, Montreal, Quebec H2L 1J6. Tel. (514)288-3384. The preparation of this bibliography would not have been possible without information and copies of plays from both these centers. They remain excellent sources for further investigation into Francophone theater.

Atlan, Liliane. *Monsieur Fugue, ou le mal de terre.* Paris: Editions du Seuil, 1967.
Mister Fugue, or Earthsick. Trans. Marguerite Feitlowitz. In *Modern Literatures Annual, 1983,* ed. Bettina Knapp. Greenwood, Fla.: Penkevill Publishing Co., 1983. Also in *Plays of the Holocaust,* ed. and intro. Elinor Fuchs. New York: Theater Communications Group, 1987.
Cast: 1 girl, 3 boys, 5 men
3 acts

Atlan's powerful drama depicts the capture and journey to the gas chambers of four Jewish children. One of the soldiers escorting them, the strange and guilt-ridden Mister Fugue, has changed loyalties and decided to accompany them to their death. At his urging the children begin to create stories and act out scenes during their trip. Through their storytelling and playacting they relive the past and create the future that will never be: escape, adolescence, marriage, child-raising, aging, and natural death.

The setting is fairly specific, though it could easily be abstracted in production: first, the flaming ruins of a ghetto, then the back of the moving truck in which the children play out their roles, and finally the "Valley of the Bones"—the approach to the flaming gas chambers. If the children have become hardened and cynical through war, moments of warmth emerge in the poetry, irony, and nostalgia of certain of their played scenes. The power of the children's theater to stave off the terror of impending death—"playing" that goes from the cruel to the tender, from the frighteningly real to the liberating fantastic within a single speech—is capable of producing both admiration and horror in the audience.

de Beauvoir, Simone. *Les Bouches inutiles.* Paris: Gallimard, 1945.
Who Shall Die? Trans. Claude Francis and Fernande Gontier. New York: River Press, 1983.
Cast: 3 women, 7 men, + townspeople
2 acts (8 tableaux)

Existentialist and feminist themes intertwine in this drama first performed four years before the publication of de Beauvoir's *The Second Sex.* The play is set in a fourteenth-century Flemish town that is running out of provisions, as it has been under siege for the past year. The governing council, swayed by a power-hungry male leader, finds a solution to the problem:

it condemns all of the women, children, the aged, and the infirm—the "bouches inutiles" (useless mouths)—to death by exposure. Two of the other city leaders, however, influenced by the three women characters, convince the council and citizens to reverse their decision. It is agreed that all of the town's inhabitants will band together and storm the enemy camp.

Theatrical space and movement in this play are quite traditional. Stage directions prescribe four different and fairly involved set changes—two interior and two exterior village scenes. Most of the tableaux include the participation of groups of people (townspeople) as well as the principals. The strength of *Les Bouches inutiles* is in its convincing, complex characters and suspense-producing moments. The play's focus on the concerns of the women gives the existential theme an interesting and moving female specificity. The women, part of the group that has had no part in determining its collective fate, finally find their voice, prompting the two main male characters to engage themselves similarly in authentic action—thus saving the city from destroying its "useless mouths."

Bellon, Loleh. *Les Dames du jeudi* (The Thursday Ladies). *L'Avant-Scène*, 1 April 1977, 5–32.
Cast: 4 women, 2 men
1 act

This play focuses on the interrelationship of three women friends throughout their childhood and adult lives. The framework for the action is the women's customary gatherings for tea on Thursdays. During the three Thursday teas presented onstage, the friends' conversations are intertwined with scenes from their past. The movements backward in time are to be made only through modifications of gesture, voice, and attitude, with no changes in costume or lighting—a technique that reinforces the importance of the past in the women's present lives. In natural, everyday language that reveals a certain comedy of character, the friends play out their present and past preoccupations and experiences. We see their aloneness and financial difficulties, their dealings with men (now absent through rejection, divorce, or death), and their relations with their children and one another. The interaction of these quite different and finally lonely women is characterized by both rivalry and caring. The tone moves delicately between the melancholic and the amusing, corresponding to the combination of the three characters' solitude and their efforts to comfort one another.

Benmussa, Simone. *La Vie singulière d'Albert Nobbs*. Paris: Editions Des Femmes, 1977.
The Singular Life of Albert Nobbs. Trans. Barbara Wright. *Benmussa Directs*. London: John Calder, 1979.
Original cast: 10 women, 2 men
12 scenes

Intriguing in its scenic presentation as well as in the political questions that it raises, this play follows the life, loves, and aspirations of a nineteenth-century Irishwoman who masquerades as a man. "Albert Nobbs" has taken on a male identity in order to be able to earn a decent living as a hotel valet. She meets a hotel guest, Hubert Page, who, it is revealed, is similarly a woman in man's clothing and who says that she has found happiness in marriage to another woman. Albert then tries to replicate Hubert's situation. She searches unsuccessfully for the right woman to share her life and, finally, resigned to her solitary fate, dies.

The set, a multilevel representation of the hotel's interior, combines both real and obviously painted characters, rooms, and furniture. This "strange mixture of banality and fantasy," in the playwright's words, is mirrored in the combination of narration and played scenes, of live voices and recorded ones from offstage, and of comic and serious tones. The recurrent attempt to undercut theatrical illusion supports the issue of masquerade that is central to the play. In Benmussa's introduction to the piece she stresses the economic necessity of Albert's and Hubert's disguises as men and insists that, if there is trangression in the piece, it is on a poetic rather than a sexual level. The presence of women in drag, however, makes the question of sexual identity—within the larger political context that the play suggests—the most compelling issue.

Bonal, Louise. *Portrait de famille*. Paris: Ligue Française de l'Enseignement de l'Education permanente / Fédération Nationale de Théâtre, 1983.
Family Portrait. Trans. Timothy Johns. New York: Ubu Repertory Theater Publications, 1985.
Cast: 3 women, 4 men
12 scenes

In Bonal's play tragedy and comedy, the psychologically probing and the abstract, successfully mix. *Portrait de Famille* examines the everyday tensions of a proletarian family, focusing on the situation of Louise, the single mother of three grown but still problematic children. The plot and tone veer from the sad to the absurd. Suicidal son Albert, who has just found a job in a funeral parlor ("I'm happy working with my dead people," he says), becomes part of his brother Patrick's plan to kidnap the body of a recently deceased man and hold it for ransom. Meanwhile, social pressure and personal jealousies fuel a plan for the double wedding of Louise's two other children. Tensions mount until the final, catastrophic clash of the family members, after which the children desert their mother. Louise then invites to the ersatz wedding banquet the questionable and ingratiating neighbor man, who has been courting her throughout the play. By including his children in her invitation, she seems to settle anew into an outwardly stable but internally fissured familial order.

The characters, though carefully drawn from everyday life and speaking a colloquial French, are sufficiently stylized to create a critical distance; they all have ridiculously fatal flaws. Louise's lines are written without punctuation to translate the speed, energy, and quirkiness of her thought patterns. Bonal's particular form of hyperrealism foregrounds and satirizes the violent hopelessness of the urban underclass.

Césaire, Michèle. *La Nef.* Centre Dramatique Régional de la Martinique: Editions Théâtrales, 1992.

The Ship. Trans. Richard Miller. In *New French Language Plays,* ed. Françoise Kourilsky and Catherine Temerson. New York: Ubu Repertory Theater Publications, 1993.

Cast: 2 women, 4 men

3 acts

In three short acts six characters on a modern-day Ship of Fools play out the moments just before they reach land, where, perhaps, they will invent a new form of community. Having chosen to wander on the sea because they do not fit in anywhere else, these six beings, each symbolic of an uneasy condition of Caribbean peoples, exercise in the cockeyed universe of the ship their individual traumas. "Misery," part sorceress, part old-maid schoolteacher, carries her African ancestors on her face and in her second voice. "Erzulie" incarnates thralldom to the voodoo goddess of love. "Cassino" is the permanent victim of European wars. "Kevin," the philosopher, never tires of reminding the rest of the crew of their liminal status midway through life and death. "Euphrarias," the captain, reinvents the world through his verse. And the child "Mimo" presages a possible future, in which hierarchy will no longer determine who has the right to speak.

This is an imaginative and potentially very lively dramatic parable. All in plumbing the meaning of their existence on-board ship, the characters sing, dance, go about their business rigging sails and climbing masts, celebrate a marriage, and stage a major tempest just for the pleasure of living through one.

Chalem, Denise. *A Cinquante ans elle découvrait la mer.* L'Avant-Scène (15 October 1980): 8–19.

The Sea between Us. Trans. Danielle Brunon, Adine Sagalyn, and Catherine Temerson. New York: Ubu Repertory Theater Publications, 1986.

Cast: 2 women, 1 girl

1 act

A young woman and her mother play out important aspects and moments of their life together in this piece. Their relationship is seen primarily from the point of view of the daughter, an author, whose "written" narrative passages provide the framework for the action. Oblivious to the setting (the kitchen, living room, and, behind a partition, the toilet of the family apartment), the daughter opens the play by reading part of the text that she is currently writing. She describes her mother, who, she writes, is "dead / in me no relief." She begins to type onstage, "When you would come home from work. . . . " At that moment time shifts backward, and the mother arrives, laden with groceries and spouting a wave of one-sided chatter. Thus begins the first of the six intimate scenes both amusing and sad, realistic and poetic, which lead us through the last years of the mother's life. Fights about the daughter's profession and life-style alternate with moments of tenderness or wild affection. The daily rituals of eating and drinking, dressing and undressing, washing up and going to the bathroom are the constants that support the exuberant highs and lows of their relationship.

Condé, Maryse. *Pension les Alizés.* Paris: Mercure de France, 1988.
The Tropical Breeze Hotel. Trans. Barbara Brewster Lewis and Catherine Temerson.
  In *Plays by Women: An International Anthology, Book 2,* ed. Françoise Kourilsky
  and Catherine Temerson. New York: Ubu Repertory Theater Publications, 1994.
Cast: 1 woman, 1 man
5 tableaux

This play depicts the encounter and separation of Emma Boisgris, former exotic dancer, and Ismaël Modestin, failed Haitian revolutionary. They meet in Paris, to which Emma had fled years before from her Guadeloupian island to lead the life of a twentieth-century courtesan. At this point in her career she lives comfortably off past investments in her "favors." Ismaël, younger, more bourgeois, and scared, has fled, but to escape his having botched an attempt to overthrow the regime of Jean-Claude Duvalier. Emma props Ismaël up and sends him back to Haiti to put his life in order, her own having been shaken by the promise of what might have been—if only they had met when they still had their innocence. Innocence, has, however, forever deserted them, and each in his or her own way pays the consequences.

This contemporary psychological drama encloses two characters within the space of Emma's apartment. They combat each other and their pasts in dialogue and monologue. They will end, however, by only being able to share nostalgia for the lands they have left and a future neither will realize. The play's interest lies in exposing the difficulties of these Caribbean exiles and in fleshing out their psychological profiles.

Delaunay, Constance. *Olympe dort: "La Donna" et "Olympe dort"* (Olympia Is
  Sleeping). Paris: Gallimard, 1977.
Cast: 3 women, 2 men
2 tableaux

Delaunay's play, *Olympe dort,* presents the ugliness of the life of a dysfunctional upper-middle-class family. Set on the back terrace of their home, it takes place during a sleepless night and on the following morning in the life of Mona and her husband, Jude, and their young-adult daughters, Marcelline and Olympe. The family members' jealousies, mutual deception, and hunger for love are brought out through tasteless joking on the part of Mona and Marcelline: the characters constantly interrupt one another in rapid exchanges, often at cross-purposes. The tension among them is released in moments of craziness—chases and verbal and physical fights that are half-serious, half–in fun, the "fun" covering up their lack of authentic contact and tenderness. At several points in the play lighting changes and song from offstage interrupt the course of events to reveal or comment on the characters' thoughts and their roles in the action. Throughout all of the activity Olympe is the absent center, offstage during most of the play. She is the subject of much of her family's conversation, the silent victim of their pettiness and insensitivity. The play's ending brings together its elements of black comedy. Marcelline discovers that Olympe has tried to commit suicide with her father's sleeping pills. The long-winded and philandering family doctor, having come by, coincidentally, to minister to the indisposed maid, rushes to "save" Olympe, proferring as he does so a final dubious homily: "Nothing's more beautiful than a young person!"

Delbée, Anne. *Une Femme* (A Woman). Paris: Presses de la Renaissance, 1982.

Director Anne Delbée has given us the intriguing story of turn-of-the-century sculptor Camille Claudel in two forms; as a successful play (written with Jeanne Fayard and performed at the Cartoucherie de Vincennes and then at the Théâtre du Rond Point / Jean-Louis Barrault, 1981–82) and as an equally popular book. Only the book is available for public distribution, but it is full of dramatic possibilities for anyone who is interested in adapting it for the stage. It provided, for example, material for actress-producer Isabelle Adjani's 1989 film based on the life of Camille Claudel.

Claudel was the sister of writer Paul Claudel and student, assistant, and lover of sculptor Auguste Rodin. Through a mixture of quotes from primary sources and fictionalized narrative, Delbée follows Claudel's life from her childhood through her thirty-year career as a sculptor until her internment at a mental hospital for the last third of her life. Delbée emphasizes the nature and strength of the social restrictions at that time upon a woman artist and a woman alone. She produces a moving and mythical portrait of the sculptor as regal, tenacious, and antisocial, misunderstood by her contemporaries.

In Delbée's theater piece three actresses played three different aspects of Claudel: the sculptor, the rebel, and the madwoman. A fourth actress, the societal voice, provided commentary and transitions. In the set representing a sculpture studio, the players, through dialogue and change of costume, presented the various stages of Claudel's extraordinary life.

Delbo, Charlotte. *Qui rapportera ces paroles?* Paris: Editions Pierre Jean Oswald, 1974.
Who Will Carry the Word? Trans. Cynthia Haft. In *The Theatre of the Holocaust,* ed. Robert Skloot. Madison: University of Wisconsin Press, 1982.
Cast: 23 women
3 acts

This tragedy tells—and paradoxically discusses the impossibility of telling—the horrors committed against the inhabitants of a Nazi death camp for women. At the beginning, middle, and end of the play two camp survivors speak to the audience, declaring that they have come back from the land of no return, from "the truth"—a truth that, they intimate, is not understandable in the context of the contemporary world. After the opening speech by present-day Françoise, we are taken back to the time and place of the atrocities. She and other characters portray and recount in agonizing, unromanticized detail the despair, sicknesses, and deaths in the concentration camp. The dialogue alternates among several groups of women onstage, who, by the end of the second act, are reduced to three survivors, and finally to two.

The production elements of the play are abstract and suggestive. Through the use of lighting, sound, and movement, the bare stage is transformed from present to past and from one part of the camp to another. Shadow and appropriate reactive movement on the part of the actresses indicate the threatening presence of the Nazi soldiers.

Much of the power of *Qui rapportera ses paroles?* resides in the tension between the stated impossibility of words to transmit the truth and the fact that the characters nevertheless persist in trying to do so. Because of its very nature, the play overcomes to a certain degree the frustrations felt by its characters. It emphasizes the ability of theater to tell through showing, not simply through words.

Dorin, Françoise. *L'Autre valse* (The Other Waltz). *L'Avant-Scène* (15 March 1976): 7–40.
Cast: 4 women, 5 men
3 acts

This elegant comedy, written by the foremost author of the "Théâtre du Boulevard" in France today, is stunning in its technique though conservative in its message and scenic presentation. The play's upholding of conventional values is part of the Boulevard tradition, as are its lightness of tone, cleverness of language, and the intricate orchestration of its plot and subplots. The main character, Alexandre, has invited Nathalie, a pretty, young, "liberated woman," to his reserve, an isolated area that he has peopled with types representative of cultured, prewar society. He intends her to be the mate of one of its members. Nathalie, however, resists this plan, attempting through persuasion and then blackmail to take Alexandre off with her to the outside world. Finally, however, the situation returns to normal: Nathalie leaves, and Alexandre is again secure in his life of refinement, tradition, and taboo.

The play's nostaglia for "things the way they were"—not without a misogynist bent—is mirrored in the static quality of the setting and of the use of space onstage. The action takes place in a minutely described formal garden just outside a palatial home. There is enough complexity in the set to permit characters to make hidden entrances and exists. The strong points of *L'Autre valse* are its quick exchanges of light, understated dialogue, the humor of the exaggerated personality types portrayed onstage, and the precision of the plot, whose twists and turns are calculated to obtain the maximum amount of surprise and delight from the spectators. In its nostaglic paternalism—typical of Boulevard theater, which reinforces unquestioningly the bourgeoisie's positive portrait of itself—it provides a disturbing counterpoint to the plays of most of Dorin's women contemporaries.

Duras, Marguerite. *La Musica deuxième* (The Musica: Two). Paris: Gallimard, 1985.
Cast: 1 woman, 1 man
2 acts

Anne-Marie Roche and Michel Nollet meet again late at night in the lobby of the hotel in which they had lived the first months of their volcanic marriage. This time, however, they are present for the finalization of their divorce. They speak until daybreak about their current lives, their past love, the town where neither lives anymore. Their conversation is a dance of desire and profound pain. Never touching, they inscribe onstage the passionately charged distance that has come to represent their life together. They will separate, each going back to the ostensibly saner structures into which they have settled. Yet, as dawn filters into the hotel, it is clear that no love will ever equal what theirs had been and perhaps still is.

The play speaks troublingly of the deception that comes with the loss of the overwhelming desire that marks the first stages of romance. As for so many characters in Duras's universe, it is this desire that alone gives meaning to existence. Anne-Marie Roche and Michel Nollet share the state of extreme alienation of those who cannot "be" unless absorbed in the other, an absorption always ephemeral and ultimately destructive.

Farhoud, Abla. *Les Filles du 5-10-15c,* MS, 1986.
The Girls From the Five and Ten. Trans. Jill MacDougall, ed. Françoise Kourilsky and Catherine Temerson. In *Plays by Women: An International Anthology,* New York: Ubu Repertory Theater Publications, 1988.
Cast: 3–5 women, 2–4 men, 1 girl, and passersby
9 scenes

Farhoud's tragicomedy, set in the Montreal suburbs of the early 1960s, presents scenes from the lives of two Lebanese sisters who have grown up in Quebec. The play explores their position in relation to the Lebanese, French, and English Canadian cultures. The sisters are ultimately "in between" those cultures and therefore truly belong to none of them. Amira, nineteen, and Kaobab, sixteen, work in their father's five-and-ten store. Amira is the contented, dutiful daughter, happy to work for the good of the family. Kaobab, the bright, rebellious one, despairs of ever being freed from her monotonous life as a clerk. In the course of the play Kaobab finally convinces her sister that they must escape the shop. Amira sets fire to it—only to see Kaobab rush headlong into the flames to rescue tapes of "memoirs" and poignant messages of frustration to her parents that she had been continuously recording throughout the play.

The sense of slow suffocation, of the immutability of "the way things are," is translated in the static and enclosed nature of the play's setting. All of the action, which we see through the store window and the continuous coming and going of passersby, takes place within the shop. A physical closing-in occurs also through the progressive accumulation of boxes that are delivered to the store but never opened. The inherent tragedy of the situation is tempered, however, by the warmth of the relationship between the two sisters and the moments of joy and clowning that such love occasions.

Gallaire-Bourega, Fatima. *Témoignage contre un homme stérile* (Testimony against a Sterile Man). *L'Avant Scène* (1 October 1987): 39–56.
Cast: 1 man, 5 women
1 act

This stunning one-act consists almost entirely of the sometimes humorous, always aggressive monologue of "Madame Bertin," shut up in an old-age home. She minces no words as she obsessively describes the vigorous sex life her husband has forced her to lead. Sometimes, it seems, she even liked it. She squeezes a confession of sexual unhappiness out of the maid who cleans her toilet. She treats the neighbor lady, the activities therapist, and the doctor who come to call with unbidden vulgarity. During all these short visits she proves to be acid-tongued and hurtfully frank but also curiously charming. Her behavior refutes all the stereotypical sweet and fragile images of the "little old lady." Her ongoing diatribe, feminist and furious, ruthlessly presents and analyzes female servitude. But "Mme Bertin" also clearly loves her husband—perhaps because he has grown so childlike and because she has to help him hide his lately declared sexual perversions.

When the real Mme Bertin arrives from the hairdresser's, panicked to discover that Monsieur Bertin has been up to his old tranvestite tricks again, the audience should experience the shock of a very unexpected coup de théâtre. M and Mme Bertin have indeed grown "alike" in old age. And the psychological realism of their encounter, their tolerance and love of each other, help mitigate the melodramatic reversal.

Gallaire-Bourega's three-act *Ah! Vous êtes venus . . . là où il y a quelques tombes ou Princesse* (Paris: Editions des quatre-vents, 1988) (*You Have Come Back,* trans. Jill MacDougall, In *Plays by Women: An International Anthology,* ed. Françoise Kourilsky and Catherine Temerson [New York: Ubu Repertory Theater Publications, 1988]) also focuses on women's enslavement and relies on melodrama for effect. In it she depicts the terrifying homecoming of an Algerian woman, self-exiled to France and married to a Frenchman. The traditional mourning for her recently deceased father turns into a torture session, as the village elders, angry female guardians of the patriarchy, condemn her to death for deserting Islam and the old ways. Gallaire-Bourega is one of the promising French playwrights able to work within and across two cultures, French and North African.

Jaques, Brigitte. *Elvire-Jouvet 40*. Paris: Béba, 1986.

Seven Lessons. Trans. Albert Bermel. For the Pepsico Summerfare Festival, Purchase, N.Y., 1988.

Cast: 3 men, 1 woman

1 act

This play, reconstructed in great part from the notebooks in which the lessons of the famous actor and teacher Louis Jouvet were recorded, traces the progress of a young actress as she refines her approach to the role of Elvire in Molière's *Don Juan*. The interaction between the actress, her two young colleagues—who play Don Juan and Sganarelle—and Jouvet is highly charged with the students' need both to assert their independence and to attain the perfection of feeling and pace that Jouvet holds out to them as the only goal worthy of actors. The intensity of this professional confrontation is further complicated and underscored by the tension only barely suggested in the noise of marching soldiers and/or sirens filtering into the rehearsal hall. It is 1940; the Germans have just occupied France; the actor learning the role of Elvire is Jewish.

The audience only recognizes her Jewishness at the end of the play as the young woman turns her back to the house, having at last conquered her role in an extraordinarily moving scene that is both her triumph and the triumph of Elvire. The Star of David sewn onto her coat helps explain retrospectively the complex subtext of the play, which is felt but not completely understood until the play's final moments: the young woman's sense of existence has been completely channeled into realizing the performance qualities that Jouvet, tough and exalted, has demanded of her. The audience is left with the haunting question: What will become of her after her actor's victory?

Laberge, Marie. *"L'Homme gris," versions française et québécoise. L'Avant-Scène* (1 March 1986): 9–36.

"L'Homme gris" suivi de "Eva et Evelyne." Montreal: VLB Editeur, 1986.

Deep Night. Trans. Rina Fraticelli. Working Draft. Montreal: Le Centre d'Essai des Auteurs Dramatiques, 1986.

Cast: 1 man, 1 young woman

1 act

This intense drama is about the breakdown of relations within a middle-class Québécois family, in particular the objectification and oppression of a daughter by her father. In the course of an evening in a motel room, the middle-aged father chronicles the family's collapse to his twenty-one-year-old daughter, revealing increasingly disturbing facts and attitudes as he becomes more and more drunk. The daughter, once anorexic, now a stutterer and the victim of abuse by her husband, remains silent throughout most of the play. As her father's accounts of his voyeurism and acts of callousness and his manifestations of resentment and self-delusion accumulate, however, she responds physically with disgust, fear, sickness, and finally violence. At the end of the play she abuses and threatens to kill herself, then lacerates her father's eyes and body.

The set—a stark motel room lit by various combinations of flashing neon from outside, room lights, and the TV—provides the perfectly cruel surroundings for the play's slowly building tension. The horror of the situation presented is underlined ironically by the natural and colloquial nature of the father's speech (the Québécois of the original version, and the beautiful adaptations in standard French and English) and by the juxtaposition of the father's verbosity with the daughter's muteness, a contrast that constitutes a challenge for both the players and the director.

Liking, Werewere. *Singuè Mura: Considérant que la femme . . .* (Singuè Mura: Given That A Woman . . .). Abidjan: Editions Eyo-Ki-Yi, 1990.
Cast: 6 women, 3 men, + 18 villagers
15 tableaux

In this dramatic ritual villagers gather under the guidance of their Wise Man to attempt to bring back Singuè Mura from the spirit world. She has killed herself in response to the community's pressure on her husband to take a second wife. University educated, politically active, a village leader, Singuè Mura has set up a school, an orphanage, a medical dispensary. She has not, however, had children, and her mother-in-law insists on her right to descendants.

The play exposes the terrifying dilemma of the modern African woman, forced to "mutilate" a part of herself and her possibilities in order to either have children or pursue the modernization of her community. Singuè Mura does eventually come back from the dead, after purging her own guilt for having aborted three times in her past. The community also comes to recognize its error and selfishness.

This is a complex piece, functioning in flashbacks and through a juxtaposition of scenes of sorcery and spiritual communion with moments of satire in which the villagers discuss their situation and argue about what they should do. Percussion, singing, and dancing are fundamental to creating the mood and involving the audience in the ritual, a ritual that, however, ends with a question. Returned to life, what will Singuè Mura do about her relationship to her husband, her co-wife, and her village?

Marchessault, Jovette. *Les Vaches de nuit: Chronique lesbienne du moyen-âge québécois. Tryptique Lesbien.* Montreal: Editions de la Pleine Lune, 1980.
Night Cows / Les Vaches de Nuit—A Story / Un Conte. Trans. Yvonne M. Klein. (Both French and English versions included.) *Fireweed* 5–6 (Winter 1979–Spring 1980): 168–79.
Cast: 1 woman
1 act

Marchessault's fairly short poetic monologue celebrates in dense and fluid language the female body and female culture. In this sonorous text the speaking voice—that of a young calf—chants the praises of her beautiful mother. She tells of the gathering of cows and other animals in the night sky, where they discuss the "time of the females," the days before their oppression. During the daytime, however, they live the calm existence of the castrated. Their hope is to keep alive the memory of the previous age in order eventually to attain the "promised land" and "give it another name." Through this expressive, sometimes humorous, and never didactic story, Marchessault presents the possibility of women together "speaking otherwise," outside the patriarchal order. The text includes no stage directions, but its highly descriptive nature and the liveliness of its characters provide more than adequate inspiration for its production.

Readers should be aware of other dramatic works by this important woman writer of Quebec, including *La Saga des poules mouillées* (Montreal: Editions de la Pleine Lune, 1981; and Montreal: Leméac, 1989) (*The Saga of the Wet Hens,* trans. Linda Gaboriau [Vancouver: Talonbooks, 1983]), which honors four French Canadian women authors; and *La Terre est trop courte, Violette Leduc* (Montreal: Editions de la Pleine Lune, 1982) (*The Edge of Earth Is Too Near, Violette Leduc,* trans. Susanne de Lotbinière-Harwood), based upon Leduc's life and works (available from Ubu Repertory Theater and the Centre d'Essai des Auteurs Dramatiques).

N'Tumb, Diur. *Qui hurle dans la nuit?* MS.
Lost Voices. Trans. Jill MacDougall. *In Afrique: New Plays,* ed. Françoise Kourilsky and Catherine Temerson. New York: Ubu Repertory Theater Publications, 1987.
Cast: 6 men, 6 women, + singers, dancers, villagers

This is a funny and highly acerbic morality play, its humor not unlike that of many contemporary West African pieces that treat the conflict between tradition and modernity. In it the character King comes back to his African village to take up his hereditary leadership role after many years of intellectual dalliance in the United States. Accompanied by his even more Westernized African girlfriend, Aya, and his advisor Mali, he is forced to set off to find his voice, which has mysteriously disappeared after only a three-month's rule. Aya wants him to give up the search and return to Boston. Mali cunningly encourages King to stay and fulfill his obligations. Various wise and foolish men and women, dancers and musicians, try to help him find his voice. Their advice and/or their talismanic performances—there is traditional dancing and singing throughout the play—are to no avail.

Although a monster brags that he has recovered King's voice, Mali convinces Aya, through a magnificent lie, that he is the real thief. Mali claims that he will only give King back his voice when Aya sleeps with him. She complies under great duress, and King, who has in fact retrieved his voice from the monster, discovers her infidelity. He has, thus, lost everything in the quest for his voice: best friend, lover, happiness, freedom and tranquility. The play asks if his voice—an obvious metaphor for political power—is worth it.

Pelletier, Pol. *La Lumière blanche*. Montreal: Le Centre d'Essai des Auteurs
    Dramatiques, 1986.
The White Light. Trans. Yvonne M. Klein. Montreal: Le Centre d'Essai des Auteurs
    Dramatiques, 1987.
Cast: 3 women
18 scenes

In this burlesque tragicomedy Pelletier examines and celebrates womanhood: the richness
of contradictions within and between women and the grounds for their coming together.
The three characters are Torregrossa, tough and agressive; B. C. Macgruge, frilly and
"feminine"; and Leude, quiet, distinguished and, at the beginning of the play, pregnant.
They meet and undertake a series of "games"—physical "scuffling" and a mock trial—
designed by Torregrossa to free them from the repression of their pasts and reveal the way
to a strong new existence. The set is open and suggestive, a "desert" that, congruent with
the "games within games within games" notion that is basic to the action, maintains a
self-conscious theatricality. Through lively metaphorical dialogue and movement, both of
which range from the brutal to the farcical to the tender, the women play out the
complexities and contrasts of the types that they represent. A series of explosive encounters, revelations, and realizations leads to Torregrossa's self-destruction; this moment is
followed in the script by a choice among three final scenes—one more exaggerated,
fanciful, and tragic than the other two. All of the endings include B. C.'s and Leude's
march into the white light of the play's title, light that is at once purifying, cruel, and
vibrating with the promise of life.

Rakotoson, Michèle. *La Maison morte* (The Dead House). Paris: Théâtre Sud /
    l'Harmattan, 1991.
Cast: 2 women, 3 men
1 act

This is an acerbic and paradoxically lyrical satire about the contemporary political situation
in Madagascar. Since independence from France, the island nation—as is true of many
African states—has undergone a series of dictatorships, most of the first leaders replaced
by their own ambitious junior henchmen. In *La Maison morte* King Randriambé, playing
cards instead of tending to the demonstrations going on outside the palace, loses the game
and his life to Rabary, the councillor he has been treating as a mere toady. In turn, Rabary
will discover that his power depends on the corporal who helped him depose the king.
    Before this cycle is set in motion again, Queen Ramoana, in strongly rhythmed
solliloquies recalling the Malagasy oral tradition of the *hira gasy*, berates the king for losing
the sense of what his mission and his country are all about. Their daughter, Ranoro, torn
between loyalty to her family and a commitment to social change, sacrifices herself to the
rapacity of a governing system that can only replace terror with more of the same.

Highly metaphorical, very intriguing in terms of the association of dance, song, and ritual to the criticism of leadership that has lost touch with grass roots, *La Maison morte* can function as live performance or radio drama. Rakotoson builds suspense through the orchestration of symbols and sounds, warning the audience well before the characters what the inevitable end will be. She also creates a splendidly imaged dialogue, with characters speaking in parables and paraphrases.

Redonnet, Marie. *Tir et Lir* (Tir and Lir). Paris: Minuit, 1988.
Cast: 1 man, 1 woman
10 tableaux

Redonnet's absurdist comedy places onstage two pathetic elderly invalids. The substance of their lives consists of the letters they receive from their children, Tir and Lir, and their own efforts to respond. The episodic structure stages ten versions of the Monday morning ritual of receiving, reading, and answering Tir's and Lir's letters. These grow increasingly dire. Tir, a soldier, has been accidently shot in the leg. Lir, whose unspecified occupation leads one, nevertheless, to suspect the "oldest profession," has caught a deadly virus from a client. With each letter the conditions of Tir and Lir, as well as of their parents, Mub and Mab, worsen. As the last-gasp letters from the four deathbeds are produced, the play fades out, echoing Mub's and Mab's situation onstage and, presumably, that of Tir and Lir offstage.

This tightly constructed and terribly pessimistic drama recalls Beckett's theatrical vision, without, however, conveying the redeeming and often breezy generosity of his characters. Mub and Mab are nightmare clowns, self-pitying and self-righteous. The children are victims of both their sluglike parents and a social system that provides very few opportunities to the poorest of the poor. Redonnet's characters live and die uniquely within the confines of letters devoid of all imagination. Life is rot and mutilation, and communication equals no more than the reworking of the same old formulas. The play's success depends on the kind of skillful timing that establishes and maintains this extreme grotesqueness without falling into unremitting nihilism.

Reza, Yasmina. *Conversations après un enterrement* (Conversations after a Burial). Paris: Actes Sud, 1987.
Cast: 3 men, 3 women
1 act

In this deft and delicate portrait of a family gathering after the father's burial the author confronts three adult children with their loss, their rivalries, and their love for one another. The play exudes a special generosity: male and female characters are intricately and complexly drawn. There are none of the usual stereotypes of bourgeois realism and no heavy-handed moralizing or facile psychologizing. Complex and sympathetic characters deal with the terrible pain of losing a beloved father and the attendant egotism, nastiness, and even decency that constitute coping strategies for what is otherwise an unbearable and incomprehensible experience.

Creation of atmosphere rather than concern for material details places this play among the best of the "neorealistic" works now being written in France. The extremely well-turned and convincing dialogue, the quality of the introspection, and the dignity of the characters, who use language as a form of action, make this play an actors' delight.

Roche, Anne, and Françoise Chatôt. *Louise/Emma*. Paris: Editions Tierce, 1982.
Cast: 3 women, 2 men
18 scenes

This play celebrates two "foremothers," the late-nineteeth-century French anarchist Louise Michel and her Russian-American counterpart, Emma Goldmann. It is an imaginative and stylized view of an encounter between them, a series of narrated and played scenes in which the characters discuss their ideas and present important moments from their pasts. Through these scenes we see women alike in their fundamental anarchism and feminism and different in their individual practice of these -*isms*, especially in their sexual mores.

The temporal and physical setting, stage movement, and character distribution are open and flexible. The action occurs in a railroad station that is transformed into other, out-of-sequence times and places through lighting, music, sound, props, and the players' words and movement. Dialogue varies from the discursive to the poetic, from the psychologically realistic to the suggestive—such as the chanting of the names of women revolutionaries that opens the piece. The players, too, have multiple dimensions, with several of them taking on a number of roles. The full exploitation of theatrical means intended by the creators of this play is detailed in extensive stage directions.

Sarraute, Nathalie. *Isma*. Paris: Gallimard, 1970.
Izzum. Trans. Maria Jolas. *Nathalie Sarraute: Collected Plays*. Ed. Marie Jolas. New York: Braziller, 1981.
Cast: 4 women, 4 men
1 act

This enigmatic radio play is about language and the power relations established through language. It consists of a conversation among four couples. Central to the discussion are the personality and habits of an absent couple named the Dubuits. This subject, first skirted by the characters, then serving as the starting point for a series of subconversations, pits two of the characters, He and She, against the others, Man 1, 2, and 3 and Woman 1, 2, and 3. Though all agree upon the unpleasant personality and evil influence of the Dubuits, He and She further maintain that the couple's evilness is evident in and transmitted by their particular pronunciation of the suffix —*ism:* "izzum." The others, opting for more obvious evidence of oddity, such as ears that protrude or an especially long upper lip, fail to be convinced by the arguments of the two main characters.

In this depiction of bias against that which is different, alliances of certain characters against others constantly and threateningly shift. The absurdity of their discussion thus possesses a hard, nervous edge. The reader or listener, introduced at what is obviously the midpoint of an endless and complex conversation, becomes, like the characters, subject to the power of the word to create isolation, claustrophobia, and fear.

Schwarz-Bart, Simone. *Ton beau capitaine.* Paris: Editions du Seuil, 1987.
Your Handsome Captain. Trans. Jessica Harris and Catherine Temerson. In *Plays by Women: An International Anthology,* ed. Françoise Kourilsky and Catherine Temerson. New York: Ubu Repertory Theater Publications, 1988.
Cast: 1 man, 1 voice-over (female)
1 act

A moving and invigorating piece, *Ton beau capitaine* speaks of the life of Wilnor, a Haitian immigrant worker in Guadeloupe, and the effect of his ten-year exile on Marie-Ange, his wife. As the play progresses, Wilnor responds to Marie-Ange's most recent cassette (their only form of communication) with a mixture of joy at hearing her voice, cockiness from needing to respond "as a man" to the disarray she describes, and, finally, near emotional collapse when he understands that she is confessing to an extramarital affair that has left her pregnant. The play exposes both the bankruptcy of the West's capitalist dream—especially as it gets played out by peoples of the "Third World" looking for a way out of their poverty—and that particular double bind of Third-World women trapped within patriarchy and neocolonialism.

Wilnor exorcises his demons through music and dance. Songs and rhythms from the French Caribbean bespeak the characters' and the author's pride in cultural specificity. Wilnor's struggle to understand what has happened to him and his wife allows him (and the audience) to come to grips with what family, community, and love might mean if possession and domination did not figure so prominently in emotional constellations.

Lo Teatre de la Carriera. *L'Ecrit des femmes: Paroles de femmes des pays d'oc* (Women's Writing: Voices from Occitania). Ed. Catherine Bonafé, Marie-Hélène Bonafé, and Anne Clément. Paris: Editions Solin, 1981.

This collection by the Occitanian (Provençal) troupe Lo Teatre de la Carriera includes three plays and one musical presentation. The pieces are based upon interviews with and research on women of the Provençal region. All of these highly imaginative, stylized pieces deal with the difficulty and necessity of their female characters' independence. In each multiple roles are played by members of a small cast (three women and one man, at the most). Traditional and original songs are mixed with the spoken dialogue, and the language switches from standard French to the Occitanian dialect to a combination of the two. This linguistic movement permits nonspeakers of Occitanian to understand the dialogue without too much difficulty. In addition, helpful French translations and a pronunciation guide are included in the text.

Except for the last piece in the collection, the plays work against psychological realism in their movement, set, costuming, and props. Exaggeration rules the stage action and the fantastic intervenes; the consequent humor balances and at the same time intensifies the gravity of the situations presented. The first play, *Saisons de femme* (Seasons of Woman) shows the various stages in the life of Aurette, a middle-aged woman, who, barred early on from entering the masculine profession of raising sheep, has become a bored, nervous housewife. In *Miroir des jours* (Mirror of the Days), a more farcical piece, the heroine has greater success in breaking with tradition. After the death of her husband, a wine producer, she rejects her suitor and, with the help of two female friends, takes over the business. *Chants de la Galine* (Songs of Galine), the musical selection on which a larger theatrical production could be based, tells the story of three young women who go to Marseilles in the 1870s—the hopes and trials of their life before, during, and after the events of the Paris Commune. In the final play, *Porte à porte: monologue pour appartement* (Door to Door: Monologue for an Apartment), a woman—through a dream in which she takes on the roles of her own mother and sister—works out the fear, doubt, and guilt surrounding her decision to leave her husband. All of the plays successfully link the political (with an emphasis upon economic and cultural conditions) to personal concerns and relationships.

Worms, Jeannine. *Avec ou sans arbres* (With or without Trees). *L'Avant-Scène* (15 April 1979): 8–27.
Cast: 1 woman, 1 man
2 acts

A couple deals with the inevitability of marital breakdown in this bourgeois tragedy with an absurdist edge. On an almost empty stage evoking a now useless cement field, Louise and Leopold, middle-class and approaching middle age, play out the mutual love and fundamental incompatability of their relationship. On this, their tenth anniversary, Louise has led Leopold to the outskirts of Paris in search of the place where they first made love. She attempts to recreate the scene of their earlier bliss, complete with picnic and the clothes that they wore at the time. The first act consists of their largely adversarial conversation and ends with her leaving him—thus carrying out a decision she had already made before their nostalgic picnic. In the second act, nearly five years later, the two arrive "by accident" at the same spot. A reconciliation seems possible, most certainly in the eyes of Leopold. But it becomes obvious that, for Louise, there remain unresolvable differences between them, not the least of which is her potential imprisonment in his routine. At the last minute Louise again leaves the bewildered Leopold.

The moments of tension and tenderness in *Avec ou sans arbres* are counterbalanced by often comedic stage play with the picnic provisions and clothing. This tone corresponds to a certain humor of character that, in an ironic, Chekhovian manner, makes this story of a conventionally dysfunctional marriage all the more touching.

Yourcenar, Marguerite. *Electre ou la chute des masques. Marguerite Yourcenar: Théâtre.* 2 vols. Paris: Gallimard, 1971.
Electra, or the Fall of the Masks. Trans. Dori Katz, in collaboration with the author. *Yourcenar: Plays.* New York: Performing Arts Journal Publications (PAJ Playscripts), 1984.
Cast: 2 women, 6 men
2 acts

This play, written in 1944, presents the mythological story of Electra and her brother Orestes. As in the classical versions of the myth, the two siblings in turn avenge the murder of their father, Agamemnon, by destroying his killers, Clytemnestra, their mother, and Aegisthus, her lover. The author sees in her piece "the frightful or sublime persistence of human beings to remain themselves, no matter what happens," for here, different from previous versions, the motives for the killing disintegrate as the play progresses. Though Orestes discovers that his father is not Agamemnon, but Aegisthus, he is unable to suppress the action that Electra has been preparing him to accomplish for years. By committing the parricide, he joins Electra, who has just killed their mother, and Pylades, their renegade companion, as part of a murderous trio that will forever be bound by its tie of criminality.

The set of *Electre* is static and the stage action minimal. The main focus of the play is its eloquent language and what this language reveals: the fascinating and frightening strength of Electra and the complicated nature of the loyalty that she has created between herself and her husband, her brother, and Pylades. In long, rhythmed; abundantly imaged speeches the characters present the complexities of their interrelationships and weave the plot of revenge, "this plan of murder . . . our baby," a project that, for Electra, replaces her "womanliness."